DID SINGAPORE HAVE TO FALL?

On 15 February 1942 Singapore surrendered. It was the beginning of the end for the British Empire. Almost before the firing stopped, the controversy started. Could Singapore have been saved if more tanks or aircraft had been provided, or if Britain had denied Japan landing sites in Thailand? Could the tide have been turned as late as 15 February if fewer Australian troops deserted? The glut of scapegoats – Churchill, British commanders, Australians – creates a need for a work which will cover the widest range of issues clearly and briefly.

This book does just that, providing an account of everything from prewar planning to postwar commemoration by Britons, Australians and Singaporeans. But it also unveils the relationship between 'Fortress Singapore' and the fall. It shows that Churchill was against a long battle for north Malaya. In his mind's eye, Singapore remained a fortress with a mota and huge coastal guns. If the defenders fell back to Johore and Singapore, the enemy would have to assemble a vast siege train in order to pulverise the bastion's strongpoints. When Churchill realised the reality – that Singapore was 'the near-naked island' – he called for a final blood sacrifice to redeem the honour of race and nation.

This book explains what Fortress Singapore was to Churchill; what it was in reality; and how it has been remembered by Singaporeans, Australians, Britons and Japanese. It also puts Churchill's decisions in the context of the struggles in the Middle East and Russia, and allows Churchill and his contemporaries to speak for themselves. It will help students and general readers make up their own minds on the most crucial question, which can be summed up as: 'Did Singapore have to fall?'

Karl Hack teaches history at the National Institute of Education, Nanyang Technological University, Singapore. He specialises in Southeast Asian history, imperialism and counterinsurgency.

Kevin Blackburn teaches history at the National Institute of Education, Nanyang Technological University, Singapore. He is an Australian historian who specialises in Australian history and in war and memory.

DID SINGAPORE HAVE TO FALL?

Churchill and the impregnable fortress

Karl Hack and Kevin Blackburn

LONDON AND NEW YORK

First published in hardback 2003
First published in paperback 2005
by Routledge
2 Park Square, Milton Park, Abingdon, Oxon OX14 4RN

Simultaneously published in the USA and Canada
by Routledge
270 Madison Ave, New York, NY 10016, USA

Routledge is an imprint of the Taylor & Francis Group

© 2003, 2005 Karl Hack and Kevin Blackburn

Originally typeset in Goudy by Laserscript Ltd, Mitcham, Surrey
Printed and bound in India by Replika Press Pvt. Ltd

All rights reserved. No part of this book may be reprinted or reproduced or utilised in any form or by any electronic, mechanical, or other means, now known or hereafter invented, including photocopying and recording, or in any information storage or retrieval system, without permission in writing from the publishers.

British Library Cataloguing in Publication Data
A catalogue record for this book is available from the British Library

Library of Congress Cataloging in Publication Data
A catalog record for this book has been requested

ISBN 0–415–30803–8 (hbk)
ISBN 0–415–37414–6 (Taylor and Francis Asia Pacific paperback edition)

I expect every inch of ground to be defended, every scrap of material to be blown and no question of surrender to be entertained until after protracted fighting among the ruins of Singapore City.
    (Winston Churchill to General Wavell, 19 January 1942)

CONTENTS

List of plates		ix
List of figures		xi
List of maps		xii
Preface		xiii
List of abbreviations		xvii
Battle chronology		xix

1 **Introduction** 1

2 **Singapore in 1941** 12

People and place 12
The 'Gibraltar of the East' 20
The sinister twilight 25

3 **The fatal decisions** 29

From Pax Britannica to Fortress Singapore 30
Churchill and strategy: from main fleet to Matador 39

4 **The campaign: from Singapore to Syonan** 56

The battle for Malaya 57
The battle for Singapore 79

5 **The guns of Singapore** 95

The myths: from impregnable fortress to guns that pointed the wrong way 102
Unravelling the myths 110
The guns in action: the War Diaries' version 114
Churchill's almost naked island 131

6 After the battle — 142

Honouring Japan's war heroes 143
The British Empire remembers 149
Between two empires: the people of Singapore remember 15 February 1942 171

7 Conclusion — 183

Appendix A: British forces in December 1941	188
Appendix B: Japanese forces in December 1941	192
Appendix C: Organisation and disposition of Malaya command	194
Appendix D: Aircraft in the far east and their disposition	195
Appendix E: War Diaries	198
Appendix F: Gun statistics	204
Appendix G: The fire commands	209
Glossary	211
Notes	212
Bibliography	272
Index	290

PLATES

Singapore as place and naval base

2.1	A Changi beach before development	21
2.2	The naval base	22
2.3	Sinister twilight	23
3.1	Underground bunker	34

Fortress construction

3.2	The railway crane	35
3.3	Gun barrel en route to its battery	35
3.4	Train and railway crane	36
3.5	A searchlight in the 'Fortress system'	37

Fortress system

3.6	The observation post for Connaught Battery	38
3.7	A rangefinder badly disguised as a local *attap* hut	38

The campaign

4.1	Japanese tanks destroyed by Australian guns	75

The close defence system

5.1	A 12 pounder at Fort Siloso	100
5.2	Modern twin-barrelled 6 pounder at Pulau Sajahat	101

The big guns

5.3	Rangefinding for the coastal guns	107
5.4	Three storeys underground, 15 inch shells wait in one of the ammunition rooms	107

PLATES

5.5 'A British gunner ...' 108
5.6 The breech of a 15 inch gun 108
5.7 Looking down the barrel of a 15 inch gun 109
5.8 One of the destroyed 15 inch guns of Johore Battery, taken in 1942 109
5.9 Local contractors removing one of the biggest guns with a crude wooden structure in 1948 110

Commemoration

6.1 An Australian flag flutters by one of the gravestones at the Kranji War Memorial 160
6.2 Changi chapel 164
6.3 Changi prison 165
6.4 The Changi murals: 'Father forgive them' 169
6.5 The Changi murals: 'Peace on earth' 169
6.6 The Civilian War Memorial (Singapore) 175
6.7 Siloso Live! Actors recreate the Fall of Singapore for schoolchildren 182

FIGURES

5.1 Profile of the 15 inch Mk. I, or Singapore mounting   116
5.2 Profile of the 15 inch Mk. II, or Spanish mounting   117
5.3 Profile cross section of the Mk. II mounting   118

MAPS

2.1	Malaya in 1941: territorial divisions	13
2.2	Singapore city in 1941	16
3.1	*Operation Matador* and *Krohcol*	43
3.2	Malayan airfields in 1941	45
3.3	The world in November 1941	47
4.1	The break-up of the Japanese invasion fleet on 7 December 1941	59
4.2	The Japanese advance – 8 to 14 December 1941	69
4.3	The Japanese advance – 15 December 1941 to 11 January 1942	72
4.4	The Japanese advance – 12 to 31 January 1942	74
4.5	The battle for Singapore – 8 to 15 February 1942	81
4.6	Japanese forces over Southeast Asia, December 1941 to March 1942	89
5.1	The guns of Singapore – 1942	99
5.2	Johore Battery – arc of fire	120
5.3	Buona Vista Battery – arc of fire	122
5.4	Connaught Battery – arc of fire and targets	125
6.1	The Changi historic area	166
6.2	The valley of death: the *Sook Ching* massacre site at Siglap – 1942 to 2002	173

PREFACE

For the strengths of the book, and for helping us to get this far, we wish to thank the many people who have helped us, directly and indirectly.

We have of course relied heavily on the accounts of other historians: Aldrich, Allen, Farrell, Kirby, MacIntyre, Murfett, Neidpath, and Ong Chit Chung to name but a few.

Then there are the organisations, enthusiasts and veterans who helped make possible research on Singapore's Johore Battery. The Johore Battery being a group of three of Singapore's biggest coastal guns, capable of hurling shells with a 15 inch diameter at their base, and the weight of a small car, 20 miles to sea.

In 2001 the Singapore Tourism Board took over responsibility for opening the site of the last remaining underground bunker of Johore Battery's three guns. The other bunkers had been cleared long ago, to make way for the runways at Changi Airport.

The authors were amongst those who descended three storeys underground, to explore flooded tunnels: tunnels that had once held scores of huge shells, as well as generators and charges and winching gear. Now they held water, bolts, the odd bottle from the 1960s and, bizarrely, a small frog which swam towards us from out of the gloom. Above ground there was even less left to tell the tale. Here stood just a few huts, a clump of banana trees, and a handful of hatches which opened to reveal shafts. Descent into these was by means of ladders, punctuated by a series of rusting platforms. At that point everyone wondered how, and if, the site could ever give visitors an idea of the sheer scale of the original guns.

A few, short months later, on 15 February 2002, the site opened to the public. Standing near to the Changi Chapel Museum and just across from Changi airport, it now has the tunnels marked out above ground, a replica of the original guns, and a copy of a shell. Sadly, there is not yet a real gun, or the chance to go underground. It is, however, a beginning.

15 February 2002 was an appropriate moment to open a site such as this. For it was the sixtieth anniversary of the Fall of Singapore. So the site opened as part of the celebrations, graced by veterans who could remember the guns, and

PREFACE

the fall of the island. For many people this offered a kind of closure. But for us, as historical consultants, our labours were only just beginning.

Having gathered the story of these guns, and the Fortress of which they were a part, we felt compelled to finish the job, and to produce a book that would make the true facts more widely available. Once we began, we quickly realised that the guns only made sense as part of the Fortress, and the Fortress if located as part of the whole gamut of Singapore strategies. We found no existing work which pulled all the different strands together in one account, and so we created our own, and located our gun story as part of the bigger picture. So began an odyssey which ended with this book, and with the realisation that the tensions between the Fortress and area defence, and between Churchill and local commanders, were central to the whole disaster that was to befall Singapore.

Three of our colleagues at the National Institute of Education played an important part on the original 'Johore Battery Project', namely: Dr Rahil Ismail; Doreen Tan; and Sim Hwee Hwang. The team worked together to produce historical advice, and a poster: *Monster Guns of Singapore: The Story of Johore Battery* (Singapore: Singapore Tourism Board, 2002).

Beyond this, a book such as this, with its focus on the guns of Singapore, would have been impossible without a great deal of specialist help. In particular, we received unstinting assistance from the following: Tresnawati Prihadi and Jimmy Yeo of Fort Siloso and other staff of the Sentosa Development Corporation, Singapore; Major John Timbers, who as editor of *The Gunner* for the Royal Artillery Association sent us many articles; John Roberts for granting use of drawings of the guns; Ian Buxton, for naval details; James J. McGrane, for photographs; Keith Andrews for details of gunners and commemoration by veterans' children; and Mark Berhow of SCDSG publications (Society of Coast Defense Studies Group) in the United States. All of them went much further in helping us than we had any right to hope. We also need to thank the following: Dag Sundkuist; David Sissons (for Japanese sources and translations); Julie Denyer of Hampshire Libraries; Marney Dunn of the University of Queensland for her research assistance on the Australian sources; Brian Farrell (for spotting errors); Lynette Silver; Jeff Leng for his help in creating the maps; Mohd. Anis Tairan for help on the 'Valley of Death' map; Tim Yap Fuan of the National University of Singapore library for helping locate the House of Commons and House of Lords debates; Leon Comber; Martin Evans; *Navy News*; Lieutenant-Commander A.K. Manning; Toh Boon Kwan and Toh Boon Ho for providing both ideas and material from *Pointer*; and Phan Ming Yen. Constructive criticism from Mr Kwa Chong Guan and Peter Stanley, as readers, also improved the work significantly.

Thanks should also go to students such as Terence Tan and Edmund Lim at the National Institute of Education, Nanyang Technological University, to colleagues such as Dr Wang Zhenping, Mr Chang Chew Hung, Dr Michael Bird, Mr Teh Tiong Sa, and Associate Professor Daniel Crosswell, and to our Head of Academic Group, Associate Professor Christine Lee. All these people were assiduous in answering questions, or supportive of our work when it mattered most.

We would also like to thank the Singapore Tourism Board and Nanyang Technological University for providing the grants that enabled the research work for various parts of the book to be completed.

Above all, however, special mention should be made of two people: Commander C.B. Robbins of the United States Navy (retired); and Roger Nixon. Commander Robbins sent a plethora of material, including indispensable documents, articles and illustrations. Roger Nixon, whose research in London has informed this project throughout, also uncovered many documents we might otherwise have missed. Neither the research for the Johore Battery site, nor this book, would have been possible without their help. They are in a way 'the third man' and 'the fourth man' in the plot that is this book.

Beyond this we must thank that indispensable group of professionals: librarians and archivists. In Singapore these include the ever-helpful staff of the National Institute of Education, and at the National Archives. The latter have made superb efforts to gather material from all over the world. Equally, the National University of Singapore's fine collection of microfilms constitute an indispensable military and colonial history collection. At Oxford's Rhodes House Deputy Librarian Allan Lodge has been a boon over the years.

Last but most definitely not least, there are the staff of the Imperial War Museum, the Australian War Memorial, and of the Public Record Office at Kew Gardens in London. Due to their efforts, we must acknowledge the Imperial War Museum for permission to use photographs it holds, the Australian War Memorial for the same, and Her Majesty's Stationery Office for the use of crown copyright material.

In the end though, the writing stemmed from the combined research efforts of the two authors, and of a dialectic (sometimes plain argument) between them. Hopefully, the result is that two cooks make the perfect number, rather than spoiling the broth, and any remaining errors are, of course, solely our responsibility.

Before we move onto the main text, a word or two is needed on terminology. Spelling and terms associated with Southeast Asia can cause confusion. The name 'Malaya' is used in this book to mean all of current West or peninsular Malaysia, so excluding Singapore and Borneo. Otherwise, spellings and names used are generally those found in documents and Malayan usage of the time, hence Johore rather than Johor, and Kuomintang rather than Guomindang. Given the use of extensive quotations in the book, the alternative, the use of modern spellings in the text and old spellings in quotations, seemed to us to be excessively messy. The exception is that places and people not mentioned in any original documents we have seen may appear with modern spellings, when these spellings are likely to be more familiar to readers.

In addition, every historian is the prisoner of their documents, and successive historians have been caught unawares by the confused trail left behind by defeat. Papers were burned, people died in battle and captivity, leaving the survivors and future generations to puzzle out the truth as best they could, and can. In particular, historians who have written on the guns have almost invariably got basic facts on Singapore's guns wrong, or omitted important details. In our attempt to overcome this legacy, we have forensically examined the widest possible range of the war diaries, and articles by gunners, as well as oral history and secondary sources on the guns. But even the 'primary' documents from 1942 were written from memory, some survivors penning their reports as Prisoners of War in Changi, others after escaping, in India.[1] Many accounts are contradictory. Like all historians, then, we are only as good as the sources available at the time of writing: tomorrow may bring a new source, a new perspective.

Finally, the opinions expressed in this book cannot be taken to represent the views of any other person or organisation. They are those of the authors, and of the authors alone.

Karl Hack and Kevin Blackburn,
Humanities and Social Studies Academic Group,
National Institute of Education,
Nanyang Technological University,
Singapore

15 August 2003

ABBREVIATIONS

ABDA	American-British-Dutch Area
AHS	*Australian Historical Studies*
AIF	*Australian Imperial Forces*
AMTB	Anti motor torpedo boat
ANZAC	Australian and New Zealand Army Corps
AJPH	*Australian Journal of Political History*
AWM	Australian War Memorial
Bn	Battalion, a unit of about 600–1,000 men, divided into companies
Bde	Brigade, a unit comprising about three battalions in the British army, or two or three regiments (each of two battalions) in the Japanese Army
CAB	Cabinet documents
CIC	Commander-in-Chief
CIGS	Chief of the Imperial and General Staff
CO	Commanding Officer
COS	Chiefs of Staff
FMSVF	Federated Malay States Volunteer Force
GOC	General Officer Commanding
H.C.	House of Commons
H.L.	House of Lords
HKSRA	Hong Kong and Singapore Royal Artillery. A force raised in India, mainly from north Indians, for service in the Far East
INA	Indian National Army
INS	*Intelligence and National Security*
JIC	Joint Intelligence Committee
JICH	*Journal of Imperial and Commonwealth History*
JMBRAS	*Journal of the Malaysian Branch of the Royal Asiatic Society*
JSEAS	*Journal of Southeast Asian Studies*
MAS	*Modern Asian Studies*
MPAJA	Malayan People's Anti-Japanese Army
NCO	Non-commissioned Officer
POWs	Prisoners of war

ABBREVIATIONS

Prem	Prime Ministerial documents
RAF	Royal Air Force
SEAC	Southeast Asia Command
WO	War Office/War Office documents

BATTLE CHRONOLOGY

The historical background

1902 Anglo-Japanese Alliance.
1905 Decision not to station a fleet in the East in peace, concentrating ships in the West against the rising threat of Germany.
1919 Ten Year Rule accepted by British Cabinet. All military planning to assume no major war for ten years.
1921 Decision to build a naval base at Singapore.
1922 Anglo-Japanese Alliance is allowed to lapse, in favour of Washington Naval Treaty of February.
1930 London Naval Treaty limits replacement of battleships, and allows Japan parity in submarines and destroyers.
1931 Japanese occupation of Manchuria.
1932 Ten Year Rule is ended.
1933 Japan leaves the League of Nations.
1934 Britain begins rearmament at a slow pace.
1935 Anglo-German naval agreement allows Germany to build a navy 35 per cent of Britain's.
1936 Rome–Berlin Axis.
1937 Sino-Japanese war begins.
      Italy leaves the League of Nations.
1938 On 14 February, the Singapore naval base is officially opened.
1939 Fortress Singapore and its coastal guns are now almost complete.

The gathering storm

3 Sept 1939   Britain and France declare war on Germany over Poland.
10 June 1940 Italy enters the war on the side of Germany.
25 June 1940 France signs armistice with Germany.

BATTLE CHRONOLOGY

Oct 1940	Commanders-in-Chief Tactical Appreciation sent to London, saying they need 566 aircraft to defend Malaya.
	Sir Robert Brooke-Popham becomes Commander-in-Chief, Far East for all land and air (but not naval) forces.
Jan 1941	British Chiefs of Staff propose 336 aircraft for Malaya by the year's end.
Apr–May 1941	British forces driven out of Greece by German forces by the end of April, and then out of Crete by 31 May.
May 1941	Lt-General Percival arrives as GOC, Malaya. Lt-General Sir Lewis Heath takes control of the newly formed Third Indian Army Corps in Malaya.
13 Apr 1941	Japan signs a neutrality pact with the Soviet Union.
22 June 1941	Operation Barbarossa. Germany invades the Soviet Union.
21 July 1941	Vichy French government allows Japan bases in southern Indochina.
26 July 1941	United States freezes Japanese assets in America.
6 Sept 1941	Japanese Imperial Conference decides to negotiate over the American trade and asset restrictions, but to prepare for war simultaneously.
Oct–Nov 1941	US–Japanese negotiations stall.
17 Oct 1941	General Tojo becomes Prime Minister of Japan.
5 Nov 1941	An Imperial Conference set a deadline of 25 November for a peaceful, negotiated end to American embargoes.

The outbreak of hostilities

2 Dec 1941	HMS *Prince of Wales* and HMS *Repulse* arrive in Singapore. III Indian Corps placed on 24 hours notice for *Operation Matador*.
	Japanese Naval and Military commanders told war would begin on 8 December.
4 Dec 1941	Japanese fleet leaves Samah, Hainan Island, off southern China.
5 Dec 1941	Brooke-Popham given authority to launch Matador.
6 Dec 1941	1212 hours (Malayan Time) Japanese ships sighted, but sailing west towards Cambodia or Thailand.
7 Dec 1941	British Catalina patrol shot down while spotting Japanese ships, but before signalling to its base. 1848 hours (Malayan Time) RAAF Hudson spots Japanese ships about 75 miles from landing sites in southern Thailand. Brooke-Popham decides it is too late to launch Matador.

BATTLE CHRONOLOGY

The Battle for North Malaya

8 Dec 1941	Japanese Army lands at Kota Bharu in Malaya, and at Singora and Patani in southern Thailand early on the morning 8 December, local time. It is still 7 December in Pearl Harbor. '*Krohcol*' force crosses the Thai border, heading for the 'Ledge'.
9 Dec 1941	British and Indian defences forced to retreat from Kota Bharu, on the east coast.
10 Dec 1941	HMS *Prince of Wales* and HMS *Repulse* sunk off the east coast of Malaya.
11 Dec 1941	Battle of Jitra (Kedah northwest Malaya) begins. *Krohcol* force abandons attempts to take the Ledge, and retreats.
13 Dec 1941	The British northwestern front retreats south of Jitra.
16 Dec 1941	Penang evacuated, Europeans being given priority.
18 Dec 1941	Percival and Heath meet at Ipoh to decide a new strategy. Heath's preference of screening a fast retreat rejected in favour of a more serious fighting retreat. This was because Percival wanted to keep Japanese aircraft and artillery away from the naval base, and so buy time for reinforcements to arrive.

The Battle for Central Malaya

23 Dec 1941	The British withdraw across the Perak River to avoid being outflanked.
27 Dec 1941	Lt-General Sir Henry Pownall replaces Brooke-Popham Commander-in-Chief, Far East, as planned well before the Japanese invasion of Malaya.
28 Dec 1941	British construct positions around west coast trunk road at Kampar, blocking the approach from Perak to Selangor and Kuala Lumpur.
29 Dec 1941– 2 Jan 1942	Battle for Kampar. Percival and Bennett discuss plans for a phased withdrawal to Singapore.
3 Jan 1942	The first British reinforcements (45th Indian Brigade Group) arrive.
4 Jan 1942	British prepare to defend the approach to the Slim River, on the road to Kuala Lumpur. General Sir Archibald Wavell formally appointed Supreme Allied Commander, South-West Pacific, to command all American, British, Dutch, Australian (ABDA) forces.

BATTLE CHRONOLOGY

7 Jan 1942	Battle of Slim River. Japanese tanks burst through British lines.
8 Jan 1942	Heath ordered to withdraw his forces to Johore, the southernmost Malayan state, thus beginning the Battle for south Malaya.

The Battle for South Malaya

9 Jan 1942	Westforce established to defend the west coast of Johore, under the Australian commander, Major-General Bennett.
10 Jan 1942	Wavell sets up ABDA Headquarters near Bandung, Java, in the Netherlands East Indies. Pownall becomes his Chief of Staff.
11 Jan 1942	British forces withdraw through Kuala Lumpur, falling back towards the southern states of Negri Sembilan and Johore.
13 Jan 1942	More Reinforcements arrive: 53rd British Infantry Brigade; two anti-tank regiments; and 50 Hurricane fighters.
14 Jan 1942	Gemas, north Johore, the Australians launch a successful ambush of the Japanese, using 2/30th Battalion of the Australian 27th Brigade and artillery. But the Japanese press on.
15 Jan 1942	Muar River, west coast of northern Johore. Japanese take the north bank of the Muar River. Two battalions of the recently arrived 45th Indian Brigade are routed. The Japanese are now in a position to outflank Gemas.
17 Jan 1942	Fight for Johore, both East and West Coast, in which many British units are defeated in detail, or cut off, by Japanese flanking movements.
20 Jan 1942	Japanese invasion of Burma begins in earnest.
27 Jan 1942	22nd Indian Brigade cut off and lost in Johore by this point.
28 Jan 1942	Bennett plans a withdrawal across the Causeway, covered by the 22nd Australian Brigade, 2nd Gordons, and the Argyll and Southern Highlanders. For these units, heavy fighting follows.
29 Jan 1942	Much of the rest of the British 18th Division arrives at Singapore.
31 Jan 1942	The retreat across the causeway, after which a hole is blown, flooding a central section.

The Battle for Singapore

4 Feb 1942	Airfields at Tengah, Seletar and Sembawang come under artillery fire. Wavell decides to divert the Seventh Armoured

BATTLE CHRONOLOGY

	Brigade, coming from North Africa, to Burma, where it plays an important role in retreat.
5 Feb 1942	The remaining troops of the British 18th Division arrive in Singapore.
7/8 Feb 1942	Imperial Guards take Pulau Ubin (island) in the Johore Strait, to draw British attention east of the Causeway.
8/9 Feb 1942	Japanese 5th and 18th Divisions attack western Singapore.
9 Feb 1942	Japanese strike inland, taking Tengah airfield that evening.
10 Feb 1942	The Japanese push inland from west and northwest Singapore. The British plan to hold a line half-way across the West of the island: The Jurong Line.
	The Japanese Imperial Guards Division have landed at Kranji, on the northwest coast but behind (east) of the Jurong Line on the evening of 9th.
	The Australian 27th Brigade stops the Japanese Imperial Guards that night, but then retreats.
	This makes the 'Jurong line' untenable. Retreat towards central Singapore.
10–11 Feb 1942	The Japanese continue to drive from the north and northwest, reaching Bukit Timah in central Singapore. They capture the hill, about five miles from the city, and repulse a counter-attack on 11 February.
12 Feb 1942	British retreat to the final perimeter around the city. Fixed coastal guns in the east destroyed to deny them to the enemy.
13–14 Feb 1942	The Japanese hold the reservoirs. The Japanese frontline on Bukit Timah Road advances to the junction with Adam Road. On the south coast, the Japanese push the Malay Regiment back from Pasir Panjang, advancing towards the harbour and city.
15 Feb 1942	Percival and his commanders agree on surrender. Approximately 1715 Percival arrives at the Ford Factory. Approximately 1810 Percival signs surrender terms. 2030 hours. Ceasefire begins.
18 Feb 1942	Japanese *Sook Ching* (screening) operation begins, aimed at identifying anti-Japanese Chinese males. It degenerates into a massacre, for which minimum (Japanese) estimates are 5,000 dead, maximum (Chinese) estimates 50,000.

1

INTRODUCTION

British forces in Singapore surrendered on 15 February 1942. This was just seventy days after 8 December 1941, when Japanese troops first disembarked on the gentle tropical beaches of Singora and Patani in southern Thailand, and Kota Bharu in northeastern Malaya. Making full use of their aerial and armoured superiority – not to mention their infantry's toughness and mobility – it had taken the Japanese just ten weeks to drive the British out of north Malaya, down its west coast (with minor thrusts in the east too), and across the causeway to their last stand in Singapore.

That the world's biggest empire should be crushed so swiftly by an Asiatic foe it assumed to despise left a sense of shock, and of betrayed trust. Perhaps this is why Singapore's fall continues to exercise fascination. It shattered mental images held for a century or more, and accelerated the end of empire.[1] The 15 February was a day that would 'live in infamy'.[2]

Hence the importance of the questions, did Singapore have to fall, and did it have to fall so soon and so ignominiously? Since 1942 there have been many suggestions as to how the island could have been saved, or defeat made less humiliating. If only there had been more guns, aircraft, tanks or men. If only *Operation Matador* had been launched in time to forestall the Japanese on the beaches of southern Thailand.[3] If only Britain's General-Officer-Commanding (Malaya), Lieutenant-General Arthur Percival, had not been fooled into thinking the Japanese would attack Singapore in its northeast rather than its northwest, or if Australian forces had not fallen apart in the last few days.

Even at the last gasp, with troops deserting, and aircraft departed to the Netherlands East Indies, some historians have spotted one last chance. What if a British counter-attack had been launched at the eleventh hour, on 15 February itself, when the Japanese were down to their last artillery shells and tanks?[4] Perhaps then the remaining force of over 100,000 men need not have been defeated by a smaller Japanese Army.

So many ways have been suggested in which disaster could have been avoided, that it has become difficult to understand how Churchill and his commanders could have missed every one of them.

INTRODUCTION

Yet blaming individuals can seem inadequate, given the scale of events from December 1941 to March 1942. The Americans lost the Philippines despite being involved in no other conflict. The Dutch collapse in the Netherlands East Indies came even more quickly. By the time Lieutenant-General Yamashita, commanding the Japanese Twenty-Fifth Army, secured Singapore on 15 February 1942, Japanese ships were rolling across the southern seas from Manila in the Philippines to Palembang in Sumatra, while Japan's forces were soon to advance to Mandalay in Burma and to bomb Darwin in Australia. They even felt able to transfer some aircraft away from Malaya in early 1942, to the Borneo front. Finally, if Malaya did not have enough forces, Burma had fewer still: less troops; less aircraft and less guns. Hong Kong's garrison of around 14,000 men and volunteers had just five aircraft.[5] By May 1942 even India did not seem safe.

So the question remains: did Singapore have to fall at this time, and in this manner? Did Winston Churchill miss his chance to save Malaya in mid–1941, when there was still time to send vital tanks and aircraft? Or did the British Prime Minister do all he reasonably could, given the constraints of a global war? Was Singapore doomed not by individual mistakes, then, but by Britain's relative decline, so that it became incapable of fighting Italy, Germany and Japan simultaneously? In short, was the Fall of Singapore avoidable, or inevitable?

The historiography on this question is so vast that, before an answer is even attempted, we need to outline the main pre-existing schools of thought. Only when a pattern is imposed on the innumerable books on this topic will we be able to start to piece the puzzle together again. Furthermore, the best place to begin this process is at the beginning, in 1942.

Several books by journalists appeared before the end of that fateful year. They gave us, amongst other things, the myth that the big coastal guns of Singapore faced uselessly out to sea. The journalists also excelled at giving the flavour of events they had witnessed. One of the best of these works was London *Times* correspondent Ian Morrison's *Malayan Postscript*.[6] Morrison covered most of the themes later authors would recycle in less exciting language, including the lacklustre performance of the civilian administration, and the need to build national armies, rather than relying on imperial mercenaries. Like many of his contemporaries, he was particularly struck by Britain's reluctant, late and minimal recruitment of Asians, including local Chinese who had every reason to fear Japanese conquest.[7]

Later works tended to serve a positive function in debunking the early myths, but they also relegated the racial aspect to the background, in favour of studies of tactics and strategy. Two of the most important of these were by Major-General S. Woodburn Kirby.[8]

Kirby was chosen to write the official British military history: *The War Against Japan*, volume one of which was *The Loss of Singapore* (1957).[9] Kirby was a natural choice, as he had experience of Singapore in the 1920s, and of India in the 1940s. He had even written a 1935 paper which foresaw Japanese landings

2

on the coast of southeast Malaya, as a prelude to the main attack on Singapore. Yet despite all this he had remained untainted by direct involvement in the Malayan campaign.[10] The resulting official history was an excellent example of the campaign study genre, but it was only in his later classic, *Singapore: The Chain of Disaster* (1971), that Kirby felt free to give full rein to his opinions.[11]

In this posthumous, 1971 work, Kirby's perspective was reflected by the subtitle: *The Chain of Disaster*. This suggested a chain of responsibility, stretching all the way from 1921, through London's decision not to send the necessary ships, tanks and aircraft, to the commanders in the field. Kirby's books thus turned out to be detailed campaign histories which nevertheless looked beyond the campaign for the ultimate causes of defeat.[12]

While Kirby stressed that the fall of Singapore was due to the whole chain of decision-making, other historians have chosen to place Britain's naval decisions to centre stage. For them, it was Britain's failure to maintain a two-ocean navy after the beginning of the twentieth century which doomed Singapore. Rather than maintaining its naval dominance, Britain chose to build a naval base at Singapore to which they might despatch a fleet in an emergency. But the plan was fatally flawed. It assumed the Japanese would only attack Singapore in the most unlikely of scenarios, that is, when the Royal Navy was not already tied down in other conflicts.

Worse still, the one force which could have compensated for a relative decline in naval power was underplayed. The Royal Air Force tried to argue that its aircraft, and especially its torpedo bombers, should supplement or even displace ships and big coastal defence guns. But the older services refused to grant it more than a marginal role, until almost the very end, by when it was too late to assemble the necessary machines.

Strategic folly was compounded by parsimony. Whether because of a genuine lack of resources or simply a lack of will in the face of pressure for disarmament, economic problems at home, and rising domestic expenditure, not enough ships were built in the 1920s and 1930s.[13] Hence when world war came in 1939 to 1940, the Royal Navy struggled to match even two adversaries: the Germans and the Italians. By 1941 it was hard pressed in the Atlantic and the Mediterranean, and no fleet could be sent to Singapore in time. This 'naval school', espoused by the likes of Neidpath and MacIntyre in the late 1970s to early 1980s, thus tended to stress Britain's long-term decline and failures, rather than short-term decisions.[14]

The entrenched nature of Britain's eastern dilemmas was also stressed by what might be called a 'diplomatic' school of historians. Books such as Ritchie Ovendale's, *'Appeasement' and the English-Speaking World* (1975) showed how British strategy was hamstrung by its global over-extension. Presented with an increasingly bellicose Germany and Italy in Europe in the 1930s, the Chiefs of Staff felt it expedient to appease in the distant Far East. To their minds, appeasing Japan was the easiest way of avoiding Britain having to face three strong enemies at once. Nor was appeasement driven only by the external threats. There were pressures internal to the Commonwealth as well. Export-oriented Britain might face economic defeat before actual war broke out, if it diverted too many of its industries into war production, to match too many adversaries, too soon.[15] In addition, Australia and New Zealand, however supportive of a strong British presence in the Pacific, did not want to antagonise Japan. So there was an economic, political and military logic to appeasement, and to the strict diet of military provision this region was placed on.[16] Until and unless concrete United States support was forthcoming, something not totally guaranteed until the attack against Pearl Harbor of December 1941, there were no obvious alternatives.[17]

These naval and diplomatic analyses would tend to exonerate both the commanders on the spot, and Churchill in London. Many other works also make light of Churchill's responsibility for the disaster, not least his own superbly crafted history, called simply: *The Second World War*.

Volume 4 of this magisterial and elegantly written work, entitled *The Hinge of Fate* (1951), argues that Churchill had no choice but to concentrate resources in active theatres in the western and northern Africa in 1941, rather than risking dispersal to passive theatres such as Singapore. Raymond Callahan's *The Worst Disaster: The Fall of Singapore* (1977) developed the classic statement of this grand strategy argument, stating that Churchill could fight one war in the west and hope to win it, or fight two, and risk losing on both fronts.[18] Like the naval school, this grand strategy school takes a strategic approach. Unlike the naval school, it places the emphasis on decisions taken in the Second World War itself, rather than beforehand.

This exculpatory grand strategy school of thought even finds supporters in Singapore. Singapore-based Canadian historian Brian Farrell took this approach at a major conference held to mark the sixtieth anniversary of the Fall of Singapore (15 February 2002). This brought to Singapore many of the world's experts on the campaign, with the resulting papers published as *Sixty Years On: The Fall of Singapore Revisited* (2002).[19]

Farrell's previous work was on British grand strategy, so it is not surprising that he chose to place Churchill's decisions in the context of a world crisis in 1941.[20] According to this argument, Churchill gambled, and, in the ultimate sense, he won. It was not the British who made the critical strategic mistakes in 1941, but Hitler, who failed to deliver the knockout blow to the Soviet Union, and the Japanese.[21]

Since the Japanese knew from mid-1941 that any further expansion in the east was likely to mean war with the United States, they should have known that that would guarantee eventual defeat. Like Hitler, they gambled that one knock-out blow would bring their opponent to their knees, or at least to the negotiating table, and they lost. By comparison, Churchill knew his main need was to conserve forces and take the risks necessary to ensure survival, in the hope that the United States would eventually enter the war.

But the grand strategy, pro-Churchill lobby has not gone unchallenged. Its critics have ranged from vocal members of the House of Commons and House of

Lords in 1941 and 1942 debates over the Malayan debacle, to Ong Chit Chung in Singapore itself. Together, these offer what might be called 'a Churchill thesis', that Churchill in particular took decisions which were not only fatal, but also avoidable.

The British parliamentary debates of 1941 to 1942 saw accusations that Churchill should and could have sent more reinforcements to Malaya, and that Britain could have produced more fighter aircraft and tanks and less labour-intensive bombers. In short, they included accusations that the seeds for what one Parliamentarian called the 'Worst Disaster since Ethelred the Unready' were sown in the corridors of Whitehall, if not on the playing fields of Harrow.[22]

At the opposite end of the twentieth century, and several thousand miles from Westminster, Ong Chit Chung also took on the role of prosecutor. Ong Chit Chung is a Singaporean historian and, at the time of writing, a member of Parliament and Chairman of the Singapore Parliamentary Committee on Defence and Foreign Affairs. His *Operation Matador* (1997) reminded us that the final defence plans for Malaya, in 1941, relied not on ships or coastal guns, but on an air and land defence of north Malaya and southern Thailand: plans which Churchill refused to back with the requisite tanks and aircraft.

Ong argued that Churchill was explicitly warned in early 1941 that a comparatively small number of modern machines could make a big difference in Malaya, but still chose to send large numbers of aircraft to the Middle East and the Soviet Union that year, and virtually none to Malaya.[23] Ong's main criticism appears to centre not on equipment sent to the Middle East, but on the despatch of more than 400 aircraft to Russia, where this material could only be a drop in a Soviet ocean. Another author has argued that 'there would otherwise almost certainly have been Hurricane squadrons in Singapore by December'. Thus, from a Singaporean perspective, Singapore never did 'fall'. It was surrendered by a British Empire that chose not to send the necessary resources, and whose commanders chose not to fight to the finish.[24]

Such postcolonial criticism has struck a chord not only in Singapore, where Ong's *Operation Matador* has been discussed in the press and reprinted in Chinese, but in Australia too. Indeed, Australia even sent a special envoy to London in late 1941. This was Earle Page, who proceeded to argue in the same terms Ong has adopted more recently, that machines wasted in Russia could make all the difference East of Suez.[25]

More recently, on 27 February 1992, Australian Prime Minister Paul Keating put the case more bluntly when he told parliament in Canberra that Britain had, 'decided not to defend the Malaysian peninsula, not to worry about Singapore, not to give our troops back'. Many veterans and opposition politicians disagreed with him, some vehemently so, but the suspicion that Britain had betrayed Australian trust, that it had taken Australian troops for Greece and Africa, and Australian pilots for the Battle of Britain, but not sent the promised fleet to Singapore in return, lingered on.[26]

In turn, some British historians questioned the performance of Australian troops in Singapore. This debate is examined in Murfett, Miksic, Farrell, and Chiang's *Between Two Oceans: A Military History of Singapore* (1999). This includes an incisive appendix covering debates such as whether Singapore could have been saved as late as 15 February, and whether Australian desertions accelerated the final surrender.[27]

Discussion of these desertions inevitably raises heckles in Australia, partly because, when the story has been told from an Australian angle, it has suggested that Australians performed not worse than other troops, or even the same, but significantly better. The Australian story has tended to emphasise their units' superior fighting spirit in Johore, even if it accepts that in Singapore a small proportion of their men did, when all seemed lost, start to lose heart and down weapons. Perhaps this tendency has been reinforced by the choice of journalists – such as C.E.W Bean for the First World War and Lionel Wigmore for the Second – as official war historians.[28]

Lionel Wigmore's *The Japanese Thrust* (1957) remains not only the official Australian military history, but one of the most detailed guides to the campaign. Wigmore's measured approach is, however, not the one most common among his scholar-compatriots. This honour goes to alternative tradition, which Keating as Labor Party leader tapped into with his 1992 comments. This tradition expressed deep scepticism about historical over-reliance on Britain, and on Britain's 'Singapore Strategy', by Australia's interwar conservative coalition governments. This vein of writing stretches back to Australian Labor Party criticisms of the 1920s and 1930s.[29] From then on, there have been suggestions from some on the left that Australia needed to build up its own, autonomous defence forces and strategy, and to rely less completely on partnership with great allies, and particularly on British strategy. Hence there was scepticism about the extent of Australia's attempts to contribute to a wider imperial strategy, for instance by contributing to Empire Air Training Schemes while receiving few modern aircraft in return, or by sending men to the Middle East in the 1940s, at the expense of theatres closer to home.[30]

In this tradition, David Day has presented works which depict British wartime policy as harshly self-interested, and willing to marginalise Australian interests where this suited metropolitan needs. In February 1942, Churchill even contradicted clear Australian instructions by turning shiploads of Australian troops, en route from the Middle East, away from their passage towards Australia, and towards Burma instead. It took a last-minute display of determination by Australia's Prime Minister, John Curtin, to reverse this imperial fiat.[31] Day is therefore critical of past Australian governments' tendency to accept British worldviews too readily, as in his *The Great Betrayal: Britain, Australia and the Pacific War* (1988).

Day's *The Reluctant Nation: Australia and the Allied Defeat of Japan, 1942–45* (1992) even carried a preface by Keating, which warned that the child's love of the parent had not been reciprocated in equal measure. In this preface, Keating overtly claimed that the 'Digger' image of heroic service to a wider British Empire had held back true, independent-minded nationalism.

There are of course other perspectives even in Australia, with the likes of John McCarthy emphasising not so much British betrayal of Australia at Singapore, but Australia's self-betrayal. For him, Australia's prewar elite relied on British plans which they knew to be flawed, rather than accepting the alternative, which meant taking on more responsibility and cost in the country's own defence.[32]

These issues continue to generate heat in an Australia which is re-examining its identity, and the balance between a British past and a Pacific and perhaps even Republican future. But less controversial and politicised analyses continue to be generated as well. In particular, Wigmore's tactical story has recently been retold and updated by Alan Warren, in his *Singapore 1942: Britain's Greatest Defeat* (2002). Warren not only brings a sense of balance to questions such as how well, and badly, Australians performed, but also makes campaign details and battle maps widely available to a new generation.

This is part of a renewed interest in the campaign itself, and issues of leadership. While few people would argue that different decisions on the ground could have avoided final defeat, this trend still serves important functions. For most military officers must operate at this level of the engagement and the battle, not at the stratospheric heights of global strategy. In this campaign school we have the official histories of Wigmore and Kirby, the more modern histories of Warren and Farrell, and biographies and autobiographies of generals such as Australia's General Gordon Bennett, and Britain's rather unfortunate Lieutenant-General Arthur Percival.[33]

At the other end of the spectrum from the individual battle or leader, there are books which focus on controversies. Amongst the best and most scholarly of this controversies school is Louis Allen's *Singapore 1941-1942* (1977). Allen covered the campaign chronologically. But he also included chapters with titles such as 'What Went Wrong?', 'Who was to blame?' and 'The Factor of Race', which examined the views of contemporaries. Like Morrison before him, and Christopher Thorne afterwards, he saw the inability of an empire to fully utilise all the races it ruled, almost the very idea of protecting power and acquiescent subject, as a major part of Britain's defensive problem in 1941.[34]

In a similarly controversial vein, but with a more journalistic and sensationalist style, Peter Elphick has provided several fascinating books, notably his *Singapore: The Pregnable Fortress*. These remind us just how flawed the defending forces were, with Elphick accusing Australian forces of mass desertion, with Indian troops (half the defender's strength) disturbed by nationalism and Japanese propaganda, and with spies inside as well as outside the ranks.[35]

In tackling the question of spies, Elphick also overlaps with an emerging intelligence school of thought on the fall of Singapore. The importance of Japanese intelligence has long been recognised.[36] But it is only recently that the works of Aldrich, Best, Elphick, and Ferris have sought to discover just how far British intelligence failure, or at least the failure to listen to good intelligence where it existed, contributed to disaster.[37]

For Ferris, British images of Japan led it to seriously misjudge Japanese capabilities and intentions. Britain was guilty of 'ethnocentrism', of judging Japan as good by Asian standards, but dismissing this as irrelevant when considering its potential against a European adversary. Alternatively, images of Japanese airpower, formed when intelligence on Japan was good in the 1920s, continued to flavour interpretation when information became scarce, in the following decade – in other words, just as Japanese airpower was dramatically improving.[38] For Aldrich, by comparison, intelligence performed well in the circumstances, and did achieve a reasonable appreciation of the Japanese. But key intelligence institutions such as the small, Royal Navy-controlled Far East Combined Bureau (FECB) lacked the clout to disseminate their findings widely, or to overcome the cognitive dissonance of London, and of commanders in the field.

The Japanese, according to Aldrich, thus achieved surprise despite their enemies being warned of when and how they would attack and, to some extent, what with.[39] All of which begs the wider question: was Singapore not better prepared and reinforced because racism, ethnocentrism and outdated assumptions negated intelligence, or was it the prior and extraneous determination not to reinforce the area which meant intelligence was downplayed? Was bravado self-consciously chosen as a form of defensive fantasy?

Despite this flow of new works on Singapore showing no sign of diminishing, with recent works touching on issues such as air power, some of the most gripping reading is still provided by older, more journalistic publications.[40] These provide essential insights into the texture, feel and psychology of the moment, the mental software which glued events together. Notable amongst these is James Leasor's *Singapore: The Battle That Changed the World* (1968), and Noel Barber's *Sinister Twilight: The Fall of Singapore* (1968).[41]

On the Japanese side, English-reading audiences have not been served quite so well. Many works make use of translated Japanese accounts of the campaign from the immediate postwar period, but these reports do not seem to have been very revealing.[42] It is just as well, then, that we also have Colonel Masanobu Tsuji's, *Shingapōru – Ummei no tenki* [Singapore – The Hinge of Fate] (1952).[43] First appearing in English in 1960, this is available as *Singapore 1941–1942: The Japanese Version of World War II*.[44] Tsuji's attraction was not only that he helped plan and execute the Malayan campaign, but that he unashamedly presented the Japanese viewpoint, that the campaign was a heroic conquest, and not merely a pusillanimous British failure.

Tsuji may have written so forcefully precisely because he was under the shadow of suspicion as one of the men behind the February 1942 *Sook Ching*, or massacre of Chinese civilians, in Malaya and Singapore. In 1945 he fled to China to avoid being captured, and as late as 1948 British authorities still wished to make an arrest. Fortunately for him, the files were closed before he re-emerged in 1950, and began a successful campaign for a seat in the Japanese Diet.[45]

Tsuji was a hard-bitten, hardline Japanese staff officer, with experience of China campaigns from 1932, and a reputation for supporting the Army's expansionist aims. He stands accused of encouraging the maltreatment and execution of both civilians and prisoners in the Philippines and Malaya. He was also adept at playing politics. In the middle of the Malayan campaign Lieutenant-General Yamashita, exasperated by Tsuji's manoeuvring, described him as 'egotistical and wily ... a sly dog ... a manipulator to be carefully watched'.[46] All of which people seemed blissfully unaware of when his book first appeared in English, complete with a preface by a fellow-professional: Australia's General Gordon Bennett.[47]

Tsuji's Japanese perspective is useful because and not in spite of his background, and also because so few historians use the many Japanese language sources. Even the easily accessible official Japanese war history, *Senshi Sōsho* [War History Series], Volume 1, entitled *Marē Shinkō Sakusen* [The Malayan Campaign] is under-utilised by historians. This is despite it being published long ago, in 1966.[48] For the moment, Louis Allen's book remains one of the few English-language works to make significant use of Japanese sources. As a wartime intelligence officer, Allen was fluent in Japanese, and so was able to use Japanese sources to inform his *Singapore, 1941–1942*. Henry Frei was one of the very few to join Allen in giving us a glimpse of Japanese perspectives.[49] In his absence, we do have a very few English-language works by Japanese authors, for instance on men such as Lieutenant-General Yamashita.[50] But we still await the translation of a more substantial slice of the innumerable sources, documentary and oral, available in Japanese. In the meanwhile, we use sources such as Shigetaka Onda's two volume, *Marē-Sen* [The Malayan Campaign] of 1977 to illuminate some of the most critical points in the Battle for Fortress Singapore.[51]

Together with innumerable others, the titles listed above give an impressive coverage of fact and argument. A short work such as this cannot supplant them. But this does not mean another book is surplus to requirements. Far from it, it is precisely this surfeit of debates and schools of thought which creates the need for a survey, for a work which offers the readers an overview of events without drowning them in detail. What is needed is one work which incorporates the basics of the naval school, grand strategy, Churchill thesis, intelligence approach, national perspectives, and postwar commemoration alike, and for a book which integrates the story of the Fortress and of its guns into the overall picture.

This last aspect is important because most existing books contain basic errors on Singapore's coastal guns, or fail to answer key questions about Singapore as a Fortress: questions such as why Singapore's naval base was located opposite the Malayan mainland, virtually inviting landward attack. There is still a need for an informed analysis which can relate the guns, and the idea and reality of 'Fortress Singapore', to the overall disaster.

INTRODUCTION

This book aims to fill that gap. While having the Fortress as one of its main concerns, it aims to introduce a wide range of perspectives – planning as well as the campaign, *Operation Matador* as well as the guns of Singapore, Churchill's decisions as well as troop morale, and recent findings – so as to let people begin to make up their own mind about the controversies. Did Churchill betray Singapore by withholding desperately needed reinforcements? Could different decisions at critical moments have significantly altered the course of the campaign? Could Churchill, the Commander-in-Chief Brooke-Popham, his General-Officer-Commanding (Malaya) Percival, or even the ordinary subaltern and soldier have made a significant difference?

In seeking to answer these questions, the book tries to let key participants speak for themselves. This is not always possible. The flow of the story has to be maintained, but where it is the words of the actors themselves have been used: of Churchill; of the Japanese military planner Tsuji; of ordinary soldiers and civilians; of veterans, and of Singaporeans after the war.

These are not mere ornamentation. It is precisely this material, much of which an austere historian might reject as anecdotal, which conveys the mentality and morale of the men involved. In a case such as this, dry and emotionless history cannot convey the essence of British failure, the way inadequate preparations led to mental as well as material inferiority. The quotations also allow the reader to judge for themselves, rather than simply being told what to believe. In particular, if Churchill is to be the principal defendant, it is only right that such a formidable writer be allowed to 'speak' in his own defence; hence the book's blend of narrative and analysis, and of fact and quotation.

As for the structure of the book, it begins with a chronology, followed by this first chapter: the introduction. The second chapter, on 'Singapore in 1941', sketches the nature and significance of Singapore before the battle commenced. Without this understanding of local terrain, both physical and human, no battle analysis is likely to be satisfactory. The third deals with the 'Fatal Decisions', from the building of the base to the adoption of *Operation Matador* in 1940 to 1941. Chapter 4 on 'The Campaign' then offers a narrative of some of the most important events after the Japanese landings of 8 December 1941. It tries to maintain the flow of the story, but it also stops to reflect at greater length at points where people have argued different decisions might have saved Singapore; or, at the least, when different decisions might have made the final fall less humiliating.

The fifth chapter, 'The Guns of Singapore', brings to bear recent research and little and never-used documents on the guns. It is also crucial to understanding why Singapore fell so rapidly, and so catastrophically.[52] This is because Chapter 5 brings into focus one of the main issues of 1941: how far should all of Malaya have been defended? How far by contrast could the defenders have concentrated their main efforts on a more limited area, such as Singapore and the neighbouring Malayan state of Johore? In short, it highlights the tension between the concepts of *Operation Matador* (the plan to defend beaches in northeast Malaya and southern Thailand) and Fortress Singapore, between the maximum and minimum options for the defence of the island and naval base. So the fifth chapter will look again at Singapore's big guns. It will subject the evidence to forensic scrutiny, especially by little-used 1942 War Diaries, in order to unravel the false trails laid down since 1942.

In this way, each chapter deals with issues vital to the book's main questions: did Singapore have to fall when it did; and did it have to fall in such a humiliating manner? In particular, what was the role of Churchill's decisions on, and his perceptions of, 'Fortress Singapore'?

Finally Chapter 6, 'After the Battle', traces the postwar history of '15 February' as an iconic date, briefly sketching in how Japanese, British, Australians and Singaporeans have sought either to ignore, or to commemorate, this date. It shows how the causes and meanings attributed to the date, and to Singapore's fall, have varied not just according to which facts people had to hand, but also due to different needs and perspectives.

We have made no attempt at covering this last, vast topic comprehensively. That would demand a new work on 'The Many Falls of Singapore', the many ways in which the campaign has been remembered by different groups. To do more than hint at these themes now, while so much research remains to be done, would betray hubris.

For the moment, the main aim of this last chapter, besides giving a skeletal survey of commemoration, is to show how the 'Fall of Singapore' remains hotly contested, controversial and shifting terrain, touching different nationalities, and different generations, from the thinning ranks of veterans and their relatives through to Singaporean schoolchildren. In Singapore, these schoolchildren are asked to remember every 15 February – sometimes even to re-enact in the face of firecrackers and smoke and 'Japanese soldiers' who herd them into dark spaces – the Fall and what it meant for their country.[53]

Before we tackle the campaign, let alone the memories, we must now start at the beginning. We need to sketch Singapore as it was on 8 December 1941: the nature of the island and people that Britain was to surrender after seventy days of fighting. Just what was 'Fortress Singapore', and what were its relationships to the region, to empire, and to the world?

2
SINGAPORE IN 1941

This book is about the fall of Singapore, Britain's tropical eastern bastion, naval base and entrepôt: that kaleidoscopic metropolis of Malays and Indians, Eurasians and Europeans, and, most of all, of Chinese who spoke a mixture of dialects and languages, some mutually comprehensible, some not: Hokkien; Hakka; Teochew; Mandarin and Cantonese.

But what was Singapore in 1941, and what were its relationships to Malaya, to the region beyond, and to the British Empire? If we want to understand why Singapore fell as it did, we must first understand what it was Britain was trying to defend, Singapore as place, as people, as imperial bastion, as communications hub and military complex.

People and place

By 1941 Singapore had grown to have an importance out of all proportion to its size. It was a diamond shaped island, about twenty-five miles from west to east and fourteen north to south. At little more than 200 square miles, this gave it a similar shape to the Isle of Wight, and a similar size to the Isle of Man. So in dimensions it had much in common with islands notable mainly for their smallness, their obscurity, and their almost total absence from military and imperial histories.

By contrast, tiny Singapore was not only a visible symbol of Britain's power in the East, but enjoyed an important position in Britain's finances and imperial communications. As Colonel Tsuji, who helped plan the island's conquest by Japan, put it, 'Singapore was Britain's pivotal point in the domination of Asia. It was the eastern gate for the defence of India and the northern gate for the defence of Australia. It was the axis of the steamship route from Europe to the Orient'.[1] In short, Singapore was an imperial synapse, a switching and broadcasting point for goods and information flowing to and from Britain's eastern territories. A place at least as vital in 1941 for British power in the East, as Malta was for the survival of British power in the Mediterranean.

Singapore, however, did not just look outward to global networks, but inwards also to Southeast Asia, and to its intimate connections with the

Map 2.1 Malaya in 1941: territorial divisions.

Malayan peninsula. On maps, Singapore looks almost as if it must have been a part of the Malayan peninsula itself, which one day cracked off and drifted the shortest of distances into the Straits of Malacca. Indeed, in 1941 there was little to distinguish the island's more outlying districts, such as Jurong in the southwest, from the Malayan mainland. As recently as the 1920s roads to outlying districts such as Woodlands and Changi, running through jungle for much of the way, saw virtually no cars. Bullock drawn vehicles and the trishaw reigned supreme until the 1930s.[2] As an island then, Singapore was separate from, and yet almost part and parcel of, the Malayan peninsula.

The link between Singapore, and the rubber and tin produced in the Malay States – over half the world's tin and nearly 40 per cent of its rubber – was the Causeway. Opened in 1923, this stretched 1,100 yards across the Johore Strait. Once across the Causeway, roads and a railway ran north, across rivers made brown by tin and by soil washed away by torrential monsoon rain. They continued past stilted *kampong* (Malay village) houses with *attap* roofs (thatch made from the *nipa* palm), through orderly estates of rubber trees. To a British infantryman going north by train in 1941, these trees might almost have looked English, except for their uniformity, and bar the occasional coconut palm or banana tree at a clearing.

A branch line split off from the main railway not far into Malaya, and ran across the centre of the country to the less developed and more sparsely populated east coast. But the main line continued up the tin-rich west coast, through a handful of the Malayan peninsula's nine Sultanates. Each of these had its own sovereign, Malay Sultan, still ruler of a Malay kingdom. From 1874 each in turn had been obliged by treaty to accept a British Resident or Adviser, and to follow their 'advice' on all matters except those of Malay religion (Islam) and *adat* (custom). The last to succumb, in 1914, was the southernmost state of Johore.

Each Sultan and his Malay subjects were the sole citizens still, though they now made up only about half the nine states' combined population. The few thousand *orang asli* or tribesmen of the jungle interior – which stretched down Malaya's central mountain spine and covered the majority of the country – had little impact on the more populated areas. But along the tin-rich coastal plains of the west, where population was densest, the Chinese had already overtaken the more rural Malays in wealth and numbers.

Here on the west coast, with its first-class system of roads, the Chinese worked tin mines and ran businesses and shops. Together with Indian estate labourers, they were mostly seen as visitors, 'sojourners' who came in the hope of sending money home. And return home the vast majority did, providing they did not fall prey to malaria or diarrhoea or dysentery, or any of the other ailments that made 'development' – Britain's main aim for the area – so deadly in tropical, forested Malaya.[3]

By contrast, there were a smaller number of Chinese who were born locally in the three main ports, which together formed the Straits Settlements Colony. For some of these 'Straits Chinese', English was now their habitual language, while for others Hokkien or even a mix that included Malay might still be used in the home.

The Straits Settlements itself had been formed back in 1826 from three of the British East India Company's trading stations: Penang, Malacca and Singapore. Singapore soon became its administrative centre, and by 1867 the

Straits Settlements had become a Crown colony under the control of the Colonial Office in London. This meant that the locally born Straits Chinese were also British subjects, by dint of birth in a British colony.

So in 1941 Singapore was the administrative centre of the Straits Settlements Colony, and it was already the global economy personified. A place where most people – even white colonial officers – were transnational workers of some sort, or at best second or third generation immigrants. In nearby Malaya, Indian rubber tappers, Malay smallholders and Chinese tin miners produced the goods on which Singapore's prosperity depended. Then European managers and traders in Straits-based companies and agency houses siphoned out the resulting tin and rubber to the United States, where it ended up in American car tyres and tin cans. This way American dollars found their way back to London, to make up for a British greed for dollar goods which Britain could not finance by its own exports. If, on the way, it kept Chinese dockworkers busy, and helped sustain British shipping and services, so much the better.

By 1941 then Singapore was much that its founder, Sir Thomas Stamford Raffles, could have hoped for at its birth in January 1819, and more besides. Then Raffles had hoped to steal away trade from the Dutch ports of the East Indies, especially Batavia on Java (now called Jakarta), by making Singapore's trade free of all taxes.

Now, in the late 1930s, Singapore was not only the free-trading port that Raffles had dreamt of and plotted to make a reality, despite dithering in Penang and India and London, but home to an imperial city of around 560,000.[4] This was a figure soon to be swollen to over a million by refugees from Malaya. In turn, Malaya's population at the time was just over 5 million.[5]

The majority of Singapore's population were Chinese, and the greatest concentration was on the southern coast, the opposite side of the island from Johore. Here in the south of Singapore Island was Singapore City, its core clustered around the southern coastline, and looking towards the ships that sustained it.

Here too the waters of the Singapore River disgorged into the Straits of Singapore. The rivers banks were lined with coolies unloading the many boats, lighters and *tongkangs* (a small Chinese ship or junk) at Boat Quay, not far from its mouth. Further inland and just round a bend in the river, there were *godowns* (warehouses) from Clarke Quay onwards.

The Singapore River ran through the very heart of the city. On the bank which faced northeast, to the right on standard maps of the island, lay the heart of the colonial administration, with the government buildings, the *padang* or recreation ground with its cricket square, and the whitewashed Anglican cathedral. From there it was just a short walk to Beach Road and the elegant Raffles Hotel.

Inland from the southwest facing riverbank, to the left on maps, was a district occupied early on by the Chinese. With Raffles' principle of free trade to

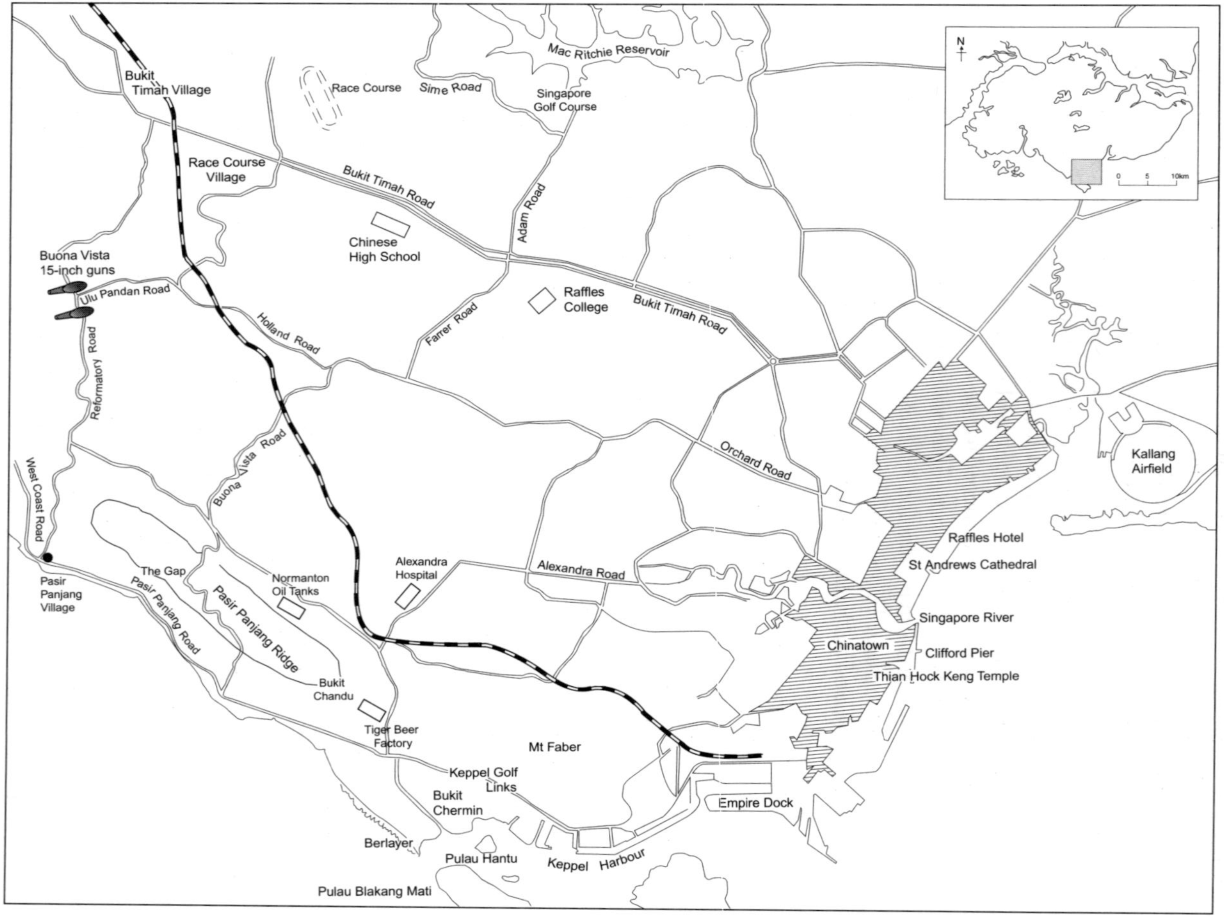

Map 2.2 Singapore city in 1941.

nurture it, this Chinese-dominated area thrived all too well.[6] By 1941 there was street after street of two and three-storey Chinese shophouses. Their upper storeys, with painted shutters in place of glass windows, were often divided into small, dank cubicles, a separate family crammed into each one. Here it was not uncommon, even in the 1950s, for twenty people to share an open-bucket toilet emptied once every two, or even three days. For the new immigrants, rickshaw pullers, and harbour workers who inhabited the cubicles here, Singapore could be an unforgiving place. Even feeding an extra mouth could prove too great a challenge. Almost 400 babies were abandoned at the orphanage of the sisters of Infant Jesus in the year of 1936 alone.[7]

The narrow streets and houses around this area, today dubbed 'Chinatown', remained crowded with people and rickshaws, with Chinese signboards, washing stuck out of upper windows on bamboo poles, and street vendors making the area alive with clutter. The gvernment decided that the area was so crowded that it was better not to build air-raid shelters here, preferring to encourage residents to take shelter away from the city. That, of course, was hardly practical for people who needed to carry on earning a living nearby.[8] So when Japanese bombers arrived from December 1941, heavy casualties were inevitable.

Sixty three people were killed in Singapore, and 133 injured, in the first Japanese air-raid alone, when Japanese bombers arrived to find Singapore illuminated by a bright moon, and with its street lights still shining, early on the morning of 8 December 1941.[9] Many more were killed when the bombers returned in January and almost daily in February, with as many as 2,000 casualties a day. The bombers came in multiples of 27: 54; 81; 108. One resident described people watching the bombers as they flew over, like silver fish in a sea of azure blue. These majestic visitors would discharge their bombs as a unit, making the ground shudder under the impact.[10] Roads were filled with debris, broken telephone lines twisted and curled, shophouses burnt In Chinatown and Orchard Road alike, people resorted to the deep storm drains either side of the roads for cover. But this was a rough and ready solution. When the bombs and later artillery shells came too close the lucky ones, who had kept their heads down, found their backsides peppered with shrapnel. When they came closer still, the drains ran with blood.[11]

This is not to say that 'Chinatown' was an unchanging place. Far from it. The shoreline receded over time, so seafront streets found themselves inland, and the temper and function of some streets changed dramatically. Smith Street and Sago Street were famous for their brothels early in the century. By 1941, these establishments, which once thrived by servicing an overwhelmingly male workforce, had been closed for a decade. The Japanese brothels clustered around Malay Street and Bugis Street, a stone's throw from Raffles Hotel, had gone as well. They had been shut down as the worldwide depression of the 1930s drove down rubber prices and slowed male migration, but not female, and as London's scruples about regulating such exploitation overcame the local government's more pragmatic approach. The inevitable result was to drive the trade, now unregulated, onto the streets, and the incidence of disease upwards.[12]

The Singapore of 1941 was, then, already very different from the Singapore of 1891 or 1914. It had changed from a late nineteenth-century town of male migrant workers, many seeking solace in prostitutes and opium (until after the First World War still the largest single source of government revenue), and help from clan houses and secret societies.[13] It had metamorphosed from a sort of oriental 'frontier' town, a vanguard for capitalism's penetration of the Malayan jungle and a staging post to China, to a relatively sophisticated and modern city.

Sophisticated in services that is, not in terms of local or national identity. Singapore remained a place where the Governor, and the white colonial officer, provided the iron framework for an impossibly varied society. It was a place where disparate races met in the market place, but went home to separate districts and worshipped in different churches, temples and mosques: St Andrews Cathedral with its whitewash; Thian Hock Keng temple (Temple of Heavenly Bliss), with its curved and dragon tipped roofs, and sturdy courtyard pillars; and the simpler mosques.[14]

If Singapore's population thought of themselves as local at all, it was probably as a resident of one of the Straits Settlements, or even of a wider area of 'British Malaya'. But most of the population still saw themselves mainly in relation to their place of origin; feeling themselves overseas Chinese, or Indians abroad, or Perak or Selangor Malays. When they thought politically, it was often in relation to overseas reference points.

In this way, most of Malaya's Chinese saw their anti-Japanese activities as an attempt to shore up a Chinese homeland, after Sino–Japanese friction developed into all-out war from July 1937. For them, this was not a Malayan, Pacific or even world war. Those are occidental ways of describing conflicts that started later on. For most of Malaya's Chinese, this was the second Sino–Japanese War (the first having been in 1894–5). For them, the Pacific War, when it did finally come, was to be experienced as a by-product of this prior, core conflict.

The plight of China stirred overseas Chinese patriotism. One student might join the communists after a lecture at a Chinese-language school; for another patriotism would be pricked by patriotic songs sung in front of Telok Ayer Street's Thian Hock Keng temple.[a] Either way, the focus was on China, and on Chinese suffering there. Later, when it came to supporting the resistance in the war, by supplying food or medicine or in person, the sentiment of the more idealistic would be that 'all lives must end, but brave hearts end worthily, and in history'.

---

a Chin Peng was recruited to anti-Japanese organisations after hearing a speaker at school. He later became Secretary-General of the Malayan Communist Party. The teenager moved by the Wuhan Choral group outside the temple was Wong Aii Wen. She was later tortured by the Japanese, *Straits Times*, 24 October 1999, p. 39.

Indians, meanwhile, might look over their shoulder at conflicts between the Indian National Congress and the British Raj, creating for some an ambivalence about their role between imperial ruler and Asian invader. It is true that some Malays, especially teachers and journalists, already had an embryonic sense of Malay nationalism, or at least of the right of Malays and Malay culture to predominate in the Sultanates. It is also true that some long-settled, English-speaking Straits Chinese felt a strong loyalty to the Crown and the Settlements, forming a 'Straits Chinese British Association'. But most other groups looked to their own parochial or overseas identities, while accepting the utility, or at least inevitability, of British rule.

Britain, in turn, accepted the inevitability of its role as protector. Even if it had not wanted the local population to concentrate on producing export-earning commodities, the very passion and overseas orientation of Malaya's Chinese made Britain doubly wary of tapping their support. Did not the communists oppose imperialism, and the Kuomintang the communists? Was the hatred for Japan which these two Chinese parties shared compatible with the British need to appease in the east, while Hitler looked dangerous in the west? From July to October 1940 Britain went so far, under Japanese pressure, as to temporarily close the Burma Road, across which supplies ran from India to China. It was only after July 1941, when the United States seemed to harden its line against Japanese expansion, that antagonising Japan could start to seem slightly less foolhardy.[15]

Hence the 'long Sino–Japanese War' of overseas Chinese, which involved boycotts and fund-raising and propaganda, and stretched back to 1937, seemed to run counter to Britain's diplomatic interests as well as its imperialist instincts.[16] A potent blend of race hierarchy, imperialism and diplomacy ensured there was little hope of Britain calling a population to arms, though newspaperman E.M. Glover claimed that 'At a word from the Governor in September 1939, they ... would have rallied as one man to the nation's cause'. If 'nation' is changed to 'China', Glover is undoubtedly right where the Chinese were concerned. Nor were such sentiments entirely restricted to the Chinese. As early as January 1941, Indian business leader R. Jumabhoy called for Indians to join the Air Raid Precautions Association. Later, when war came to Singapore itself, all races lined the streets to donate blood.[17]

For want of a will or a way, this potential remained largely untapped. Britain continued to look askance at recruiting too many local residents, preferring to send troops from India or Burma to garrison Singapore, and when war threatened, yet more Australian and British troops.

The foundations for more broader, more inclusive local identities were being laid, but only very slowly. The 1930s depression played a role in this, slowing male immigration from China to a trickle. But female migration continued, with more and more people now settling as couples, or becoming couples on settling. In turn, the Second World War was soon to cut these people off from China for a long period, so that for some, at least, 'Singapore' and 'Malaya' became more a home, and less a temporary adventure overseas.

So Singapore City was changing, with an increasing proportion of people being born locally, rather than being sojourners or first-generation immigrants. But the Singapore Island Britain sought to defend was much more than a bustling city.

North of the city's outskirts, there were reservoirs with names such as MacRitchie and Pierce. These were essential to the water supply, which in normal times was also supplemented by a pipeline to Malaya.

Still around the centre of the island, and about five miles northwest of the city, was Bukit Timah (Malay for 'Tin Hill'). The latter was a steep hill, characterised more by granite than tin, despite its name, and covered in virgin forest. It had been declared Singapore's first nature reserve back in 1883. But its significance for 1941 to 1942 was that, at over 530 feet (162 metres) above sea-level, it was the highest natural point in Singapore. Only Mount Faber, which overlooks the south coast just west of the city, matches it as an obvious vantage point.[18] If an enemy could capture Bukit Timah Hill, they could look down Bukit Timah Road, towards the city itself.

Travelling further away from Singapore City, moving west, north and east, well-built colonial bungalows gave way to Chinese farms and Malay *kampongs*, interspersed by forest. Beyond these there was the coastline, much of which looked back to Malaya. This was fringed with mangrove swamps, intersected by creeks, and in some case backed onto jungle.

The main break in this pattern of farm and forest was the massive British naval base, on the northern coast about three miles east of the Causeway. The base was built in the 1920s and 1930s, unfortunately as it was to turn out, barely more than a stone's throw from the coast of Johore.

The 'Gibraltar of the East'

At first, the location of the naval base seems a puzzle. It faced the Johore coast, across a Johore Strait that ranged from 600 to 2,000 yards across. This meant it would be extremely vulnerable to bombardment from Johore, should the latter ever fall into enemy hands.

But in the 1920s, when construction of the base began, landward attack seemed unlikely. Indeed, at the time it was unlikely, since Britain then had few obvious naval rivals in Europe. There was not likely to be any significant impediment to mustering a fleet to relieve Singapore, and once on its way this could reach the island in just forty-two days.[19] With Johore's east coast roads still primitive, and Japan's nearest base over 1,500 miles away, in Formosa, it seemed unlikely that a landward attack on Singapore could succeed in the time available. Certainly, no aircraft could fly that far, even in 1941.

In the 1920s, then, the overriding consideration was how to shield the base against naval attack in the period between the outbreak of war, and the arrival of the Royal Navy. For this purpose, the location chosen for the base at Sembawang was ideal. By positioning the base next to the Causeway, with its

Plate 2.1 A Changi beach before development. A beach in the Changi area in eastern Singapore, in pristine state before the area was covered in neat barracks.

Source: James J. McGrane.

back to the Malayan mainland and right in the middle of Singapore's northern coast, Britain kept it as far from the open sea as possible.

Attacking battleships would have an extreme range of 40,000 yards. That is, well over 20 miles. Placing the base in the middle Singapore's northern coast meant the base's guns could be pushed up to 20,000 yards in front of the base, to the southern and eastern extremities of the island. Since the biggest of these coastal guns were themselves 15 inch battleship guns mounted on land, with a range of 36,900 yards (21 miles), they would be able to fire on attacking ships well before the latter's guns came within range of the base.

The first money was for the base was authorised by British authorities in 1923. Afterwards, contributions flowed in from Hong Kong, the Straits Settlements, the Malay States and New Zealand; but not Australia, which preferred to spend the money on building up the Australian navy as its

Plate 2.2 The naval base. Building the naval base also involved turning swamp and forest areas into acres of modern facilities. Here a Royal Navy ship is refitted in a huge floating dock, moored in the Straits of Johore.

Source: Australian War Memorial: negative number 007748.

contribution to Imperial defence. In total the base was to cost £63 million, the contributions being a good symbol of Singapore's position as an imperial base and communications centre.

As it took shape, the base was to supplement one of the world's most impressive military routes. After Gibraltar, Malta, Suez and Aden, Singapore (some 7,000 miles from Britain via Suez) formed the next link on a line stretching over 10,000 miles from Southampton to Shanghai, on the River Yangtze. On the Yangtze itself, there were still fourteen British gunboats in 1921: the year the decision to build the base was taken.[20]

The decision to build a base at Singapore had in turn been caused by the obsolescence of existing docks and stores. The launch of the bigger Dreadnought class battleships from 1906, and the conversion of the Royal Navy to using oil rather than coal as fuel, meant that by 1918 there was no eastern base that could support a modern fleet. While Singapore itself already had five docks, none could take the biggest battleships of the Royal Navy.

The new Singapore base was designed to fulfil these needs. Notwithstanding brief delays during periods of Labour government in 1924 and from 1929 to

Plate 2.3 Sinister twilight. Smoke from the naval base blackens the sky in 1942. Seen looking back from the mouth of the Singapore River. The clock tower belongs to the Victoria Memorial Hall, the nearby dome to the Supreme Court. To the right of that there are the Corinthian columns of the City Hall, which overlooks the *padang*, and the sea beyond. In the distance is the spire of St Andrew's Cathedral.

Source: Australian War Memorial: negative number 012468.

1931, for reasons of parsimony and peace-mongering, it was all but complete by 1938. The base's King George VI dry dock, capable of taking the largest capital ships afloat, was opened on 14 February 1938. At 1,000 feet long, 130 feet wide, and 35 deep, it joined an equally impressive floating dock, already anchored in the Johore Strait.

Presiding at the dock's official opening was Sir Shenton Thomas, the Governor of the Straits Settlements. Eleven thousand people attended, including the Indian and Chinese construction workers, the Duke of Sutherland, the First Lord of the Admiralty, and Sir Charles Vyner Brooke, white rajah of Sarawak. Twenty-five British naval ships paraded as aircraft from HMS *Eagle* flew overhead, as the Japanese Consul-General looked on.[21]

Britain's naval base and 'Gibraltar of the East', as the *Daily Express* put it, was all but ready. The docks themselves, with their huge cranes capable of lifting a whole battleship turret, were the crowning glory. The base beyond them covered several square miles, with seventeen football pitches, endless workshops and storerooms, and streets of English-style houses.[22]

Some of the best of the houses, around Admiralty Road, were excellent specimens of the colonial architecture of the time, with its 'black and white' painted bungalows. Their shutters, verandahs, and the upper floors jutting out and supported by pillars, were a little reminiscent of stilted Malay dwellings. But these houses also had distinctly English-style gardens, large and landscaped, creating a fusion of east of west, of England and Malaya. The area around about had its own 'village church', and road-names which mapped out the empire: Bermuda; Ottawa; Malta and Gibraltar Crescents; and King's and Queen's Avenues.

Nor was the naval base at Sembawang, and the airstrip built nearby, the only major development. Beyond the naval base, new air bases were constructed at Tengah in the northwest, Seletar in the northeast, and at Kallang just to the east of the city for commercial traffic. Other areas of Singapore were also developed, as Singapore transformed, in two decades, from being a sparsely defended commercial port, with a concentration of guns around the southern coast and a small garrison, to becoming Britain's major strongpoint east of India.[23]

The Changi district was foremost amongst those transformed, as international politics and strategy impinged on Singapore's life. The Changi area, where the River Changi flows into the South China Sea, is at the easternmost extremity of the island. It is about fourteen miles from the heart of the city as a bird flies, rather more by winding roads. Here, in the early 1920s, the coast was still picturesque and undeveloped. Here too the forest gave way to a narrow strip of sandy beach, to a handful of Malay houses and government bungalows, and to a wooden Japanese hotel built on stilts over the sea.

Then came the decisions to build the naval base, and to protect it with new coastal guns. Changi was to house many of these, arranged in an arc from the mouth of the river Changi in the east, to the site of the present Changi airport on the coast just to the south. The planners also decided the gunners should live at Changi, for reasons which suggest the 1927 Gillman Commission on coastal defences did not find Singapore welcoming:

> They... suggested that, in view of local conditions such as the enervating climate, endemic malaria and venereal disease among the local population and a high level of 'murders, robberies and strikes', the garrison should not be scattered in isolated detachments but concentrated in high-standard barracks, with good amusement facilities.'[b][24]

---

b Strikes were then on the rise. On 12 March 1927 a procession commemorating the second anniversary of Sun Yat Sen's death was hijacked by activists. After a trolley bus tried to force its way through, and an arrest was made, it culminated in an attempt to storm Kreta Ayer Police Station. The police fired warning shots. The attackers persisted. The police fired for real. The result: 2 Chinese dead, 4 mortally wounded, and 11 others injured. Kuomintang activists, anti-imperialist sentiment among Singapore's Chinese youth, radical Hainainese night-school teachers, and incipient communism were responsible. One banner read: 'Abolish all unequal treaties', another, 'Eternal success to the world revolution'. Banishments and police informers then kept these forces within limits until war intervened.

These facilities were to be built just inland of the guns themselves.[25]

In 1927 the Royal Engineers arrived to begin work. At first there was not even suitable accommodation for working parties, so one officer, one foreman and eighteen 'coolies' travelled the road from Singapore City each day, to clear ground and build huts. Only then could more men come in, building themselves a pier and installing electricity (candles had to be resorted to at times) and still later connecting Changi to Singapore's mains water supply. The Royal Engineers brought in Chinese contractors, who in turn hired Tamil coolies, so that within a year the site was abuzz with activity.[26] Land was drained, trees felled, earth moved, roads laid, workshops constructed, a quarry started for stone and a factory for making concrete. Stretches of railway track were built, including one to run supplies to the big 15 inch naval guns, which were installed in the 1930s, just inland from the coast.

Where pythons and cobras were common before, there were soon good roads, comfortable Royal Artillery messes and fine recreation grounds. Squadron Leader H. A. Probert's *History of Changi* simply states that

> In fifteen years a piece of virgin jungle had been transformed into one of the most modern and best equipped military bases in the world. The Royal Engineers in Kitchener Barracks, the Gordon Highlanders at Selarang stood ready, yet the chances of war ever coming to Singapore looked remote.

There was to be an irony to all this. Changi prison was completed in 1936 and the nearby Selerang Barracks about the same time, just in time for the Japanese to capture them and fill them with interned civilians and allied prisoners. The coastal guns were also finished by 1939, though in 1941 Changi still did not have an airstrip. That had to await the Japanese, who used Prisoners of War to build the first runways here from 1943.[27] The Royal Air Force took these over in 1946, and got Japanese Prisoners of War to reciprocate by laying a runway of pierced steel planks. The Royal Air Force continued using Changi until after the confrontation with Indonesia in the 1960s, destroying the site of two of Changi's three 15 inch coastal guns as they improved the runways. In this way, the origins of the modern Changi airport, Singapore's main civil airport since 1981, lay in the defeat of Fortress Singapore, not in its construction.[28]

The sinister twilight

But defeat still lay in the future, and for the moment even an attack was all but unthinkable. To the residents of Singapore, military and civilian alike, the changing landscape and the filling airwaves and sky must have made the British Empire seem as strong as ever in the early 1930s. It would have been difficult to persuade many British here, the commercial classes surrounded by servants and fine roads and with packed *godowns* on the river bank, or the many officers and men in their new barracks, that they belonged to a declining empire with a shrinking fleet. For many Chinese, Indians and Malays too, at least those outside of plantations and remote *kampongs*, the proliferation of roads and doctors spoke of development, not decline.

A quarter of the world was still painted red on British atlases, empire flying boats and radio waves linked together territories as never before, and new territories, such as Palestine and German East Africa, had come under British influence, as League of Nations mandated territories, since the First World War.[29]

The very experience of travelling to Singapore would have reaffirmed the faith of the newcomer to Malaya in the British Empire. A new recruit to the Malayan Civil Service, or to a rubber plantation in Malaya, would sail the slow, red route from Britain, through Gibraltar, Malta, Port Said, the Red Sea, and on to Aden and Ceylon, before arriving at Singapore. Except for a stop at Marseille, the experience of travel mapped out dominance. To see the map coloured red was one thing, but to experience such cartographic domination first hand must have been as intoxicating as it was illusory.

Once in Singapore, or even dispatched to some *ulu* (upriver) district in Malaya, the impression of dominance would have been confirmed. A young British bachelor, not long out of university, could hope to rise to District Officer, supervising local justice and taxes and administration for a whole area. They could expect servants to make their lives comfortable as well, or at least as comfortable as club and servants could make life confronted by squadrons of mosquitoes, ants in your tea, and a climate that could punish a moderate walk with a layer of hot, slimy sweat.[30] Being British, for many, still meant privilege and power in the East.

If less wealthier Europeans now took Japanese and other Asians as mistresses, as many had until just before the First World War, even this was partly due to progress.[31] With improving health care, clubs and British styled 'Cold Storage' grocery shops, life became increasingly suitable for wives and families. The Singapore Cold Storage Company sold the first locally produced ice cream in 1923, and began baking fresh bread from 1930.[32] Malayan Breweries started up in 1932, giving birth to the still-popular Tiger Beer.[33]

The elite amongst the white community, meanwhile, could enjoy Raffles Hotel on Beach Road, with its potted palms, sunblinds and lazily whirring fans.[34] Right into 1941 it was possible to take a five-course dinner here, and dances continued to be advertised into 1942. Indeed, the increasing threat to the island intensified Singapore's nightlife.

Officers poured in, and as a result overcrowding on Raffles Hotel's dance floor, 'gave birth to a syncopated, close embrace to music which was known locally as crush-dancing. It was part of an atmosphere that was distinctly hectic for the normally decorous social life of the colony and was almost certainly attributable to the proliferation of uniforms among the evening gowns'[35] European goods could still be bought at Robinson's store on Raffles Place, 'Singapore's direct equivalent to Harrods', and coffee taken in its restaurant. By

1941 this restaurant even had air-conditioning, as did cinemas, cabarets and even a house or two.[36] Even after Robinsons suffered bomb damage on 8 December 1941, it continued to offer 'a cheery smile', wryly advertising special lines in 'perforated teapots and specially cut glass (cut to bits)'.[37]

As if this combination of tropical splendour and European comforts was not enough, for many Europeans, *amahs* to look after the children were an affordable luxury, with some having an impressive array of servants: water carriers, gardeners, and cleaners included.

The outbreak of European war scarcely changed this pattern. Even Churchill later confessed that the Japanese menace remained 'in a sinister twilight' in his mind.[38] Soldiers flooded into Singapore not so much to fight Japan, as to ensure by their deterrent effect that there never would be a battle for Malaya.

While newly arrived officers easily fitted the local social life of the European community, the rank and file were another matter. From 1939 the other ranks coming off the transports helped push up prices, indirectly causing hardship to those rubber tappers and ordinary workers whose wages did not keep pace with inflation. The troops also brought with them the 1940s hits from England. Men whose canteens one newspaperman recalled offering 'complex permutations on an invariable theme of sausages, beans, toast, eggs and chips with mugs of tea' for breakfast, despite Malaya's steamy climate, added hearty and exotic choruses of 'Run Rabbit Run ... Run Adolf, Run' and 'Roll out the Barrel' to Malaya's previous repertoire.

Beer, football and the occasional fight kept Australian and British other ranks busy, even when drill did not. Perhaps they also made petty restrictions more tolerable, such as their effective exclusion from innumerable hotels, and the lack of Western women. With so few Western women in town, unattached girls could take their pick of dates from the over-abundant supply of officers. Besides, daughters of colonial civil servants and businessmen were not an obvious match for privates and corporals. Rank and race alike continued to mark a man out in prewar Singapore, dictating what club he could attend, which doors were opened to him, and which remained firmly barred. Later on, when the going got tough, some soldiers were to ask themselves why they should die for a country which had done so little to make them welcome.[39]

War was making Malaya and Singapore livelier places, and arguably wealthier too. Officers and nurses added spice to prewar social life. War in Europe also meant more demand for Malaya's rubber and tin. European men were discouraged from abandoning plantations and mines to go and fight in Europe, since Malaya itself became an essential 'dollar arsenal'.[40] Rubber and tin from Malaya were sold to the United States, and therefore they provided Britain with the 'dollars' that were desperately needed to buy war equipment from America. No wonder that Malaya and Singapore came to seem, in the light of defeat, a fool's paradise, where the good life continued after September 1939, and where the war in Europe, the blitz of London, blackouts, and rationing seemed worlds away.[41]

Singapore was, then, many different things. It was a symbol of Britain's imperial domination of much of the east, stretching from Karachi to Hong Kong, and from Upper Burma to Sydney. It was a colony where a few white civil servants provided the iron framework for a mosaic of peoples. It was an entrepôt and free trade port which funnelled tropical goods to the West. It was a naval base and imperial garrison, with the myriad of barracks, magazines and workshops this implied. It was an exotic posting for British, Australian and Indian troops alike, with its striking combination of blue sky, red earth and palm trees; and with its vibrant flowers and its almost overwhelming range of smells, from spices to the stench of drains and of fish drying on the streets.[42] It was a 'fortress' area which covered Singapore and part of the south Johore coast, consisting of fixed coastal guns, and all the supporting apparatus needed to fire these accurately at approaching ships. It was also a city of 560,000, crowded in some places, green and elegant in others, Singapore City. But it was a city on an island also called Singapore, much of which was still covered with forest, mangrove and farms. Finally, it was a money-making, or more strictly speaking, a dollar-making machine, a role crucial to Britain's survival, but which made preparing for war psychologically and mentally difficult.

All of these characteristics, from the social structure to the geography, were to have an important impact on the island's defence, and it is to the planning of that defence that we must now turn.

3

THE FATAL DECISIONS

If Malaya's concentration on production, and its remoteness from the Europe's traumas, made it difficult to envisage war, propaganda about British strength and Japanese deficiencies gave a false air of security.

For Malaya's leaders, though, this was in large part knowingly false, a bravado affected to cover their knowledge that decisions taken from 1921 had left Malaya and Singapore without the ships, without the aircraft, and without the tanks it needed to meet a Japanese attack. In August 1941 the British Commander-in-Chief, Air Chief Marshal Sir Robert Brooke-Popham, stressed the importance of giving the Japanese 'an exaggerated impression of our strength, and of our confidence in our security'. In October 1941 he also wrote that, 'The main thing I try to do is to convey an impression of confidence'. British commanders and officials were most reluctant to tell the people of Malaya, who they were supposed to protect, and the troops, about half of whom were Indian, just how threadbare Britain's position was. The problem being, of course, that the propaganda may have fooled too many on their own side, and a few historians as well.[1]

The story of the fatal decisions which Brooke-Popham sought to obscure goes back at least as far as June 1921. For that was when the British Cabinet agreed that a new naval base should be built at Singapore.

This was the first of many decisions which together proved disastrous, a chain of disaster running through the building of the base and the failure to provide the necessary ships to defend it, to the adoption of *Operation Matador*: a plan which Churchill, as British Prime Minister, would not back with the necessary resources.

This chapter examines these decisions, which shaped the 'Fortress' and its defences, and Churchill's particular role in them, asking why they were taken and, to a lesser extent, what the alternatives were.

It divides these decisions into two very distinct types: the long-term 'strategic' and naval decisions which led to a base being built, and a naval strategy evolved for its defence; and the shorter-term, wartime decisions on what resources to commit to Singapore's defence.

From *Pax Britannica* to Fortress Singapore

The long-term context for the Singapore strategy was Britain's declining naval dominance. What might be termed a 'Naval Base' school of thought has attributed Singapore's loss to a supposedly pusillanimous willingness to accept this naval decline, and it is certainly true that naval power lay at the root of Britain's dilemma.[2]

The Britain which had claimed Singapore in 1819 had had no need to post large garrisons there. For just over 100 years after Raffles secured Singapore for the East India Company, in 1819, its local defences remained more remarkable for their weakness than for their strength. Singapore's real protection had then come from the Royal Navy's global dominance, backed when necessary by the Indian Army.[3]

But the *Pax Britannica* could not last forever. Japan's forced opening to the West by American ships, in 1853, ultimately led to its industrialisation, and to its expansion in Asia. Japan defeated China in a war of 1894–5, leading Britain to try and harness Japan's rising power by the Anglo-Japanese Alliance of 1902. Then the Russo-Japanese War of 1904–5 suggested Japan and Russia would remain preoccupied with each other for some time, preventing them from coveting other areas of Asia, or from interfering too greatly in China. With the Russian threat reduced, and Japan friendly, Britain concluded it no longer needed to maintain a major fleet in the East.

The Royal Navy responded by concentrating its capital ships in the West, where German naval building threatened Britain's traditional naval dominance. This made sense for just so long as Japan remained friendly. In January 1915, however, Britain detected signs that Japan would not be satisfied with the status quo. Under cover of the war, Japan issued Twenty-One demands to China. The Chinese were told they must cede German rights in the Shantung Peninsula to Japan, recognise a special Japanese position in South Manchuria, and accept Japanese political, financial and military advisers. Though Japan reduced these demands before China accepted them in May, it was clear Japan wanted to drastically increase its influence in China. This meant it might not remain a natural ally of Britain, which favoured keeping China as a sovereign and independent country, open for all to invest and trade in, and with no further concessions to foreign powers beyond existing treaty ports and areas.

With this in mind, Britain allowed the Anglo–Japanese treaty of 1902 to lapse in 1921, when it came up for renewal. Instead, it joined the United States in securing the Washington Naval Limitation Treaty of February 1922. This set a 5: 5: 3 ratio for American, British and Japanese capital ships, and a limit of 35,000 tons for any replacement battleships. At the time the treaty looked a good way of avoiding an expensive naval race with Japan and the United States. A race which Britain, hit by a postwar slump, could ill-afford. There was a further London Naval Limitations conference in 1930, which set a similar ratio for cruisers, and gave Japan parity in destroyers and submarines. In June 1935 an

Anglo–German Naval agreement was signed as well, allowing Germany to build a navy up to 35 per cent of the strength of Britain's.

This limitation in British naval building was a critical first stage in determining Singapore's fate. But it would be naive to assume that any increase in ships launched earlier would have turned out to Britain's advantage later. The Washington Naval Limitation Treaty of February 1922 did have short-term benefits. It resulted in Japan abandoning some work, notably plans for *Kaga*, *Amagi* and *Kii* class battleships, all of which would have used a 16 inch (41 cm) gun. Plans for a still larger 18 inch (46 cm) gun were also shelved.

Japan only formally renounced the Washington naval limitations in December 1934; the same year British rearmament began to take effect. This meant Japan was free of restrictions after the stipulated two-year wait, in 1936, when it commenced a crash-building programme. The ensuing construction added no less than four aircraft carriers to Japan's fleet by 1941. Japan's first battleship with 18 inch guns, the *Yamato*, was also completed in late 1941, just in time for the Pacific war. Had Britain committed itself to an earlier naval race, it is by no means clear its extra building would have compensated for that of other countries. Nor is it obvious that Britain would have concentrated extra building on aircraft carriers, which were to be the key to naval dominance in the Pacific.

By September 1941, then, Japan had no less than ten aircraft carriers, meaning it had the capacity to counter whatever naval moves Britain, by then facing Germany and Italy, had planned. Only the intervention of the United States, which had several carriers of its own, could tip the balance. It was to be 1 December 1941 before the United States belatedly promised to support Britain against any Japanese aggression.[4]

The reality is that the 1930s represented a concentration of all the threats Britain faced, as a result of the late nineteenth-century emergence of new, industrialised, competitor nation-states. Before 1860 there had been no Italy, no Germany and little development in Japan. By the mid-1930s all these countries were naval competitors. Any British rearmament could result in countermoves by at least three countries. In this way, and in the space of a few decades, Singapore's position changed out of all recognition. Once effectively shielded by the Royal Navy's global supremacy, it increasingly had to look to defend itself. It would have to be able to survive at least until the Royal Navy could muster a relieving fleet, and rush this eastwards from the Mediterranean and Atlantic.

This changing situation demanded that there be a Far Eastern base to receive and service any reinforcing fleet. The answer was to create a naval base at Singapore. Singapore was chosen because Hong Kong was too close to Japan and Formosa to be safe and to be reinforced in time, and Sydney too far away from China and Southeast Asia to be a main base. Besides, Hong Kong could not be fortified further under the terms of the Washington treaties of 1921–2.

The British Cabinet endorsed plans to build a new naval base at Singapore in June 1921. By 1923 the initial funds had been voted. Building continued from then on, with only brief interruptions under Labour governments, which favoured military economies domestically and disarmament talks internationally, in 1924 and 1929–31. By 1938 the base was virtually complete.

The decision to build a major base at Singapore also raised the question of how to defend it in what came to be called the 'period before relief'. That is, the period between a crisis breaking out, and the arrival of a main fleet which must come from up to 8,000 nautical miles away. Initially, this period was put at twenty-eight days if there was plenty of warning and good weather, up to forty-two if conditions were unfavourable.

Then, even as the base was being built, conditions became progressively worse. There was the rise and increasing aggressiveness of Mussolini in the 1920s, and Hitler and Japan in the 1930s. Against this background, the estimated period before relief rose from forty-two days in the 1920s to early 1930s to seventy days in 1937, ninety in June 1939, and then to 180 upon the outbreak of war in Europe in September 1939. The Fall of France in June 1940 then removed one allied fleet from the reckoning.

With Britain deprived of its French ally, and facing both the German and Italian navies, it could no longer be sure how long it would take to assemble a main fleet for the East.[5] It also became wise to avoid using the Suez Canal wherever possible, because ships using this route would have to run the gauntlet of German and Italian aircraft in the Mediterranean.

By late 1941 the hope was that a small fleet could be gathered in the Indian Ocean early the following year, in spring 1942. This fleet was to include several capital ships, at least one aircraft carrier, as well as numerous cruisers and destroyers. But there was no guarantee that hope would turn into fact. In the meanwhile, Churchill insisted on sending a small 'deterrent' force of the most modern ships, rather than the larger number of older, slower vessels preferred by his naval advisers. Eventually the battleship *Prince of Wales* and battlecruiser *Repulse* were sent out as a token force: Force Z. The capital ships arrived in Singapore in early December 1941, where their progress up the narrow Straits of Johore to the naval base presented a magnificent spectacle.[6]

Each time the expected period before relief was lengthened, or Japanese conquests and bases moved nearer, it had implications for Singapore's defence. Initially, the forty-two day period was so short, and the nearest Japanese bases in Formosa so far away, that it seemed unlikely Japan would have time to land troops in Johore and mount a landward attack before British capital ships could appear off Singapore. This was not, at the time, wishful thinking. The jungle of the Johore coastline opposite Singapore, and that state's poor road system, were real limiting factors for any invader. Troops landed at Johore's most obvious ports, at Endau or Mersing on its east coast, would initially have to navigate poor roads and tracks. If an invader failed to take Singapore before a British fleet could arrive, the plight of their troops, stranded in Malaya, would be dire.

Despite the short period before relief, however, Japan might have enough time to send battleships to raid the island. Japan itself was 3,000 miles away,

THE FATAL DECISIONS

with forward bases not much more than 1,500 miles away, in Formosa. This meant Singapore's existing defences were inadequate. These then consisted of a small garrison of regular troops, local volunteers and five 9.2 inch guns. The problem with these was twofold.

The first problem was that the existing guns were located mainly in the south at the offshore islands of Blakang Mati (present-day Sentosa) and nearby Pulau Brani, to protect Keppel Harbour. Keppel Harbour was Singapore's commercial port, lying along the shoreline of Singapore City itself, to the west of the Singapore River. Yet the chosen location for the new naval base was on the opposite, northern shore. From the old guns on Pulau Blakang Mati to the new base in the north was a distance of over 14 miles.

The second problem was that Japanese warships already boasted guns which could out-range the 9.2-inch specimens at Singapore. What Singapore would need, the Admiralty concluded in 1922, was no less than eight 15 inch guns, of the type then common on battleships. Six of these could be located to the east, to guard the approaches to the new naval base from Japanese bases.[7]

For the rest of the 1920s there were squabbles over finance, what to build and where, and over whether the Royal Air Force (RAF) could replace many of the biggest guns with torpedo aircraft. But aircraft ranges were still short and airborne torpedo attacks were unproven against capital ships. In addition aircraft, which could be moved away, were less certain to be available when needed than fixed coastal guns. So a compromise emerged.[a] First, in 1928, it was agreed that Singapore should get three heavy guns and most of the 6 inch and 9.2 inch guns in the first stage of building, pending final decisions. Then, after a Labour government suspended work in 1929 to 1931, came a final compromise in 1932.[8]

The 1932 compromise was that Singapore would get a 'fortress system' to include five modern, heavy 15 inch naval guns, six 9.2 inch guns, and eighteen 6 inch guns. The RAF, meanwhile, won recognition that it had an auxiliary role. It would provide reconnaissance, fighter aircraft, and torpedo bombers to hit battleships.

By 1934 the first 6 and 9.2 inch guns were in place. By 1935 Japan and Germany had renounced armaments limitation. Authority was now given for a second stage of building, to include two additional 15 inch guns, and two more

---

[a] The RAF never forgave this defeat. Lord Tedder claimed that even in 1938 he felt 'there was something pathetic about the 15-inch gun turret', especially when, at the ceremonial opening of a gun, he saw on the breech a broad arrow and the figures 1915:

> The general asked me if I would fire the first shot. I declined the honour and am afraid I could not resist saying that I did not feel the gun would ever fire in anger for it covered the main entrance to the Singapore Straits and one could not expect an enemy to break in the front door'.

The 1915 date means the gun he recalled must have been at Johore Battery. Lord Tedder, *With Prejudice* (London: Cassell, 1966), pp. 6–7.

Plate 3.1 Underground bunker. The construction of the three-storey underground bunker for one of the 15 inch coastal guns (Mk. II mounting). Ammunition and equipment to provide electric and hydraulic power was located in the arms seen left and right. There were further tunnels behind. The gun was mounted in a 'turret' like structure over the central circle in the picture. Shells were fed to it from directly underneath, by means of a winch. This gun could traverse 240 degrees, 290 if safety stops to avoid damage to hydraulic cables were removed, and nearly all-round if power for the gun was disconnected.

Source: James J. McGrane.

airfields. The first 15 inch gun was installed in 1936, and by 1939 Singapore's 'fortress system' was almost complete.[9]

Here it is worth noting an important distinction. Singapore itself was not a fortress. It was an island, containing a naval base, with the naval base being defended by a fortress system. The fortress system comprised fixed guns with overlapping fields of fire, observation posts set in concrete on hills, searchlights and rangefinding and plotting equipment, working together to provide an integrated defence against seaward attack, from the south or east. At its best (for the big 15 inch guns), information on range and bearing from the observation posts was converted into firing data by a plotting room, and fed directly, by electrical cables, to guns positioned out of sight of the coast. Their indirect fire would then keep them unseen by the enemy.

Plate 3.2 The railway crane. The 100-ton railway crane lowers part of the 15 inch gun platform into place.

Source: James J. McGrane.

Plate 3.3 Gun barrel en route to its battery.

Source: James J. McGrane.

Plate 3.4 Train and railway crane.
Source: James J. McGrane.

The armament of this fortress system comprised one set of guns in the south, on and close to Blakang Mati and commanded from Mount Faber (Faber Fire Command); and another guarding the eastern approaches to the island and naval base, commanded by Changi Fire Command. In each case, the name derived from the hill which the main fire command post was placed on: Mount Faber; and Changi Hill.[10]

Each fire command had one battery of the biggest, 15 inch guns: Buona Vista Battery of two guns in Faber Command; Johore Battery of three guns in Changi Fire Command. Each also had a share of the 6 inch and 9.2 inch guns, and of smaller weapons for close defence.

Many of the guns could be turned to face landward, if obstructing concrete and trees were removed. The truth, though, was that there were no defensive works to link up these widely dispersed guns, the guns themselves would be far more effective against ships than men, and the northern side of the island was defended by the jungle of Johore and the Strait, rather than by fortifications.[11]

So for Singapore the word 'fortress' did not mean citadel or fortified place, but a system designed to allow twenty-nine large, modern coastal guns to fire accurately at approaching ships. The 'fortress system' was based as much on islands around Singapore (and in the case of one battery on the south Johore coast) as it was on Singapore itself.

Plate 3.5 A searchlight in the 'Fortress system'.
Source: James J. McGrane.

From the 1920s to the 1930s, the defensive concept was that the 'fortress' would repel seaward attacks, with only limited defence required to counter landing parties on Singapore's northern shores, and in Johore. The rest of Malaya could be left to locally raised volunteer forces, and perhaps to the Malay Regiment. The latter was raised in the early 1930s at the request of the sultans, starting on a small, experimental basis to test the 'martial' qualities of the Malays.[12]

The late 1930s saw this strategic conception, with the emphasis on seaward defence of the naval base, totally overturned. The outbreak of the Sino–Japanese conflict from July 1937 was not enough by itself, and neither were the improvements in roads in Johore and the west coast, and increasing aircraft ranges. But the creeping advance of Japan towards Southeast Asia, and the lengthening of the period before relief until it became indeterminate after June 1940, gradually eroded old certainties.[13]

Plate 3.6 The observation post for Connaught Battery.
Source: James J. McGrane.

Plate 3.7 A rangefinder badly disguised as a local *attap* hut.
Source: Public Record Office (UK): W0203/1 539.

These changes came together in 1940. The Sino–Japanese War had been dragging on for three years, and Japan was anxious to persuade Western powers to discontinue supplying the Chinese government. This included pressure on Britain to close supply routes from Burma to China, the Burma Road, and attempts to gain more influence on the borders of southern China. As part of this process, Japan secured bases in French Indochina, in its north, in September 1940. In July 1941 it moved into southern Indochina as well, though it stopped short of ousting the Vichy French colonial government.

This meant everything had changed from the 1920s. Then a distant power which accepted naval limitation, Japan was now rapidly building new ships. In taking positions in Indochina, it had also secured access to bases just 650 miles from Singapore, and 400 miles across the Gulf of Siam from north Malaya. These advance bases in Indochina made a sudden and large-scale attack on south Thailand and Malaya's east coast possible. From these landing sites invaders might cross to Malaya's west coast, where excellent north–south communications would open the road to Singapore.

All of which raises the question: how far was the fall of Singapore due not to naval decline, itself an almost inevitable symptom of the erosion of technological and industrial supremacy, but rather to strategic decisions taken in the last years and months? Here a sharp debate emerges, between those who blame Churchill for taking the wrong decisions, and those who emphasise Britain's strategic dilemma in standing alone against Germany, Italy and Japan from June 1940.

Churchill and strategy: from main fleet to *Matador*

I take the fullest personal responsibility Churchill to Parliament, 27 January 1942, justifying the priority he had given Russia and 'the Nile valley' over Malaya for tanks, ships and aircraft.[14]

Strategies which had been sound in the 1920s had now became redundant. But British commanders had long anticipated this. As early as 1936 Major-General William Dobbie, General Officer Commanding (Malaya) since 1935, had asked if more forces would be required on the mainland. These might guard against the threat of the Japanese landing there and grabbing forward bases for an attack on Singapore. He also got his Chief Staff Officer, Colonel A. E. Percival, to draw up an appreciation on how the Japanese were most likely to attack.

Percival's late 1937 report duly confirmed that north Malaya might become the critical battleground. He said the Japanese might seize east coast landing sites in Thailand and Malaya, in order to capture aerodromes and achieve local air superiority. This could be the prelude to further Japanese landings in Johore, to disrupt communications northwards, and the construction of another main base in North Borneo. From North Borneo, the final sea and air assault could be launched against eastern Singapore, against the Changi area.[15]

Dobbie and Percival made it clear that Singapore could no longer be seen as a self-contained naval base. Instead, its fate might become intimately intertwined with that of the mainland. In May 1938 Dobbie wrote that, 'It is an attack from the northward that I regard as the greatest potential danger to the Fortress. Such an attack could be carried out in the northeast monsoon. The jungle is not in most places impassable for infantry'.[16] By the end of 1938 the Chiefs of Staff (COS) had accepted that there was now a real danger that Singapore could be attacked by troops who had established themselves in Johore. Dobbie also told them that an attack might be possible between November and March, despite the high winds and waves produced by the northeast monsoon. The recent landing of '5,000 smuggled coolies' in this period had blown any idea that the monsoon offered protection. Quite the reverse, the monsoon would provide cloud cover for an invader.[17]

Events now served to make Dobbie's warnings seem more and more realistic. The Japanese took Hainan Island off the southern coast of China in 1939, and developed a substantial fleet of motorised landing craft. The scale of threat was increasing, and this was reflected in the British COS's August 1940 'Far East Appreciation'.

The August 1940 appreciation showed that London increasingly accepted that it was important to hold all of Malaya, not just the area around the naval base. It emphasised the importance of holding the north. This was now vital if Japan was to be prevented from establishing forward airfields, which could then be used against Singapore. The report also recognised that, once established in the north, the Japanese might advance overland to take the naval base. Malaya's existing eighty-eight aircraft were now manifestly inadequate. The COS suggested 336 would be ideal. But, in what was to become a pattern, they said they could not manage this in the short-term. For the moment, Malaya would have to make do with more infantry.[18]

The figure of 336 aircraft became a target to be attained in 1941, but even this proved unrealistic. The problem was that Churchill had to balance Home, Atlantic, Bomber offensive, Mediterranean and Middle East conflicts, as well as Malaya. Each seemed vital: without the Home front there was nothing; the Atlantic was Britain's umbilical cord to Empire and American supplies; the Bomber offensive the only way of hitting back at a Germany triumphant on the Continent or, later, of relieving pressure on the Soviet Union; and the Middle East seemed to be the key to oil, Africa, and the allegiance of countries beyond.

In his attempt to square the circle, Churchill soon insisted that the active Middle East theatre take precedence over still peaceful Singapore. Churchill's logic was that the chance of an attack on Singapore remained remote, and anyway its ultimate guardian was not the army and air force, but the Royal Navy. In September 1940 he argued that:

> The prime defence of Singapore is the Fleet ... whether it is on the spot or not ... The fact that the Japanese had made landings in Malaya and had even begun the siege of the [Singapore] fortress would not deprive a superior fleet of its power. On the contrary, the plight of the besiegers, cut off from home while installing themselves in the swamps and jungle, would be the more forlorn ... The idea of trying to defend the Malay peninsula and of holding the whole of Malaya ... cannot be entertained.[19]

On this occasion, reinforcements were routed to the Middle East rather than Singapore. But herein lay a tragic division: Churchill continued to insist Singapore would not be attacked, that if attacked it must be defended as an island and limited hinterland, and ultimately rescued by a relieving fleet. Consequently, in 1941 it was to receive very few aircraft and no tanks, yet his commanders in London and Malaya continued to assume the whole of Malaya must be defended. Rather than forces and plans being coordinated, local commanders were allowed to plan for an all-Malaya defence that Churchill would not back with the necessary resources. Yet all-Malayan defence seemed to become even more necessary when Japan secured bases in northern Indochina in September 1940.

With the Japanese now in Indochina, the commanders in Singapore drew up a tactical appreciation in early October 1940. They recommended that, with Japanese forces closer than ever, they now needed 566 aircraft and twenty-six battalions, and that they should consider the possibility of seizing Thai ports in an emergency, to deny them to any Japanese advance. Later in the same month a meeting of the Commanders-in-Chief in the Far East, including those of Australia and New Zealand, increased the air requirement to 582 aircraft.[20]

Meanwhile, Air Chief Marshal Sir Robert Brooke-Popham was appointed to the new post of Commander in Chief, Far East, in October, and arrived in November. In fact the grand title was a misnomer. He was really a coordinator for the army and RAF in the region, with no power over the Royal Navy. The appointment was, however, aimed at resolving local disputes about whether to defend all of Malaya, or just part, and at ending inter-service squabbling. The main cause of friction was the issue of whether the new, bold plans for forward defence could or should be preferred, while the resources to mount them were still manifestly inadequate.

In late 1940 the General Officer Commanding (GOC) of Malaya (Lionel Bond) preferred a more limited defence, possibly of Singapore and Johore. This was not because he doubted the importance of the north, but because he insisted Malaya lacked the men and machines to make a forward strategy work. He was right, but being correct is not always a defence when your conclusions are impolitic.

In appointing Air Chief Marshal (and former Governor of Kenya) Sir Brooke-Popham as Commander-in-Chief, the COS must have known they were settling the issue. A sixty-two-year-old RAF officer, a veteran who had joined the service at its inception in 1918, was hardly likely to accept that Malaya's northern and eastern air bases could not be defended.

Brooke-Popham concluded that forward defence would be critical even before he left England. He reasoned that his mission was to keep the naval base operable, and open to reinforcing convoys, and that this meant keeping enemy aircraft at a distance.

Hence Brooke-Popham endorsed the plans for northern defence, and the idea of a pre-emptive seizure of key landing points in southern Thailand should war seem imminent, in order to deny them to any Japanese attack. By March 1941 the Chiefs of Staff (COS) had also become more receptive to the idea of a pre-emptive seizure of southern Thailand.

That same month, Brooke-Popham became confident enough, as more troops arrived, to direct his commanders to start preparing the plans for a Thai operation. At first codenamed *Etonian*, these were the genesis of *Operation Matador*, as it came to be called from August 1941.

This was the situation when Percival, now promoted Lieutenant-General, returned to Malaya in May 1941 as its General Officer Commanding (GOC). Again, senior commanders were choosing the men they knew would back existing policies. Percival, in his 1937 paper on the most likely route for a Japanese attack, had already identified the north of Malaya as vital. Given his past views, and given that his Commander-in-Chief was an RAF man determined to support all-Malayan defence, it is scarcely surprising that Percival did not revive Bond's practical objections. Instead, he oversaw final planning for *Operation Matador*.

This triumph of *Matador* and banishment of doubts represented an almost total change in strategy for defending the naval base, from relying on Singapore's coastal guns until a relieving fleet could arrive, to relying on the RAF and army to meet the enemy in the north, on the beaches and off the coast.

The plan that emerged under Percival envisaged a rapid advance into southern Thailand at brigade strength, and at short notice, in the event of a Japanese attack seeming likely. The aim would be to deny ports, beaches and airfields there to Japan, There would be two main objectives.

The first objective was Songkhla (sometimes called Singora). Songkhla was an east coast Thai port around 50 miles from the nearest point on the Malayan border, around 80 miles from where British military forces would set out from the northwestern state of Kedah. The British had correctly guessed that Singora's charms would attract the attentions of the Japanese. Its gently sloping beach beckoned any invader. Its harbour would provide protection for boats once a landing was made. There was a crude airfield nearby, and the rice fields behind would allow Japanese forces to fan out quickly. Once Singora was theirs, it would be just a few miles inland to the town of Haadyai, where the rail tracks from east and west Malaya met. It would also be a short distance across the peninsula at this, its narrowest point, so giving easy access to Malaya's west coast.[21]

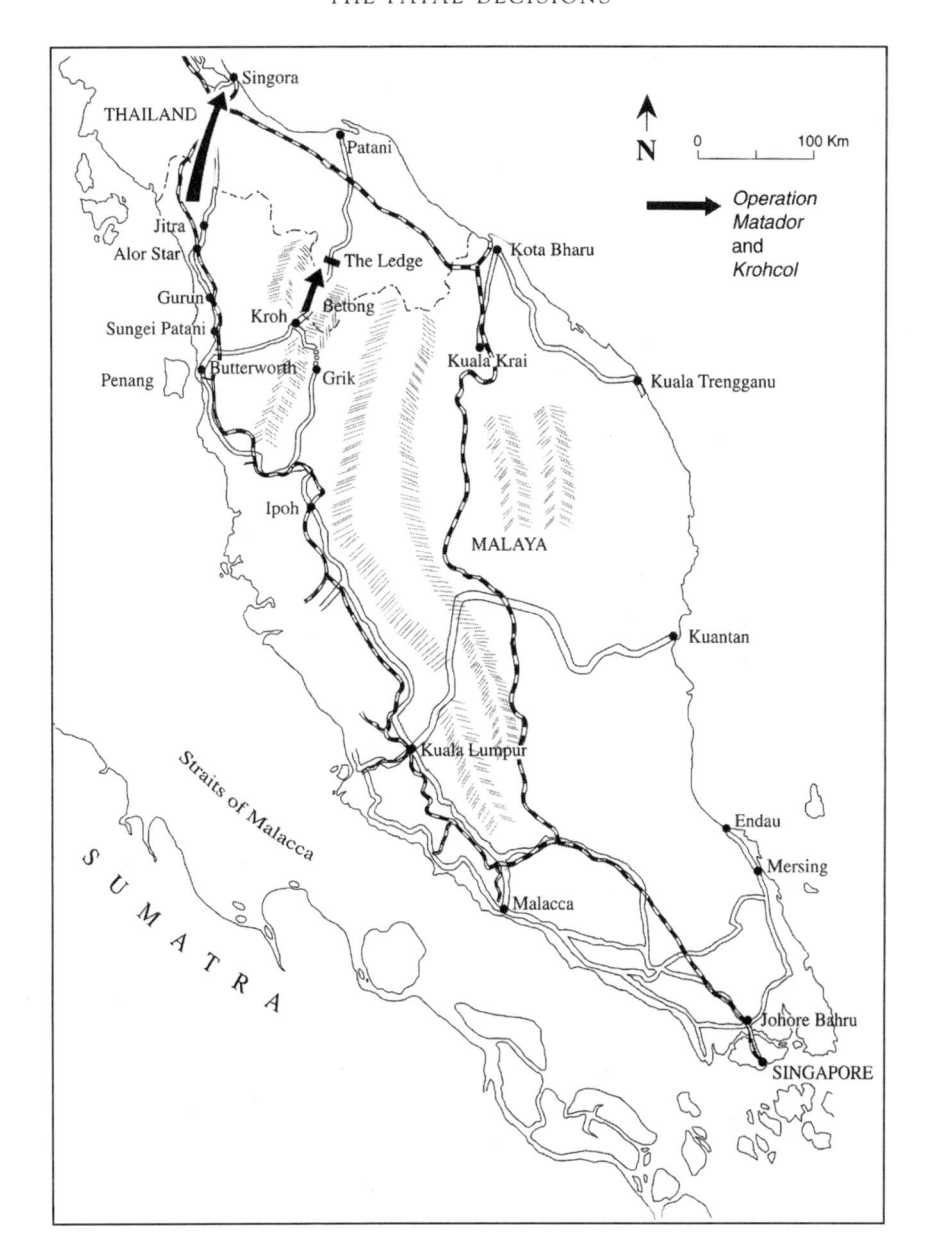

Map 3.1 Operation Matador and Krohcol.

The second British objective at the outset of war would be the 'Ledge'. The force responsible for securing this position was called 'Krohcol' force, after its starting point on the Malayan side of the border: the small town of Kroh. The 'Ledge', meanwhile, was a position on the road which ran from Patani, a small

Thai port a little to the south of Singora, across the peninsula and into Malaya near Kroh. From there the road continued into west Malaya, running on a line well inland from the coastal plain. The Ledge itself was about 35 miles from the Malayan border. Here the road was cut from a steep hillside, which the defenders hoped might be blocked by well-placed explosives.[22]

In many ways the Ledge was even more important to the plan than Singora. This was because the road from Patani would allow the Japanese to bypass not just Singora, but also any British positions in the northwest Malayan state of Kedah. They would be able to drive down central Malaya, inland of the coastal plain. Japanese forces taking this route would have the option of coming out south of the airfields of Kedah and their defenders, by striking across towards Penang. Alternatively, they could continue to drive southwards towards Grik, before cutting towards the coast. Clearly, the road into Malaya from Patani and the 'Ledge' was vital if the Japanese were not to be in a position to outflank British positions on the west coast.[23]

There were several additional reasons for trying to hold any attack so far forward, in north Malaya and southern Thailand. One was to guard aerodromes in the north, which had been built there in the 1930s to receive air reinforcements from India and Burma, and for forward reconnaissance in the South China Sea and Gulf of Siam. There were three airfields in Kelantan alone. Forward defence would also deny the Japanese access to the excellent road and rail system of west Malaya. During the northeast monsoon of October to March the ground near Singora would also be very wet, and so less suited to tanks than the drier west coast. Only the Japanese had tanks.[24]

Finally, *Operation Matador* would secure a position enjoying good east–west communications across the peninsula at its narrowest point. The next such position was almost halfway to Singapore, since Malaya's backbone of mountains began near the Thai border and rose to heights of up to 7,000 feet. Surrounded by mile upon mile of jungle, these central hills formed a daunting barrier to east–west communications across the Malayan peninsula.[25]

Planning for *Matador* proceeded, but no one could guarantee that such an operation would be authorised when the moment came. The United States refused to make even a Japanese invasion of Thailand a certain justification of war, and American cooperation would be vital if there was an eastern conflict. In these circumstances, it proved impossible to get the British COS to agree to any pre-defined circumstances that would automatically justify launching Matador.

Worse still, Churchill remained determined not to disperse resources way from the Middle East and towards to Malaya. As he put it on 10 April 1941:

> There is no objection in principle to preparing the necessary plans ... but we must not tie up a lot of troops in these regions which we can so readily and rapidly reinforce from India ... I view with great reluctance the continued diversion of troops, aircraft and supplies to a theatre which it is improbable will be lighted up unless we are heavily beaten elsewhere.[26]

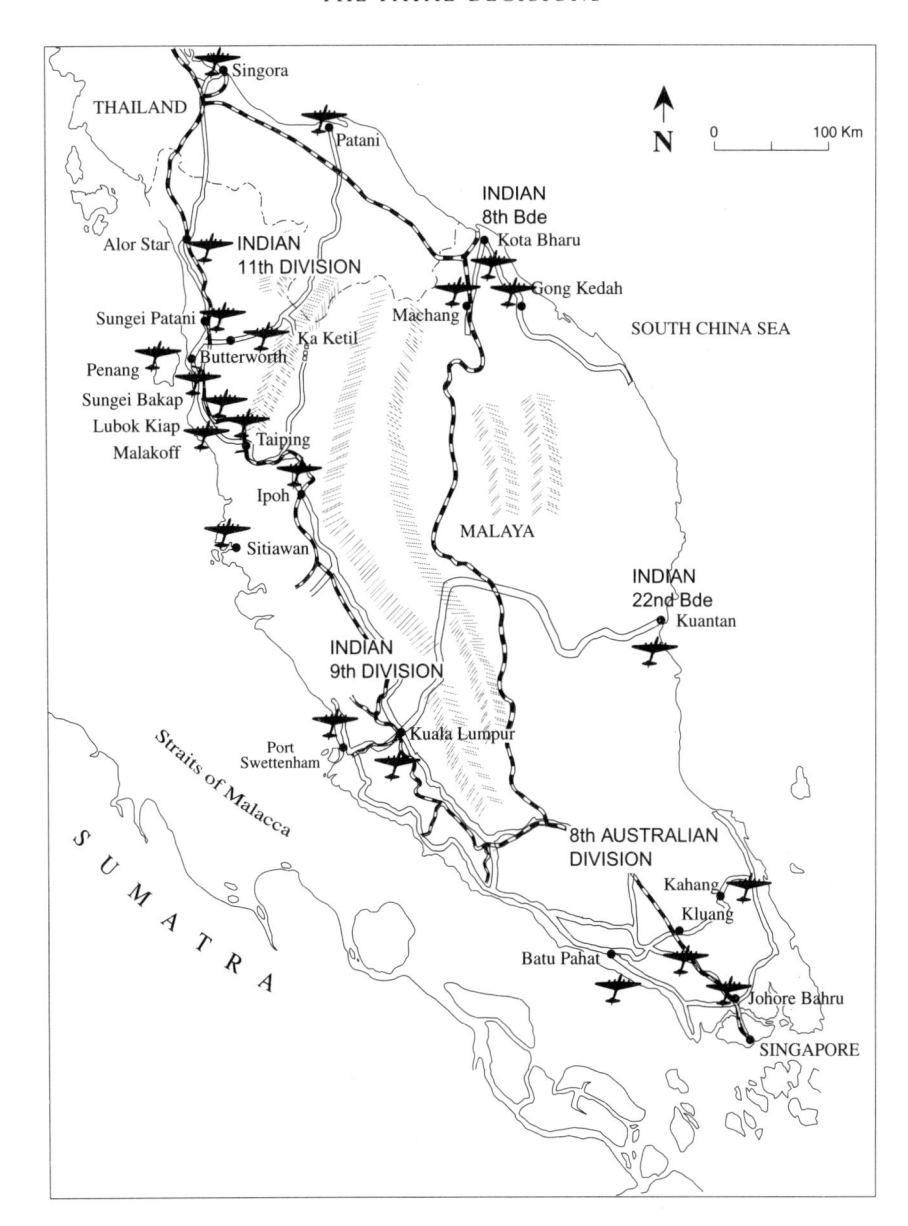

Map 3.2 Malayan airfields in 1941.

Churchill confirmed this attitude when he told his COS (in a 28 April 1941 Directive) that all reinforcements must go to the Middle East, not Singapore. He maintained this determination despite professional advice to the contrary. On 15 May his Chief of Imperial General Staff (Sir John Dill) told him that, the defence of Singapore requires only a fraction of the troops required for the defence of Egypt ... This is the very reason why I am so anxious not to starve Malaya at the expense of Egypt. Quite a small addition at Singapore will make all the difference ... The same resources put into Egypt would add comparatively little to the strength of its defences. But since three months must be allowed for shipments to reach Malaya, it is necessary to look well ahead. If we wait till emergency arises in the Far East, we shall be too late.[27]

The implication of Dill's position was clear: Singapore needed reinforcements, but though these might be critical to the island, they would not be on a scale that would adversely affect other theatres.

Dill's warning suggests one of the most important debates about Singapore's fall. Was Churchill the pivotal decision-maker, and the period April to September 1941 the critical period? Or could Churchill's stance be justified, at least in terms of the information he possessed and the global conflict he had to wage, taking risks in one area in order to survive overall?

In this debate, the best accuser of Churchill is Churchill himself. On 27 January 1942 he told an uneasy House of Commons that,

priority in modern aircraft, in tanks, and in anti-aircraft and anti-tank artillery was accorded to the Nile Valley ... for this decision in its broad strategic aspects, but also for the diplomatic policy in regard to Russia, I take the fullest personal responsibility. If we have handled our resources wrongly, no one is so much to blame as me. If we have not got large modern air forces and tanks in Burma and Malaya to-night, no one is more accountable than I am.

Churchill was facing the first of three days of debate, during which he hinted that worse was still to come. Fortunately for him, he still seemed the best there was, and more than a few of his audience agreed with the basic premise, that one could gamble on the periphery, but never the central European conflict, on which the fate of the world might hang. On 29 January the House of Commons, though appalled by the disaster unfolding in the East, and after much bitter talk, nevertheless recorded its confidence in the government by 464 votes to one.[28]

Churchill's mindset, and his determination that he had nevertheless done the right thing, needs to be seen in terms of overlapping sets of ideas. In his determination to favour active over passive theatres, and the Middle East and Russia over Malaya, he seems to have followed five main assumptions.

First, that while Singapore was a passive theatre it did not merit higher-grade reinforcements.[29] Certainly not until attack was imminent, by when of course, there was likely to be insufficient time for men and machines to arrive and prepare. In August 1940 Churchill went further. He told the Prime Minister of

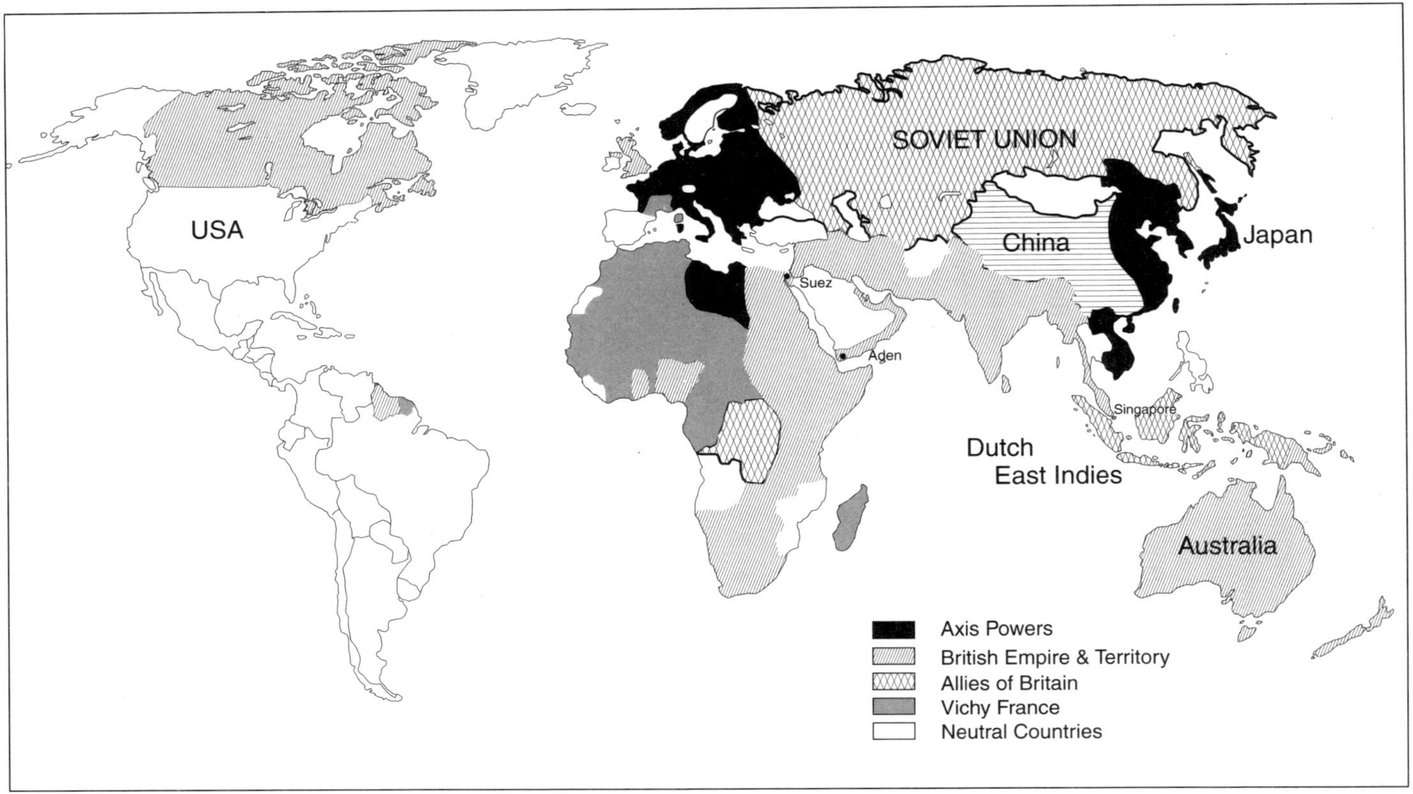

Map 3.3 The world in November 1941.

Australia, Robert Menzies, that he would prefer to delay the dispatch of a fleet from the Mediterranean even if the Japanese did attack, until it became vital for Australia and New Zealand's safety. The reason was his fear the fleet's departure would cause 'the complete loss of the Middle East, and all prospect of beating Italy'. If winning wars requires taking calculated risks in order to concentrate forces, Singapore was to be the area Churchill would gamble on.[30]

Second, Churchill calculated that any Japanese thrust beyond Indochina must bring the United States into the conflict. This meant the Japanese would probably not risk overextending themselves to Southeast Asia, leaving thousands of miles of communications back to Japan vulnerable to American attack. It also meant that Singapore was, in the long-term, safe. If it was attacked, the United States would probably become involved, and Singapore and every other British territory become safe. In short, at a strategic level he guessed it was almost impossible to lose Singapore. Hence when Churchill first learnt the Japanese had attacked the Americans in the East, his response was 'So we have won after all!' That first night he 'went to bed and slept the sleep of the saved and the thankful'. Even in the short-term, it was difficult to envisage Singapore's loss, unless the attack on Pearl Harbor, so daring, so successful, and ultimately so futile, could be foreseen.[31]

Third, however, Malaya was still the empire's dollar arsenal, its rubber and tin being vital exports to the United States. Singapore was also psychologically important. Australia and New Zealand contributed pilots and troops in the Middle East, in the expectation that Singapore would remain a forward shield for them. So it was worth pumping in enough forces to form some sort of deterrent to enemies, and reassurance to friends. Hence Malaya did receive large numbers of men.

Fourth, such a deterrent force was doubly worthwhile, because it might suffice to hold Singapore itself until reinforcements, or American action, stabilised the situation. Here Churchill was lax. He allowed the COS to authorise defence on the basis of holding the whole of Malaya. But he himself continued to believe the country's main defence might ultimately depend on an area around Johore and the 'Singapore Fortress'.

This belief, that defenders could fall back to a final defence of Johore, if not a citadel at Singapore, was his fifth, final and fatal assumption. He talked as if Singapore were a crusaders' castle, the defeat of which would require an enemy to concentrate 50,000 men and a large siege train, before storming across its 'moat'.[32]

Churchill's position was difficult, but that is precisely the reason that Dill, on 15 May 1941, told Churchill he did not have to drain other theatres to save Malaya, and that Malaya's requirements were relatively small. In addition, to Dill's plea, British estimates of the possible scale of Japanese attack already suggested that this was far greater than existing Malayan forces could deal with.

Malaya never had more than 181 serviceable aircraft, and had armoured cars but no tanks.[b] Yet in August 1940 the COS's 'Far Eastern Appreciation' had suggested the Malayan area (including Borneo) might need 336 frontline aircraft, and theatre commanders subsequently suggested 566 or even 582. As early as April 1941 some British estimates of Japanese strength for a Malayan attack already suggested up to 600 aircraft.[33] In addition, Dobbie, as GOC Malaya, had asked for fifteen tanks as early as July 1938, when planning was only just shifting from the basis of defending Singapore alone, to that of protecting landing sites in Malaya too. By April 1941 one British estimate had suggested Japan might deploy up to 360 tanks to Malaya.[34]

Malaya's neglect looks even worse if it is compared to British production. Britain produced over 15,000 aircraft in 1940, over 20,000 in 1941. In the latter year the Soviet Union also produced 15,000 aircraft.[35] Nor did critics fail to notice that hundreds of aircraft were poured into Britain's bomber offensive against Germany. In January 1942 Mr Pierce Loftus (Member of Parliament for Lowestoft) raised this issue in the House of Commons:

> I believe one giant bomber takes 80,000 to 100,000 man-hours of labour to make. Are we overdoing the time and energy spent in building these big bombers and not building enough torpedo-carrying planes and so on? ... As night after night in my home on the East Coast I hear masses of heavy bombers going overseas to bomb Germany ... I ask myself whether some of the immense effort which has created those machines might not have been diverted to make lighter machines, in greater numbers, to be sent out to defend this vital naval base of the British Empire ...[36]

Malaya needed only about 500 extra modern aircraft to bring it up to the levels its commanders wanted. Instead, serviceable *frontline* forces there went from a meagre eighty-eight in late 1940, to about 167 in late 1941. The mathematics does look damning.[37]

These figures are even more interesting when read alongside those for tanks. The Middle East received 770 tanks and 600 field guns between July and October 1941. Between May and November 1941 it received 1,776 aircraft. Then there was the Soviet Union, to which Britain sent 280 tanks and 493 aircraft in October, as part of plans to send a stream of equipment there.[38] All this was noted in the House of Commons in 1942, with another Member of Parliament melodramatically asking if 'one week's supply diverted from Russia would have made all the difference'.[39]

---

b We must distinguish between total *serviceable* aircraft, and the proportion of these which were also *frontline* (operational). Brooke-Popham's figures, those most commonly cited for 7 December 1941, count aircraft which were both serviceable and frontline. He therefore excludes the Maintenance Unit (MU) and an unspecified number of serviceable reserves. By contrast, Probert counts every single serviceable aircraft. Hence Probert says there were 181 serviceable aircraft in December 1941. Deduct 14 in the MU, and that leaves about 167 serviceable, frontline aircraft compared to Brooke-Popham's 158. See Appendix D below for details.

Anglo-American production clearly did leave some scope for supplying Malaya with more machines. Pilots may have been a more tricky issue. Brooke-Popham later recalled that, even with Malaya's tiny air force: 'the majority of the pilots had to be brought from Australia and New Zealand ... straight from the Flying Training Schools ... it took over four months from the time that the pilots arrived in Malaya before the squadrons could be considered fit for operations'.[40]

Even at the time, people divided were sharply for and against Churchill's neglect of Malaya. Immediately after the Fall yet another member of Parliament, one Commander Robert Bower (Member of Parliament for Cleveland) refused to accept Churchill's logic in starving Malaya of resources:

> ... I do not think that this House or the country has been in any way helped by the Prime Minister's disposition to attribute all our misfortunes to a fortuitous concatenation of adverse circumstances ... Malaya, Singapore and our Eastern position were not lost among the swamps and jungles of Malaya; they were lost in the corridors of Whitehall and the Palace of Westminster. It might very well be true that Singapore was lost on the playing fields at Harrow.[c][41]

While many criticised the neglect of Malaya, others came to Churchill's defence, seeing his decisions as justified risks, taken in a finely balanced struggle, one in which errors east of India were always redeemable, but those made closer to Europe could spell total disaster. The MP for Renfrew Western captured the essence of Churchill's defence a little later, on 20 May 1942, when he told the Commons that: 'The hard truth is that if Russia is victorious, it will be very easy to recover those parts of the Empire which we have lost, while if Russia is defeated, we shall lose a great deal more of the Empire ...'. He might almost have added, 'a great deal more than the empire'.[42]

Nor were such views restricted to London. In Malaya, Australian gunner Russell Braddon's main fear in mid-1941 was 'that the Russian Front would not hold fast for the hundred days which American experts said was the minimum allied requirement if Germany was not to sweep the world'.[43] Even rickshaw pullers in Singapore contributed to Russian war relief.[44]

The debate has not stopped since, so that Britain's parsimony towards Malaya, and Churchill's decisions still demand explanations which need to divide into two periods: spring 1941 (April to May); and mid-1941 (especially July to September). This division is necessary because the global situation changed drastically from one period to another.

For the period April to May 1941 the obvious defence of Churchill is that neither the Soviet Union nor the United States had yet entered the war. Germany and Italy could still, if they chose, concentrate most of their forces

c Harrow was Churchill's old school.

against Britain. Up to this point everything suggested that the German blitzkrieg, armoured offensives combined with air power, was likely to rapidly defeat any British forces it met, unless the latter could boast far greater numbers. Hitler's forces had rapidly defeated Poland in September 1939, seized Norway against British opposition in spring 1940, and then crushed France in May to June 1940. After the Dunkirk evacuation of defeated British and French troops in the latter month, an invasion of Britain seemed a distinct possibility.

Hitler's failure to defeat the Royal Air Force in the summer of 1940 bought time and postponed the prospect of invasion, but it did not guarantee Britain's survival.

Then came events in the Balkans, where Britain went to the aid of Greece against an invasion by Mussolini. In April to May 1941 German forces intervened, resulting in yet another British disaster. British forces were driven out of the Balkans in April, and lost the Aegean island of Crete by the end of May.

German victory in the Balkans left their forces stationed to the north of Africa, pointing like a dagger at Egypt and the Suez Canal. It also threatened to release German resources to reinforce Rommel. Rommel's Africa Corps had arrived in Africa in February, and was already driving along the coast towards Egypt.

These were desperate times for Britain, and the see-saw movements of British and German-Italian forces across Libya and Egypt of 1941 to 1942 add a new perspective to the numbers of aircraft Malaya needed. In November 1941 British forces in North Africa mustered around 680 tanks against Rommel's 399, and 1,000 aircraft to Rommel's 320. With superior numbers, British forces did manage to relieve the besieged garrison at Tobruk on 8 December 1941. But even then danger remained. After forces were diverted to Malaya, the British army in North Africa began to retreat again from 22 January 1942.[45] Despite numerical superiority in the Middle East, then, no decisive victory was achieved until El Alamein in October 1942. That is, until well after the United States had joined the war, and after Germany had begun to struggle in Russia.

In 1941 itself, the issue in the Middle East still looked likely to be difficult. There always remained the danger that aggressively led German troops might repeat earlier successes, capture the canal, seize the region's oil, impress more countries into joining their fate with its cause, and even lead the United States to despair of Britain's chances.

Churchill also had to consider other problems, such as the possibility of having to intervene to save Spanish and Portuguese islands in the Atlantic if Germany made a move for them. These islands might provide Germany with advance airbases against British shipping in the Atlantic. In turn, the Atlantic provided an indispensable umbilical cord to the United States and the empire.[46]

By contrast with Germany, with its series of rapid victories, Japan had been bogged down in the interior of China since 1937, with no prospect of final victory. It seemed likely Japan would be reluctant to drive southwards, and so risk further antagonising the United States. This was especially the case before June 1941, while the Soviet Union's forces lay unoccupied to Japan's north. As recently as May to June 1939, these Soviet troops had tangled with the Japanese Army in Mongolia, with Marshal Zhukov inflicting significant losses on Japan.[47]

So in April to May 1941 Churchill headed a country rapidly going bankrupt, standing alone and yet fighting several campaigns: the Battle of the Atlantic; the bomber offensive against Germany; the Balkans; Mediterranean; North Africa and the Middle East. In the circumstances, his guess that Malaya did not at that time need reinforcements turned out right. There was no Japanese attack in mid-1941, when reinforcements sent in the spring would have arrived.

Yet the assessment which proved correct in the spring, seems to have changed little into summer, though the situation in Asia was by then deteriorating. This makes the period June to September 1941 one of the most fascinating.

This is the period when London and Churchill seem to have seriously misread the shifting global situation. The most dramatic changes of this period came in the Soviet Union. In April 1941 Japan and the Soviet Union signed a neutrality pact. If this made the Soviet Union less of a worry to Japan, events were soon to remove its northern enemy from the reckoning almost entirely. Germany attacked the Soviet Union on 22 June 1941, beginning *Operation Barbarossa*. Soon the German army was surging across the Russian steppe, only to grind to a halt in December 1941, just short of Moscow. From the Japanese viewpoint, German progress freed it to neglect the north, and to increase its pressure to the south, in the hope of ending the China conflict there.

Japan duly moved into southern Indochina in July 1941, though nominally Vichyite French forces were left in control. This caused the United States to impose crippling financial sanctions on Japan from the same month, freezing its assets in the United States. One conclusion might have been that Singapore was now in much greater danger, as Japanese aircraft would be able to reach northern Malaya from their new bases, and Japanese planners might now eye the resources of Southeast Asia jealously.

Unfortunately, not everyone saw it this way. As early as August, the Joint Intelligence Committee in London believed Japan might strike south, even seizing southern Thailand. But they still did not rule out the idea of Japan attacking the Soviet Union instead, even into September.[48] Brooke-Popham, now Commander-in-Chief, Far East, also told London on 4 August 1941 that Japan was likely to concentrate its main resources for a campaign against the Soviet Union. He continued to hold this view until October of the same year, by when southern Thailand was awash with Japanese spies. From then on there could be little doubt that something was afoot, even if Brooke-Popham still doubted if an attack on Thailand would automatically be extended to Malaya.[49]

Such calculations may have seemed logical in the light of the Japanese–Soviet conflict at Nomonhan in 1939, Russia's role as Japan's number one enemy in Asia going back to before 1904, and the global implications should a joint German-Japanese attack knock the Soviet Union out of the war. A strong case could be made that Japan did keep the northern option open until very late in the day, that it should have attacked the Soviet Union, and that only the fall of the communist state could have decisively altered the balance of power in favour of Germany and Japan.[50] But Brooke-Popham should have been pleading his theatre's case for reinforcements, not undermining it. Meanwhile, the contradictory and uncertain guesses about Japan's next move meant Churchill was not getting clear guidance that Japanese intentions were changing. Instead, Japanese pressure in southern China, and moves into Indochina in 1940-1, could still be interpreted as attempts to seal off China from outside help.

Even if Japan did turn its attention southward, it seemed increasingly likely that the United States would react to any further Japanese expansion. President Roosevelt confirmed this impression in early August 1941.[51] Churchill persuaded Roosevelt to agree, early in that month, to warn the Japanese that any further encroachments in East Asia could lead to American countermeasures, 'even though these might lead to war'. Admittedly, Roosevelt's advisers had this toned down. The final warning issued to Japan on 17 August was disappointingly vague, dropping the reference to war in favour of 'any and all steps' necessary to protect American interests. But at least Churchill had a private intimation that Roosevelt's thinking was hardening.[52] In short, in August and September 1941 it could be argued that, in Churchill's grand strategic calculations, a Japanese attack on Singapore itself was far from certain, while any such attack was increasingly likely to turn into a suicidal war with the United States.[53]

Unfortunately, that was not how it seemed in Tokyo. On 6 September 1941 a Japanese Imperial Conference decided to negotiate with the United States for the removal of trade and financial restrictions, and yet to prepare for war simultaneously. It was recognised that increased financial and trade restrictions by the United States – which Britain and the Dutch were now backing – would gradually bleed its oil stocks dry, making the oil of the Netherlands East Indies an attractive target. The Japanese could either go to war to seize extra resources, and in the hope of dealing a blow so hard that the Americans would sue for peace early, or they could retreat in East Asia in order to repair relations with the United States.

It was not a real choice. Indeed, a retreat from hard won gains in China and Indochina might have been suicidal for any statesman who endorsed it, given the real possibility that it would provoke assassination or coup attempts.

On 17 October 1941 General Tojo became Prime Minister, replacing civilians who were less willing to face the issue of war. 5 November saw an Imperial Conference set a deadline of 25 November for a peaceful, negotiated end to American embargoes, with forces to be ready for war by 1 December.[54]

From July, then, Japan had started slithering, or being pushed, down, the path to war. There was simply no question of easing pressure on China, which the United States was demanding as the price for resuming supplies. Nor could

THE FATAL DECISIONS

there be any question of allowing American restrictions to gradually tighten the noose round Japan's supply of materials until it was garotted.

Meanwhile, *Barbarossa* may have resulted in Singapore getting even less reinforcements than it might have, as British aircraft and tanks were routed to the Soviet Union. Japan made its final decisions on the shape of its invasion in November itself, so setting the scene for December. By the beginning of the latter month, Japanese transports were already heading westwards towards Cambodia and Thailand. In Malaya, there were approximately 87,000 British and allied troops and volunteers, 167 frontline aircraft, and no tanks. But Malaya's British commanders remained committed to the forward defence of Singapore, and to *Operation Matador*. On sighting Japanese convoys they were to hold Malaya's east coast, while also rushing men forward to grab southern Thai ports, and so deny the Japanese landing points. Britain's defensive plans now relied overwhelmingly on land and air forces, while a major eastern fleet had become a hope for 1942, rather than a fixed part of the plan for the present.

The man who would have to launch *Matador* was Air Chief Marshal Sir Robert Brooke-Popham, as Commander-in-Chief of land and air forces in the Far East. As negotiations between Japan and the United States broke down, it did at least bring increased likelihood that the United States would stand by Britain, if its eastern territories were attacked.

On 3 December London received American assurances that the United States would not only support Britain if attacked by Japan, but would give military support if Britain felt compelled to launch *Matador*. As a result, on 5 December London authorised Brooke-Popham to launch *Matador* on his own initiative. He needed only convince himself that a Japanese attack on Thailand or Malaya was imminent.

On 6 December, Japanese convoys were spotted by aircraft. But they were heading west across the Gulf of Siam, so their final destination was unclear. Was it Cambodia, or Thailand, or Malaya itself? British and Indian troops were ordered to stand by for the order to launch *Matador*. Further aircraft were dispatched to look for the Japanese transports, and Brooke-Popham waited for news that the Japanese convoys were turning south, which would confirm Malaya as the target. Confirmation came, but only on the evening of 7 December. This was too late for British forces to have time to rush to Singora, and then to dig themselves in there, before the Japanese transports arrived. Brooke-Popham now decided not to authorise *Operation Matador* and, less justifiably, failed to order *Krohcol* to advance.

Did Brooke-Popham miss a vital opportunity to stall or delay the Japanese? He was not helped by the intelligence situation. This showed a Japanese attack in the east was imminent, but not whether Malaya would be included. A telegram intercepted on 29 November also showed some pro-Japanese ministers in Thailand hoped Britain would attack first. This might justify calling Japan for help. Brooke-Popham had to make the call in the most difficult of circumstances, yet he had been told as early as 5 November that he was to be replaced by a man with more up to date knowledge. Duff Cooper, who was Britain's Resident Minister at Singapore from September to December 1941, unkindly declared the slightly elderly Brooke-Popham to be 'damned near gaga'.[55]

It is impossible to know whether Brooke Popham might have acted more decisively, had he not been hampered by the knowledge that he was now a stop-gap, holding the baby for his successor. But we do know that Brooke-Popham failed to take a risk and authorise *Matador* when Japanese ships were sighted on 6 December. Then late on 7 December, when it was confirmed that they were closing in on Malaya, he decided it was too late.

Operation Matador would never be launched. The Japanese would land at Singora virtually unopposed in the early hours of 8 December 1941, and against thinly spread British forces in northeast Malaya. But just how deadly was the legacy of the decisions taken up to 8 December? How far, by contrast, was there still room for London and Singapore to avoid destruction, to delay disaster, or at the least to salvage some semblance of honour from defeat?

4

THE CAMPAIGN

From Singapore to Syonan

Sunday, 15 February 1942 was Chinese New Year. It should have been a time of celebration in Malaya, of family, of looking to the future. But for those penned inside the final defensive perimeter in Singapore, there was little to celebrate. The water supply was failing as pipes disintegrated, and an artillery duel raged over the city. Few could have guessed that both sides were running short of shells.

The end was palpably near. The day held out the prospect of British surrender, or of a final storming of the city by Japanese troops. Already the Governor had ordered alcohol stocks be destroyed, to prevent any repeat of the invading army's drunken rampage through Chinese cities. One policeman described working like a robot to help destroy the city's 1,500,000 bottles of spirits and 60,000 gallons of Chinese *samsu*: 'bend, grab, hurl, bend grab, hurl. Bottle after bottle, thousands of them, the stuff ran ankle deep. In a short time, we were half-stupid with the fumes'.[1] Others destroyed their personal stocks, mindful of the actions of victory-drunk invaders in the 'rape of Nanking' of December 1937: with its large-scale killing and raping of Chinese civilians.[2]

Percival still held it in his power, in theory at least, to make Singapore suffer a final battle. Did he want to salvage a last shred of British imperial pride, or to accept defeat? On 19 January Churchill had demanded 'no question of surrender to be entertained until after protracted fighting among the ruins of Singapore City', officers to die alongside men.[3] As late as 10 February Churchill was still insisting his forces make a last stand as the Americans were on Luzon, writing that 'the whole reputation of our country and our race is involved'.[4] Percival's first requests to be allowed to consider surrender were rebuffed. It was 14 February before Churchill relented, giving Wavell, Supreme Commander of Allied Forces in the South West Pacific since early January, permission to judge when further fighting would serve no purpose. The consequences of a Churchillian last stand, had Wavell or Percival insisted on this, do not bear contemplation. Not if events at Alexandria Hospital on 14 February are anything to go by.

On that penultimate day of battle there had been fierce fighting around Alexandria Hospital. When the Japanese finally pushed the defenders back, they massacred patients and staff alike. Whether or not their behaviour was sparked by the use of the hospital grounds by some defenders, as later reports suggested, it augured evil for further resistance.[5]

Fortunately for Singapore, Churchill did allow the possibility of a last-gasp surrender, and Percival's commanders were in no mood to make the Japanese pay for every street. At 0930 hours on 15 February Percival met his commanders at his Fort Canning bunker. Rather than argue that a last stand would help allied strategy elsewhere, or save imperial prestige, he presented his commanders with a choice he must have known was no choice. They must counter-attack and take back essential stores and reservoirs, or surrender.

After being told that the water supplies might fail within a day, and knowing their forces to be incapable of effective counter-attack, Percival's commanders agreed on surrender. From this moment, Singapore's fate was sealed. That afternoon Percival went to meet Yamashita at the Ford Factory, on Upper Bukit Timah Road, starting discussions sometime shortly after 1700 hours. The aim was not to decide whether to surrender, but to discuss how to put into effect what had already been decided. Singapore had fallen. All that remained was to confirm in writing what had happened on the battlefield.

After a short discussion about details, Percival signed the surrender documents. Shortly afterwards, at 2030 hours, the formal ceasefire came into effect. From that moment, the forces of the British Empire in Singapore, British, Australians, Malays, Chinese, Garwhals and Gurkhas, Sikhs and Jats, Chinese volunteers in Dalforce, and Eurasians in the local volunteers, were surrendered.[6]

So how did Fortress Singapore become *Syonan-to* (pronounced Sho-nan-toh): Shining Light (*Syowa*) of the South Seas (*Nanyo*): the epicentre of Japan's new empire in Southeast Asia? Was the timing and nature of defeat all but inevitable, given the lack of ships, aircraft and tanks, or could British leaders still have performed better with the cards they had been dealt? How did commanders manage the tension between the desire to keep Japanese aircraft and artillery as far away from Singapore's naval base as possible, with the reality that they lacked the aircraft and ships for effective defence of the Malayan peninsula? In short, what chance, if any, was there of making an effective defence of Singapore Fortress?

These questions demand an account of the campaign in Malaya and of the final battle for Singapore: an account which could take the form of a story, unfolding events up to the point of surrender, or the form of an analytical study, focusing on moments when different courses might have been chosen. This chapter attempts both, unfolding a narrative, but stopping to look at some of the more critical moments in more detail.

The battle for Malaya

Brooke-Popham's decision not to launch *Matador* meant the Japanese could land unopposed at Singora. Their problem, in the early hours of 8 December, was not so much to fight their way inland, as to find someone who would acknowledge their arrival, and the beginning of the glorious liberation of southern Asia. Coming ashore in rough seas, the Japanese troops 'were delighted to see lamps burning brightly from the homes of the town'. But thereafter they had a frustrating time:

> ... we spoke to the residents but they could not understand us. We proceeded to the Japanese Consulate ... Evidently they were still not aware of our landing. A company of troops was sent to the British consulate .... We were met by the consul. He spoke to me in English. I could not understand him.[7]

In fact it later turned out the Japanese Consul was asleep and he was woken up, and some Thai forces did fire on Japanese troops.[8] But no matter, the Japanese brushed them aside and set off for the border. The first waves of landings comprised about 26,000 men, the vast majority of them combat troops.[9] Colonel Tsuji, who helped plan the campaign, claims they eventually landed over 400 guns and 120 tanks and armoured cars, and over 60,000 men (including at least 42,000 frontline infantry). When the immediate support troops, such as artillery and engineers, are added, the total came to considerably more.[10] They also had at their disposal the reserve 56th Division, which in the end was not needed. Those who were landed included the 5th and 18th Infantry Divisions, both well seasoned by fighting in China, and the unblooded but highly regarded Imperial Guards Division.[11]

Meanwhile, the unfortunate troops of the defending 11th Indian Division, of the British Imperial forces, were still on alert for *Matador*, waiting, in incessant rain, for an operation that would never be launched. Brooke-Popham only gave the order to cancel *Matador* on the morning of the 8 December, and the order only trickled through to the troops early that afternoon.

More than one historian has argued that, even at this late moment, and even without the requisite tanks and aircraft, *Matador* could have worked, but for Brooke-Popham's dithering.[12] Worse still, it has been claimed that the disorganisation caused by the late abortion of the plan left British forces reeling backwards.[13]

Was there a missed chance? Brooke-Popham later argued that without the aircraft and tanks required, any *Matador* force would have been cut off. We would expect him to argue that, given that he was the man who blinked at the crucial moment.[14] But he is not alone. Percival has also questioned whether the operation had been sound given the forces available.[15] General Wavell, who had less reason to make excuses, agreed that *Matador*, 'without denying the enemy in any appreciable degree ... [gave] every possibility of losing an entire brigade'. That is, troops put in an extreme forward position, and without any dynamic plan to back them up, would have been rapidly outflanked, as subsequently happened all down the Malayan peninsula.[16] The official historian, Kirby, went further, and dismissed *Matador* as a foolish idea from

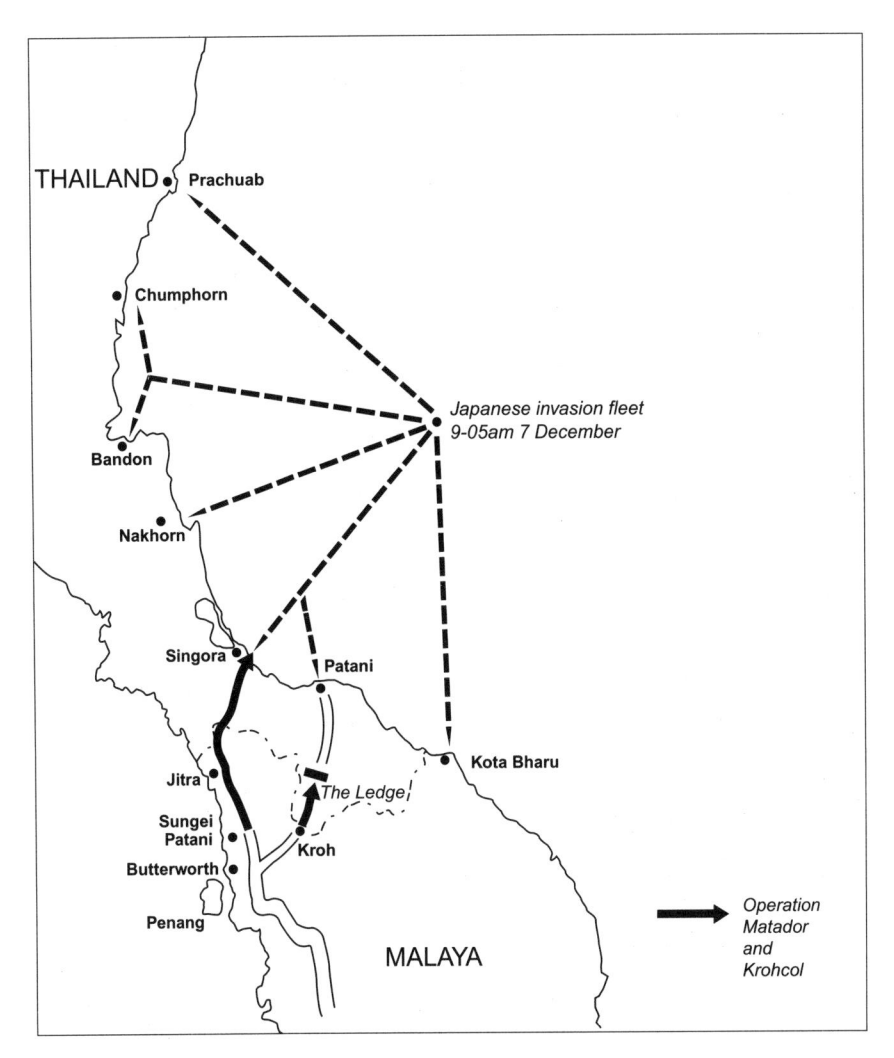

Map 4.1 The break-up of the Japanese invasion fleet on 7 December 1941.

the start. In his *Chain of Disaster*, he argued that it required thirty-six hours warning for preparation, and another thirty-six hours for troops to arrive at Singora and dig in. Kirby concluded that 'It should have been evident that *Matador* could never be launched in sufficient time to have a real chance of success ... the idea should have been dropped'.[17]

Even if *Matador* had been launched in good time, Japanese forces ultimately landed south of the position, in both Thailand and Kelantan, and north of it too. The Japanese commanders had orders to abort the Singora part of their landing if opposed, so the result might merely have been to reinforce Japanese landings to the south or north of Singora. With landings to either side of any

Matador force, and Japanese air and sea superiority, the result could hardly be in doubt, even if the Japanese might have been delayed a little.

In what circumstances might *Matador* have been worthwhile? Ideally, it required a steely political resolve to violate Thai neutrality as soon as Japanese transport ships left Indochina or Formosa. It also needed enough British aircraft to match Japanese airpower, or at least to come close to this. Finally, it required at least one of two additional elements. The first of these would have been a serious British defence not just of Singora, but of the main landing sites to its north and south. To the south, that meant Kelantan and Trengganu's miles of beaches, as well as the Thai town of Patani. To the north, it meant the Thai beaches and ports which dotted the Kra peninsula beyond Singora. A second option, if there were not enough troops to cover all these landing points, would have been to assemble mobile reserves, ready to be rushed to support the initial brigade in mobile fighting behind Singora. Neither of these elements was included in *Matador*, or was possible with the limited forces available.[18]

Clearly air superiority was out of the question by late 1941. The one area where British forces did have the upper hand was in numbers of men. But even here, all was not what it should have been. The British forces' psychological and physical lack of preparedness for the war was to place them at a severe disadvantage. Lieutenant-Colonel Ian Stewart, who commanded one of the more successful battalions in the campaign, the 2nd Argyll and Sutherland Highlanders, ranked this British mentality amongst the major causes of defeat. He argued that a lack of tough, combined training by different arms meant British staff and men alike were 'clumsy, unaggressive, and slow through practical unfamiliarity with job in a war whose tempo was extreme'. Defending fixed positions, British-led troops were disastrously quick to retire, leaving other units exposed. Stewart argued that 'Whenever the Japs got behind, the reaction was "We are outflanked, we must withdraw", instead of the reverse of the coin, "Good, we outflank him"'.[19]

In some units, the situation was worse than mere indifference or lack of preparation. In 1940 and 1941 there were outbreaks of disaffection in newly arrived Indian units. The Japanese worked hard at this:

> By means of radio and pamphlets dropped from aircraft, they flogged the point that they were fighting only the white man; that the British were putting Asiatic troops in the front line as cannon fodder, while the white soldiers remained skulking in the background ... Subsequently, the stories of some of the men [Indians who surrendered] were broadcast from Penang and Bangkok and in some cases the men themselves spoke into the microphone.

To Indian troops sent ahead to delay the Japanese advance, or facing Japanese attacks on the east coast with little or no air cover, this must have seemed a plausible message.[20]

One Indian State unit, a battalion of the 1st Battalion Hyderabads, had to be disarmed just a few days into the campaign, on 14 December. Given that about half the British-led forces were Indian, even a few such instances did not augur well for the defenders' chances. In short, too many Indian units had been milked of experienced officers and non-commissioned officers to seed new units in the Indian Army's never-ending expansion, or were led by officers not accustomed to their languages, even if they were not affected by Japanese propaganda.[21]

The defenders' emotional coldness can also be illustrated by comparing what British and Japanese troops were given to read at the beginning of the campaign. First, there is the limpid tone of Air Chief Marshal Brooke-Popham and Vice-Admiral Geoffrey Layton's Order of the Day for 8 December 1941:

We are ready. We have had plenty of warning and our preparations are tried and tested. We do not forget at this moment the years of patience and forbearance in which we have borne, with dignity and discipline, the petty insults and insolences inflicted upon us by the Japanese in the Far East. We know that those things were only done because Japan thought that she could take advantage of our supposed weakness. Now, when Japan herself has decided to take put the matter to a sterner test, she will find out that she has made a grievous mistake.

We are confident. Our defences are strong and our weapons efficient. Whatever our race, and whether we are now in our native land or have come thousands of miles, we have one aim and one only. It is to defend these shores, to destroy such of our enemies as may set foot on our soil, and then, finally, to cripple the power of the enemy to endanger our ideals, our possessions and our peace.

What of the enemy? We see before us a Japan drained for years by the exhausting claims of her wanton onslaught on China. We see a Japan whose trade and industry have been so dislocated by years of adventure that, in a mood of desperation, her Government has flung her into war under the delusion that, by stabbing a friendly nation in the back, she can gain her end. Let her look at Italy and what has happened since that nation tried a similar base action.

Let us all remember that we here in the Far East form part of the great campaign for the preservation in the world of truth and justice and freedom; confidence, resolution, enterprise and devotion to the cause must and will inspire every one of us in the fighting services, while from the civilian population, Malay, Chinese, Indian, or Burmese, we expect that patience, endurance and serenity which is the great virtue of the East, and which will go far to assist the fighting men to gain final and complete victory.[22]

Brooke-Popham's statement comes across as negative and vague in some places, and in others nonsensical, as when calling his mainly non-Malayan army to defend 'our soil'. Above all, however, it was also irresponsible in not facing squarely the likelihood of being opposed by an enemy with superior equipment, and calling for heroism to combat this. Finally, references to eastern 'serenity' combined empty stereotyping with an apparent call to civilians to assist by doing nothing. Perhaps the message looks worse than it was in retrospect, but it was hardly the stuff to inspire a vast, multiracial army about to fight an enemy with aerial and armoured superiority.

By contrast, Japanese preparation, though begun only a few months before, was thorough, and the guidance given to the troops blended the practical and the spiritual. Colonel Manosubu Tsuji had been sent to Taiwan early in the year, to help plan for an attack on Singapore. He was to help compile every conceivable detail on tropical warfare, which was a far cry from campaigns in northern and central China, and to help plan practice landings too. He even flew with an unarmed reconnaissance mission over the British airfields at Alor Star and Sungei Patani in the north. His own account of the war describes leaning out of the cockpit and into the freezing air to take photographs of the airfields and aircraft below.[23]

Amongst Tsuji's detailed preparations was a booklet called 'Read this Alone – And the War Can be Won'. Its authors envisaged Japanese soldiers reading it lying down in the invasion fleet, as it crossed the Gulf of Thailand and headed for Singora and Kota Bharu.

'Read this Alone' epitomised Japanese thoroughness. Invoking 2,600 years of Japanese history, it called on the troops to free 'South Asia ... a treasure house of the Far East', from subjection, to complete the Meiji revival by breaking the grip of 300,000 whites over 100 million Asians, and to break the supply lines by which British and American supplies had been sustaining China against Japan since 1937.

The Japanese soldier was told American embargoes of oil and steel were killing Japan 'Slowly, little by little, like a man strangling his victim with a soft cord of silken floss'. He was to consider it both a war of national survival, to secure resources, and as Asia's final liberation. The booklet finished with the verse:

Corpses drifting swollen in the sea-depths,
Corpses rotting in the mountain-grass-
We shall die, by the side of our lord we shall die
We shall not look back.

Ironically, relatively few Japanese were to die, with only a few thousand casualties for the whole campaign. But 'Read This Alone – and the War Can be Won', however stirring compared to Brooke-Popham's 'Order of the Day' of 8 December, was no idle breastbeating. Indeed, the notion of the Japanese soldier as an almost inhuman automaton, a robot programmed to obey unquestioningly, and able to survive on virtually nothing, betrays just how badly Britain was prepared. Characteristics that might have been regarded as heroic if shown by allied troops have since been caricatured. Again, caricatures build on the truth – Japanese obedience (rather than British-style parade drill) and application to task was deservedly legendary. Japanese soldiers did travel lightly, able to survive on a little rice, perhaps some pickles, salted fish and plain tea, and whatever could be found locally.[24] But the Japanese soldier was not simply schooled in sacrifice. To the contrary, Japanese tactics in Malaya suggested a high degree of tactical training, of restraint against the temptation to simply attack, and of initiative when in action. One British telegram of January 1942 summed up these characteristics with commendable brevity:

> Tactics. Rigorous advance. Roads used till contact gained. Direct frontal attack avoided but outflanking through rubber and jungle and by river and sea in small parties to attack flanks and rear thus causing general withdrawal. Considerable initiative displayed in these tactics.[25]

This emphasis on tactics and timing, and on detail, is also seen in 'Read this Alone and the War can be Won'. Japanese troops, some coming from China, none of them having experience of fighting in the tropics, were told how to treat water-oxen, throwing water over them and rubbing in mud regularly. They were told how to preserve rice and cereals against the humidity, and how to fend off the malarial mosquito and treat sunstroke. However accurately or unfairly, troops were also warned that,

> Since the natives defecate and urinate quite freely in all the lakes and streams ... it is safest to drink only water which has been properly purified by filtering.

The Japanese soldier was to be preserved against the hygiene dangers of the *ulu*, the upriver areas which development had as yet hardly touched. This, combined with taking creosote pills, and dissolving 'about' 0.8 pre cent of salt in warm tea, would keep the Japanese army from illness and dehydration. The list goes on. Horses should be given sun hats to avoid sunstroke, and men should avoid marching in the midday sun if possible, while at the day's beginning tyres should be deflated 10 per cent, to allow for expansion in the heat.[26] The booklets lack many military details, such as on outflanking enemy positions, were almost swamped by instructions for the practical care of man and machine. As the booklet warned,

> It is an historical fact that in all tropical campaigns since ancient times far more have died through disease than have been killed in battle ... To fall in a hail of bullets is to meet a hero's death, but there is no glory in dying of disease or accident through inattention to hygiene or carelessness. And a further point you would do well to consider is that native women are almost all infected with venereal disease ...

The last, lurid exaggeration may have been in the hope of avoiding any repeat of the Rape of Nanking in 1937.[27] We can never know the exact number of Chinese who were raped and killed in the wake of Nanking's fall, but we do know how the Japanese tried to limit such depredations for the future.

The Japanese Army regularised, regimented, and expanded the provision of sex for its soldiers, setting up houses for 'comfort women', with strict regulations, on paper if not in reality, for hygiene and pay, and different rules and hours for men and officers. Regular Japanese prostitutes were soon joined by Korean women, many impressed on the false hope of good work, and in Malaya by local women. Some of the latter, the least lucky of those to fall victim to rape by the invading army, were dragooned into service in more dramatic and brutal circumstances.[28]

Even if the Japanese soldier might view warnings about widespread sexual disease with scepticism, the booklet was a brilliant combination of attention to the men's welfare, and exhortation for them to ignore their own welfare if necessary, to die in the cause of home, and of Asians in general. In this context, the final verses, the invocation of 'Corpses drifting swollen in the sea-depths', may have come across as poetic, rather than trite.

So the contrast between Japanese practicality, thoroughness, and motivation, and 'British' troops' indifferent performance, is more than justified. This was compounded by the British approach to training. To a great extent, the British Army of the time left the details of this up to individual commanders. Where a General such as Montgomery provided a clear lead and coordination, this might mean training was tailored to the particular theatre. In Malaya this lead was not given, and the result was that some unit commanders provided good anti-tank and jungle training, and others little, if any. In this way there was a lack of 'operational' effectiveness', that is procedures for standardising best training practices, and for drawing up ever-better theatre training manuals and battle drills.[29]

By contrast, the Japanese 25th Army's 5th and 18th Divisions were selected for Malaya from amongst the best of those units which had been seasoned in the China campaign. They were not novices, but veterans for whom the Malayan campaign was an extension of the war in China. Tsuji has described feeling, as he drove past the Chinese shop-houses on entering Kuala Lumpur in January 1942, 'as though we had entered the crossroads of the central provinces of China'.[30]

British forces were not only less effectively trained and less experienced, but were frankly imperial as well. The 'Asiatic', local troops formed a tiny proportion of the starting force of around 87,000 men, and an even smaller percentage after British and Australian reinforcements arrived. Locals were to be defended, not to be motivated to form a national army. This despite the plentiful raw material for resistance, especially amongst Chinese outraged by the Sino–Japanese war. But prewar offers of help from the banned Malayan Communist Party were spurned until December 1941, when some of its members were belatedly trained as part of the irregular Chinese 'Dalforce', and

THE CAMPAIGN

as the stay-behind parties which later formed the nucleus for a 'Malayan People's Anti-Japanese Army' (MPAJA).[31] Local forces were to be minimal, and the battle for Malaya above all a test of the fitness of the old system of imperialism.[32]

On the British side it remained a case of too little, too late. But 'Read This Alone – and the War Can be Won', indeed the whole planning of the Japanese operation in 1941, from a standing start, is illustrative of the Japanese professionalism and focus. They were also more than willing to learn from German campaigns in the West, and to emphasise a 'blitz-advance' that on paper looked absurdly risky.[33] Tsuji himself claimed that

> my mind was filled with one thought how to carry this unusual strategy with success. One night, as I went to sleep after a whole day's thought over the forthcoming operations, I dreamed that the Japanese forces, with the cooperation of Thai troops, had succeeded in capturing a bridge spanning the Perak River.[34]

By contrast, British training remained patchy. In the final analysis, Lieutenant-Colonel Stewart concluded that:

> The Jap. was ardent, and in consequence had all the characteristics in action we lacked. . . . Our troops were not cowardly, but we thought all the time of how we could avoid being killed. The Jap was not fanatically brave, but he did not mind being killed.

Here was a real and pervasive difference between the two sides. There was rigorous preparation, high morale and clear motivation on one side, including an almost brutal training regime, providing bicycles for rapid transport, and seizing sawmills in each new region taken to secure wood for bridge repairs. On the other side there was poor preparation, and sometimes indifferent motivation. This difference was about to be exposed to the full, as Japanese troops came ashore in southern Thailand and on the east coast of Malaya on 8 December.[35]

On the morning of the 8 December Brooke-Popham finally cancelled *Matador* and authorised *Krohcol*, the orders reaching the commanders in the north just after lunch the same day.[36] 11th Indian Division's troops, having waited in the rain for the order to advance, then found themselves falling back towards the Jitra position in northwest Malaya.[37]

The Japanese had by now successfully landed at Kota Bharu on the northeast coast of Malaya, as well as at Singora, Patani and at locations a little north of these sites in Thailand. They had also mustered over 600 aircraft, which soon asserted crushing air superiority over 167 inferior, frontline Allied adversaries.[38]

Excluding reserves and unserviceable machines, there were 167 frontline aircraft in Malaya, but British planners had always known this was not enough.

In October 1940 theatre commanders had asked for 566 frontline aircraft, which, at reserve rates of about 50 per cent, would have implied an additional 283 reserve aircraft. In January 1941 the COS suggested 336 might be a more realistic target for later in the year. But that was before Churchill and his commanders routed most modern aircraft to the home theatre, the Middle East, and then to Russia as well. As a result, the aircraft in Malaya were too few and often outclassed. Even the Dutch in the Netherlands Indies had 144 aircraft. Northern Malaya's several airfields also lacked radar and did not have enough anti-aircraft guns. So they had only a limited chance of scrambling aircraft in time to intercept Japanese bombers, or of shooting them down when they did arrive.[39]

Too often, British planes were caught on the ground. As December wore on, the number of aircraft available sometimes dipped towards the 100 mark, with these increasingly operating from south Malaya. Some British infantry dubbed the dwindling airforce the Penguin Club, 'because they had wings but didn't fly'. Lieutenant-Colonel Ian Stewart, commanding the 2nd Battalion Argyll and Sutherland Highlanders, claimed he 'did not see one British aircraft ... between the 10 December and the 14 January', while his battalion suffered 'about 50 air casualties in the campaign'.

When British aircraft did fly, the results were scarcely more reassuring. The Japanese navy *Zero* fighters proved able to climb higher and faster than the RAF's *Brewster Buffalo* fighters. The pilots of the *Wildebeeste* torpedo bomber, which made little more than 100 miles per hour (as opposed the Japanese fighters clocking over 300 miles an hour) dubbed their machine 'The Flying Coffin'. Such statements may exaggerate the technical gap between the two forces a little. In reality few of the much-vaunted navy *Zeros* made an appearance, and the Japanese Army's more numerous *Nakajima* Ki-43 fighter was a less impressive machine. But the Japanese were also vastly superior in combat experience. British novices scarcely out of flying training school were no match for China veterans, notwithstanding that some of their squadron leaders, and even a few flight commanders, did have European experience.[40]

In these circumstances, even the late-arriving Hurricanes' proved slightly disappointing, though the Japanese did note their January arrival with distaste. Before, Japanese forces had largely ignored British aircraft, pressing on along roads at speed even when aircraft passed over in broad daylight. Now they found it wise to take cover from time to time, as the Hurricanes flew in low over rubber trees to strafe troops and transport.[41]

Notwithstanding the temporary boost the British received from the January arrival of the Hurricanes, the Japanese position improved over time. They started out using airfields in Indochina, with extra fuel tanks attached where necessary, before taking aerodromes in southern Thailand, and then in northern Malaya too.[42]

Just as the Japanese were asserting mastery of the air over northern Malaya, the Royal Navy's performance added to the gloom. On 8 December, Singapore's mini-fleet, Force Z, headed out of Singapore to try and intercept Japanese transports off the east coast of Malaya. With the RAF too hard-pressed to offer much cover, even if the force had not maintained radio silence, it was a risky move. Spotted by Japanese aircraft, the battleship HMS *Prince of Wales*, battlecruiser HMS *Repulse* and their four-destroyer escort, headed back for Singapore. Unfortunately, they made a diversion to check reports of landings at Kuantan. None were discovered. According to some accounts, the culprits were unlucky water buffalo which had drifted onto a minefield, according to others, Japanese infiltrators, or unlucky Malay fishermen who were later found in their boat, dead.[43]

The cause can be disputed, but the result cannot. A Japanese submarine, one of a number on patrol, spotted the delayed ships. When they resumed their retreat to Singapore they were caught east of Kuantan, and without air cover. The two capital ships were then destroyed by Japanese bombers and torpedo-bombers about 50 miles off the east coast, on the early afternoon of 10 December.[44]

Given Japanese air superiority, this had been the almost inevitable result, unless the Royal Navy had been willing to skulk off and abandon the army to its fate.[45] It is true that a quirk of fate had deprived the force of its intended aircraft carrier, HMS *Indomitable* running aground off Jamaica on 3 November. A determined move north by *Indomitable* and the two capital ships around 6 to 8 December could have created havoc with Japanese transports.[46] But whether even *Indomitable*, with about 50 aircraft, could have changed the final outcome is doubtful. The number of quality Japanese aircraft available, and the possibility the Japanese would have sent extra ships or men in response to the arrival of a British carrier, both have to be considered.[47]

To tip the scales, Britain would have needed to send significant extra forces, and as far as aircraft carriers are concerned, these were not available. Britain did have five modern aircraft carriers in early November, the United States about seven in service. But circumstances temporarily favoured Japan.

The United States had not accepted that the defence of Singapore warranted the dispersal of its Pacific naval forces. Indeed, Anglo-American discussions from January to March 1941 had resulted in a so-called A.B.C.1 Plan, or 'Hitler First' strategy. This involved increasing American naval forces and patrols in the Atlantic, and standing on the defensive in the East even if Japan attacked. By December 1941 there were just three American carriers in the Pacific. Against this Japan could muster ten, including six fleet carriers and four light carriers, two of the latter being kept in Japan for training duties.[48]

The Japanese committed all six of their fleet carriers to the operation against the American Fleet at Pearl Harbor. Only two light fleet carriers were left over for other tasks, in addition to about 150 naval aircraft operating from Indochina.[49] But Britain was in no position to take advantage of this. Two of Britain's five modern carriers were in repairs for battle damage. A third, the *Indomitable* ran aground on 3 November, delaying its departure. A fourth, HMS

Ark Royal, sunk on 14 November, while under tow after being torpedoed by a German U-boat. That left just one modern fleet carrier for the Home Fleet, and three or four older carriers.

The older vessels were unlikely to intimidate Japan, even if they were sent. Typically, HMS *Eagle* and HMS *Hermes* both started construction as battleships. They had been converted to carry about twenty aircraft or less, inferior to Japan's light carriers, and about a quarter of the number Japan's fleet carriers were capable of.[50]

Britain did, it is true, assemble an eastern fleet of sorts by April 1942. This was already being planned for in late 1941, and eventually boasted five battleships (four of them old and slow), and three carriers, including both *Indomitable* and *Hermes*. But even this was not enough. When Admiral Nagumo's main battlefleet made its solitary foray into the Indian Ocean that month, it came with five of the Pearl Harbor carriers, with another operating separately. Faced with the choice of running or facing defeat, the Royal Navy managed both. On 9 April HMS *Hermes* was sunk off Ceylon by Japanese carrier-borne aircraft. Having suffered further losses, the rest of the British Indian Ocean fleet scurried back towards the Indian and East African coasts.[51] It would take the American victory at the Battle of Midway, in June 1942, to decisively turn the tide against Japanese naval forces.[52]

In the end Force Z, Churchill's deterrent force of the *Prince of Wales* and *Repulse*, was caught without air cover and went down fighting. The Japanese pilots who sunk the capital ships left the British destroyers to pick up survivors. Next day Japanese bombers dropped a bouquet of flowers over the ships' graveyard, and the final resting place of 830 officers and men.[53]

Even before the *Prince of Wales* went down, British land forces were reeling backwards. Part of their problem was that they were hopelessly dispersed from the start, in order to cover all possible Japanese landing sites. In the northwest, and originally scheduled to launch *Operation Matador*, was the 11th Indian Division. On the northeast coast was the 9th Indian Division, attempting to defend miles of gentle, idyllic, palm-fringed beaches. Meanwhile, the Australian 22nd and 27th Brigades were miles away, watching Johore in the south, while more troops and aircraft guarded Singapore. Here was a force outnumbered and outclassed in the air, and hopelessly dispersed on the ground.

Nor was the armoured situation better. There were literally no British tanks until late in the campaign, though there were armoured cars, leaving a terrible onus on the artillery to stop Japanese armour breaking through. What followed was a Malayan campaign in which a Japanese *Kirimomi Sakusen* [driving charge] tactic – their version of *blitzkrieg*, featuring tank thrusts, outflanking movements and interpenetration of British units – were pitted against British attempts to hold fixed positions.[54]

Japanese speed was such that some British forces did not even reach their starting positions. Critically, *Krohcol* failed to take the 'Ledge', the position just inside the Thai border, and blocking the road from Patani. The handling of

THE CAMPAIGN

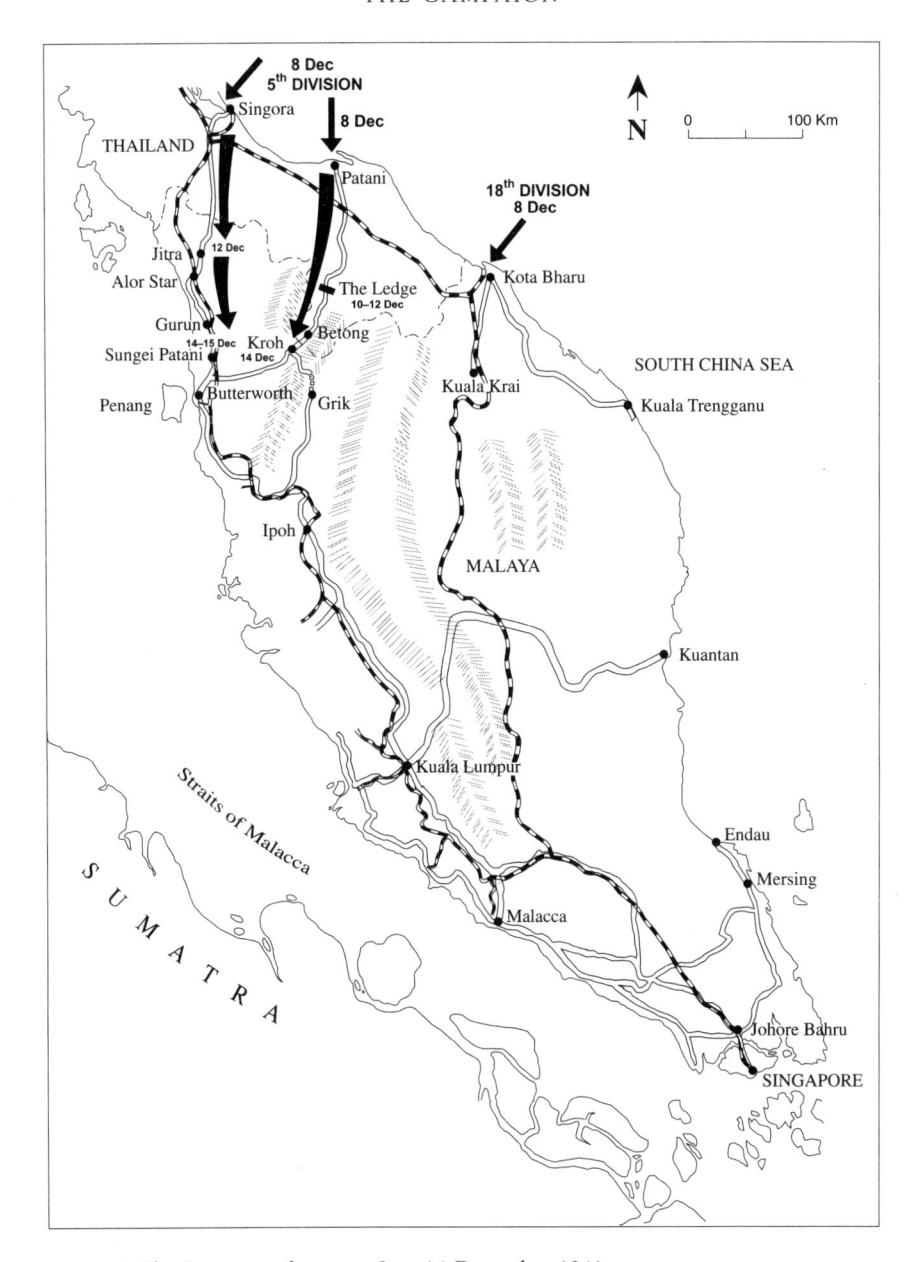

Map 4.2 The Japanese advance – 8 to 14 December 1941.

Krohcol was symptomatic of the British failures. First, Brooke-Popham and Percival should have authorised the operation on 7 December at the latest. This is because *Krohcol* was essential if the nearby Jitra position in Kedah was not to be outflanked. Second, the force allocated consisted of only two battalions and a

69

battery of artillery from the Federated Malay States Volunteers. This, especially the use of volunteer artillery support (which was still not fully mobilised) was not commensurate with the importance of the task. Third, only one battalion was ready when the order to advance came just after 1300 hours on 8 December.

This understrength *Krohcol* force duly set off around 1500 hours on 8 December, only to be delayed by roadblocks and by about 300 Siamese armed policemen. *Krohcol* only had about 30 to 35 miles to advance, but by the morning of the 10 December was still several miles from its objective. By this time the Japanese had already covered 75 miles from Patani to race beyond the Ledge. *Krohcol* was sent reeling backwards when it came across them, and their light tanks.[55]

One Royal Artillery officer later recalled with evident frustration how his unit had trained for *Krohcol*, only to be switched 'at the last minute ... to supporting 1/14 Punjab with whom it had not trained'. So *Krohcol* was deprived of some of its artillery support, only for this to go to Jitra. Yet the Jitra position would be vulnerable to being outflanked if *Krohcol* failed.[56]

The whole *Krohcol* episode was indicative of abysmal British planning, training, and initiative, and suggestive of how *Matador* might have fared. Unless this disaster could be reversed, and the road held further down, this meant the Japanese were already on their way to flanking British positions at Jitra, not far from the Thai border in Kedah.[57]

The Jitra position had always been the fallback position in case *Matador* was aborted, or defeated. By now it was being manned by troops of 11th Indian Division, who until the afternoon of 8 December had been waiting to launch *Matador*. The position itself was about 18 miles south of the border with Thailand, just in front of the town and road junction of Jitra.[58] It thus stood in the way of the Japanese advance to airfields at Alor Star behind, then Sungei Patani, and further back still at Butterworth opposite Penang.

The 11th Indian Division had started to prepare this as their fallback position some time earlier, with pillboxes and an anti-tank ditch, though supporting works were sparse. The troops at the Jitra position now stood astride the main road from Thailand, blocking the Japanese route down the west coast. This position had marshes guarding its left flank, beyond which the sea lay some 12 miles away. To the right there were hills, and artillery had been positioned to counter Japanese tanks.

In order to buy time, two battalions (1/14th Punjabis and 2/1st Gurkhas) were sent ahead piecemeal to delay the Japanese, only to be badly mauled by tanks. The 1/14th was caught on the move by Japanese tanks on 11 December and overwhelmed. Amongst their captives, the Japanese discovered one Captain Mohan Singh. By the beginning of January he was to agree to help form an Indian National Army (INA) from Indian captives. The INA was run down on his resignation at the end of that year, but the idea of Japan using Indian troops lived on to bear fruit in Burma in 1944, by then under the leadership of Subhas Chandra Bose.[59]

For the moment, however, the rapid defeat of the two Indian battalions meant the main Japanese attack would come quickly. When it did, later that day the Japanese were true to their tactics of *Kirimomi Sakusen* or a driving charge. Just two Japanese battalions, with a company of tanks in support, concentrated on interpenetrating the gaps between the units of two Indian Army Brigades.[60] This forced partial retreats by some, which caused others on their flanks to fall back in turn. In this way the whole British position crumbled, without the Japanese even needing to launch a major outflanking operation.[61]

Ultimate withdrawal had anyway been inevitable, as Japanese forces that had landed at Patani were now driving past the Ledge and into west Malaya, pushing southwards on a line some miles inland from the coast. In this way they were threatening to come round behind the British forces at Jitra. By the end of 12 December British forces had begun to abandon the Jitra position. By 14 December, the Japanese were installing their own aircraft at the newly captured Alor Star airfield just south of Jitra. Another delaying action at Gurun ended just as badly by 15 December, and British commanders agreed the port of Penang just to the rear should be evacuated.[62] The evacuation followed on 16 December, the sight of whites leaving the town to the Japanese doing nothing to improve Britain's image. The Japanese soon had the radio transmitter at Penang beaming their propaganda to Singapore.[63]

By 18 December all of the State of Kedah was gone. The next in line was the west coast State of Perak, with its rich tin fields. Even here the situation was becoming desperate. Shaken and reduced units had to be amalgamated, one example being the 6th and 15th Brigades turning into the 6/15th. Percival now decided to pull his troops back further to regroup. Perak's busy, Chinese-dominated mining town of Ipoh was evacuated by 28 December.

The battle for north Malaya was over. The battle for central Malaya was about to begin. At first this involved numerous delaying actions against Japanese thrusts, these coming from both the northwest, and from Japanese forces still making their way down the road from Patani. The Japanese increasingly employed flanking movements as they advanced, moving by river, and later along the coast too. At Kampar on the west coast for instance, 20 miles south of Ipoh and about 90 miles north of Kuala Lumpur, British and Indian forces stalled the Japanese from the dying moments of December 1941 until 2 January 1942. Here a determined stand was made for once, in a position with a good, open field of fire to its left, and with ridges and mountainous jungle to the right. The ridges on the right flank ran up to the 4,070 foot high *Bujang Melaka* mountain, and here successive Japanese attacks were held.

Yamashita was furious about the delay at this 'rocky bastion'. Tsuji momentarily withdrew from the General Staff when reinforcements were refused.[64] But ultimately it became futile to persist, as Japanese forces both landed on the coast to the south of the defenders, and sailed reinforcements down the Perak River behind them. By 2 January, after six days' fighting, British forces were again retreating, rather than risk being cut off and destroyed.[65]

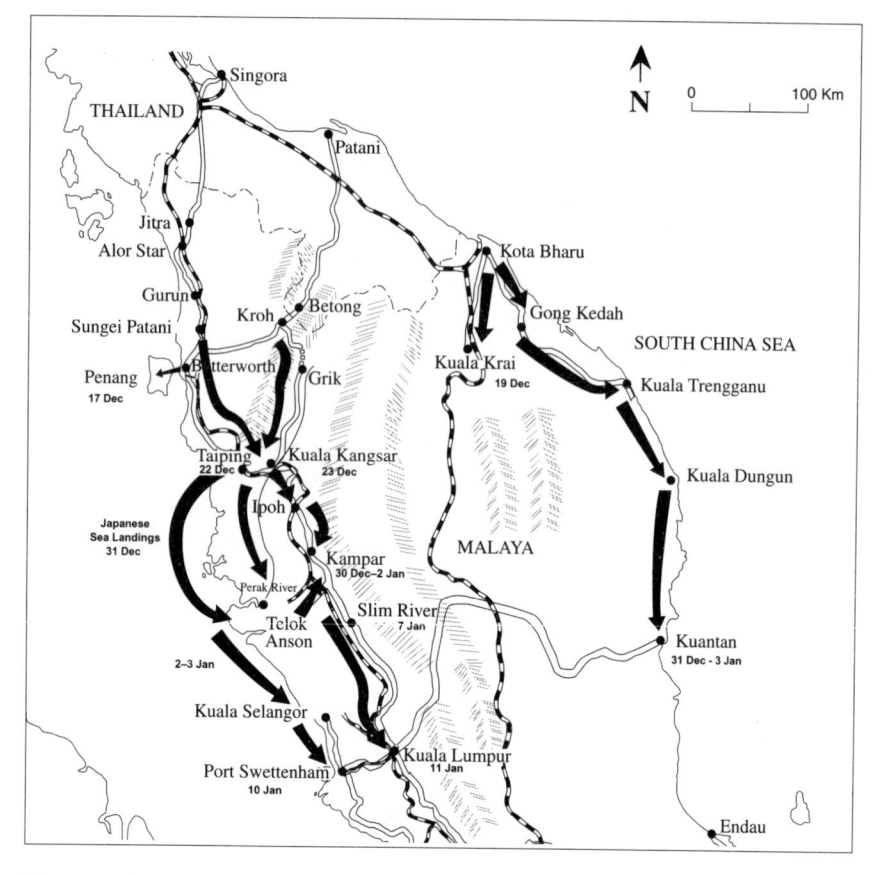

Map 4.3 The Japanese advance – 15 December 1941 to 11 January 1942.

By early January the Japanese were advancing out of Perak and down the west coast towards Kuala Lumpur. British troops were by now not above absurd fears, claiming to see 'arrows cut in the grass and arrows formed by clothes put out to dry, pointing to battery positions', despite the fact that most bomber pilots, at speed and height, would have been hard put to make sense of such signs. Sentries sometimes blazed away at imaginary signalling fifth columnists, only to discover 'nothing more harmful than a glow-worm'. Instead, and despite some real traitors in the ranks, the most deadly 'fifth column' in Malaya was increasingly fear itself.[66]

Brooke-Popham and Percival, meanwhile, still wanted the Japanese delayed as far to the north of Singapore as possible. Two recurring concerns patterned their thinking. They wanted to keep airfields, this time in central Malaya, out of Japanese hands, and to delay the Japanese advance so as to allow ships carrying reinforcements to arrive in Singapore relatively unmolested by Japanese aircraft and artillery.[67]

For these reasons, and in line with British conception of the campaign as a fighting retreat, forces now took up positions in depth at Trolak in central Malaya. The Trolak position covered the approach to the Slim River, and so the final road to Malaya's biggest town: Kuala Lumpur. At Trolak the main road and railway towards the Slim River ran close together, with rubber plantations and in places dense jungle to either side. This seemed to provide an excellent funnel through which Japanese forces would be forced to advance.

British forces sat themselves astride the trunk road and the railway, and when the Japanese arrived from 5 January their initial attacks were beaten off.

Then pandemonium broke loose. Under a brilliant moon, between 0300 and 0400 hours on 7 January, the Japanese launched a frontal assault. Tanks, interspersed with infantry-packed lorries, rolled down the road. Where the resistance was too stiff, they took loop roads left disused after a recent road-straightening.[68] Too few anti-tank guns had been positioned, and preparations made, to the front. In this way, twenty or more Japanese tanks were able to adopt 'human bullet' tactics, punching their way down the road and taking bridges before they could be blown.[69]

By dawn the Japanese tanks were mauling and scattering successive units, until they captured the road bridge over the Slim River itself. British artillery was not in short supply, just unprepared or too far back. Finally:

> They were stopped after a 16-miles run, by a truly gallant effort of a 4.5 Howitzer of the 155th Regiment. One of their batteries was at the time going up to the front, when the leading tank knocked it out; the second gun was just in time to be able to come into action on the road and fire at point blank range at the leading Jap tank which it destroyed, the knocked out gun and the tank thus forming a very efficient road-block.[70]

British forces now fell back towards Kuala Lumpur in disarray. An April 1942 Japanese article claimed that the Slim River battle 'completely choked the life out of' the British forces'.[71] Certainly the retreat, well underway by the end of 8 January, found the 12th and 28th Infantry Brigades in a desperate state after their mauling. The day after the disaster, less than 1,200 out of their 5,000 men could be mustered.[72]

On a brighter note, the first reinforcements were arriving at Singapore. The 45th Indian Brigade disembarked as early as 3 January. But the danger was that the army they were due to reinforce would be ruined in its retreat. As a Japanese article of April 1942 put it:

> The enemy troops escaping from Sulim [sic, Slim] fled to Kuala Lumpur, but even there they had no time to rest. From Kuala Lumpur they fled to the northern part of Johore, but the Japanese troops were close on their heels, and they had to flee again ... Troops were ... sent to Gemas from Kuala Lumpur, including a tank corps and an engineering corps. The distance was 160 kilometres.[73]

THE CAMPAIGN

In other words, the defenders now retreated from central Malaya, where the abundance of good roads made outflanking by armour or by troops landing along the coast almost inevitable. They scuttled back to north Johore, where they hoped to set up a final shield for the Singapore naval base. On the east coast too, the defenders fell back to Johore, after the Japanese captured Kuantan just ahead of New Year's Day, 1942.

So January 1942 found the defending forces trying to construct a defensive line across north Johore. In effect this meant two separate lines, one west of Malaya's central spine of hills and forests, one east. The battle of Johore would also be fought by relatively fresh units, as the severely battered 11th Indian Division was placed in reserve.

It was a case of fresh troops, new commander. The Australian's combative Major-General H. Gordon Bennett, was given control of 'Westforce', which was tasked to defend Johore.[a]

The Australian 22nd Brigade was left to cover the east coast.[74] Bennett took the other Australian Brigade, the 27th, and joined it to the 9th Indian Division in the west. He chose to use the resulting 'Westforce' to make a main stand at the inland town of Gemas.

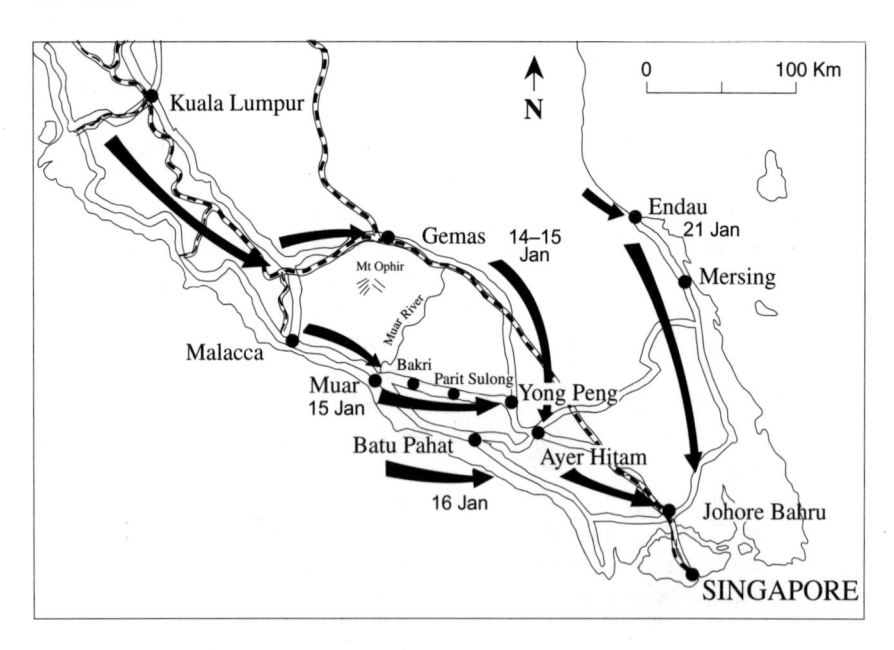

Map 4.4 The Japanese advance – 12 to 31 January 1942.

---

a Major-General H. Gordon Bennett. He joined the militia in 1908, rising to command the 6th Battalion AIF at Gallipoli and in France. By 1939 he was one of the most senior ranking, and outspoken, generals on the Australian Army List. As well as remaining a militia officer, he was a highly succesful businessman. In 1940 he was appointed to command the 8th Australian Division.

THE CAMPAIGN

Gemas had much to recommend it. The rail track coming across country from the east coast merges with the main west coast line near here. So the main road and rail links to Singapore could be covered by one position. Even better, the approaching road had jungle right up to its fringes in places, with some ideal spots for ambushes.

When the Japanese attacked, Gordon Bennett's strategy of defending the Gemas position in depth at first seemed to pay off. First, a company-strength ambush was set at Gemencheh, about 7 miles ahead of Gemas, and just ahead of a wooden bridge. An advance company of the Australian 2/30th battalion allowed the leading Japanese on bicycles to get across the bridge on 14 January, before blowing it and pouring fire into the Japanese trapped on the road. They left many Japanese dead before withdrawing, and so held out the hope of inflicting more serious casualties on their opponents.[75] At Gemas itself the following day, the same battalion's supporting anti-tank guns helped knock out several tanks before massing Japanese forced a withdrawal.

Plate 4.1 Japanese tanks destroyed by Australian guns. Three Japanese type 95 Ha-Go light tanks destroyed near Bakri (between Muar and Parit Sulong) by gunners of the 13th battery, 4th Australian Anti-Tank Regiment. Still more were destroyed nearby and at Gemas.

Source: Australian War Memorial negative number 011301.

75

The performance was impressive, but even so the battalion involved had taken almost 10 per cent casualties (about eighty including wounded, of these seventeen dead and nine missing), and had had to leave behind all but one of their supporting anti-tank guns in the retreat. In addition, the stringing out of units along the road made effective, sustained counter-attacks and outflanking of the enemy unlikely, since the Japanese arrived in waves, each capable of wider flanking movements. By 16 January, the Japanese were already massing men and tanks, and starting to try to outflank the entire 27th Australian Brigade on the road south from Gemas.[76]

Worse still, the Gemas position had a major defect: Mount Ophir stood between it and the west coast. If the Japanese successfully landed on the west coast, near the Muar River, they would be able to cut inland. Following the road from the coast, they could join the main Gemas to Singapore road well to the south of the Gemas position.

The job of defending the coast at a position astride the Muar River, about 80 miles north of Singapore, fell to the 45th Indian Brigade.[77] The Brigade was fresh, having arrived in early January, but unfortunately fresh to the point of being unready. Too many new officers were unfamiliar with their Indian troops, and not yet competent in their languages. One Australian gunner caustically said, of the young recruits of 45th Indian Brigade, that 'none of them had even the smallest idea about how to aim and fire anything', and that they were to flee the coming battle all too readily.[78] There was also insufficient artillery.

When the central Japanese thrust slowed down at Gemas, the initiative passed to the Imperial Guards Division on the coast. They forced the Muar River from 15 January, finding some of the defenders totally unprepared. Within two days, the 45th Indian Brigade was sent spinning backwards as the Japanese made repeated outflanking movements by land and along the coast. This was a double blow: the coastal force faced destruction; and the Japanese now threatened to cut off the main part of Bennett's 'Westforce', still situated around Gemas. In its turn, this caused yet more fresh units to be fed in to the deteriorating situation behind the Muar River. The British 53rd Brigade, newly arrived on 13 January, and scarcely recovered from nearly three months at sea, was the main candidate. Its men were ordered to try and link up with the retreating 45th Brigade.

There followed a disastrous retreat for the 45th Brigade, and two Australian battalions which had been sent in to support them, fighting their way back along the road to Yong Peng to the rear. They were repeatedly harassed by Japanese flanking movements and by roadblocks. Their fate was sealed when the British 53rd Brigade failed to fight its way forward to secure a line of escape. The 45th Brigade and accompanying Australian units, bombed and strafed all the way on their retreat, eventually found the Japanese barring the crucial bridge at Parit Sulong. With no hope of breaking through, these units shattered. On 22 January, their commander ordered them to disperse into the surrounding rubber trees to try and make it back, in small groups, across jungle, swamp and *padi*.[79]

By 19 to 20 January, Percival had already concluded that northern Johore would soon be lost, and decided to fall back to a new line, in yet another bid to buy time for Singapore.[80] That new line would run from Mersing on the east coast, through the trunk road between Gemas and Singapore, to Batu Pahat on the west coast. This latest battle, for a line across the middle of Johore, turned out as a replay of Gemas. The 15th Indian Brigade was outflanked by 25 to 26 January and had to disperse into jungle to try and escape, over 2,700 reaching the coast. The gunboats *Dragonfly* and *Scorpion* combined with small craft from Singapore to rescue them. But there was no such lucky escape for the 22nd Indian Brigade. Cut off on the retreat, its commander surrendered.

The defence of Johore was all but over. It had cost two more brigades, and still more in abandoned equipment and damaged morale. There now followed the final retreat to Singapore, from 27 January. A retreat which might have been more disastrous, had the Japanese not already diverted some air power to help capture Borneo.

Back in Malaya, Lieutenant Hayes, a naval liaison officer with III Indian Corps, was at the Causeway. Early on the morning of Saturday, 31 January, he saw the retreating army cross the Causeway in all its variety: Bren carriers; troop carriers; artillery; field ambulances; and finally the infantry, the 'tramp of their feet on asphalt ... the only sound in the stillness ... a tired tramp'. At dawn khaki forms were still plodding across, 'as the full moon was setting amongst the buttresses of the Sultan's Palace' on the Malayan side of the causeway. The sun was beginning to rise, 'impossibly coloured'. Soon the Japanese would use the tower of the Sultan of Johore's Green Palace, which looked towards Singapore from the Johore coastline, as their command post for landings on Singapore itself. But that still lay in the future. For now, Lieutenant-Colonel Stewart's 2nd Argyll and Sutherland Highlanders marched, last across, with bagpipers playing. A hole was blown in the Causeway just after 0800 hours on 31 January.[81]

That the Japanese had come so far in such a short time begs the obvious question: could the defenders have delayed the Japanese more in Malaya? The answer is: almost certainly. But would this have made a substantial difference to the outcome?[82] Churchill did not think so.

As early as 16 December the British Chiefs of Staff received Churchill's warning to 'Beware lest troops required for ultimate defence of Singapore Island and fortress are used up or cut off in the Malay peninsula. Nothing compares in importance with the fortress'.[83] Brooke-Popham, however, seems to have seen things very differently. A few days later Churchill, by now irritated, was insisting that 'He [Brooke-Popham] should now be told to confine himself to defence of Johore and Singapore and that nothing repeat nothing must compete with maximum defence of Singapore. This should not preclude delaying tactics and demolitions on the way south ...'. Churchill's logic was that, following naval disaster, 'we have no means of preventing continuous landings by Japanese in great strength ... It is therefore impossible to defend ... anything north of the defensive line in Johore ...'.

Churchill then watched his worst fears become reality from the United States, where he went to try and cement the Anglo-American alliance that the Japanese had kindly created by Pearl Harbor. On the night of 26 December, while still in the White House, the combined strain of the war on this 67-year old, not to mention his passion for food, drink and cigars, culminated in a mild heart attack.[84]

Churchill shrugged off the warning, which remained a secret at the time, only to see his fears for Malaya further confirmed, as the Japanese again and again used river, sea and rubber plantations for flanking movements. With Japanese aerial and armoured superiority, as well as their speed and outflanking tactics, Lieutenant-Colonel Stewart later lamented that there was, 'a false tactical conception – that defence of a "position" was possible, hence Jitra ... and Muar'. Yet the Japanese tended to simply 'fix' such positions by a frontal attack, prior to finding a way through or round British units. Even the Battle of the Slim River is presented by one Japanese source as originally conceived not as a frontal attack, but as developing 'in the course of a flanking movement ...',[85] Only the pleas of Major Shimada had resulted in him being allowed to try his tanks first.[86]

There was another peculiarity to the Malayan campaign. Stewart on the British side, and Tsuji for the Japanese, both recognised the battle in Malaya had to be for the roads, off the roads.[87] The battle was for the roads, because roads were more vital than ever in a country where jungle and rough terrain could splinter large military units. Tsuji ascribed the ease of success partly to a combination of excellent paved roads the British had built, combined with cheap Japanese bicycles. Since cheap Japanese bicycles had invaded the Malayan market in advance of the Japanese army, replacement parts were everywhere available. Good roads made it possible for the bicycles to continue even after their tyres had given out, making a noise Tsuji described as like that of tanks.[88]

But the battle had to be fought off the road, because of Japanese flanking tactics, and because the surrounding terrain usually gave excellent cover for infantry. This cover was not usually 'jungle' in the first instance. Typically there might be cultivated rubber plantations, with rows of well ordered and tended trees, allowing troops to be deployed on a narrow front of a mile or a few miles either side of the road. Beyond that there might be jungle, marsh and hills, though of course roads did at some points cut through forest and defile as well, as they did where the Australian's set their ambush near Gemas.[89]

Even if British-led troops had performed better in the terrain off the road, Japanese control of the strategic environment made the defence of any position on the mainland difficult, if not impossible, as Churchill recognised. Bad training and tactical errors compounded this already bad situation. Lieutenant-Colonel Stewart later recognised that 'some A.Tk gunners, certain Inf. Units, and certain of R.A.F ground staff ... chucked in their hand'. The latter was true at Slim River, where Japanese accounts suggest British forces were utterly unprepared, some weapons and vehicles having been left unattended in the torrential rain. Nor was this the only time units were caught without weapons at the ready.[90]

How far many troops' poor performance was caused by the hopelessness of their situation is in turn open to debate. Stewart recognised the practical limitations, Japanese tanks made effective counter-attack difficult in the absence of British tanks, and many others joined him in noting that Japanese air superiority constantly sapped morale.[91] The combined effect of poor British preparation compared to the seasoned Japanese 5th and 18th Divisions, and Japanese superiority in tanks and aircraft, also ruled out another possibility. British forces could not fight a war of movement, attempting their own encircling movements and counter-attacks. Not even if they had not been over-equipped and over-reliant on mechanised transport; dressed up like Christmas trees in some observers' eyes. These troops would be too slow, counter-thrusts would risk annihilation by Japanese tanks, and Japanese aircraft would give the enemy the edge in intelligence. In these circumstances, it is difficult to see how any single decision here, or there, could have made a worthwhile difference.[92]

Come 1 February, the chance had passed anyway. Malaya was gone. Singapore was besieged, even if the hole blown in the Causeway did turn out to be just four foot deep at low tide.[93] The men who would bear responsibility for Singapore's final defence would be Percival, as General Officer Commanding (GOC) Malaya, Lieutenant-General Sir Henry Pownall (Brooke-Popham's successor, now styled Chief of Staff to the Supreme Allied Commander, South West Pacific) and the Supreme Commander himself, General Sir Archibald Wavell. Wavell was formerly Commander-in-Chief India, and before that in North Africa as Commander-in-Chief, Middle East. He had become Supreme Allied Commander, South West Pacific on 3 January 1942. He controlled not only British possessions, but the wider ABDA (American-British-Dutch-Australian) command based in Java.

The battle for Singapore

Even before the Causeway was blown, way back in mid-January, the newly arrived Wavell had realised that Singapore had scarcely been fortified to the north. This was mainly because it had always been assumed it would be defended at a distance. When he informed London, a bitter exchange followed from 19 January, between Churchill and his high command in London. Churchill demanded to know why the island had not been made into a citadel, and his commanders responded that this was scarcely possible for a mangrove-swamp fringed island, and anyway, everyone had always known that the naval base, facing Johore, could only be defended in Johore, or further north.[94]

The Strait between Singapore and Johore, which Churchill insisted on thinking of as a splendid moat, shrank in places to between a half a mile to a mile across. The Japanese Headquarters, now positioned in the tower of the

Sultan of Johore's green palace (Bukit Serene) in Johore Bahru, had a commanding view of Singapore's northwestern shore. London *Times* correspondent Ian Morrison reported that some soldiers, who arrived after the Causeway had been blown, 'swam the Strait with ease'.[95]

Despite the length of Singapore's coast, and despite the frequent Japanese air-raids from mid-January, there should have been enough troops and food and ammunition to make a fight of it. Except that the troops in Singapore, and those still struggling back through Johore, were for the most part wearied, and accustomed now to expect defeat. Churchill's mood was not that of his commanders. He determined the island should die in a manner honourable to his now thoroughly dishonoured empire, calling for protracted fighting.

In the east of the island, meanwhile, the naval base was being rendered useless: not so much by the Japanese, as by the British. Much of dockyard staff were evacuated to Ceylon on 31 January, and by 5 February the floating dock had been wrecked and a denial scheme had been put into partial effect. The base was already useless anyway, as it was within easy range of Japanese artillery and mortar fire. But the nearly empty base also meant that, in a way, the defenders had failed in their mission before the Japanese so much as set foot on Singapore.[96]

For Yamashita commanding the Japanese 25th Army, however, the final aim was the capture of Singapore itself. To achieve this, he had 168 artillery pieces to the defenders 226 (including fortress guns), and far less than the defenders' 85,000 regular troops (perhaps 70,000 of whom were combat ready).[97] Yamashita later said he used a mere 30,000 men for his final attack, a figure which probably includes only to the 5th and 18th Divisions used in the initial thrust on the night of the 8 to 9 February. But even with the Imperial Guards joining from in from the latter day, and further artillery, tanks and support, he certainly had fewer troops than Percival, who claimed the real number of attackers was 60,000. This made surprise essential.[98]

The defenders were to be kept dispersed and guessing at Japanese movements, while directing their own thrusts so as to concentrate troops towards one focal point. To achieve this, they removed all people from the west Johore coast, kept their own troops back, and made a faint attack in the east. Entering the Strait in the northeast, about 400 Japanese troops landed on the island of Pulau Ubin on 7 February. Artillery was then moved onto the island to make as much noise as possible.

Percival and his commanders had already decided the east might be the critical front anyway, despite Wavell suggesting otherwise. So the freshest troops, the British 18th Division, were kept on the right, in the northeast. The centre of the island was guarded by the Indian 9th and 11th Divisions, both much ravaged by the mainland campaign. The south, where the fortress guns were numerous and an attack less likely, was given to 1st Malaya Brigade, which included the Malay Regiment's two battalions. Again, Percival tried to cover everywhere, and in the process ended up being strong nowhere. This proved fatal on Singapore's northwest coast, where the Johore coast was closest to

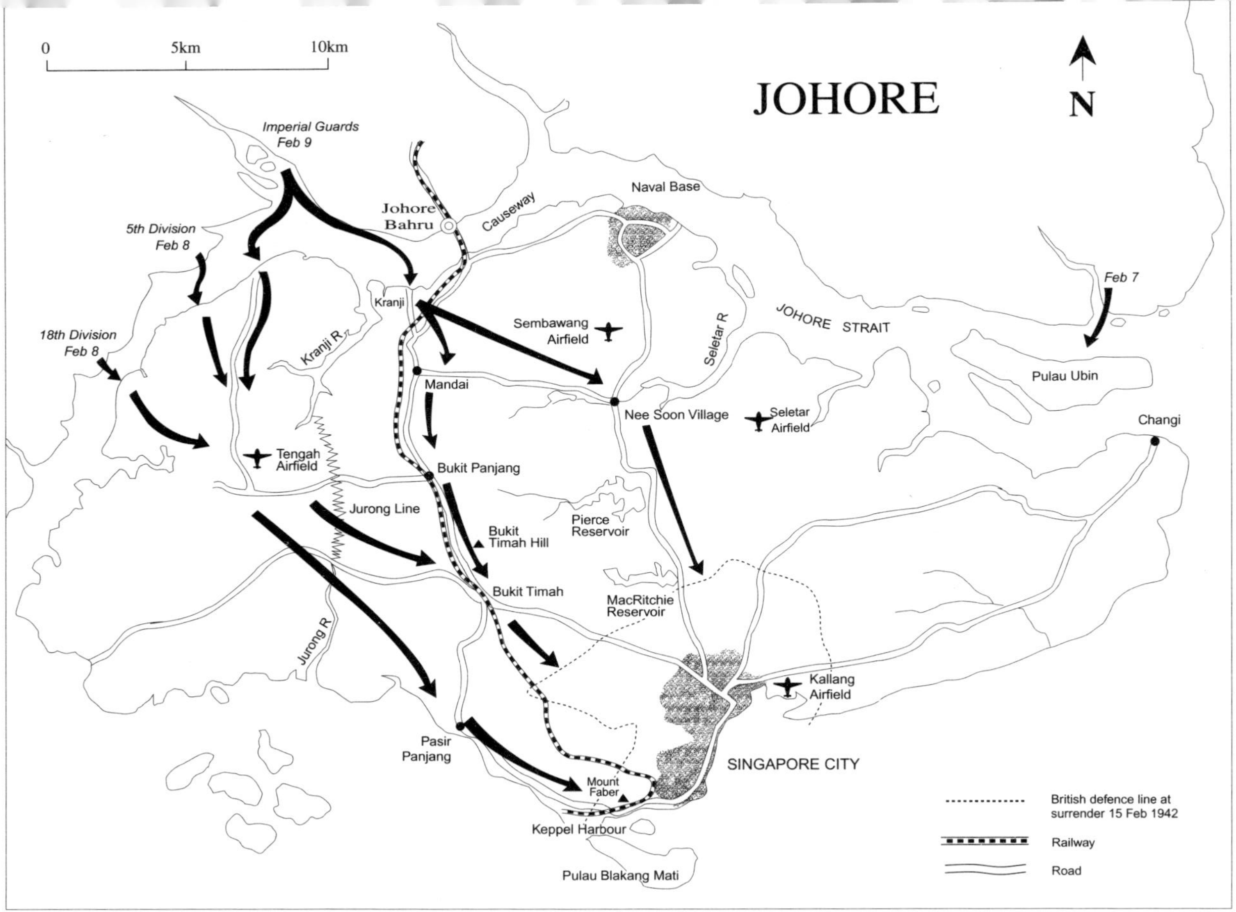

Map 4.5 The battle for Singapore – 8 to 15 February 1942. For detail on Singapore town, see Map 2.2 Singapore city in 1941 (page 16).

Singapore. This section fell to Gordon Bennett, who had just two Australian Brigades and the fresh Indian 44th Brigade. It was not enough.[99]

In the middle of the night of 8 to 9 February, the Japanese 5th and 18th Divisions started landing on the northwest of the island.[100] In the first landing areas, the unfortunate Australian 22nd Brigade had just three battalions, with a smattering of artillery support, to cover several miles of mangrove. With as little as one or two companies of men to a mile, and no sizeable reserve close enough to plug holes or counter-attack, a repeat of Japanese infiltration and bypassing was inevitable. Besides, the Japanese had amassed the entire 5th and 18th divisions on the shore opposite, ready to cross on a front held by just one Australian brigade. The initial Japanese bombardment also cut communication lines, so the defenders were unable to call on large-scale artillery support at the outset. So, despite their overall numerical inferiority, the Japanese forces again achieved massive local superiority.

By daylight on 9 February those Japanese who had not been killed in the first wave were in possession of the coast. Further waves were landing, and much of the Australian 22nd Brigade, like other formations before, had been reduced to tatters retreating across mangrove and rough terrain.[101]

So it was that, on 9 February, Percival committed first the 12th Indian Brigade (badly beaten up at Slim River) and then the 6/15th Indian Brigade (the remnants from Jitra) to help the Australians and 44th Indian Brigade hold a line further into Singapore.

This was the Jurong line. From the northern coast, the line traced the Kranji River, and from its southern coast, the Jurong River. In between the two rivers was a gap of about 3 miles. Here it seemed was a reasonable defensive front: one which might quarantine the rest of Singapore from the Japanese now pouring into its western sector. It might also shield the approach to Bukit Timah Hill, Singapore's highest point, which if lost would open the final road to the reservoirs, military supplies and dumps nearby, and then to the city itself. Four Brigades were committed to this line.[102]

Unfortunately, three of these four brigades were already substantially reduced in strength. In addition, this western defence could only make sense if the Australian 27th Brigade could hold the remaining stretch of the north coast between the Kranji River and the Causeway.

On the night of 9 to 10 February the Imperial Guards fell on the Australian 27th Brigade.[103] Initially they found it hard work, and some guards were caught up in oil released onto the water by the defenders, and now blazing fiercely. But then Brigadier Maxwell, the 27th Brigade's commander, ordered a premature withdrawal. Maxwell had been a captain in the First World War. But in civilian life he was a doctor, and he had only recently returned to military service. He turned out to be a dreadful choice for the situation in hand, telling one officer as early as 9 February that he wanted to ask Percival to surrender. By early on 10 February one of his brigade's battalions had retreated about 3 miles inland, to the Mandai Road.[104]

This was a disastrous call, since the guards had been finding the crossing hard going, and had even considered abandoning it. Had the guards taken a more severe mauling, it would have placed the overwhelming burden of the Japanese attack on the two divisions advancing from western Singapore. This might have allowed more British forces to concentrate there. As it was, the guards were able to land, and to help keep the defenders dispersed, by constantly threatening an additional attack from the north.[105]

With the Imperial Guards now consolidating east of the Kranji River, they were behind the Jurong Line. Faced with this, and with some commanders knowing of Percival's secret, reserve plans to withdraw to a tighter defensive perimeter later on, the defenders retreated. They moved back from the Jurong Line and towards the centre of the island.[106]

With commanders always nervous they might be outflanked and cut off, as had happened so often on the mainland, units tended to withdraw when the Japanese advanced to either side, rather than counter-attacking. This meant any defensive line tended to move backwards in response to Japanese attacks in just a few locations. On 10 February the front finally came to rest just west of the causeway on Singapore's northern coast. From there the front ran southwards across the island to Pasir Panjang on the opposite coast, running just to the west of Bukit Panjang and Bukit Timah as it did so.[107] On the same day the last of the defending aircraft flew off to Sumatra.[108]

All this time Percival kept most of the Indian 11th Division and British 18th Division to the centre and east of the island, nervous of committing too many of his forces at once. His problem was that he did not know if there were more Japanese units waiting to attack elsewhere, especially as he thought the Japanese might have five divisions or more. This meant he was never likely to commit enough men to make any counter-attack effective, and so the same pattern continued on 10 and 11 February. In the north of the British line, there was relatively little trouble. But orders for a counter-attack towards the Jurong line had little effect.

Japanese tanks helped clear their troops' way to Bukit Panjang in the island's centre.[109] Below Bukit Panjang, there was fierce fighting on the slopes of Bukit Timah from the afternoon of 10 February. The Japanese finally secured its heights on the next day. From Bukit Timah Hill, Bukit Timah Road stretched ahead towards the city, now a few miles away. The Japanese had hoped to subdue Singapore by 11 February, which was *Kigensetsu*, the anniversary of the coronation of the ruling dynasty's mythical founder, Jimmu Teneo, in 660 BC. For Tsuji, Bukit Timah stood for the whole of the island. He later wrote that, 'We felt assured that we had occupied Singapore for the first time when Bukit Timah was taken'[110]

A respectful invitation to the British to surrender was sent by an air-dropped leaflet the same day that Bukit Timah fell, warning that further resistance was futile, and would merely increase the danger that the city's 1 million inhabitants would face 'pain by fire and sword'. Percival was asked to send envoys up the Bukit Timah Road, bearing both a Union Jack and a white flag.[111]

THE CAMPAIGN

Percival ignored the invitation. Instead, British forces attempted to retake positions around Bukit Timah on 11 February, resulting in hand-to-hand fighting as ammunition ran out. Lim Chok Fui, then a young resident of Bukit Timah, has recalled the aftermath:

> we saw the British soldiers being killed while retreating into Holland Road. Their heads and legs were cut off, leaving only the torsos which were thrown into a drain. Some of the soldiers' hands were pierced through with wires and their bodies were slashed with swords ... They were stripped naked and with both their hands tied, were hung on trees by the Japanese.

This was not to be the last time that fierce resistance resulted in brutal reprisals.[112]

Meanwhile, the Japanese drive from the west was coming closer to the city itself. From 12 February, the Japanese 18th Division drove along close to the southern coast, towards Pasir Panjang Village, with Mount Faber and the city centre just beyond.

In the centre of the island on 12 February, meanwhile, the Japanese 5th Division pushed on past Bukit Timah Hill and down Bukit Timah Road, tanks assisting.[113] They came to a halt where Adam and Farrer Roads cross Bukit Timah Road. They were now just short of Raffles College.[114] Except for the defending troops before them, the Japanese were little more than a short tank or bus ride, 5 miles or less, from Orchard Road and the heart of the city.

The Imperial Guards were now on the move too. They had landed just west of the Causeway. Now they moved to a line just east of the Causeway, and of the island's central reservoirs. They then advanced southwards towards the city.[115] In response, Percival called in the forces still in the north and the east of the island, hoping to construct a tight perimeter defence around Singapore City. On the evening of the 12 February the Changi area was abandoned, and its coastal guns blown up. By the morning of 13 February the Japanese had taken control of the MacRitchie Reservoir.[116]

One positive effect of this retreat to a City perimeter was the concentration of artillery in an increasingly small area, which subjected the Japanese to more intense fire. As one gunner recalled: 'Every available open space on the outskirts of the town held some form of gun, whether 25-pounder, 4.5 Howitzer, 6-inch Howitzer, 2-pounder, anti-Tank, Light AA or Heavy AA.'[117] To at least one Japanese officer, the bombardment seemed to intensify, until on the 15 February, as Japanese troops prepared for the final conquest of the city: 'houses were blasted to pieces. The roar of explosions was deafening and we could not hear one another even if we yelled at the top of our voices. Shrapnel and fragments of shells ... hit the steel helmets worn by the lying soldiers and made metallic sounds every time they struck ...'[118]

The Japanese now ground forward. Breaking the resistance of the Malay Regiment on the southwest coast, at Pasir Panjang Ridge, on 13 and 14

THE CAMPAIGN

February they pushed past Alexandria Hospital, coming to a halt at a line just in front of Mount Faber. There the defenders stitched together yet another defensive line. With the Japanese so close to the harbour in the south, and actually in the outskirts of the city, forces further inland were vulnerable to having their flanks turned.

Worse still, by 14 February parts of Percival's forces were beginning to fall apart. Australians troops, whose battalions had borne the brunt of the fighting in Johore and in the west of Singapore, were prominent amongst those seen in town and around the harbour. Some were merely lost, others determined not to go back, and a few were intent on an early escape from the island. On Blakang Mati (Sentosa), meanwhile, where remnants of the island's coastal artillery forces were gathering, some Indian forces started to act independently. Ordered to proceed to Connaught Fort on the island, where there were three 9.2 inch guns, some threw down their arms and changed into civilian clothes. Others made for barracks and hoisted a white flag. Second Lieutenant Colchester, trying to restore order, was told by one Indian 'that the British Raj was coming to an end'.[119]

There were, of course, many men, and many Australian and Indian soldiers, still in position, but by the morning of the 15 February the impossible seemed near. The larger British-led forces had been brought to the point of defeat.

Lieutenant-General A.E. Percival was now in charge of a disintegrating army, with the remaining defenders entombed within Singapore City itself. He had by now seen a Resident Minister, Duff Cooper, go in December 1941. One who unfortunately had had enough power to interfere – some dubbed him 'Tough Snooper' – but not enough to impose order and inspire action.[120] Percival had seen Air Chief Marshal Brooke-Popham transferred out at the end of the same month, according to a schedule decided upon before the attack. Then he had come under Wavell, controlling the battle from a safe distance in Java. By now even the aircraft had been withdrawn to the Dutch East Indies.

This was a cruel fate for a man who had long ago forecast the nature of a likely Japanese attack, and whose army career had started with volunteer service on the Western Front in the First World War. He had predicted what was coming, and eastern commanders' demands for nearly 600 aircraft had come close to matching what the Japanese had thrown at them. But the equipment had not come, and he had compounded that nightmare by lacking the ability to take calculated risks, and to leave some areas thinly defended in order to concentrate on others. Where Churchill had taken too many risks, Percival had taken too few.

Now, on 14 February, Percival was penned into Singapore city, faced with desertions, and considering the imminent likelihood that the Japanese, who already held the reservoirs, would soon cripple the town's water supply. Near Mount Faber on the south coast, 'the supply of water had just about dried up. In fact, troops were having to break into houses to get at the water remaining in the cisterns ...'[121]

It has been suggested that, despite all this, 14 to 15 February saw one last chance for the defenders to turn the tables. According to some Japanese sources, the fall of Singapore was still not inevitable. Yamashita's attack on Singapore had been a bluff, to cover up his small forces and lack of supplies.[122] It was also a bluff based on the assumption that British forces, demoralised by their retreat, and led by a man who had already abandoned several cities, would give up early. By the end of 14 February this bluff was in danger of backfiring. The Japanese were running short of ammunition and tanks. According to Tsuji's accounts, there were just 200 shells per field gun left on the morning of 15 February,[123] and 100 shells per gun left by the afternoon, so that heavy reliance was now placed on large mortars loaded on handcarts.[124] Yamashita had vaingloriously pushed on, two weeks ahead of his original timetable and, at the limit of his logistics, despite his troops placing a heavy reliance on 'Churchill rations', captured supplies, for food. On 14 February they began to fear that they had miscalculated. That the heavy British artillery barrage meant the defenders intended to engage in street to street fighting, for which Yamashita now had neither the numbers nor the ammunition. In short, 'they feared they might be the ones to surrender'.[125]

If Yamashita had pushed his men and his supply lines to their limit, and the German model of blitzkrieg to breaking point, it has also been argued that the defenders did not push him as far as they might have done. Many of the post-defeat reports on the Fall, whose authors were trying to explain the disaster, settled on Australian failures as one critical problem of the last days. According to the G.W. Seabridge, editor of the local *Straits Times*, some Australians failed to follow orders from early on, some forward posts were withdrawn, on occasions without a fight – and consequently the Japanese quickly established a bridgehead on Singapore. Seabridge also said a senior Johore official had offered 'incontrovertible proof' the Australians were guilty of rape and pillage in Malaya.[126]

Nor did such information come from British sources alone. One Australian Provost unit reported increasing problems persuading stragglers to return to the line from 12 February, with 'AIF soldiers' 'very reluctant' by the next day, and by 14 February, 'all imaginable excuses being made to avoid returning to the line', and arms and equipment being abandoned, while men crowded the wharves in the hope of getting away by boat.[127]

To be fair, Seabridge and Wavell both recognised the Australians received the heaviest artillery fire, and that they had virtually no air cover. The Australian Provost unit cited above also noted British and Indian troops wandering around aimlessly from 13 February, and claimed British wearing Australian style slouch hats (especially those rescued from stricken ships and then provisioned by the Australians) were sometimes mistakenly identified as Australians.[128] Recent works have argued the Australian plight was more symptomatic of defeat than causative of it, and some of their reinforcements were almost entirely untrained. Their battalions on the northwest coast had also taken the full brunt of the initial Japanese attack. However, the sheer number of reports which criticised the Australians' performance, including people who stressed they had admired Australian fighting qualities elsewhere, is difficult to dismiss. If one took seriously the idea it was a close run thing, then it could be argued that the failure of general morale, combined with Australian failures from 9 February, whether in command or at the frontline, were just one more 'cause' which, if removed, might have helped to save Singapore.[129]

According to this interpretation, all previous mistakes made defeat likely. But it was not inevitable even at the very end.[130] On this interpretation, every single mistake was vital. Almost any improvement in Britain's previous record, more equipment, better training, launching *Matador*, or abandoning it earlier, recruiting a more formidable local army, the aircraft carrier *Indomitable* not running aground en route to Singapore in 1941, the Australians and other key forces performing better at key moments, any one thing might have tipped the balance: the fall of Singapore was never inevitable; it was always avoidable.

The problem is that such arguments are rarely followed through. The extra step, of asking how the Japanese would change their plans in response to British moves, is not pursued, or not pursued far enough. The final judgement must depend on the flexibility of the Japanese. The temporary Japanese control of the strategic environment has already been noted. Japan began the land invasion of Burma on 16 January. At dawn on 14 February airborne troops were sent from southern Malaya to seize advance positions in Sumatra, more following the next day.[131] On 19 February Japan launched a mass air attack on the Australian town of Darwin, using over 180 aircraft from four carriers. Its forces overran the East Indies and attacked New Guinea within a month of Singapore's fall. In the Philippines, the Americans held on for weeks on the Bataan peninsula and then on the island of Coreggidor. Unlike Singapore, these were places lending themselves easily to defence. But such defiance did not affect the final result. Manila, a better comparison for Singapore, was declared an open city and abandoned as early as 2 January.[132] The South Seas, meanwhile, were awash with Japanese men and machines, moving in waves towards the resources of the East Indies.[133]

These later attacks make a simple point. Assume Yamashita had failed to take Singapore on 15 February itself. Assume British forces had fought better in Singapore. The Japanese could no doubt have suffered setbacks, especially since Japanese commanders were notoriously jealous of each other, and might have proved reluctant to help Yamashita. But the fundamental strategic environment favoured Japan. It had the regional superiority in machines, and control of the seas. Any marginal improvement in British resistance could be countered. When Japanese sources claim a few days more resistance could have exhausted them, we must bear in mind their desire to emphasise their heroism taking on a numerically superior force, and the ever-present danger of death and failure.

The reality was that the Japanese temporarily dominated the theatre. Put bluntly, Japan may have been in a position to counter reinforcements of the scale Britain was to be able to spare, especially as Malaya had priority.[134]

THE CAMPAIGN

The Japanese deployed just three divisions in Malaya, Yamashita keeping one in reserve for this area. Beyond his command, Japan had eleven divisions for Southeast Asia as a whole, another thirty-five in China, and forty mostly in reserve in Japan. Though they were pushing the limits in 1941–2, the overall strategic domination (and the availability of ammunition for subsequent campaigns in Burma and the East Indies) meant they retained flexibility. Since they were not at war with any major naval or air power before 7 December 1941, they also had flexibility over how to deploy their aircraft and ships. The result of all this is that, despite naval defeats from Midway in 1942, American ships did not enter the South China Sea again before 1944. On dry land, meanwhile, the Japanese reached the high tide of their fortunes as late as May 1942, by when their troops were in New Guinea just off Australia, and on the border between Burma and India.

By contrast, Britain's short-term problems in 1941, combined with its long-term decline relative to its main competitors, made an adequate response difficult.[135]

On this scale, the Fall of Singapore seems a tragic reflection of larger events, a catastrophe waiting to happen as Britain continued to control one quarter of the globe, but saw its industrial lead eroded. Britain had continued expanding its empire after 1918, even as its financial strength started to falter. By the 1930s it controlled a quarter of the earth's land with only a tenth of its military might. By contrast one potential enemy, Germany, had increased its share from an insignificant level to 14 per cent in a few decades. Another potential enemy, Japan, which in 1853 had been largely isolated from the world, was now also a major competitor. Once both these powers, as well as Italy, were at war against Britain simultaneously, Britain would be hard-pressed to keep itself in house and home, let alone worrying about Singapore.[136] It was this dilemma which had made every minor decision over Singapore from the 1920s on a matter of financial bickering, and which ate away at the ability to do what was needed, when it was needed. In this sense, it was not the individual decisions that mattered, but having sufficient reserve capacity to outbid opponents who were willing to risk everything.

This was Churchill's problem. Come mid-1941 the Middle East, bomber offensive and Russian fronts were all active theatres, but up to December 1941 Singapore was not. In these circumstances, Churchill could move more resources to Singapore, but there would always be pressure to limit the numbers of tanks and aircraft involved. As early as 27 January Churchill put this case to parliament:

> While fighting Germany and Italy here and in the Nile Valley, we never have had any power to provide effectively for the defence of the Far East ... It has been the policy of the Cabinet at almost all costs to avoid embarrassment with Japan until we were sure that the United States would also be engaged.[137]

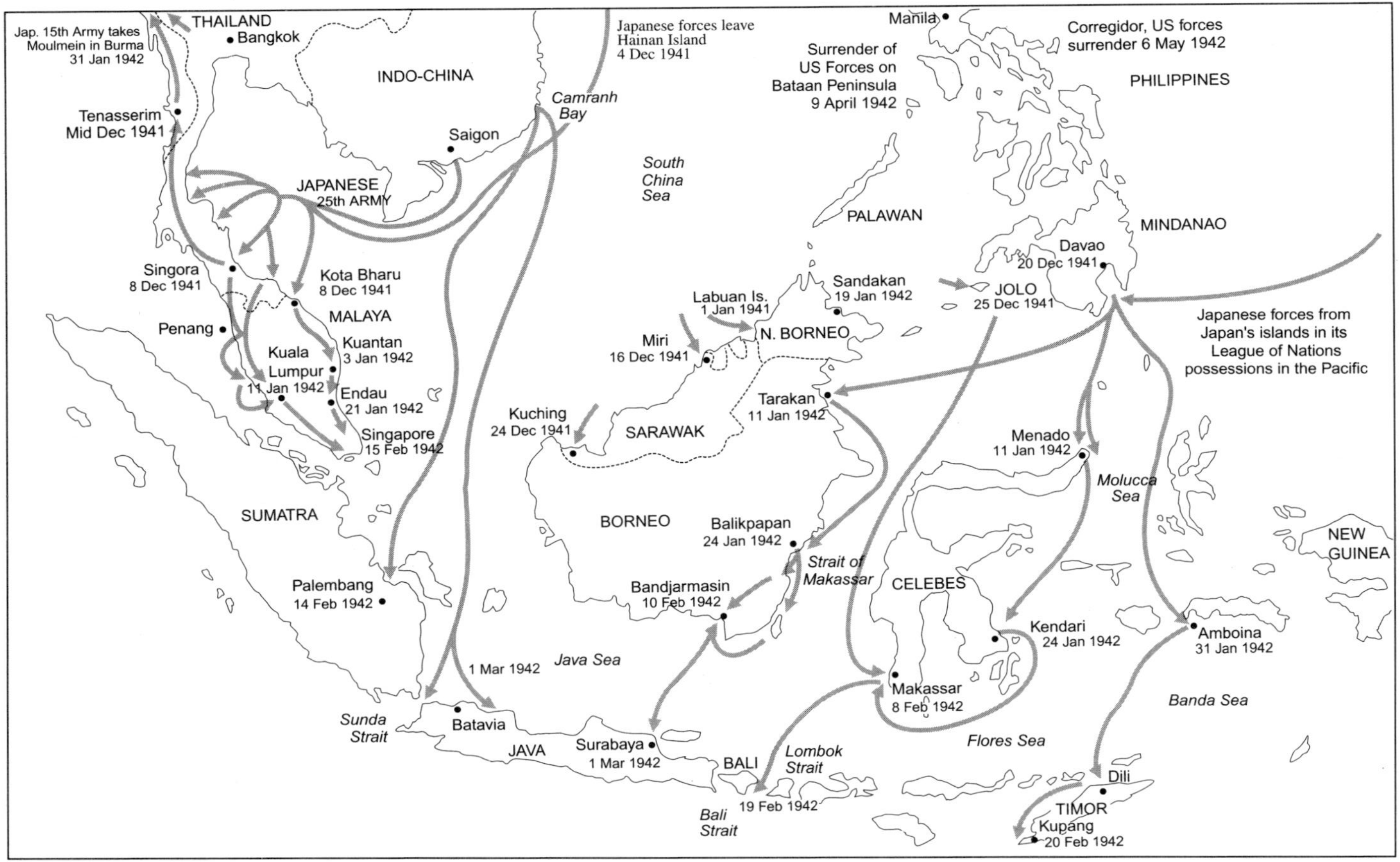

Map 4.6 Japanese forces over Southeast Asia, December 1941 to March 1942.

Every tank, aircraft and ship diverted from Egypt, Russia, the Atlantic, or the Home theatre, increased the danger Britain would be outbid or the Soviet Union defeated. The consequences of a Soviet defeat and all Italy and Germany's might turn on Britain then seemed too terrible to contemplate. So though it could be argued that other theatres might survive some diversion of resources towards Malaya's needs, the penalty for any miscalculation could be costly, if not terminal.[138]

The likelihood that any further, pre-December reinforcements for Singapore would have been limited raises a further question. If the battle for Singapore really was a close-run thing, could moderate additions of British aircraft and tanks have altered the short-come outcome, as Dill had suggested to Churchill in May?

It is certainly conceivable, but begs yet another question: how would Japan have responded to changes in British forces? Given the number of Japanese civilians in Malaya and the additional presence of spies, it is almost certain that changes of a significant scale would have been reported to Japanese planners. In the unlikely event that Malaya's 5,600 Japanese civilians had failed to notice reinforcements, there were also spies, including one British officer of the Indian Army.[139] This was Captain Patrick Heenan of 300 Air Intelligence Liaison Section. We do not know why this New Zealand born, and British public-school educated man turned 'traitor', probably sometime around his trip to Japan in 1938 to 1939. Discrimination or being the 'odd man out' has been suggested, with speculation that this might have been fuelled by his illegitimacy, the Irish Republican sympathies of a father who died before he could get to know him, possible mixed race origins, or even disgust with British racism in Burma, where he spent his childhood. We can speculate that attending a British public school with this background, as he did, was an uncomfortable experience. What we know for certain is that Patrick Heenan was discovered in Malaya with a two-way radio receiver. Just before the surrender of Singapore it seems he was marched down to the harbour, shot in the back, and pushed into the water.[140]

In these circumstances, Japan was likely to be able to respond to changes in the defending garrison. Small additions of men or equipment were not likely to make a critical difference. Even if all the 200 Hurricanes which went to Russia in the second half of 1941 had gone instead to Singapore, it might have merely prolonged the period before Japan achieved mastery of the air.[141]

Indeed, the Japanese may have felt that the 600 aircraft they provided were sufficient to counter at least 300 British aircraft anyway. This is because we know that one of the highest level British reports, the Chief of Staff's August 1940 Far East Appreciation, suggested Malaya needed 336 aircraft. A copy of this report was despatched to Singapore on the British merchant ship SS *Automedon*. And the *Automedon's* cargo fell into enemy hands. On 11 November 1940 the German merchant raider *Atlantis*, disguised as a Dutch merchant vessel, sighted the *Automedon*. By a twist of fate, one of the first shells the *Atlantis* fired landed on the bridge of the British ship, killing most of the officers, who would normally have destroyed all confidential documents. This meant the Germans were able to seize the vital report intact. After the war British counter-intelligence units found the original copy of the report in the rubble of Berlin, with a comment scrawled across the front in what they believed to be Hitler's handwriting: 'This is a document of first importance and should be sent to NA [German Naval Attaché] Tokyo'. This is exactly what happened, and some Japanese historians claim the document played an important part in encouraging Japan to attack not only European territories, but to take on Pearl Harbor simultaneously.[142]

In short, a besieged British Empire would have been hard-pressed to up the stakes beyond Japanese capacity to respond. In a classic scenario, an overstretched empire, losing an original economic lead, and faced with a major war, would find it extremely difficult to hold an outpost such as Singapore against a determined attacker. On this reading, and given world war and France's fall, Singapore's fall became almost inevitable from the moment Japan decided to take it.[143]

According to this interpretation of events, Lieutenant-General Yamashita's last-gasp problems in Singapore, as commander of the 25th Army, were symptoms of justified confidence. Having taken Malaya with a speed that surprised himself, by January 1942 he had Singapore at his mercy. It could be contained, attacked at convenience or bypassed. The decision to attack immediately was not so much a 'bluff' intended to cover up supply shortages, but a result of the exhilaration of chasing a defeated army, of Yamashita's impatience, and of the Japanese accepting a carefully calculated risk that Singapore's obviously demoralised garrison could not resist for long. Even on 15 February, he seems to have been contemplating one last night attack, so as to concentrate the remaining tanks and artillery shells, punch through the shrunken defensive perimeter, and cut up the remaining defenders.[144]

For Percival to have fought to the last as Churchill wanted, let alone manage a counter-attack, he would have required an army far less advanced in its disintegration. Examples of this were legion, so one will suffice. On 15 February, Second Lieutenant Griffiths of the 9th Coastal Regiment, Royal Artillery (at this point promoted Acting Captain) was commanding a company of gunners of the fixed coastal batteries. The regiment had been reorganised as infantry after the Changi area guns had been blown up on 12 February. His unit was holding a section of the perimeter defence around Singapore city, with orders to 'hold out to the last'.

In the afternoon, stragglers came flowing through his lines, many claiming they had been told to ceasefire. This reflected a general rumour that fighting would stop around 1600 hours. On this occasion the subaltern was able to 'stop the rot' in his sector and add some of these men to his own, but not without cost: 'He had to shoot two officers killing one'; an action that later earned him the praise of his commander.[145] Stragglers and deserters whose numbers had been swelling from 9 February, as well as those who no longer believed there was anything left to fight for, were becoming a critical problem. Wounded now lined the aisles of St Andrew's Cathedral. The Raffles ballroom was awash with empty beer bottles and sometimes drunken soldiers too. The editor of the *Straits Times* later wrote of 'the almost complete demoralisation of the defending troops' in a city that reeked of smoke and decay.[146]

What would have happened if Percival's forces had not been this forlorn? Yamashita might have sensed this, and delayed his initial assault on Singapore. Quite why Japanese planning and intelligence, up to this point superb, should suddenly be incapable of detecting, and adapting to, different British capabilities, is never made clear. Had the improbable nevertheless happened, Yamashita would have been in trouble. For the Japanese forces were in such a race against time that each element had its own task to achieve, and he had accepted the risk of pushing his supplies to their extreme limits.

What we do know is that British forces were in no position to break out of Singapore, so that their best hope by February was to hold on to all, or some part of, a burning and battered island, just as American forces did in their ultimately futile last stand at Corregidor, before surrendering on 6 May.

Percival's commanders were not in the mood for such defiance. At 0915 hours on 15 February they agreed on surrender. Just after 1700 hours Percival arrived at the Ford Factory on Upper Bukit Timah Road to meet Yamashita. Unconditional surrender was quickly agreed, with the final ceasefire to commence at 2030.

The realisation was that it was over did not take long to seep through to the troops:

> the gunners manning the Command Post on Mount Faber had been joined by a small Indian Commando unit and were holding a line across the main road near Keppel Golf Course below Mount Faber. At about sunset we distinctly heard Japanese troops farther up the road shouting *Banzai! Banzai! Banzai!* Shortly afterwards orders were received from Fort Canning that we were to cease-fire and we were informed that the great fortress of Singapore had been surrendered.[147]

For most of the defenders of Singapore it was over. In all, more than 100,000 allied military personnel were surrendered.[148] On the 16 February they awaited their fate, while an eerie silence heralded the fall of Britain's eastern empire, and smoke from blazing oil tanks blackened the sky.

But it was not over for all the defenders. As the Japanese had advanced, some British officers had encouraged Chinese, Malay and Indian forces to slip away to avoid reprisals. Other men had done so on their own initiative, and a few had been trained by the British for sabotage and guerrilla warfare. So as far as the Japanese were concerned, the battle would not be over until they had identified these, and neutralised the most dangerous of them. Besides, Japanese troops had already learnt distrust and brutality towards the Chinese in China itself, terming

THE CAMPAIGN

them *chancorro*, which implied something less than human, on a level with a louse. In January, Tsuji had already been reminded of central China while driving into Kuala Lumpur, where the heads of Chinese soon adorned intersections.[149]

Come 18 February, it was Singapore's turn. Japanese commanders gave the order for a cleansing or sifting out of anti-Japanese elements from the Chinese population. To be precise, Yamashita, who knew most of his troops had to be moved on quickly to Sumatra and Burma, gave the order. He left it to his Chief of Staff, Lieutenant-General Suzuki, to clarify the details, and Suzuki specified the *genju shobun* [severe disposal] of hostile Chinese as part of a mopping-up operation. In military terms, that meant execution without trial.[150]

By 21 February this order had begun a slaughter more cold-blooded and calculated, if smaller in scale, than that of the frenzied events at Nanking in December 1937. This was the *Sook Ching*, the 'screening' or 'cleansing' of anti-Japanese Chinese at locations scattered across the island, such as Chinatown, Tanjong Katong, Happy World Amusement Park and Dhoby Gaut. Signs were posted ordering Chinese males to report to points such as these, with food for three or more days. These areas were then cordoned off, and troops posted around about. The Japanese had lists of prominent Chinese, but they also made men pass by Chinese detectives and even criminals from the gaols, whose job it was to pick out 'communists, terrorists, Dalforce members, volunteers and bad hats'. The results could seem almost random, but the outcome was not. Selection was followed by transport to one of the beaches stretching from Katong to Changi, to a lonely inland spot, or by a boat ride, ending in death by bullet or bayonet.[151]

The Japanese later admitted 5,000 had been killed, the Chinese claimed ten times that number if executions in Malaya were included.

Despite the senselessness of much of the selection, the operation was originally conceived by the Japanese as the closing shot in the battle: a cleansing which would pave the way for peaceful administration. It is, in many ways, the right moment to end an account of the battle for Singapore.

The *Syonan Times* of 23 February 2602 (1942) put it this way:

> It is hereby declared that the recent arrests of hostile and rebellious Chinese have drastically been carried out in order to establish the prompt restoration of the peace of 'Syonan-Ko' (port of *Syonan*) and also to establish the bright Malaya.
>
> Chinese in *Syonan-Ko* have hitherto been in sympathy with propaganda of Chunking government, and majority of them supported the aforesaid government and taken politically and economically the same action with Britain against Japan and moreover they have positively participated in British Army, in forming volunteer corps and still have secretly disturbed the military activities of the Nippon Army as guerilla corps or spies they, in spite of being Eastern Race, were indeed so-called

traitors of the East Asia who disturbed the establishment of the Great East Asia ...

Thus it is the most important to sweep away these treacherous Chinese elements and to establish the peace and welfare of the populace.[152]

By 26 February, '138 dead bodies of Chinese were washed up at BLAKANG MATI [Sentosa] ...' in one area alone, as many as 500 overall, tied together in twos and threes. Some of the gunners at Fort Connaught, on the hills to the island's south, watched as Chinese were brought out of the city on boats and tugs, and pushed overboard. Looking through binoculars one European planter saw 'firing over the bows at "something red", which he presumed to be blood-stained bodies bobbing up and down in the water'. Each boat circled for a few minutes, and then turned back towards Singapore Harbour.

Some of the victims were subsequently washed ashore on the beaches of Blakang Mati tied up in twos and threes, and became entangled on the barbed wire: many Chinese and a few Malays; workers with harbour-board armbands, and occasionally a woman, one with two babies still tied to her. British and Indian troops buried some of the bodies, almost their last act on the island. On 27 February these troops were, at last, evacuated: 582 British going to Changi; 750 Indians to Farrer Park.[153]

For Singapore the battle was finally over, as anti-Japanese resistance switched to the jungles of Malaya, under the leadership of Malaya's Chinese communists.

In London, meanwhile, the war of words over Singapore's fate had already begun, and a significant part of that debate revolved around the role of the gunners just mentioned and the system they supported: the role of Fortress Singapore.

5

THE GUNS OF SINGAPORE

No one should ever have been fooled by the legend of the mighty fortress of Singapore. The place had none of the natural characteristics of an old time fortress like Gibraltar; nor was it 'fortified' in any way, though it had been armed with guns which were useless against anything but a sea-borne assault.
> C. A. Vlieland (Secretary of Defence for Singapore, 1939–41) writing in the 1960s.[1]

Singapore was naturally easy to defend, and with consolidation of its equipment could be shaped into an impregnable fortress. Facing the sea coast a battery of fifteen inch guns ... dominated the eastern mouth of Johore Strait and protected the vast military barracks at Changi ... We know however that in the rear of the fortress the defences are weakest ....
> Tsuji, Singapore 1941–1942, pp. 217 and 214[2]

Lord Jellicoe has declared that Pearl Harbour is so well fortified as to be impregnable, the implication being that Singapore can also be rendered impregnable. But we know how delusive is the term; we remember how once Port Arthur was deemed impregnable and how, notwithstanding its garrison of 45,000 men and 500 guns, it fell.
> Australian author Tristan Buesst, 'The Naval Base at Singapore' *Pacific Affairs* 5, 4 (April 1932), p. 315, arguing the Base threatened disarmament.[3]

The defences of Singapore have ... been rendered as nearly impregnable as modern military science can approach.
> Naval correspondent, 'Singapore and the Services', *The Times* (London) Weekly Edition, Thursday 3 March 1938, p. 41.

For Churchill, 'Fortress Singapore' implied a place that could hold out for weeks against a siege, much as Tobruk had from April 1941 until it was relieved on 8 December of the same year.[4] For his commanders, 'Fortress Singapore' was a naval base opposite Johore, whose guns could secure it from sea attack, but which remained vulnerable to its landward side. For them, the only way to defend it was to keep attacking forces as far to the north, in Malaya, as possible.

In this way, there was between Churchill and his commanders a serious, if not fatal, gap in understanding: a gap which gives 'Fortress Singapore' an important place in the bigger story of how Singapore fell.

The story of 'Fortress Singapore', and its coastal guns, began in the 1920s, when Britain planned to build a 'Fortress' to defend its new naval base. Chapters 2 and 3 have already touched upon this, starting with the 1921 decision to build a naval base, but not to provide a main fleet for it in peacetime. Instead, Singapore was to be reinforced with a main fleet only in an emergency. This meant Singapore would have to survive in the so-called 'period before relief': the time a fleet would take to arrive from the Mediterranean or Atlantic. For this period, initially set at forty-two days, big coastal guns were a necessity in order to keep Japanese battleships at bay.

When British officials and officers began to plan Singapore's coastal defences, in 1922 to 1923, the Admiralty at first wanted Singapore to have eight of the biggest coastal guns. That is, about the same number as a modern battleship, such as Japan's *Nagato* (commissioned in 1920 with six 16 inch guns).

The army was happy with a solution based on coastal guns, which they would man. But the RAF was not convinced. They had only recently achieved status as a separate service, in 1918, and were fighting to increase their size and prestige. The Air Ministry argued aircraft were cheaper, more mobile, had a 150-mile range against a big gun's 20-mile range, and could even be stationed elsewhere in peacetime.

It was a bold move considering the embryonic state of development of military aviation, and one destined for only limited success. In the end, the Admiralty and War Office preferred the bird in the hand (guns which could not move) to two in the bush (torpedo bombers which might not even be stationed in Singapore, and whose range, effectiveness, and reinforcement routes, though improving yearly, were still questionable). In May 1932, and after much tiresome debate, a final compromise emerged. A Coast Defence Committee in London agreed Singapore would get five big 15 inch guns, but the RAF could have a subsidiary role.[5]

Though airpower was later to prove triumphant against capital ships, it would be naive to assume that a different decision at this point would have helped later. The fixed defences cost under £5 million, equivalent in 1920s prices to a small capital ship or little over thirty modern aircraft, the latter having very high costs of maintenance and rates of obsolescence.[6] Even if all the guns had been replaced with aircraft, and even if those aircraft had not been out-dated by 1941, experience was to show that few of the latter were likely to be stationed permanently in Singapore. The assumption was that aircraft could be mustered and flown in quickly if need be. By contrast, coastal guns, whatever their limitations, tended to see slower technological change, and were not going anywhere.

Beyond the guns versus air debate, the real significance of the final decisions was this: that Britain could quibble over costs of giving Singapore fewer big guns than a single Japanese battleship.

Serious planning for these fortress guns began in 1927 with the visit of the Gillman Commission to Singapore from April of that year.[7] This was a group of three artillery and engineering officers led by Lieutenant-General Sir Webb Gillman, who later became Master General of Ordnance for the Royal Artillery.

The committee recommended work on the Fortress start immediately, with a first phase of works to include three big 15 inch guns. They suggested the precise, final balance of guns and aircraft could be decided later.[8] From then on work progressed, notwithstanding brief delays when Labour governments were in power in 1924, and in 1929 to 1931.[a][9]

The succession of events from 1931 – the Japanese invasion of Manchuria, its pressure on Shanghai in 1932, the League of Nations' condemnation of Japan as an aggressor the next year, and Japan's renunciation of the Washington Naval Treaties at the end of 1934 – then produced cumulative pressure to accelerate building. In April 1933 the British Cabinet gave the final go-ahead for Phase I of the Fortress system, including three 15 inch guns.[10] In July 1935, the second phase was endorsed, including two more 15 inch guns (to make a total of five). By 1936 several of the smaller guns were in place, and the first of the big 15 inch guns was being readied.[11]

It should be noted that, regardless of which direction these coastal guns were pointed when they were emplaced, the image of them pointing out to sea could be misleading. The five biggest guns were deliberately placed out of sight of the sea. There were suggestions in the 1920s that one 15 inch gun should be located on the island of Pulau Blakang Mati ('Island behind Death' in Malay, renamed Sentosa or 'Island of Tranquillity' by the Tourism Board in the 1970s).[12]

Blakang Mati was a stone's throw from Singapore's south coast, next to the commercial Keppel Harbour and the west of the city. But this was ruled out as a location for the 15 inch guns precisely because the Blakang Mati position would be visible from the sea, and so from attacking battleships.[13] Instead, all the 15 inch guns were placed slightly inland, often surrounded by rubber or coconut trees.[14]

Indirect fire from these big guns, guided by observation posts on nearby hills, would make it difficult for an attacker to spot them. Their foundations on *terra firma* also meant each gun had to be taken out individually. Even if bombers were to spot the clearings necessary for the gun emplacements, and the railway tracks which supplied them, and even if the guns could not evade shells as ships

---

a The War Office in London was not too concerned with the 1924 Labour Government's halt. This was the first such Government that Labour had formed. It relied on Liberal support, and looked fragile from the start. The Singapore military were ordered to 'carry on with all our defence investigations, so that if it is decided at some future date to develop the base, we shall have all the necessary data at our disposal'. WO32/3622, Colonel Wavell to Major Harrison, 15 April 1924.

could, their destruction would be no easy task. Singapore was in effect turned into a battleship, a sort of becalmed 'HMS *Singapore*', more lightly armed than the best battleships, but in turn unsinkable.[15]

In some instances, Singapore's guns had quite literally come off battleships. The 15 inch gun had been developed from 1911, first seeing service on HMS *Queen Elizabeth* in 1915. The guns were rotated off ships for servicing, with some ending up on Singapore. Of Johore Battery's three 15 inch guns, two had been at the Battle of Jutland in 1916, one on HMS *Barham*, the other on HMS *Valiant*.[b][16]

Despite delays, all the bigger coastal guns were ready in time for war. With the exception of some close, harbour defence guns, anti-aircraft defences and final touches, they were all in place by 1939. By December 1941, the completed Singapore 'Fortress' had twenty-nine large coastal guns: five 15 inch, six 9.2 inch and eighteen 6 inch. These larger guns were intended for counter-battery work against enemy warships, with ranges of 10 to 20 miles.

In addition, a slightly smaller number of guns was provided as a parallel close defence system. One set of these was located on the coast and islands in the Changi area in the east. Another was arranged around Keppel Harbour, which lay on the coast just west of Singapore city itself. These latter weapons straddled the harbour, being placed on the surrounding islands of Pulau Blakang Mati, Pulau Hantu (ghost island – sitting in the narrow channel between Blakang Mati and Singapore), and at Berlayer Point, on the mainland.[17]

These close, harbour defence weapons were a mix of one obsolete 18 pounder, four equally obsolete 12 pounders,[c] and of modern, twin-barrelled six pounder guns which could spit seventy rounds a minute at motor torpedo craft speeding in at 40 knots. At night the twin-barrelled six pounders would get the briefest glimpse of their targets, as searchlights illuminated craft for as little as a minute a time, hence their emphasis on a high rate of fire. They could be controlled remotely by a 'Director No. 13', ranges and bearing passing to the guns electrically by means of Magslip cables. But ultimately they could also resort to the guns' own auto-sights as the target closed in. Their job was harbour and close defence, and they were generally termed 'Anti-Motor Torpedo Boat' (AMTB) weapons.[18]

The combined counter-battery and AMTB guns were organised into two fire commands: Changi Fire Command and Faber Fire Command.

Changi Fire Command guarded the eastern approaches to the Straits of Johore and the naval base. As such, two of its six inch guns were on the Johore

---

b   HMS *Barham* was a Queen Elizabeth class battleship of 31,100 tons. Built by John Brown & Co. Ltd, Clydebank and completed in October 1915, it was the flagship of Rear Admiral Sir Hugh Evan-Thomas, commanding the Fifth Battle Squadron at the Battle of Jutland on 31 May 1916. It fired over 300 shells and took five hits itself. But it survived to fight with the Mediterranean Fleet in the Second World War, before being sunk off Sidi Barrani by U-boat 331, on 25 November 1941. Alongside it in the 5th Battle Squadron was HMS *Malaya* (built from Malayan contributions) and HMS *Valiant* and *Warspite*.

c   In service since 1894, the 12 pounders fired 15 rounds a minute with a range of up to 10,100 yards.

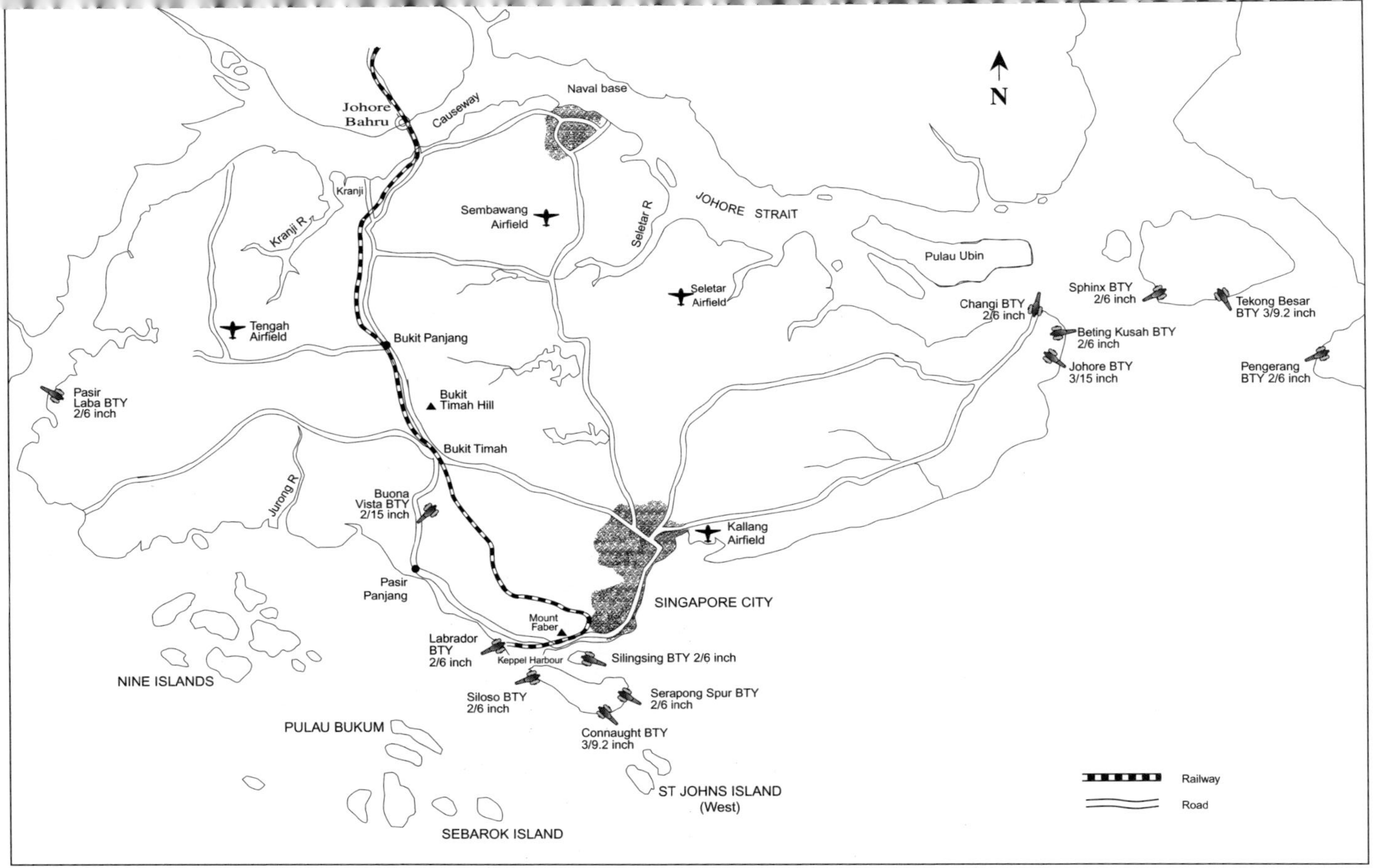

Map 5.1 The guns of Singapore – 1942.

THE GUNS OF SINGAPORE

coastline opposite, at Pengerang, while Pulau Tekong Besar, an island sitting in the middle of the entrance to the Johore Strait, boasted one battery of 9.2 inch guns, and one battery of 6 inch guns. Changi Fire Command's job was not to defend 'Singapore' as such, but to straddle the Johore Strait and repulse any enemy approach to the Johore Strait, and so the naval base.

Faber Fire Command, by contrast, had most of its guns in the south of the island around the city and Keppel Harbour. The largest concentration of these was on the island of Pulau Blakang Mati (Sentosa). Indeed, little Blakang Mati, with its several batteries, barracks, underground tunnels, generators, and even its own underground fresh water reservoir, was the nearest Singapore had to a real fortress.[19]

Each fire command had some of the biggest, 15 inch guns. When mounted, these 15 inch guns looked like battleship turrets, each with a single barrel,

Plate 5.1 The close defence system. A 12 pounder at Fort Siloso.
Source: Public Record Office (UK): W0203/6034. Appendix Y.

Plate 5.2 The close defence system. Modern twin-barrelled 6 pounder at Pulau Sajahat (1946).
Source: Public Record Office (UK): WO203/6034. Appendix E.

which had been unceremoniously dropped on dry land. Faber Fire Command had the Buona Vista Battery on the mainland with two guns facing south. Changi had Johore Battery, with its three guns facing southeast. Contemporary photographs sometimes labelled these biggest weapons 'monster guns', an understandable epithet given their 54 foot (16.5 metre) long barrels, and the combined, 100 ton weight of the barrel and breech mechanism. They were designed to propel armour piercing shells the weight of a small car 21 miles (36,900 yards) to sea. The shells themselves had thick casing, to help them penetrate battleship armour, after which they would explode into a few large pieces, each capable of destroying vital machinery. Given the sheer scale of the guns, and of Singapore's new barracks and airfields and naval equipment, it is scarcely surprising that just before the outbreak of war in September 1939, people started to view Singapore as a solid Fortress, a place secure against attack. This was the first of the myths about the Fortress: myths not myth, because there are at least three.

The myths: from impregnable fortress to guns that pointed the wrong way

The first myth, dating to before 1941, was that Singapore was the 'Gibraltar of the East', a strong fortified place. In November 1941 Singapore's *Straits Times* gave prominence to the words of Earle Page, special envoy to Britain and one-time Prime Minister of Australia, when he described Singapore as 'impregnable'.[20]

Churchill also seems to have believed that Singapore's defences were formidable, later writing that: 'I had read of Plevna in 1877, ... and I had examined Verdun in 1917 ... I had put my faith in the enemy being compelled to use artillery on a very large scale in order to pulverise our strong points at Singapore, and in the almost prohibitive difficulties and long delays which would impede such an artillery concentration and the gathering of ammunition along Malayan communications'.[21]

For Churchill, Singapore was a fortress surrounded by a glorious moat, and protected by naval guns. Whether his experience with Turkish guns at the Dardanelles, the straits leading to Constantinople in 1915, had left an indelible mark on his mind is not clear. As First Lord of the Admiralty he had championed a plan to force the straits, menace the Turkish capital, and so impress upon the Turkish government the wisdom of inclining towards the Entente powers. The subsequent mauling of British battleships as they ran the gauntlet of Turkish mines and guns had been a low point in Churchill's career. Forts won, battleships lost, and Churchill had left the Admiralty by May 1915.[22]

Whatever the impact of these now ancient events on Churchill, it is certain that large coastal guns continued to exercise his imagination. Not only did he take Singapore to be a fortified place, and personally order its large guns be prepared to fire landward in January 1942, but in June 1940 he instigated the placing of battleship guns on land near Dover as well. Two 14 inch guns were emplaced there, in August 1940 and February 1941, promptly being dubbed 'Winnie' and 'Pooh'. In 1942 they were joined by a further pair of 15 inch guns, which tried to deny the channel to German shipping, and to silence enemy guns on the opposite shore. Unfortunately the residents of Dover were less than grateful, complaining that the guns' duels with their German counterparts, across the Channel, resulted in unnecessary damage to the town.[23]

The second myth about Singapore arose directly from the realisation that the first had been wrong. When planning the Japanese attack on Singapore, Tsuji had quickly concluded that the Fortress was 'solid and strong on its sea front, but the rear facing Johore Province was practically defenceless'.[24] After Japanese troops attacked the Fortress from Johore in February 1942, subduing it in a week, the idea took root that the fortress guns had been useless, that Singapore had been, in Churchill's later words: 'the almost naked island'.²⁵

The most extreme stories that followed were to claim the coastal guns faced uselessly out to sea, while the Japanese came in through the unbolted back door. The origins of this myth lie with veterans and civilians who escaped from Singapore in early February 1942, just before the city fell.

These people had often seen only limited sectors of the island, sometimes only those sectors where the coastal guns had been relatively quiet. Basing their accounts on what they had seen, they suggested that few coastal guns had fired.

In 1942 one volunteer who had served at Fort Berlayer (adjacent to Labrador battery with its two 6 inch guns and within sight of the island of Blakang Mati), noted that the Buona Vista Battery of two 15 inch guns 'never fired a shot'. He wrote that: Singapore's fire defences were largely condemned to idleness ... I am aware of only three forts ... whose guns were actually used to aid our troops fighting on the island.²⁶ All the batteries this witness mentions were on or near Pulau Blakang Mati, near to where he was based.

This sort of comment provided an early basis for the myth that the guns faced uselessly to sea. If someone who fought with the coastal artillery, in this case manning their searchlights, could go this far, it is hardly surprising others went further.

That is precisely what happened, as journalists turned pen to paper in 1942. Ian Morrison, a London *Times* correspondent who covered the campaign firsthand, rushed out his *Malayan Postscript* before the year was out. Writing about the naval base he commented that:

> The huge naval guns which protected it pointed out to sea. They were embedded in concrete and could not be turned to point inland. Most of them were never fired. People had sheltered, not behind the naval base, but behind the defensive concept of which the naval base was the chief visible expression. Other people had done the same thing behind the Maginot Line.²⁷

For Morrison, this image, of the guns facing the wrong way while Japanese infantry lobbed 'two-inch mortar shells' at an unprotected £63 million naval base, served to produce the right note of irony and pathos.

Another newspaperman, Edwin Glover, came to similar conclusions. He had arrived in Malaya in the early 1930s, and had achieved a meteoric rise from journalist to Managing Editor of the *Malaya Tribune* newspaper. In 1942 he left Singapore, escaping on 10 February. Before the year was out Glover had written most of the book he would publish in 1946 as *In Seventy Days: The Japanese Campaign in Malaya*. Glover wrote that, 'The island's east coast defences, with their sixteen-inch [sic] guns and heavy howitzers ... could not be brought into play in the case of a landing from Johore ... To the best of my knowledge these guns never fired a shot – they were pointing the wrong way'.²⁸

To be fair, Glover professed to have written not a history, but a 'newspaperman's perspective' and survivor's account. As an example of this genre, his book was a success, but therein lay the problem. Glover's instinct as a journalist gave birth to a phrase about the guns 'pointing the wrong way', a phrase which would prove irresistible to others.

Morrison and Glover's images, of guns and commanders facing the wrong way, and no doubt many similar stories from other witnesses, soon caught on.[29] In 1943 the reputable *Pacific Affairs* journal repeated the accusation that the 15 inch guns 'could not be turned to fire upon an enemy approaching down the peninsula'.[30] By 1945 Lieutenant-Colonel A.H. Burne, who had commanded the guns in peace, was lamenting to the Royal Artillery journal *The Gunner* that, 'the legend that Singapore fell because the guns could only shoot out to sea is now world-wide'.[31]

Not even Churchill's War Memoirs on the Fall, published in 1951, could stop the myth from flourishing. Churchill stated that many of the guns did fire landward, albeit to little effect. But he also quoted at length telegrams from Wavell which may have given the wrong impression. These included telegrams of 19 and 21 January 1941, the former of which emphasised that

> The fortress guns are sited for use against ships, and have mostly ammunitions for that purpose; many can only fire seawards .... I do not want to give a false impression of the island fortress, Singapore defences were entirely constructed to meet seaward attack'.

Without being incorrect, and despite Churchill noting many guns could fire landward, it is easy to sea how Wavell's dramatic telegram could have caught the careless reader's attention. If you wanted to believe Singapore's guns faced uselessly to sea, you could find the evidence you wanted.[32]

From then on all was confusion, some works correctly noting some guns could fire landward, others confusing matters further. Even C.N. Parkinson (then Raffles Professor of History at the University of Malaya), managed to have the myth replicated in his work. A 1956 article of his on the naval base featured a picture of one of the guns under the title 'The Folly of Singapore'. The caption read:

> Singapore's great defense guns, installed in the mid-thirties, were especially designed to fire seaward, but the Japanese attacked from the Malaya Peninsula in December, 1941, and these guns were of no use.[33]

Whether or not some of the guns could fire landward did not matter for this myth. The point was that the guns were used to symbolise the lack of landward preparations: 'The Folly of Singapore', and an imperial power looking the wrong way. Given this symbolic role, it is scarcely surprising that the guns' role in Singapore's Fall has continued to attract attention, being repeated in newspapers, on television, across the Internet, and even in otherwise reliable books, into the 1980s and even 1990s.[34]

For a few people, the myth may have been further cemented by images of other guns, fictional as well as real. There is the film, *The Guns of Navarone*, where German guns built into the cliff-side of the Aegean island of 'Kheros' are destroyed by British commandos. The subconscious impact of seeing Gregory Peck and David Niven descend a cliff face to destroy guns which, without a doubt, can fire in only one direction, is incalculable.[35] In Singapore, meanwhile, there is the sight of old 9.2 inch gun barrels on static mounts at today's Fort Siloso. Some Americans may also be familiar with pictures of United States' 16 inch coastal guns of the same era, some of which were set in implausibly massive concrete bunkers or 'casemates', opening only to the front; or of the fortified islands which guarded the entrance to Manila Bay, including Corregidor with its vast tunnel system.[36]

For Singapore, the myth was also fuelled by the perception that British of all ranks and types had lived a life of ease in prewar Singapore, and had failed to prepare themselves for war, physically or psychologically. This was the opinion not only of some of the escaping troops and newspapermen, but of the Japanese who surveyed the fortress not long after its surrender.[37] Two Japanese officers assessed the fortress in mid-1942, noting that only one 15 inch gun, at Buona Vista, was salvageable, together with one or two of the 6 inch guns. They stated the defences were not very impressive, but took note that the surrounding amenities were very comfortable indeed.

The reason for this was that when the fortress had been built, the Royal Engineers had taken great pride in the barracks, recreation grounds and tree-planting. One officer later recalled that

> Changi... had a garrison of two infantry battalions, two gunner regiments and some sapper and service units, together with a number of married quarters. It was a delightful setting complete in itself with the messes set on top of small hills with views overlooking the Johore Straits and the open sea.

For the officers there was 'a palatial mess... and the quarters all had verandahs, their own bathroom and we each had our own Chinese boy as batman'.[38] The reference to servants should not come as a great surprise, and should be set against the role of the Hong Kong and Singapore Royal Artillery (HKSRA), an Indian-raised force whose origins went back to 1847, in manning the 6 inch guns.[39] But Changi, an area mainly of forest, swamp and beach in 1927, had indeed been transformed to provide excellent amenities.

Looking at the half-destroyed remnants of the guns, the Japanese concluded that: 'It would appear that the military was primarily interested in placing their efforts and funds in living, transportation and defense establishments, rather than in the various installations in the fortifications'.[40] They took this as evidence of a lack of martial determination, adding that: 'It is felt that the fact the British concentrated on the housing and transportation systems rather than on military preparedness is a direct reflection on their national character'.[41]

At one level, this Japanese stereotyping was little more convincing than the beliefs by some British servicemen that Japanese pilots might be short-sighted. The Japanese acknowledged some of the British rangefinders and equipment were of high quality. But the colonial and military lifestyles of interwar Singapore must have come to seem manifestly soft to those who saw Japanese discipline in 1941.

For the artillery officer, life in prewar Singapore had meant drill and target practice, a pride in regular exercises and a job well done. But for some it also meant a round of cinema, hockey, rugby, the Tanglin Club and Singapore Swimming club, and up-country practices which were a good excuse to travel. Singapore had in many ways become a good posting for a young officer, with some unusual highlights.

One senior officer later recalled an army 'rugger team' taking on a 'Siamese XV'. It looked as if dinner afterwards would be marred by the British side's inability to wield chopsticks. Then:

> Noticing that the Army chopstick technique was at about starvation level, our host promptly summoned a bevy of taxi-dancers[d] from the nearby dance hall, and these gorgeous little girls were deployed one to each army lap, gleefully operating our chopsticks.'

Polo, meanwhile, was made easier by the possibility of getting Indian other ranks to volunteer to look after the ponies.[42]

No doubt this was little more than what one would expect from the upper ranks of the privileged, officer class of any of a number of first-class nations in the 1930s. It also paled in comparison to the 'lavish civilian style of entertaining with which Army officers could not afford to compete and so could not accept'. In addition, some officers were frustrated by the sense of unreality in Singapore, especially if they had brothers or fathers serving in the Middle East and Europe.[43] But Malaya's main war role, as a dollar arsenal by way of its rubber and tin exports, probably fuelled the image of excess as war conditions boosted the area's earnings. This and the contrast between the preparations of British and Japanese in 1941 was so great, and the guns of Singapore such a good symbol of British unpreparedness, that memories of prewar lifestyles could only fuel the myth.

The resulting legend has since proved impervious to proof and reason, because it provides such a satisfying symbol of everything that went wrong. As Lieutenant-Colonel A.H. Burne (then editor of *The Gunner* magazine) put it:

---

d Taxi-dancers attended the big 'worlds' in Singapore, such as Happy Valley World, which were halls and complexes with cabarets and dancing. They were obliged to dance with any man who bought and presented a ticket. For many if not most, that was all that was involved.

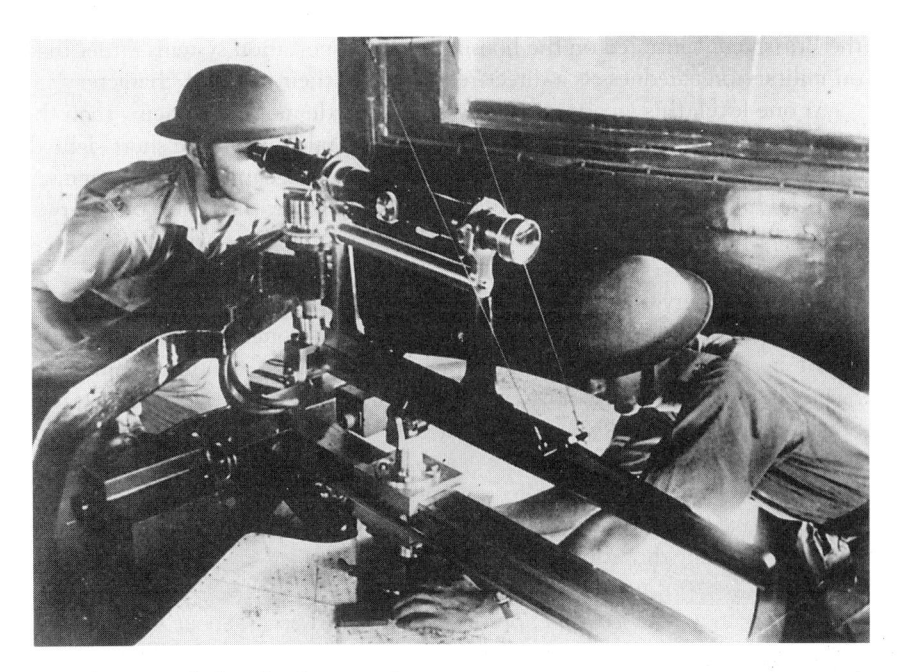

Plate 5.3 Rangefinding for the coastal guns.
Source: Courtesy of the Imperial War Museum: negative number K706.

Plate 5.4 Three storeys underground, 15 inch shells wait in one of the ammunition rooms.
Source: Courtesy of the Imperial War Museum: negative number K703.

Plate 5.5 The original caption reads 'A British gunner stripped to the waist for coolness deep below ground, swings a shell towards the elevator which will lift it to the gun's breech'.

Source: Courtesy of the Imperial War Museum: negative number K756.

Plate 5.6 The breech of a 15 inch gun.

Source: Courtesy of the Imperial War Museum: negative number K754.

Plate 5.7 Looking down the barrel of a 15 inch gun.
Source: Courtesy of the Imperial War Museum: negative number K758.

Plate 5.8 One of the destroyed 15 inch guns of Johore Battery, taken in 1942.
Source: Tim Bowden, *Changi Photographer: George Aspinall's Record of Captivity* (Sydney: ABC, 1997).

THE GUNS OF SINGAPORE

Plate 5.9 Local contractors removing one of the biggest guns with a crude wooden structure in 1948. It was destined for the UK, for use as scrap.

Source: Courtesy of Stan Bowyer.

'It is an unfortunate fact that if you give a lie enough start you cannot catch it up'.[44] Consequently, the myth has survived regardless of works by historians and participants which note some of the guns not only could, but did, fire landward.

Unravelling the myths

Even as the myth of the guns pointing the wrong way gained ground in popular consciousness, specialist historians were rejecting it. As early as 1951 Churchill's *The Second World War* Volume 14: *The Hinge of Fate* told readers the majority of the guns could fire landward.[45] Churchill also quoted a Wavell telegram of 16 January 1942 which said 'fortress cannon of the heaviest nature have all-round traverse'. Some artillery officers made similar claims.[46] Kirby's *Singapore: The Chain of Disaster* took a similar view as late as 1971, saying that 'Many of the 6 inch guns had inevitably a limited field of fire because of their particular tasks, but the 9.2 inch and the modern 15 inch guns had all-round field of fires; there was, however, no fire-control system developed to cover the north of the island, since this was to be defended, if attacked, by mobile columns'.[47] The officer commanding Royal Artillery on Singapore had raised the issue as far back as 1924, saying that:

110

Presumably the new mountings for both 15" and 9.2" guns will permit of 'all-round' arcs of fire? This is very desirable, as it is conceivable that the heavy and medium armament might, in an emergency, be called upon to oppose a landing or engage a hostile force already landed. This would not be their normal role, nor would their normal ammunition ('Armour Piercing, Capped' and 'Common Pointed, Capped') be suitable, but the eventuality might arise, and 'all-round' traverse and suitable ammunition (Shrapnel and H.E.) call for consideration.[48]

As the archives on the period were opened, in the 1970s and 1980s, academic historians started to build on these foundations. It soon became obvious that, while some of the guns had been used in the land battle, Churchill and the official historian had exaggerated in the opposite direction. Not every 15 inch gun could or did fire to the rear, towards Johore.

Far from it being all or none of the guns being able to fire all-round, it now seemed that every historian had their own theory. One witness said four of the 15 inch guns had all-round traverse.[49] Later works suggested the real figure might be three, or even two.[50]

No two works seemed ever to agree. But a rough consensus did start to emerge. This suggested that many, if not all, 6 inch and 9.2 inch guns could traverse 360 degrees, and that most joined in the battle for Singapore.[51] Most works also agreed that the 9.2 inch guns had fired at south Johore.[52] The consensus also accepted that the guns had a limited effectiveness when firing inland, at troops. This was because they had a low trajectory, and their ammunition was not well suited to hitting large numbers of infantry or enemy guns. Most of them had a limited supply of High Explosive ammunition, designed to disintegrate into many pieces and so kill large numbers of infantry.

The biggest guns, 15 inch guns in particular were condemned to fire only armour piercing shells, excellent for penetrating ship's armour, but of limited use against infantry. Armour Piercing shells were designed to explode only after penetrating several inches of a battleship's armour plating, with a relatively small amount of explosive relative to a thick casing resulting in the shell breaking into a few large pieces. Excellent for destroying ships or mincing large items of machinery, their main effect against infantry would be to produce large craters in the ground. There were last-gasp attempts to acquire more High Explosive ammunition from late January 1942, but by then time had run out. It never arrived.

As for the biggest, 15 inch guns' ability to fire landwards, by the 1980s to 1990s this was said to vary between the two 15 inch batteries. Faber Fire Command's Buona Vista Battery, to the south of the island, was wrongly said to have had a limited traverse of around 180 degrees, facing southward towards the sea. If true, this would have meant that it could only reach the southwest coast of Johore.

Why was Buona Vista Battery supposedly so limited? One argument was that 'Magslip' cables were fitted around 1938 to transmit fire control, concerning the bearing and traverse required to hit targets, directly to the guns. These would have made the process of firing quicker and more accurate, but they were (according to Macleod-Carey, a Faber Fire Command officer) too short to allow full traverse. As a result, gun-stops were installed to limit the guns' ability to turn and so damage their cables. This is the explanation for the biggest guns' limitation which most authors accept.

The 15 inch gun manuals from the war period, however, suggest that most books have been wrong. These manuals, and information from one of the men who helped to fit Singapore's biggest guns, show that the main reason for fitting gun stops was to protect the guns' 'walking cables'.

The 'walking' cables allowed pipes to carry hydraulic power to the gun mounting, while still allowing the mounting to turn. The power helped with traversing the gun, elevation and loading. Manual operation beyond the guns' normal traverse was possible, in theory at least. It required the gun stops to be removed and, for all-round traverse, the hydraulic cables to be disconnected.

The problem was that disconnecting the power in this way would make life extremely difficult. Without the power, the gun would have to be loaded and targeted manually, an exhausting job when dealing with 1936 lb (879 kg) shells. If ships had appeared offshore when the power was disconnected, guns modified in this way would have been severely limited. Even the gunners of Connaught Battery, when forced to manhandle its much smaller, 380 lb, 9.2 inch shells, ended up totally exhausted.[53]

This meant that the traverse of the 15 inch guns was likely to be limited by the movement of its hydraulic cables. As fitted in Singapore, these cables limited the traverse of the four 15 inch guns on MKII platforms to 240 degrees when spring-loaded buffers or gun-stops were in place to prevent damage to them. With the buffers removed, the traverse would have been increased to 290 degrees. If the hydraulic cables were totally disconnected, and power movement and loading foregone, then the traverse would then have approached 360 degrees.

In truth, one of Faber Fire Command's War Diaries states that one of Buona Vista Battery's guns was mounted to allow it to turn as far as 301 degrees clockwise, if due north is taken as zero degrees. This means that Buona Vista's guns could reach targets as far round as Sungai Pendas on the southern Johore coast. In layman's terms, that meant Buona Vista Battery could fire to its west, but not at an enemy directly to its rear, to the north. The same document then noted that the enemy landing was well north of this arc of fire.[54]

The figure given by the War Diary makes it almost certain that neither the cables nor the gunstops were removed in this case. In other words, Buona Vista could traverse from 61 to 301 degrees clockwise, with true north as zero degrees. That meant they could turn slightly to the guns' rear, which in turn meant almost all Japanese troops remained too far north to hit.

By contrast, recent studies have argued Johore Battery's three 15 inch guns not only could turn landward, but that they did, firing on the town of Johore Bahru just across the Causeway, and directly to its rear.[55] We even have Tsuji's gripping account of coming under what he says was 'probably' '15-inch or 16-inch' fire, near Tengah airfield in northwest Singapore, on the night of 11 to 12 February 1942:

> When we reached the southeastern extremity of Tengah aerodrome, we found that bombs or heavy-calibre shells were blowing large holes in the roadway ... Abandoning the car the orderly and I continued on foot. ... Just at that moment there was a shellburst which shocked our eardrums, while the blast jarred our spines. The flash seared my eyes, and I was thrown into the roadside ditch. In my agitation I thrust myself into an earthenware drainage pipe. The heavy shelling continued ... Up to this moment I had had no experience of such heavy projectiles, which tore holes in the ground fifteen or sixteen metres in diameter and four or five metres deep. They were probably the fifteen or sixteen-inch [there were no 16-inch guns] fortress guns which had been swung round 180 degrees to fire over the land instead of over the water out to sea ... Crouching like a crab inside the earthen pipe, I imagined what would happen if a shell fell on me.[56]

The shells came one every few minutes. Since most existing accounts agree that Buona Vista did not fire, it is usually assumed that Tsuji was hiding from 15-inch shells from Johore Battery's three guns. The reality is that the war diaries do not mention Johore Battery firing anywhere near Tengah, but do mention repeated fire on Tengah from Connaught's 9.2 inch battery. So these were almost certainly Connaught's 9.2 inch guns.[57]

Taken together, most pre-existing accounts make it clear many of Singapore's guns could fire landward. They also mistakenly suggest three of the 15 inch guns of Johore Battery did fire landward, and appear to answer the vast majority of questions.[58]

In addition, Ong Chit Chung's work on *Operation Matador* goes further. It places the guns of Singapore into the wider context of British plans to defend Singapore by meeting the Japanese at landing grounds to the north, in Malaya and Thailand. According to this version, the guns were largely irrelevant. They belonged to a 1920s strategy when Singapore would act almost as an island battleship, until a relieving fleet could arrive. By 1941, however, the plan was to defeat an invader on the beaches of eastern Malaya and southern Thailand, so as to prevent them seizing airfields and thrusting down the peninsula. If this plan, *Matador*, failed, and if the Japanese were not kept well away from Singapore's northern shore, Singapore would be as good as lost. At the least, the naval base, the raison d'être of British plans, would be rendered unusable as soon as Japanese artillery reached southern Johore. This is exactly the situation Morrison describes, with Japanese mortars lobbing shells into the naval base in early 1942.

In this wider context, it seems it did not matter greatly whether the Fortress guns could turn and fire landward or not. They were fixed coastal guns, designed for use against ships, while local commanders had determined that Malaya's fate would be decided on land, in northern Malaya.

There is, however, now a danger that a final myth may form: that almost all guns had all-round traverse, that the majority did fire landward, but that they were ineffective, while Singapore's defence would anyway be decided by *Matador*, in northern Malaya and southern Thailand. In this '*Matador* and the guns facing the right way' version, not just the fortress guns, but the fall of Singapore itself seems to become a mere footnote to the real battle: the battle for northern Malaya.

All of this raises the questions: what did the guns really do; and what was the significance of 'Fortress Singapore' for the campaign as a whole? Given that almost every journalist and historian has given a slightly different account since 1942, the only way to answer these questions is to go back to those sources closest to the action: the various witness accounts from 1942, and to the War Diaries written by artillery officers in that same year.

The guns in action: the War Diaries' version

Chief amongst these diaries is the combined War Diary for all Singapore's coast defences. This consists of the diary itself, and a brief analysis. The whole document is entitled 'FIXED DEFENCES SINGAPORE in relation to OPERATIONS ON and NEAR SINGAPORE ISLAND February 1942', and is signed by 'A. D. Curtis Brigadier Commanding Fixed Defences Malaya'.[59] This takes up the story from early January 1942:

> Early in January it became apparent that the guns of the Fixed Defence Singapore might be called upon, in the not far distant future to fire upon land targets in the state of JOHORE in the areas opposite the North and West coasts of SINGAPORE and the area North and East of the PENGERANG defended perimeter [an area of the south Johore coastline opposite Singapore's northeast tip] ...
>
> ... the only battery that could reach the town of JOHORE BAHRU and the Causeway ... was the 15 inch battery at Johore Fort – of this battery only the two Mk.II equipments could bear. The 15 inch battery at Buona Vista was useless for this purpose as the dead arc prevented any firing northwards ...
>
> In order to diminish the threatened danger from low-flying ... aircraft, 6-inch batteries had been fitted with overhead concrete cover. This considerably diminished the landward arc of these batteries ...
>
> Ammunition for landward firing was scanty, only 50 rounds H.E [High Explosive] being allowed for 6 inch guns, 25 rounds H.E. for 9.2 inch guns and none at all for 15 inch guns' ...

3. (a) ... .'everything possible that could be done was at once put in hand to increase the arcs of fire of the 6 inch batteries by demolishing part of the concrete overhead cover (at the expense of protection) and at all batteries by cutting down trees obstructing lines of fire to the North and West.

(b) The Naval authorities were asked if they could supply any 15 inch H.E. projectiles but were only able to find one which was transferred to JOHORE Fort.

This means that only two of Johore Battery's three 15 inch guns could fire to the rear.[60] Finally, according to Curtis's document there was some H.E. ammunition for the 15 inch guns, namely one solitary projectile. What happened to it is not recorded.

The Johore Battery, incidentally, was not so-called because it was built to fire at Johore. Far from it, its name derived from a £500,000 gift from the Sultan of Johore, made in May 1935 towards King George V's jubilee year – the twenty-fifth year since he acceded the throne. £400,000 of this helped pay for the two guns which in February 1942 shelled Johore Bahru, the capital of his state.[61]

If only two of Johore Battery's guns fired at Johore, this was because the third was already there in 1936–7, on an earlier mark of gun emplacement. This gun was positioned on a Mk. I concrete emplacement (called a barbette), with a limited traverse, and with the tunnels for its ammunition positioned a little to its rear. Its concrete emplacement described only a partial turning circle, and had supports for lifting machinery built into it.[62]

These restrictions left this gun with a traverse, or clockwise swing, from about 67½ to 247½ degrees, measured from an imaginary line pointing due north. Since the guns were positioned facing south, this translated into a 180 degree sweep to the south. In short, the Mk. I mounting could face out to sea, but it could not turn to face Japanese troops attacking from its rear, to the north.[63] This gun stood at the site where the Singapore Tourism Board erected a replica 15 inch gun in February 2002, at one end of Changi airport.

The Mk. I was, however, the only one of the five 15 inch guns on this earlier mounting.[64] After it was installed, it was decided that it would be more efficient to mount these guns in the same way as a battleship turret, with the tunnels for ammunition directly below, and a greater traverse. Consequently the remaining four 15 inch guns were mounted on Mk. II emplacements which featured naval, battleship-type 'turrets' with the potential for all-round traverse, if the obstructing cables and gun stops were removed. In the case of Johore Battery, these guns could fire on a large swathe of Johore, even with the gun-stops in place.[65]

So Changi Fire Command's guns could, and did, join in the battle for Singapore from 5 February, when two of Johore Battery's guns, and the 9.2 inch and 6 inch guns on Tekong island, commenced firing against Johore. From then on these guns shelled the Johore coast repeatedly.

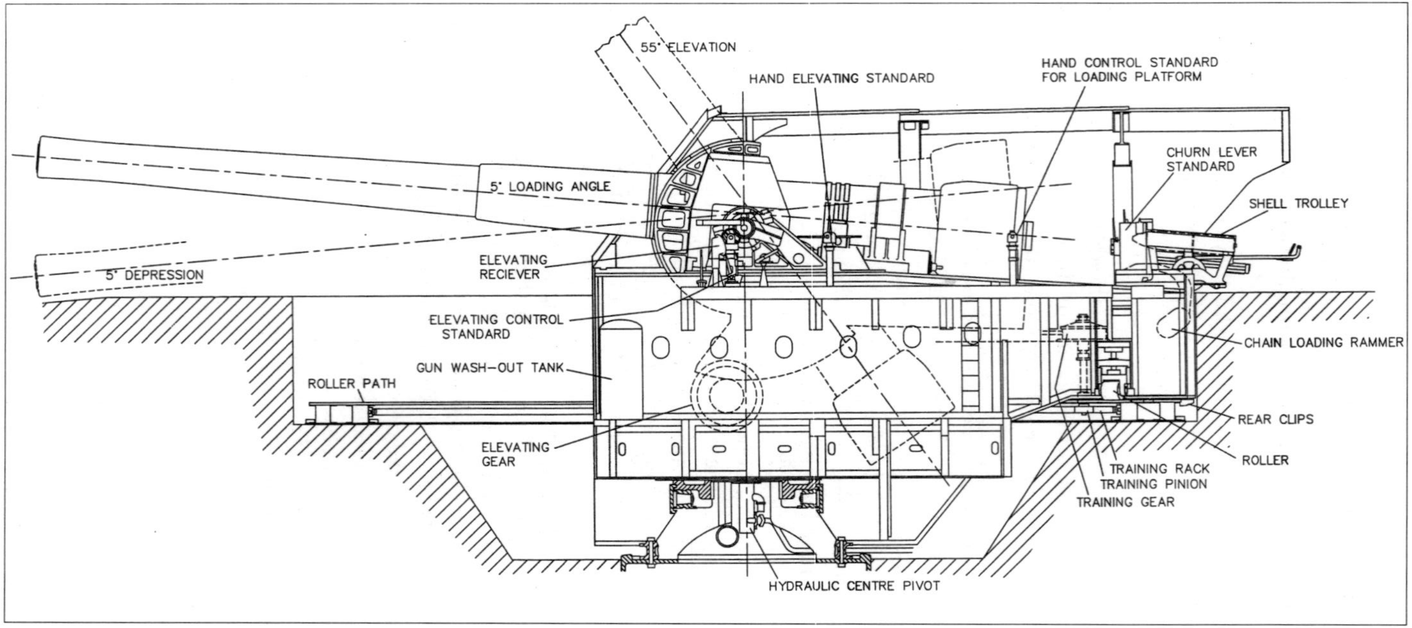

Figure 5.1 Profile of the 15 inch Mk. I, or Singapore mounting.

Source: John Roberts.

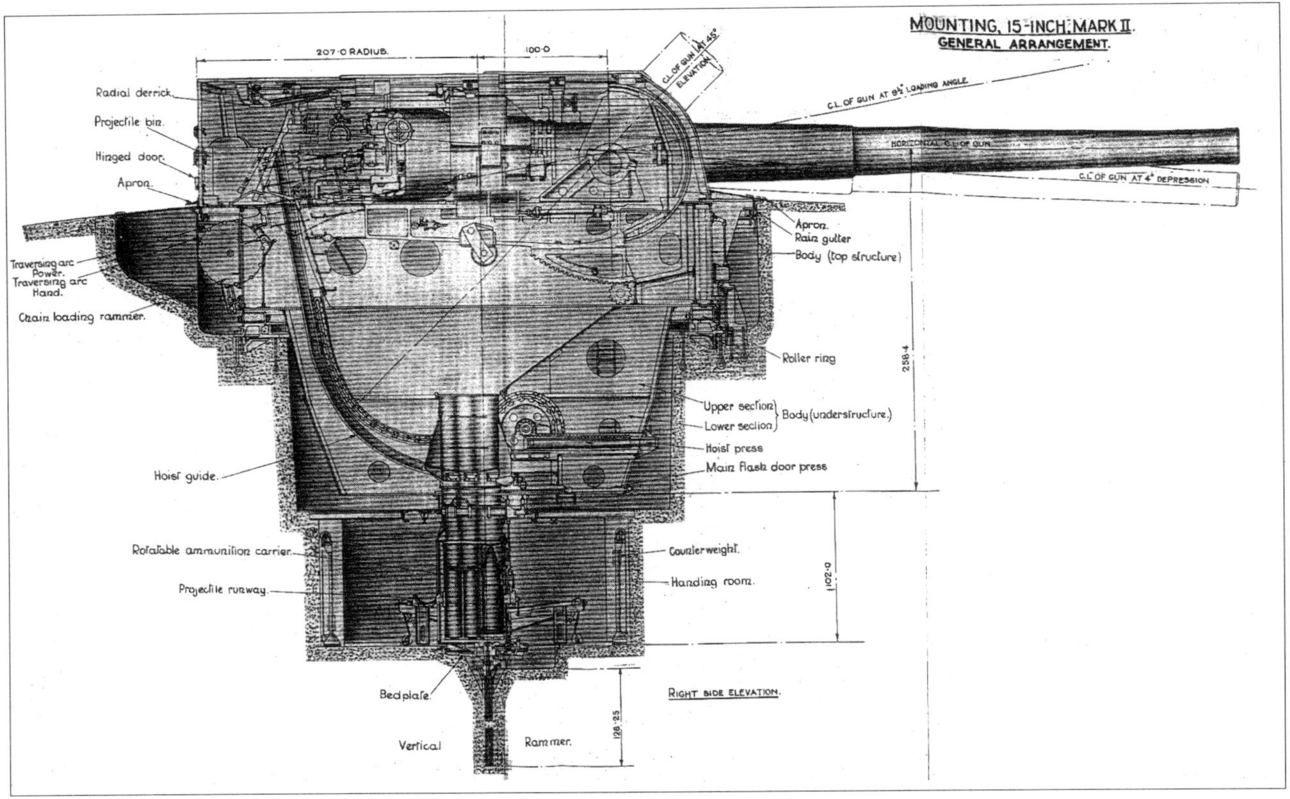

Figure 5.2 Profile of the 15 inch Mk. II, or Spanish mounting, four of which, together with the Mk. I, formed the heavy coast defence batteries of Singapore.

Source: John Roberts.

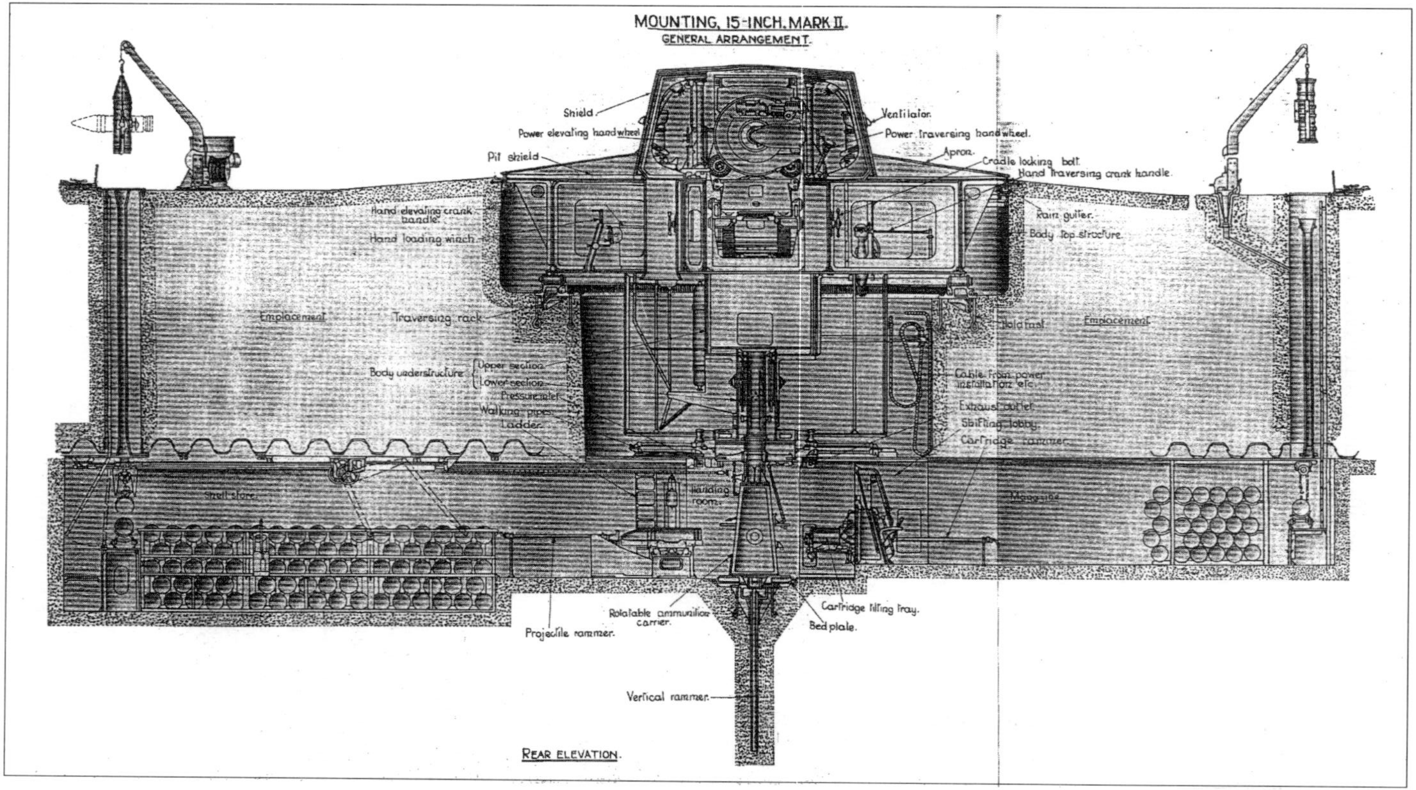

Figure 5.3 Profile cross section of the Mk. II mounting.

Source: John Roberts.

Nor was this shelling without effect, despite the use of Armour Piercing shells. Lieutenant-Colonel Tawney recalls that as a prisoner he was taken to various places to be interrogated on artillery matters, including north Johore. There he was told destroyed buildings were the work of the coast defence guns:

> The Japanese had erected a *jinja* or shrine at this spot which was pitted with huge craters, and I further gathered that this shrine was in honour of a large number of dead, including those of some formation Headquarters which had been occupying some of the buildings ... .[66]

On the British side, both civilians and troops were reassured by the roar of the 15 inch guns in these early actions. On 11 February J. Hodder noted in his diary that: 'A terrific noise went on all night. The big naval guns had been reversed, and were firing towards Johore, the Japs being concentrated there and a crossing on S'pore Island had been made.'[67] Lieutenant-Colonel A.A. Tawney adds that he: 'saw 15-in. and 9.2-in. batteries firing towards Johore Bahru, and on other occasions heard the heartening noise of their shells passing overhead'.[68]

Johore Battery also joined in some of the bitterest battles on Singapore Island. It fired at Japanese forces advancing near the southwest coast, from west of Pasir Panjang village, on 10 to 12 February. On the morning of 12 February Johore Battery also fired towards the Bukit Timah Road and the Racecourse area. This was designed to cover a calculated retreat from near Bukit Timah Village, down the Bukit Timah Road to new positions a couple of miles closer to the city. Japanese troops and tanks were too close to the retreat for comfort. Thrusting past Bukit Timah Hill and down Bukit Timah Road they were soon approaching the Chinese High School. Together with extra pressure from troops to the south of the road, covering fire from the coastal guns allowed the retreating forces to successfully make a point a couple of miles back, where Bukit Timah Road intersects Adam and Farrer Roads.[69]

Having swung round to fire westward then, Johore Battery's guns hit targets on a line running from Bukit Timah in the centre of the island, to Pasir Panjang on its south coast.[70] In this way, Changi Fire Command's coastal artillery joined the battle for Singapore early and in full. This only ceased on the evening of 12 February, when the retreat to a final perimeter around the city put the eastern guns outside the defenders' area, and so demanded their destruction.

The story for Faber Command is very different. It seems Faber Fire Command joined battle much later, and even then with only a fraction of its guns.[71]

This can be seen if we use a 'Report on the Surrender of Singapore', written by a member of the volunteer forces serving on searchlights at Fort Berlayer, and mentioned earlier. This states that:

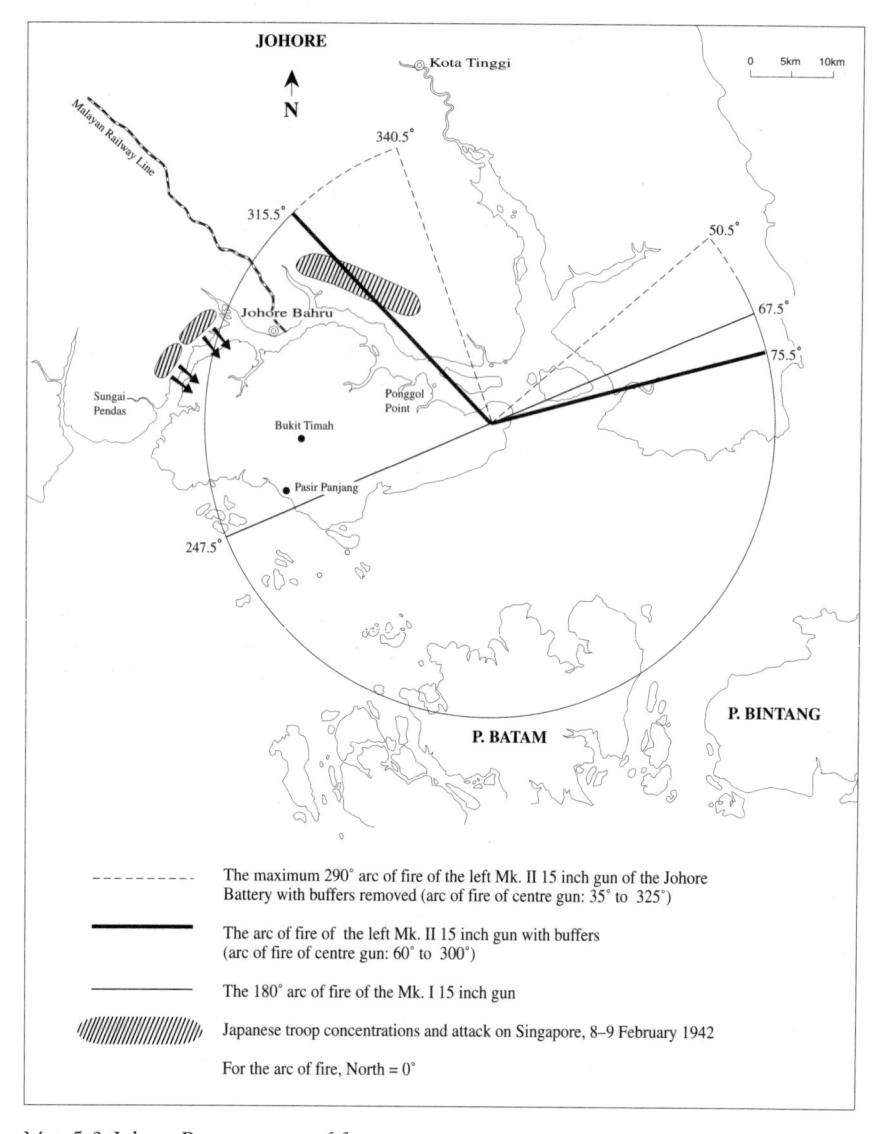

Map 5.2 Johore Battery – arc of fire.

The point remains, however, whether ... there could not have been an improvised adaptation of the guns and defences of the harbour to meet the changed strategy of the Malayan war, when it became clear that the attack on Singapore, if and when it came, would be from the north across the Straits of Johore. Admittedly, the harbour defences had to be preserved but nevertheless the guns could have been used if the back walls of the forts had been knocked down.

It seems clear that the higher authorities refused to contemplate or allow this. I heard that Captain Pickard, R.A., of Fort Berlayer, was refused permission to knock down his obstructing back walls, even though he was prepared to do it with his own men. He was realistically aware, long before the end, of the changed strategy but all he was able to do was to make apertures in the back walls to take small arms in the event of an attack from the land. I believe, also, that the men on Buona Vista, whose 15 [inch] guns never fired a shot, requested their officers to knock down obstructing walls but nothing was done on the grounds that there were no orders to that effect from Fire Command

Thus Singapore's fire defences were largely condemned to idleness ... I am aware of only three forts, Connaught, Labrador and Serapong [sic, he probably means Siloso, which he could have seen from his position],[72] whose guns were actually used to aid our troops fighting on the island.[73]

This suggests a sharp difference between Changi and Faber Fire Commands. Why was Faber Fire Command's role more limited? Why were Buona Vista Battery's 15 inch guns not adapted to fire landward? The Faber Fire Command War Diary has their traverse from a line due north limited to 301 degrees by the 'dead arc'. But they were on similar Mk. II mountings, in naval-type 'turrets', to the Johore Battery, which had a similarly limited arc if unmodified, that is, if walking cables for transmitting hydraulic power were left intact, and the training stops to protect those cables were not removed. We know that two of Johore Battery's guns could fire at Johore in their rear even with their gun stops in place, and that, if their gun-stops were removed, at least one could traverse as far as 340 degrees before the cables would be damaged.[74]

A May 1945 Southeast Asia Command (SEAC) report on the guns goes further, stating Buona Vista's guns could turn as far as 320 degrees as opposed to 340 for Johore Battery. This was of more than academic interest, since British attempts to blow the guns up before retreating had left one of Buona Vista's guns intact. An Australian Prisoner of War had spotted the Japanese loading and operating this gun manually, before his escape. SEAC planners presumably did not want to send any reoccupation fleet straight into the path of a 15 inch gun. It would have been ironic indeed if the Fortress guns' main victims had ended up being British.[75]

In other words, it seems that Faber Fire Command chose not to make the more radical adaptations necessary in order to get Buona Vista's guns further round. They seem to have chosen not to remove the gun stops, let alone disconnect the hydraulic power, and not to waste armour piercing ammunition against infantry targets.[76] These decisions preserved the full efficiency of Buona Vista's 15 inch guns in case of a naval attack. But such an attack never came.

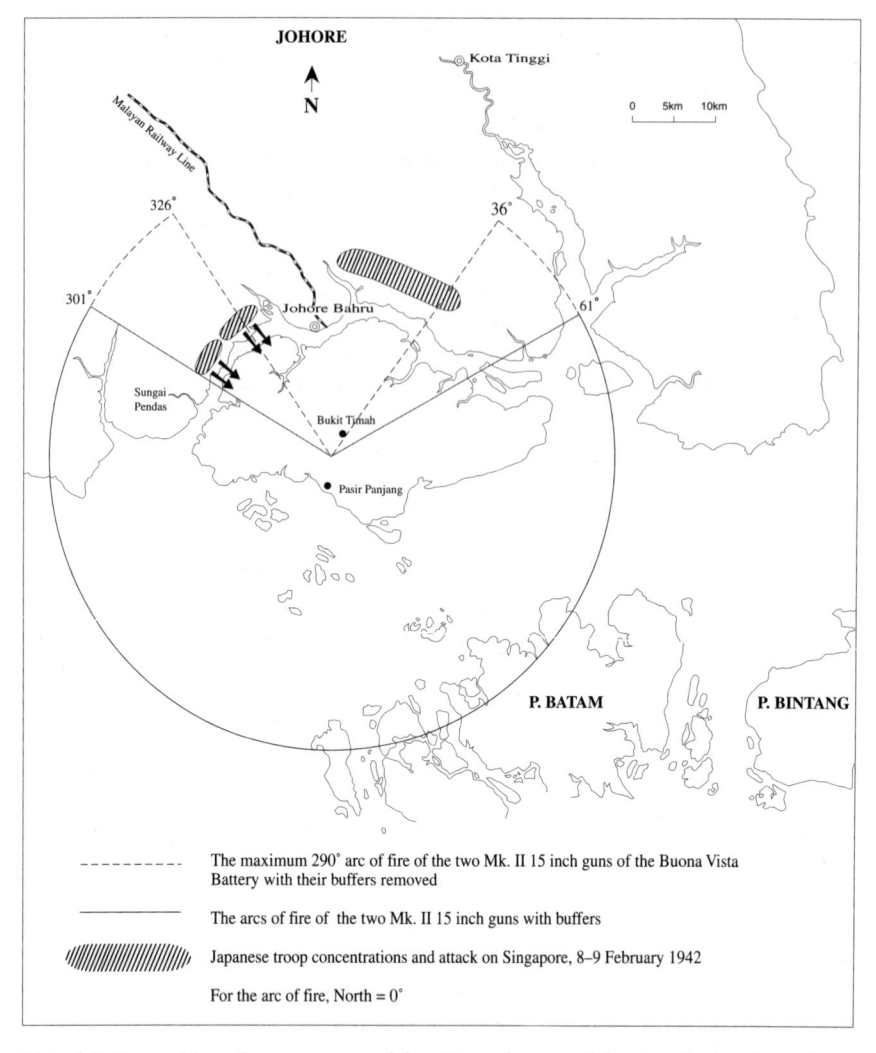

Map 5.3 Buona Vista Battery – arc of fire. How the arc of fire is calculated: we have extrapolated the above arcs using the relevant War Diary and gun manual as starting points.[77]

Instead, the Japanese landed on the night of 8 to 9 February, coming from the northwest. With their gun buffers or stops in place, Buona Vista's guns could not reach the southernmost fringes of this attack. The Japanese advance that followed gave little time for modifications, due to the battery's position. It was inland, about halfway between the South Coast and Bukit Timah Hill.[78] Consequently, there were fears it might be quickly overrun. As early as 0900 hours on 9 February Buona Vista Battery was ordered to prepare in case demolition was required.[79]

Then the Japanese attacked Bukit Timah on 10 February, as they moved across the island from the northwest. South of Bukit Timah, the frontline moved close to the battery's position.[e] There was confusion and firing around it on the night of 10 to 11 February. At one point close to dawn the gunners wondered if their area had been overrun, and an officer was sent out to reconnoitre. The confusion was partly a result of Australian troops moving into a sector the 44th Indian Brigade were vacating. The Australians did in fact manage to establish a line in front of the guns until that afternoon. But the threat was near and real.[80]

Demolition was duly carried out around 0600 hours on the morning of 11 February. The remaining gunners withdrew, the frontline then sweeping on past Buona Vista's position that afternoon. The battery's crew reformed as infantry, without having fired a shot in anger.[81]

Buona Vista Battery is one example of Faber Fire Command's more limited impact on the battle. It seems Faber Fire Commands guns generally started firing later than those of Changi Fire Command, when they fired at all.

Despite this, many of Faber Command's guns could fire landward, and the majority were eventually to be used in anger, though only after Buona Vista Battery had been abandoned. By then it was becoming obvious the choice was between the rest of the guns firing, or being overrun without defending themselves.

Up to the point of Buona Vista's destruction early on 11 February, however, it seems just one of Faber Command's batteries had opened up. That one was Pasir Laba, which happened to be in the front line when the Japanese landings started. Pasir Laba Battery (two 6 inch guns) was the only one of Faber's batteries not concentrated close to the south coast and to Keppel Harbour. It lay several miles away, halfway along the west coast. Its position was a little to the south of where Japanese troops launched their first assault on Singapore Island on the night of 8 to 9 February.

As Japanese poured across the strait in the early hours of 9 February, Pasir Laba, by removing its concrete overhead cover, managed to bring one gun to bear on points on the Johore Coast where Japanese were likely to embark.[82] The other could not be turned round far enough.

But the Australian troops on Singapore's west coast were far too few anyway, and too thinly spread, to hold off the two Japanese divisions which were pouring into this sector. By 0700 hours most of the Indian and Australian infantry in the area were withdrawing.

The Japanese also decided to deal with Pasir Laba's gunners. The battery was subjected to heavy dive-bombing and shelling. Its observation post was hit. Both gun emplacements were struck, number one gun rendered unusable except in dire emergency, the overhead covering of gun number two smashed. Several

---

e The battery's two guns were positioned, about 500 yards apart, close to the junction of Ulu Pandan and Clementi Road.

of the Hong Kong and Singapore Royal Artillery's (HKSRA) Indian gunners, who manned all Singapore's 6 inch coastal guns, were injured. Captain Asher, the British commanding officer, prepared to blow the magazines, but before he could finish he emerged to drag a wounded colleague to safety. A shell killed him outright. With the guns silenced they attracted less attention from now on, but retreat was only a matter of time. That evening the remaining gunners destroyed their guns and fell back.[83]

Pasir Laba was exceptional. As Japanese troops quickly thrust inland from the north and the west, the rest of Faber Command's guns remained silent, holding fire until 11 February.

Then came Buona Vista's demolition early on the morning of 11 February, as Japanese troops drove from the west, closing in on the outskirts of the city. With the futility of waiting for an attacking fleet now apparent, Faber Command seems to have ordered as many of its guns into action as possible. The various batteries at Blakang Mati Island, a few hundred yards south of Singapore itself, as well as Labrador Battery on the coast opposite, came into action that afternoon. From midday Siloso and Labrador fired at the coast to their west.[84]

Connaught Battery on Blakang Mati (Sentosa) followed at about 1430 hours on 11 February. Its three 9.2 inch guns were turned round from facing seaward, southeast, to fire over the heads of people waiting at docks on the south coast, and across to targets in the centre, west and north of Singapore. Its shells may even have reached targets at its extreme range, just across the Causeway in Johore, which its commander later reporting firing at.[85] It was busy from then on, expending much of its ammunition in just two days, and all but wearing its gun barrels' rifling smooth in the process.[86] Observation was from Mount Faber on the mainland opposite, which sent directions for firing, and for correcting aim.[87]

On 11 February itself, as the Japanese surged across the island from the north and west, Connaught Battery's three 9.2 inch guns shelled the Jurong area and Ulu Pandan Road.[88] That night Connaught put down three concentrations of fire on Tengah airfield back in the northwest of the island as well, where the Japanese had established their forward headquarters, and which reports said was being used by Japanese dive bombers. Its guns expended sixty-three Armour Piercing rounds on Tengah alone between 0130 hours and dawn on the night of 11 to 12 February.[89]

Connaught fired at Tengah again on the following night. On 13 February it took over the task of shelling the Japanese around Bukit Timah Road as well. With the Johore Battery having been destroyed by the British on the evening of 12 February, and Japanese reported to be massing for another attack down the road, Fort Connaught's three 9.2 inch guns were now brought into play here.[90]

Japanese historian Yoshiki Saito recorded the effect on Japanese troops of the 5th Division, then positioned near the reservoirs in the very centre of Singapore:

JOHORE

Johore Bahru

Sungai Pendas

Tengah
Bukit Timah
Jurong
Ulu Pandan
Pasir Panjang

Fort Connaught

P. BATAM

////// Japanese troop concentrations and attack on Singapore, 8–9 February 1942

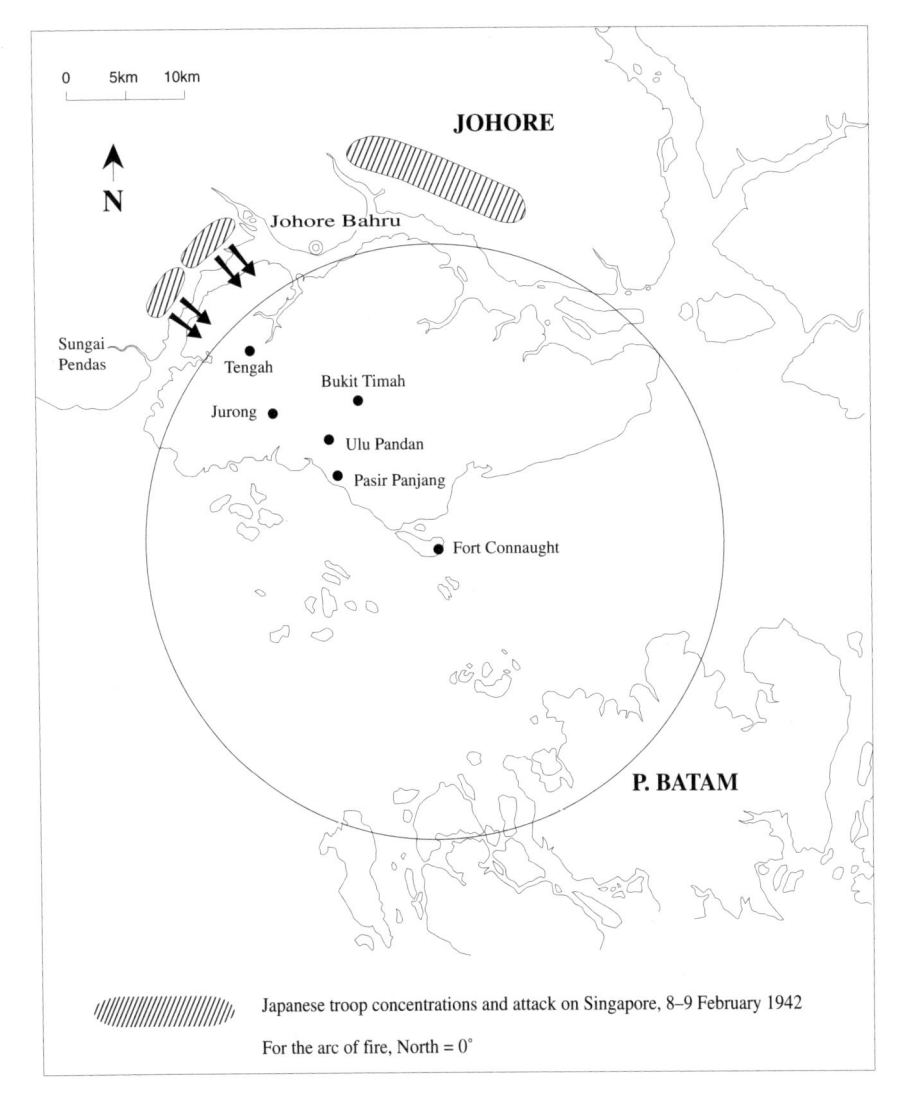

For the arc of fire, North = 0°

Map 5.4 Connaught Battery – arc of fire and targets.

> ... on Feb. 13 and 14. Under bombardment we had no chance of leaving our fox-holes. Often the enemy's shells hit the water sending up huge columns of spray. Huge limbs from the rubber trees were blasted into the air. Shells like petrol drums with their baleful whine and their fragments fell among us. When that happened the walls of our fox-holes caved in.[91]

Captain Ezumi of the 21st Infantry Regiment in the 5th Division, an eyewitness to bombardment on the northern fringe of the Racecourse on 13 February, recalled 'large calibre shells that we called "the petrol drums" ... they did not fragment. I saw there the whole nose-cone of a 40 cm calibre shell that landed in front of our HQ.'[f][92] In these circumstances, the line on Bukit Timah Road stabilised. The Japanese shifted their main weight of attack to the west of the city.

Not that all this firing, most with the 'petrol drums' (armour piercing shells) mentioned, was very effective. In one instance Macleod-Carey's binoculars came to rest on a brave Japanese soldier who had climbed a telescopic mast behind the grandstand of the racecourse, just east of Bukit Timah. Macleod-Carey, at the time a Major and second in charge at Faber Fire Command, later recalled that, 'I turned the Connaught 9.2 in battery on to him and fired about 30 rounds. The little man disappeared in a cloud of smoke, dust and debris most of which came from the grandstand'. Whether the victim was hit, or scampered off, is unclear, but it certainly would have put a stop to his spotting.[93]

Connaught Battery achieved a complete, 360 degree traverse in the campaign, and was one of the busiest, firing only at land targets. It continued firing after the magazine lifts broke down, the men resorting at the last to bringing shells up from the guns' subterranean bunkers manually. With tropical heat, and each shell weighing 380 pounds, it is not surprising the crews had exhausted themselves by the penultimate day of battle.[94]

By that same morning, another of Faber Fire Command's Batteries had also played a significant part in supporting the land battle. This was Labrador Battery, situated on Singapore's south coast, just west of Blakang Mati and Keppel Harbour. Its two six inch guns helped sink an abandoned *tongkang* (a small civilian boat) on 11 February, to keep the harbour area clear, and to provide practice and morale for its HKSRA gunners.[95] The next day it joined in sinking another ship, probably a *tongkang* drifting with oil drums aboard.

Labrador also fired landward salvoes at Japanese infantry of the 18th Division advancing up the west coast from 11 to 13 February. In this way the battery supported the Malay Regiment's attempts to stop a final Japanese drive into the city: attempts which culminated in fierce fighting along Pasir Panjang Ridge. Pasir Panjang Ridge was about half a mile inland, running parallel to the coast for about four miles, before it stopped a few hundred yards short of Labrador. Sections of the Malay Regiment were all but wiped out trying to hold positions on this ridge on 13 to 14 February, despite support from Labrador on the former day.[96]

By 13 February, however, Labrador's gunners, Indians of the HKSRA, were becoming tired of repeated bombing. Japanese aerial dominance was again important, both for bombing and spotting, while the coastal guns had been

---

f If it was a 40 cm (around 15 inches) shell it must have been left over from the day before, when Johore Battery bombarded the area. We are very grateful to David Sissons for locating these accounts of Japanese soldiers coming under artillery fire from the large coastal guns, and for translating them.

given very little anti-aircraft protection.g For protection the 6 inch guns did have some overhead concrete cover, as well as armoured shields, but even the armoured mountings of the 9.2 and 15 inch guns gave scant protection against sustained bombing and shelling. At some batteries, men resorted to nearby slit trenches during bombing raids.[97]

The HKSRA which had to keep on manning Labrador in the face of the repeated attacks was an old regiment, raised in India for service in the East from about 1847. The military had considered recruiting personnel locally, in Singapore, but had ultimately decided that the local population was unsuitable. This was in contrast to Hong Kong where a few hundred Chinese were recruited for the coastal and anti-aircraft guns from 1937.[98] The HKSRA now manned all of Singapore's 6 inch guns. They were mainly North Indians, with a few Viceroy Commissioned Indian officers, and a British commanding officer with each battery. But the HKSRA had, like most other Indian regiments in Malaya, been milked of some of its better men, this time to supplement British batteries. Recruitment had also suffered as the wartime expansion of the Indian Army forced a resort to less promising recruits.[99]

This was to prove significant as the Labrador gunners came under repeated bombing over several days. As if the bombing, in the absence of a worthwhile sea target, had not been bad enough, things got worse. Just after 1400 hours on 13 February Japanese artillery got the range of Labrador. A shell hit the overhead cover of one of the fort's guns. Another sent splinters through the steel door of a magazine, killing three men and wounding more. Many of the Indian gunners took off for old magazines nearby, hoping these would be safer. Their officers cajoled them in every way short of shooting men. But they could only coax enough back to man one gun. Then enemy shelling recommenced, and all the Indian other ranks disappeared for good.[100]

By the afternoon of 13 February the Japanese were closing in on Labrador. Most of the HKSRA gunners had gone, and the guns themselves could only turn to 310 degrees. This meant that if the Japanese came any nearer the guns would not be able to turn round far enough to hit them anyway. With the Japanese now so close, Labrador and Fort Berlayer, the latter with its old twelve pounders, were blown up on the evening of the 13 February.[101]

A little to the east of the advancing Japanese, and of Labrador's destroyed guns, was the command post at Mount Faber, while offshore there was Pulau Blakang Mati with its several batteries. The infantry's retreat on the mainland now had knock-on effects on nearby Blakang Mati. Just after midnight Berlayer's crew went by *tongkang* to Siloso Pier. The same night Indian and Australian stragglers landed on the island. These movements were wrongly interpreted as Japanese landings, with immediate consequences for Blakang Mati's guns.[102]

---

g The exception to this rule was the 15 inch batteries, which were given several Bofors 40mm guns in January, manned at first by survivors from Force Z: The *Prince of Wales* and *Repulse*. But even then, Buona Vista had two out of three of its Bofors transferred away before 8 February.

From the viewpoint of the command on Blakang Mati, the latest reports made a deteriorating situation seem desperate. Visibility from the island's observation posts was down to 1,000 to 2,000 yards, due to black clouds from burning oil. Its own guns had contributed to this, when they helped set fire to oil tanks on Pulau Bukom to the west on 12 February. Japanese artillery had also set alight oil tanks onshore, at Normanton.[103] The water supply was failing; roads were cratered, and communications between Faber Fire Command and Blakang Mati were temporarily broken. Fearing the worst, at 0415 hours on 14 February commanders on the island ordered the guns prepared for demolition, to be carried out when it became essential.

As false reports of Japanese landings on the island came in, Siloso Battery was first to be destroyed, at 0500 hours, then Connaught from 0715, several of the close defence guns following. Even the demolition proved dangerous, one British artilleryman losing most of the fingers on one hand, and three Indians being wounded while helping to destroy a magazine.[104]

Despite the false reports, the Japanese did not attack Blakang Mati that day, or any other. They simply ground along the coast, taking Pasir Panjang Ridge and reaching Alexandra Road just beyond. By the day's close they had almost reached the shoreline opposite Blakang Mati's western tip. Early next morning, on 15 February itself, the very last of Faber Command weapons, one of Serapong Battery's pair of 6 inch guns, was disabled.

Now all the coastal guns were silent, though on Singapore Island many of the gunners fought on, reorganised into infantry companies.[105] On Blakang Mati itself, most men retired to the hilly area to the east, around Fort Connaught and Mount Serapong, to fill sandbags and prepare for a final infantry defence.[106]

In this way, the two fire commands differed in their response to the siege of Singapore, which started on 31 January 1942. Changi Fire Command arranged observation of the north of the island and the Johore coastline opposite early on, opening fire on Johore from 5 February. Faber Fire Command, meanwhile, shepherded its guns until the eleventh hour, then threw as many as it could into frenzied action from 11 to 13 February, before destroying most of its guns the following day. For Changi Fire Command, the guns on and near Pulau Tekong were demolished that evening. Had a last British counter-attack been launched on the final day of battle, there would have been no coastal guns left to support it.

One explanation of Faber Fire Command's tardiness in joining the battle is that the defence of the south of the island was left mainly to volunteers and the Malay Regiment, and a naval attack could not be ruled out. So it may have been wise to retain the effectiveness of the guns in their anti-naval role there.[107] Especially as their effectiveness against infantry would be limited in the absence of adequate observation, and given the limited number of high explosive shells. An editorial in *The Gunner* of October 1947 put this case forcefully:

... it should be remembered that the Japanese fleet might have put in an appearance at the last moment, and criticism would have been universal if at that moment the 15-inch guns had expended all their ammunition. It is easy to be wise after the event![108]

The writer might have added that the 15 inch barrels would need replacing after firing about 200 shells, a difficult operation when they weighed around 90 tons, even if there were railway cranes to assist.[109] Indeed, the artillery's main defence of the coastal guns was precisely that they had worked. When the searchlights for Labrador and Siloso Batteries discovered what Faber Fire Command identified as a 'Japanese landing craft' in the dark, late on 12 February, its fate was sealed. Macleod-Carey recalled that:

I gave the order "Shoot" and within seconds all ... guns opened up with a roar ... their instruments and range-finding gear was so accurate that preliminary ranging was unnecessary. Direct hits were scored at once. Flames, sparks and debris started flying in all directions. The crew could be seen frantically trying to lower boats but it was all over in a matter of minutes, after which the ship simply disappeared into the sea.[110]

The Faber Fire Command War Diary shows that the ill-fated ship was almost certainly nothing more sinister than a drifting *tongkang* with oil drums on board – not the troop ship Macleod-Carey at first suspected – but either way this is one of several instances when the guns fired at vessels, including Chinese junks.

Occasionally the guns were too efficient. One small craft, which was spotted trying to enter Keppel Harbour on the 13 February was summarily dispatched by two shells from Siloso's 6 inch guns. When the sole, wounded survivor swam ashore, it emerged that he was a straggler from an Australian unit. He may have saved not just himself, but others too. A boatload of Australian stragglers which approached early next morning was identified and allowed to land.[111]

One senior artillery officer has argued this efficiency of the guns was well understood by the Japanese. This meant the guns' main achievement was not that they fired in anger, but their deterrent value: 'the Gunners achieved their primary role – they deterred the Jap fleet from venturing within range of their formidable guns'.[112] Just as the American guns at Corregidor persuaded the Japanese to take the back route to Manila and its Harbour, so Singapore's defences ruled out the seaward approach.

What seems certain is that Singapore's guns were designed to fire seaward and had a role in deterring naval attack, that their ammunition was mainly suited to that role, and that only two out of the five biggest guns were ever used in the land battle. All this seems as certain as is possible, after a Fall which saw many documents lost or destroyed.

This means that it was true all along that the majority of Singapore's biggest guns were facing seaward. It was also true all along that most could not be used, or at least were not used, to fire at the Japanese massing in Johore. It also suggests Morrison was right in 1942 when he suggested that the problem was they were built facing seaward, with concrete protection or emplacements limiting their ability to turn. Morrison's argument had been that, 'The huge naval guns which protected it [the naval base] pointed out to sea. They were embedded in concrete and could not be turned to point inland. Most of them were never fired'.[113] 'Embedded' was too strong a term for concrete stops which limited the traverse of the four 15 inch guns with naval type mountings. These obstructions could be removed if the resulting reduction in anti-naval capacity was accepted. But Morrison's statement, if half false, was also half true.

It was even truer for the smaller guns. The 'myth' that many of these could not or did not fire landward was not baseless, and the later idea that all these guns could turn 360 degrees was a misleading simplification.[114] The overhead concrete protection they had added, as protection against air attack, had to have solid supports or back-walls. These did in many cases limit their turning circle.

Given the final demoralisation of the gunners at Labrador, unwillingness to compromise this protection was not without logic either. Indeed, it could be argued that it was partly the presence of thick concrete casements, giving virtually all-round protection, which made American artillery on Corregidor and surrounding forts far more durable when under attack than Singapore's guns.[115] When the Japanese took Hong Kong they also recognised the importance of such protection, encasing some of the colony's guns in 'igloo' shaped concrete huts featuring four feet of concrete.[116]

Singapore's guns, then, were not sufficiently protected to withstand significant shelling or bombing. This limited protection did restrict their movement, but only partially so. The result was that many could traverse much of the way round, and did fire landward, at least in the last few days. In the case of the 9.2 inch guns all six were used extensively in the land battle, with targets including Tengah, the important battles around Bukit Timah Road, and in at least some cases, the southern Johore coastline.[h][117] But only a fraction of Singapore's eighteen 6 inch guns were used against land targets. Other 6 inch guns meanwhile fired at small naval targets.[118] In total, it seems around two-thirds the modern guns were fired, possibly slightly under half of them at land targets, though most had very limited amounts of the high explosive ammunition most suitable for this purpose.[119]

In terms of the guns' ability to turn landward the situation now turns out a mixed one. More significantly, it could be argued that Singapore's main hope of survival lay not in a last-ditch battle on its own soil, at Kranji or Bukit Timah or anywhere else on the island. If Singapore was to survive it was best defended as a whole, preferably in conjunction with some of south Johore. In this sense, of

---

h The same was true in Hong Kong, where Brigadier John Major reported the 9.2 inch guns had been effective in breaking up Japanese attacks.

being able to repel an enemy from penetrating the island in the first place, the guns were of less use. They would need to be able to hit targets in Johore or the Straits of Johore, not just in Singapore itself.

If we count only the guns which defended Singapore island by firing at land targets outside Singapore, then a minimum of ten guns were used (two 15 inch at Johore Battery, three 9.2 inch guns on Pulau Tekong, and five 6 inch, perhaps as many as thirteen if Connaught's three 9.2 inch guns really did reach Johore.[120] So the original myth about the guns facing uselessly to sea, while half-wrong, was also half-right.

Churchill's almost naked island

Does this mean the myth of the wrongly positioned coastal guns is better forgotten? After all, they were of marginal relevance to the land battle and *Matador*. Their real role was naval gunnery and in this it has been claimed they were successful, and yet some of the guns did fire landward. If anything, it could be argued that coastal guns needed more protection from shelling and bombing, not less, and that this might even have justified a more limited traverse.

The problem is that one cannot jettison a half-false myth entirely. An alternative would be to accept the myth's complex nature, while also refocusing the debate. Perhaps we should look not so much at what Fortress Singapore did do, but at the way the defenders failed to prepare and defend Singapore as a properly fortified place. This makes sense, because the myths about the Fortress and its guns always had a symbolic role: they symbolised the lack of preparations on Singapore itself, especially on Singapore's northern shores.

The debate about 'Fortress Singapore' can be refocused back to the discussion Churchill tried to start when he complained in mid-January 1942 that Singapore was not a citadel. There is room for cynicism about Churchill's attempt to write his own history of the Second World War, one which we would expect to serve his own interests. He would claim that he had warned his commanders to prepare Singapore for a final defence. Especially as he himself had had a major role in denying Malaya the reinforcements it had needed.

But Churchill's comments on Singapore were not mere retrospective pleading. His war memoirs show that he repeatedly made clear Singapore's main defence should be mounted close to Singapore itself, and that he regarded it as a fortress which would need storming. Yet as late as mid-January 1942 no extra high explosive shells had been ordered for Singapore's biggest guns, and beach obstacles and defence systems on Singapore's northern shores were minimal. On 9 January Wavell, standing next to the Causeway, angrily demanded Percival fortify Singapore's northern shores. He dismissed the local commanders' claims that building defensive works would harm morale, arguing that morale would be harmed far more if the Japanese were allowed to pour across the straits onto unprepared shores.

Still preparations proceeded fitfully, and beach defences marked on maps sometimes failed to appear in reality. Notwithstanding problems raising civilian labour early on because of low War Office rates of pay, and later on because of the effects of Japanese bombing, this failure to fortify better Singapore's north was not one troops were likely to forgive – certainly not those who had made a fighting retreat on the mainland in the belief they were buying time for Singapore to be prepared. They marched back to find its northern shores badly neglected.[121]

This leaves two questions concerning the 'Fortress' at Singapore.

First, why did the original plans for the fortress not envisage some defences to the north, given that the Japanese already had a well-established reputation for trying to take fortresses, such as at Port Arthur in 1904 and Tsingtao in 1914, from the rear? Attempts to construct a defensive line in South Johore, including pillboxes, were started in the 1930s, but abandoned half-completed, the money only half-spent.[122]

Second, given Churchill's insistence that Singapore's last hope lay in its defence as a citadel, and that forces should not be frittered away to the north, did he have just cause for complaint against his Chiefs of Staff and commanders, who appear to have managed to ignore his ideas virtually to the last? How was it that Churchill continued to envisage Malaya's defenders retiring to Johore, and then to a Singapore well fortified and protected by a 'gorge' or moat, and yet its commanders and the Chiefs of Staff chose instead a protracted fighting retreat? Put bluntly, in 1940–1 Churchill seems to have waged guerrilla war against the concept of an all-Malayan defence, and *Operation Matador*. This seems to be the tension Churchill wanted to expose in his war memoirs in 1951. Churchill's implicit point, that his commanders had let him down by ignoring his preferences, stands regardless of the comparatively trivial question about which guns could or could not fire landwards. Hence Churchill could present himself as misinformed by his commanders, while asserting in a footnote (incorrectly as it turns out) that all the biggest guns had all-round traverse.

So for Churchill the real debate about 'Fortress Singapore' was not about how many guns could fire landward or at Johore. Instead, the central question was: how far did Churchill's Chiefs of Staff and local commanders both insist on making a more determined fighting retreat in Malaya than Churchill wanted, while failing to fortify Singapore island and Johore? In this connection, Churchill's complaints of 19 January 1942 are worth restating.

The background to Churchill's complaints was this. On 15 January Churchill telegraphed Wavell asking what Singapore's landward defences were: 'Are you sure you can dominate with fortress cannon any attempt to plant siege batteries', he added.[123] The next day Singapore time Wavell sent a blunt reply:

> Until recently all plans were based on repulsing seaborne attacks on island and holding land attacks in Johore or further north and little or nothing was done to construct defences on the north side of the island to prevent crossing the Straits.

The only good news was that preparation had been made for blowing the causeway, and 'fortress cannon of the heaviest nature have all-round traverse'. Even the latter news, however, was only half-true (only a few of the heaviest guns having been adapted for this), and Wavell also stated that their flat trajectory made them unsuitable for counter-battery work.

On 19 January Wavell telegraphed Churchill with still more depressing news:

> I must warn you ... that I doubt whether island can be held once Johore is lost. The fortress guns are sited for use against ships, and have mostly ammunition for that purpose; many can only fire seaward ... I do not want you to have a false picture of the island fortress. Singapore defences were entirely constructed to meet a seaward attack.[124]

This included beach defences running along the south coast from Pasir Panjang to Changi, with 20 miles of concrete pillboxes at 600 yard intervals, beach lights, and 18 pounder guns. But little in the west or north, while in Johore Dobbie's line of pillboxes and defences had been abandoned half-finished.[125]

Having insisted all along that the main defence be mounted in Johore after a limited delaying action, and having all along described Singapore as a fortress, Churchill was understandably furious that so little had been done to correct this situation, or at least to correct his misperceptions.[126]

On the same day, 19 January, Churchill drafted a minute for his Chiefs of Staff. He demanded to know why the necessary defence works were absent on Singapore's northern shores, and

> How is it that not one of you pointed this out to me ... [when] ... over the last years I have repeatedly shown that I relied upon this defence of SINGAPORE ISLAND against a formal siege and have never relied on the KRA ISTHMUS [Matador] plan.[127]

Churchill's use of capital letters made his position doubly clear. He had emphasised Singapore all along, not *Matador*. In effect he accused his chiefs and commanders of having squandered their forces on flawed plans and defensive concepts, while ignoring the value the Prime Minister had put on Singapore. He also made it clear that he regarded his commanders as having failed to tell him the real situation:

> I must confess to being staggered ... it never occurred to me for a moment ... that the gorge of the fortress of Singapore with its splendid moat half a mile to a mile wide was not entirely fortified against an attack from the northward. What is the use of having an island for a fortress if it is not to be made into a citadel? To construct a line of detached works with searchlights and cross-fire combined with immense wiring and obstruction of the swamp areas, and to provide the proper ammunition to enable the

fortress guns to dominate enemy batteries planted in Johore, was an elementary peace-time provision which it is did not exist in a fortress which has been twenty years building ...

Seaward batteries and a naval base do not constitute a fortress, which is a completely encircled strong place. Merely to have seaward batteries and no fort or fixed defences to protect their rear is not to be excused on any ground ... I warn you that this will be one of the greatest scandals that could possibly be exposed.[128]

Having made clear his view that this was a scandal, and one not of his making, Churchill then directed that there should be 'an attempt to use the fortress guns on the northern front by firing reduced charges and by running in a certain quantity of H.E. if none exists'. He added a long list of measures to be taken to prepare for a siege, demanding every strong point be defended. The Prime Minister was in apocalyptic mood: 'Finally, the city of Singapore must be converted into a citadel and defended to the death. No surrender can be contemplated, and the Commander, Staffs and principal Officers are expected to perish at their posts'.[129] After citing the critical minute of 19 January in his war memoirs, Churchill added that 'I ought to have known' ... but 'the possibility of Singapore having no landward defences no more entered my mind than that of a battleship being launched without a bottom'.[130]

Churchill's complaint was not just that there were no permanent guns or fortifications to the rear (there were in fact guns to the north, notably on the island of Pulau Tekong), but that few perimeter defences of any sort had been prepared. Above all, he later argued that,

All that I had seen or read of war had led me to the conviction that, having regard to firepower, a few weeks will suffice to create strong field defences, and also to limit and canalise the enemy's front attack by minefields and other obstructions.

Field defences, barbed wire, mines, earthworks, did not require a great deal of money, or time, and here Churchill seems to have some cause for complaint.

Churchill's complaint about the deficiencies in more permanent fortifications were on top of this, and less convincing. He admitted that

it had never entered my head that no circle of ... forts of a permanent character protected the rear of the fortress. I cannot understand how it was that I did not know ... I had put my faith in the enemy being compelled to use artillery on a very large scale to pulverise our strong points at Singapore ...[131]

A War Office reply to Churchill's minute of 19 January dryly countered that the Singapore 'Fortress' was originally built to protect the naval base from seaward attack, and that Singapore's mangrove swamps and manifold creeks impeded defence works on its northern coasts. Churchill's imagination may have ranged from South African plains to Turkish citadels, and across the high seas, but it did not seem to encompass the reality of tropical coastlines. Churchill was also reminded that, though he had been reluctant to reinforce Malaya sufficient for an all-Malayan defence up to the Kra, he had still allowed the Chiefs of Staff and Far Eastern Commanders to the plan on this basis. Anyway, the whole Singapore strategy was designed not to save Singapore City, but to preserve the naval base, which was positioned at Sembawang on Singapore's northern shores. Since this faced the nearby Malayan mainland, across a narrow Strait, it could only remain operational if enemy aircraft and artillery were kept well away, up-country in Malaya.

If Churchill is to be allowed to conduct his defence in his own words, however, it is as well to quote his military advisers' own defence as well, as it appears in a document dated 21 January 1942:

> The SINGAPORE fortress was designed to protect the naval base which is located in the Strait at the extreme North of the island. Effective protection from landward attack can only be given by holding the Peninsula in Northern Johore and beyond ... The mangrove swamps which border most of the thirty miles or so of the North Coast of the island are unsuitable for the construction of defences covering the Strait. ... the period before relief was fixed at 180 days. If our policy had been to retire to the island at once, or even to a line in JOHORE, our chances of holding out for this length of time would have been non-existent; and the Naval Base would have been so damaged by Japanese air attack that it would have been useless when the Fleet arrived ... The whole basis of the plan was to fight delaying [action]. Owing to the almost complete absence of the naval and air elements of this plan, the arrival of the Japanese forces has been unimpeded and the scale of attack has been far greater than any army we could have put there could cope with.[132]

Local commanders also pleaded that early construction of defences on Singapore would have sapped morale, and that army rates of pay for civilian labour were too low. By the time they were raised, increased bombing and the Japanese approach meant labour was even more difficult to obtain.[133]

The replies to Churchill's questions were as tendentious as Churchill's original queries. Churchill for one was not convinced:

> I am aware of the various reasons that have been given for this failure: the preoccupation of the troops in training and in building defence works in Northern Malaya; the shortage of civilian labour; pre-war financial limitations and centralised War Office control; the fact that the Army's role was to protect the naval base, situated on the northern shore of the

island ... I do not consider these reasons valid. Defences should have been built.

The Japanese estimate was that shore defences, behind barbed wire, were well sited but 'little more formidable than ordinary field entrenchments' and easy to neutralise 'with field guns lighter than 15 centimetres'.[134] On the west coast of Singapore, their artillery barrage was so effective that it cut communications to the beaches, leaving the defenders isolated at critical moments.

Clearly, more beach lights, communication systems, minefields, underwater obstacles and the like might have been prepared on Singapore's northern shores, if not in Johore as well, and on 19 January Churchill cabled ten specific measures he wanted taken. These included using the coastal guns to fire northward and acquiring for them high explosive ammunition, and using if necessary 'rigorous compulsion' to marshal the entire male population on works.[135]

His urgency reflected the fact that relatively little had been done by mid-January, despite calls from some quarters for more urgency. As far back as August 1941, the new Chief Engineer, Brigadier Ivan Simson, had come to similar conclusions. Indeed, there must be some suspicion that Simson's views influenced Churchill's later writing.

After two years helping with defences in Britain, Simson had arrived in Malaya with instructions to modernise defences. He almost immediately urged anti-tank defences be constructed in depth along Malaya's north–south road system, with obstacles and works on the flanks to channel attackers into killing grounds. He even saw Percival in mid-October 1941, outlining how effective defences had been previously against Japanese attack, at Port Arthur. Like Singapore, Port Arthur was a fortified naval base. The Japanese isolated it in 1904 by a surprise attack on the Russian fleet, but were prevented from seizing the base itself by fortifications to its landward side. These works had allowed the defenders to hold out for five months and inflict heavy casualties on the Japanese before Port Arthur fell.

Simson now advised Percival that field fortifications in south Johore be improved, and stressed that it was vital to construct such works before war started and labour became scarce. At first, he was ignored, and by October 1941 defence works planned included little more than the Jitra line, and additional work on Singapore's south coast, where the coast guns made direct attack less likely anyway. Simson's appeal to develop the island's northern shores went ignored. He called for

> field and permanent defences in depth consisting of mutually supporting wired trenches, switch lines, pillboxes and various underwater obstacles, mines, petrol fire traps, anchored but floating barbed wire, and methods of illuminating the water at night' so that 'the water surface and shore line should always be the main killing ground'.[136]

Other ideas included preparing detonation chambers for bridges, something that might have reduced the number of failed demolitions due to wet charges in 1942. As with Lieutenant-Colonel Stewart's ideas for jungle training, and for holding the road by fighting the battle for the road off the road, overall command failed to harness the best and most vigorous ideas.[137] According to Simson he saw Percival again on 27 December. Then he had a request by Lieutenant-General Heath, commanding the forces retreating on the peninsula, to prepare defences in Johore before his battle-worn troops reached it. Percival later did order some work in Johore, but too little, too late. For Singapore the story was even less inspiring.

Simson later claimed to have worked on Percival for over two hours on 27 December, telling him 'that time was rapidly running out for the construction of permanent and field defences on the north shore of Singapore Island; because once any area came under enemy fire civilian labour would vanish'. Now, he said, was the time to marshal both civilian labour, and the 6,500 Commonwealth Engineers, to do what could be done. The answer from Percival, and the Fortress Commander, Major-General Keith Simmons was supposedly that defences were bad for civilian and military morale.[138]

Orders to develop northern defences were finally given in early January, after Wavell expressed horror at seeing the largely unfortified landward side of Singapore. But even then they were too timid. Anyway, War Office payscales for civilian labour still remained below those obtainable on plantations, and became yet more inadequate as wartime inflation pushed up costs. By the time they were increased bombing meant it was too late.[139]

There was also debate about just how to defend a mangrove-fringed northern and western coast. On 23 January Percival emphasised that

> The northern and western shores of the island are too intersected with creeks and mangroves for any recognised form of beach defences,' recommending instead 'small defended localities to cover known approaches, such as rivers, creeks and roads to the coast ... supported by mobile reserves in suitable assembly areas'.

This was a fine theory, except that British communications broke down as Japanese bombardment damaged surface lines and neither troops nor commanders were geared to rapid and decisive counter-attack. Besides, more mines, oil traps and underwater obstacles would still have helped soften an enemy up, even if beach defence was not the main plan.[140] Instead, there was confusion to the last.

Simson, meanwhile, reconnoitred the coast of Johore and decided the swamps to the east of the Causeway would make a poor jumping off point for an attack on Singapore, compared to west Johore, where there was good road access to the coast. At the same time, the Japanese concluded British defensive positions would be stronger east of the Causeway because of the Naval Base.[141]

So Simson had mines, booby traps, Lyon lights, petrol drums for setting alight the water, barbed wire and obstacles dumped along Singapore's northwest coast, ready for use. Unfortunately Percival read the situation differently, so Simson was ordered to move these stocks to the west, completing the task by 5 February. Whereupon the sighting of Japanese in west Johore prompted orders by 6 February to switch some of the supplies back. Again, it was all far too late.[142]

Tragically, the material needed for defence works had been present in Singapore all along, even if the willpower and organisation to use it effectively was not. The War Office had sent large quantities of the supplies necessary to build defences to ports such as Aden and Singapore as early as 1938 to 1939. This had specifically been intended to ensure the stockpiles were there before wartime conditions placed a premium on shipping space.[143]

We do not know when Churchill learnt that Simson had advised the very defences whose absence he himself lamented in January. But he was impervious to Percival's reasoning anyway. Churchill himself had argued for a relatively early withdrawal to a well fortified Johore and Singapore from the early stages of the campaign, though accepting the need to delay the Japanese as far as possible.[144] On 16 December Churchill had warned the Chiefs of Staff to, 'Beware lest troops required for ultimate defence of Singapore Island and fortress are used up or cut off in Malay peninsula', adding for emphasis that, 'Nothing compares in importance with fortress'.[145] Yet both the Chiefs of Staff and Brooke-Popham seem to have largely ignored Churchill's views. In part this may have been because they wanted to screen the naval base, in part because Churchill's instincts ran against the grain of general military thinking on defending Malaya.

Whatever the reason, a few days after his first telegram on this subject, an evidently annoyed Churchill was again putting pressure on the Chiefs of Staff. On 19 December he demanded that:

> He [Brooke-Popham] should now be told to confine himself to defence of Johore and Singapore and that nothing repeat nothing must compete with maximum defence of Singapore. This should not preclude delaying tactics and demolitions on the way south ...

Given Churchill's repetition, that 'nothing repeat nothing must compete with maximum defence of Singapore', the Chiefs of Staff could hardly complain that Churchill had not been clear. Indeed, Churchill also read the strategic situation of December accurately. He pointed out that, following the sinking of the *Prince of Wales* and the *Repulse*, 'we have no means of preventing continuous landings by Japanese in great strength ... It is therefore impossible to defend ... anything north of the defensive line in Johore ...'[146] As late as 14 January he cabled the Australian Prime Minister that,

The only vital point is Singapore Fortifications and its essential hinterland. Personally, my anxiety has been lest in fighting rearguard action ... to gain time we should dissipate the force required for the prolonged defence of Singapore. Out of the equivalent of four divisions available for that purpose, one has been lost and another mauled to gain a month or six weeks' time. Some may think it would have been better to have come back quicker with less loss.[147]

One of those who did think this might have been wise was Tsuji, who wrote that 'If it was considered that the enemy would rely on Singapore Fortress, and hold out there to the last man, then the military strength that had been poured in north of the Perak River was excessive ... Pouring in fresh reinforcements to support the forces destroyed in the opening battles was like pouring water on thirsty soil'. In December, these British tactics reassured Tsuji that there was reasonable hope of Japanese success.[148]

Churchill's instinctive preference was still 'to fight the battle for Singapore in Johore, but to delay the enemy's approach thereto as much as possible'.[149] Churchill's fears for a mainland battle were duly realised, as British forces were repeatedly outflanked. Indeed, the whole notion of a substantial fighting retreat was, in these circumstances, flawed. Britain could never commit enough forces to win a single engagement, for fear they would be outflanked by sea or land and lost in totality. As Tsuji noted, 'The enemy were ... preparing fortified positions; yet their resistance lacked sincerity and showed a reluctance to fight a decisive battle with us'.[150] So each fixed line was doomed before it started, and attempts to shore up the situation or save troops when a line crumbled sometimes resulted in further units being drip-fed into battles, so that the Japanese were able to mangle them one by one.

Against these odds, Brooke-Popham and Percival persisted in mounting a determined fighting defence of Malaya itself. Their perspective was that they had to keep Japanese artillery and aircraft well away from the naval base, and from convoys on the way to Singapore with more troops, for as long as possible.

The real tragedy of Singapore may be that Churchill failed to force a decisive debate on these differences at any stage from late 1940 to mid-January 1942. A debate whereby he would accept plans for all-Malayan defence and provide the necessary reinforcements, or the Chiefs of Staff would enforce a more limited defence based mainly on Johore, and a more thorough fortification of Singapore as security against the worst.

Churchill and his commanders clung to very different visions of the defence of Singapore, right down to the bitter end. Churchill had one conception of strategy, of Singapore and Johore as a fortress, defensible as a hedgehog, and to be retired to relatively quickly. From his perspective, it turned out that Singapore was never properly fortified, not because his commanders were surprised by a northern attack, but precisely because they concentrated too much energy on meeting that attack in the north. Indeed, the impetus of planning to meet an attack from the north, slowly building up from Dobbie's reports in the mid-1930s, may have made it difficult for the military to make a paradigm shift when they found the resources for *Matador* lacking.[151] Only very briefly, in early 1940, did a local commander (General Bond as GOC Malaya) seem to realise that all-Malayan defence, while theoretically ideal, might prove disastrous with the limited resources available.[152]

From the perspective of Churchill's commanders, *Etonian* and then *Matador* remained vital, even if the aircraft were not there. For them, fortifications seem to have been viewed as a distraction, excepting perhaps those at Jitra in the far north, and on Singapore's seaward coast in the far south. To them fortifications seem to have been regarded almost as bookends, something desirable only to support the northern and southern extremities of their defensive area.

We shall never know if Churchill's preferred option, a more concentrated defence around Johore and Singapore, with a less committed delaying action to the north, would have worked better. It might have changed things only marginally. It might even have allowed the Japanese to bring their full naval and air superiority to bear on Singapore even more quickly, causing still earlier demoralisation.

The example of American resistance in the Philippines might at first suggest an early retreat would have worked well. American resistance lasted much longer, in part because of a very early withdrawal to the Bataan peninsula. But Bataan and Corregidor are not very useful comparisons for Singapore. While Singapore Island is flat, bar a small number of hills, the Bataan peninsula, which overlooks the entrance to Manila Bay, is rugged, mountainous country.

Even after Bataan had fallen, some men could retire to the string of four fortified islands which protected the entrance to Manila Bay, strung across it like teeth. While Singapore's coastal guns had little more than some concrete overhead cover, and thin armour, these islands boasted extensive protection. Corregidor and Fort Drum, two of the four islands, had thick reinforced concrete walls. Some of their guns were protected by almost fully enclosed casemates.

Fort Drum in particular illustrates the difference between the two defensive positions. Fort Drum was one of the four island fortresses strung across the entrance to Manila Bay. It was a 350 foot long 'concrete battleship', built on a levelled island. With concrete walls up to 36 feet deep, four 14 inch guns in turrets, and four casemated 6 inch guns, it lacked the soft underbelly possessed by Singapore's scattered batteries. The island of Corregidor, meanwhile, was just 3 miles long by up to half a mile wide. It was closer in size to Blakang Mati than to Singapore. Yet it had a complex of tunnels and even an underground hospital. The main Malinta Tunnel shaft alone was 1,400 feet long. The island also bristled with twenty-three batteries, including seven 12-inch guns and mortars. All were First World War vintage, with inadequate ammunition suitable for infantry targets, but defensively it presented a much more compact and well-protected site than anything on Singapore, and defended at the last by several thousand men.

It is clear that Singapore was no Corregidor. Whether it would still have been served better by a more limited defence, we shall never know, because Churchill's commanders clung to their conception of Singapore as a naval base needing shielding as far to the north as possible. The local commanders only really abandoned their attempt at a substantive fighting retreat in late January 1942. By then it was already too late to provide more effective all-round fortifications for 'Fortress Singapore', and the troops available were either fresh off the boat, or much-battered and demoralised by the string of defeats and retreats. When Churchill finally realised how bad the situation was, in mid-January, he was distraught. As he wrote in his *The Second World War*:

> I had put my faith in the enemy being compelled to use artillery on a very large scale to pulverise our strong points at Singapore. . . . Now, suddenly, all this vanished away, and I saw before me the hideous spectacle of the almost naked island . . .[153]

6

AFTER THE BATTLE

They shall grow not old, as we that are left grow old,
Age shall not weary them, nor the years condemn,
At the going down of the sun and in the morning,
We will remember them.
> Ode from Laurence Binyon's 'The Fallen', first published in the *The Times* on 21 September 1914.[a]

End of Occupation,
rapture of sudden peace!
Their mighty drums booming and brave pipes swirling,
The British come
Marching back their good old Singapore,
Re-planting the empire flag,
Re-union with Jack ...

And into the night, young Singapore ponders:
'The British are back! Good God!'

Eyes Having seen,
Minds having thought,
Can live once more the old days? Were they not stripped and thrashed,
Forced to kneel to
Yellow men they taught us to spit on? ...

Light shines forth from the eastern sky
The hour is coming,
The dawn of freedom ...
'Merdeka!'[b]
> Goh Sin Tub, 'Re-union with Jack', from Robbie B.H. Goh (ed.), *Memories and Desires: A Poetic History of Singapore* (Singapore: Unipress NUS, 1998), p. 24.

Churchill's angry exchanges with his military chiefs of mid-January 1942 began what has turned into a never-ending post-mortem, and one conducted as much in the public eye as on the pages of books. Almost as soon as he had dashed off instructions to prepare Singapore's coastal guns for landward firing, Churchill was faced with a secret debate in the British House of Commons. Beginning on 27 January 1942 this ended, after three days, with an overwhelming vote of confidence in his government. British parliamentarians knew that Churchill was the best they had, whatever happened at Singapore.

By the time the House of Commons expressed its confidence in the Prime Minister on 29 January, Australian newspapers also had some harsh things to say. Even British and Australian prisoners of the Japanese, squashed into Pudu gaol in Kuala Lumpur, were debating what was happening. Australian gunner Russell Braddon talks of prisoners having 'threshed it out' in the hot prison exercise yard over four days of fierce debate: debate which was interspersed by working trips into the city, where human heads already adorned intersections; and by the rumble of Japanese tanks heading south.[1]

Those tanks would eventually reach Singapore, where it would all end. So it was the Japanese who would control Singapore on the first anniversaries of the war: 8 December 1942 and 15 February 1943. This meant they would be the first to control how the Fall of Singapore would be commemorated, and what it would be allowed to mean.[2]

Honouring Japan's war heroes

The Japanese were all too happy to adapt the image of the impregnable fortress to their own purposes. The more formidable Singapore and its defenders had been, the more heroic have been Japan's seventy day conquest. For the Japanese, frustrated by endless war in the vast expanses of China, 15 February 1942 marked one of their greatest victories. It was a highpoint in *Dai Tao Senso*, the 'Greater East Asia War' against 'Western imperialists'.[3]

Even after the war Tsuji, who helped plan the campaign, would emphasise not British incompetence, but Japanese heroism in overcoming the odds, in executing a blitzkrieg of breathtaking daring: one which, according to Tsuji, succeeded only by the skin of its teeth as Japanese ammunition all but ran out on 15 February. Serious Japanese reflection and debate over massacres in Malaya and Singapore, over how far they were oppressors, would take decades to mature, and even then would be overshadowed by 15 August, and the Japanese sense that they, too, had been the victims of war.[4]

---

a This ode was quickly taken up for British and Commonwealth memorial services after the First World War, including Remembrance Day on each 11 November, and Anzac Day in Australia.

b *Merdeka!* meaning 'Freedom'! Goh Sin Tub's stories and poems capture the ambivalence as well as the horror of occupation. His poem 'My Friend, My Enemy', talks of learning 'enemy ways' – 'Nippongo, Yamato-damshi, Bushido ...', while 'you see as I see, you understand the things done ... A shame you cannot speak.'

Meanwhile, exhilaration was the order of the day. In Tokyo in 1942 poets wrote odes to commemorate the event. Tatsuji Miyoshi (1900–64), considered Japan's finest at the time, wrote 'The Fall of Singapore':

And Singapore has fallen.
The fierce soldiers of the Divine Land with
godlike speed
Have pursued the old and ugly thieves
from north to south
And swept through a thousand miles of
jungles; today the fortress has fallen.

For Haruo Sato's (1898–64) 'The Song of the Dawn of Asia' it was not just the end of the old, but the dawn of the new:

Singapore, the celebrated
Showcase of modern weapons,
The bastion of infamy, has fallen.
The heads of the hobgoblins have dropped
Under keen Japanese swords.
Ah, the calamity of Asia
Surely now will be extirpated.[5]

For the Japanese, the capture of 'an impregnable fortress' had been not just a practical affair of steel and flesh, but a symbolic ending of an era, a liberation of Asians from white rule, and from imperialist time. The 100 day South Seas campaign of 1941–2 was the culmination of a project to regain Asian honour. A project which can be traced back to the moment when Commodore Perry and his ships forced Japan to open itself to the world in 1853.[6]

The Japanese army liberates Singapore from British imperialist time

This meant the Fall was much more than a military victory. It was a seismic shift, a rupturing which implied a racial, cultural, and even a chronological transformation.[7] On the day Singapore fell, its *Straits Times* brought out a last Sunday edition. When it reappeared on 20 February it was no longer the *Straits Times*, but the *Shonan Times* (spelt *Syonan Times* from the next day). *Syonan-To*, or 'Light of the South' being Singapore's new name.

The date on the paper had changed too. It was 20 February, Showa 17, 2602. So it was no longer 1,942 years after Jesus's birth, but the seventeenth year of the reign of Japan's Emperor Hirohito, an era he had entitled 'Showa' ('Illustrious Peace'). And it was the 2,602nd year since the legendary founding of Japan's Jimmu dynasty in 660 BC, a dynasty which claimed descent from Amaterasu Omikami, the Sun Goddess no less.

AFTER THE BATTLE

With a chronology older than the Christian and Muslim calendars, and a sense of history to match, it is not entirely surprising that the Japanese felt themselves the chosen people of Asia, and their victories to signal the resurgence of Asian civilisation. Thus they even discarded with time zones set according to Greenwich Mean Time, standardising everything on Tokyo time. Singapore's clocks were moved forward one and a half hours, in defiance of the logic of the rising and setting sun. As the newly reset clocks of *Syonan-To* approached 7 a.m., dawn would now be a couple of hours away. As they approached 8 p.m., the sun would scarcely be starting to set.[8]

This shift from one world to another meant the Fall of Singapore would first be commemorated not in Christian chronology, but Japanese, recalling not 1942 but 2602. Even then, a choice had to be made. Should the campaign be commemorated by marking the start of the campaign, or its end; the landings on the beaches to the north, or the Fall of the Fortress in the south?

The start of the campaign commended itself on a number of levels, not least because the Malayan campaign marked the start of the whole of the war to liberate 'Greater East Asia'. The initial attack on Malaya had occurred on 8 December in local time, about an hour and a half before the Japanese bombed Pearl Harbor. The Americans only recorded Pearl Harbor as on 7 December because the International Date Line, which ran through the Pacific Ocean, meant they were a day behind. For the Japanese, the sequence of events was as follows:

1.40 a.m. on 8 December, Kota Bharu attacked from the sea.[cd]
3.05 a.m., landings on the beaches of Singora and Patani in Southern Thailand.
3.20 a.m., Pearl Harbor bombed.
4.20 a.m., Ambassador Nomura hands Japan's 'final note' to American Secretary of State, Cordell Hull.
6.10 a.m., Singapore bombed.
11.40 a.m., Emperor Hirohito issues Imperial Order declaring war on Britain and the United States.[9]

This chronology added extra meaning to the Malayan landings in December. But February 1942 became the first moment of commemoration, since the end of the campaign was the obvious first moment to honour fallen comrades.

Immediately after the surrender Yamashita attended services for the fallen with each of the three divisions. He himself made a small statue of the God of Mercy and offered daily prayer. Each subsequent 15 February he held a

---

c In Singapore Time, Kota Bharu was attacked between midnight and 0100 on 8 December, and Singapore bombed at around 0340 hours.
d In London time (then 7½ hours behind Singapore), Kota Bharu was attacked between 1700 and 1800 on 7 December.

memorial service, even when stationed in Manchukuo and the Philippines. So two dates resonated powerfully from the very beginning.[10] Given additional pride at seizing the 'impregnable fortress' of Singapore, it is scarcely surprising the Japanese soon began to build major monuments in *Syonan-To*, in order to commemorate 8 December 2601, and 15 February 2602.

Building Singapore's 'Yasukuni' Shrine[11]

One obvious model for a monument was Japan's *Yasukuni* Shrine, in Tokyo.[12] Its huge *torii* gates, cherry trees, gingko trees, and the cooing of its doves, can evoke a strong atmosphere, even without seeing the oak cases in its museum, crammed with relics: medals, swords and maps. But in addition since 1869 it has been the spiritual centre for honouring the souls of over 2 million Japanese war dead. It is for this reason that, every year on 15 August, there is pressure on Japanese ministers to attend the shrine: to attend on a date which emphasises Japanese as victims of Western imperialism and the atomic bomb, rather than the horrors and crimes of war.

When a minister succumbs, as Prime Minister Junichiro Koizumi did in 2001 (eventually visiting two days before the 15 August), it inevitably reopens old wounds. For the shrine includes Second World War war criminals amongst the *kami* or 'deities', the spirits of the fallen which are honoured. Among these are the actual remains of Hideki Tojo, the wartime Prime Minister who the allies hanged as a war criminal in 1948.[13]

In this way Yasukuni combines Shinto, in 1941 a state religion which deified the Emperor, commemoration of the spirits of the 'dead', and the honouring of a martial tradition. Equivalents were built across the Japanese Empire, in Korea, Taiwan, and Manchuria. Hundreds of Japanese Shinto shrines were styled on the Yasukuni Shrine in Tokyo. They were also run by the military, which compelled their colonial populations to pay respect to Japanese deities and Japan's war dead at the shrines as signs of their obedience to the Japanese Empire.[14]

In order for its conquest, its ingestion into Japan's cultural and cosmological order, to be complete, *Syonan-To* needed its own memorials: its own 'Yasukuni'.[15]

From April 2602 the Japanese set about building two sacred sites, the *Syonan Chureito* (Light of the South Cenotaph) and the *Syonan Jinja* (Light of the South Shrine). The *Syonan Jinja* was to be a replica Japanese Shinto shrine and compound constructed near MacRitchie Reservoir in the centre of the island, complete with pools, pebbles and specially imported Japanese plants, and consecrated to the sun-god Amaterasu Omikami. That is, to the divine ancestor of the Imperial House, and so of Hirohito himself.[16]

Amaterasu Omikami was referred to by the Japanese military in Singapore as 'the Eternal Protector of Malaya and Sumatra who is to be worshipped by the local inhabitants'. The shrine thus encouraged, as did the many other local versions of Yasukuni built across the Japanese Empire, devotion to the Emperor almost as a 'deity in human form'.[17]

The *Syonan Chureito*, by contrast, was a more austere monument. It was a giant wooden obelisk built to pierce the sky on top of Bukit Batok Hill, not far from Bukit Timah and the Ford Factory. On 7 May 1942, Lieutenant-General Tomoyuki Yamashita himself laid the symbolic foundation stones for both the *Syonan Chureito* and the *Syonan Jinja*. The *Syonan Times* dutifully reporting that

> the purpose of these is to perpetuate the memory of the Nippon heroes who laid down their lives at the battle fronts of Malaya and Sumatra; also to enable the *Nippon-jin* and the newly attached nationals of different races in the Southern Co-Prosperity Sphere to respect the ideal of the founding of the Dai Nippon Empire.[18]

The Japanese also erected a similar monument, a ten-foot-high granite obelisk inscribed with Japanese characters, on Lido Beach in Johore. It marked the spot where final assault against Singapore had begun.[19]

Allied prisoners of war (POWs) were brought to work on the *Chureito*. POWs laboured to cut away the jungle under the command of Japanese engineers. While some, such as the young Bombardier Stanley Warren, made the access roads, others constructed flights of steps up the hill, to where the monument would hail 'Nippon heroes'.[20] The Japanese also allowed the POWs to construct a more modest monument close by, a wooden cross for the allied dead. Quite apart from the propaganda this provided, Japanese culture did respect the dead of both sides. It was those who had surrendered, who worked now as POWs, who they viewed as disgraced.

So it was at these monuments, on 8 December 2602 (1942), that some of the earliest commemorations of the Malayan campaign were staged. The choice of date was, fittingly, not that of the Fall of Singapore.[21] Instead, the date was the anniversary of the commencement of Japan's campaign to liberate 'South' Asia or the *Nanyo* (the South Seas).

On 8 December 2602 400 of Singapore Island's young people were marched several miles out of the city to the *Syonan Chureito* to 'pay homage to the souls of the war heroes enshrined there'. The local press showed front-page photographs of several Chinese students demonstrating gratitude for being 'liberated' from European colonial domination by laying wreaths in the presence of Japanese soldiers. Japanese propaganda also showed British prisoners of war commemorating the anniversary.[22]

The 8 December seems to have become the preferred date for local representatives and schoolchildren to go to *Syonan Chureito* each year, to pay homage to the war dead. In many ways it was a more fitting date than 15 February, if the aim was celebration, and commemoration of fallen conquerors. It was also one which placed the Fall of Singapore in its proper context, as just one part of Japan's 'World Shattering' campaign, as one Japanese newspaper article of April 1942 had termed the hundred days from 8 December.[23]

Despite the symbolic resonance of 8 December, the Japanese also chose to mark 15 February as a public holiday. On 15 February 2603 (1943), they held a ceremony at the *Syonan Jinja*. Local leaders were invited, and even encouraged to join the Japanese in prayer. In turn they were reassured that this indicated only obedience to the Emperor, rather than subscription to Shinto beliefs, and so was not a betrayal of their own religions.[24]

By encouraging local representatives to join in events at the monuments on occasions such as the anniversaries of 8 December and 15 February, and on the Emperor's birthday, the Japanese provided a theatre of commemoration.[25] Participants showed submission to the Emperor and empire, and were united to Japan and its designs.[26] In this ritualistic sense, Singapore shifted from being Fortress of the British Empire, to being a participant in the world of Nippon, from being integrated into a Western-dominated system of celebrating the King's birthday and Empire Day, to an Eastern one of celebrating *Tenchōsetsu* and *Kigensetsu*.[e]

By 1945 the Japanese system of time and commemoration was well established. Even men such as Chin Kee Onn, a former teacher in an English-language school and badminton champion, now believed Malayans might be well on their way to becoming Nipponified.[27] Only the changing tide of war from 1943 kept at bay the move towards learning Japanese language and Japanese ways. By 1945 everyone knew the Japanese were close to defeat, and losers no more get to set the pattern for commemoration than to write history.

The Japanese knew this as well as anyone, and so when their country surrendered on 15 August 1945 they hurriedly set about dismantling their monuments. They removed the sacred symbols and objects at the *Syonan Jinja*, and then destroyed the monuments according to Shinto rituals, which in some cases call for a periodic burning and renewal of temples.[28] The *Syonan Chureito* was also destroyed, and the ashes of the Japanese war dead transplanted to a quiet corner of the Japanese civilian cemetery, a place used by the Japanese community since 1891. On 9 September 1945, when British troops arrived to blow up the *Syonan Chureito*, they were duly disappointed. All they could find was the stump where the Japanese had sawed off the 12 metre wooden obelisk. The Christian cross behind it had also gone. The British troops had to be satisfied with blowing up the concrete base, leaving the flights of steps intact in Bukit Batok Park to this day.[29]

---

e The 11 February, *Kigensetsu*, the day celebrating the foundation of the Jimmu dynasty, replaced Britain's Empire Day, 24 May. Celebration of the King's birthday on the Second Thursday of every June made way for *Tenchōsetu*, the Emperor's birthday on 29 April.

The British Empire remembers

Choosing not to mark the Fall of Singapore

After Japan capitulated on 15 August 1945, there was a formal surrender ceremony on 2 September 1945 on board the USS *Missouri* in Tokyo harbour. Douglas MacArthur, Supreme Commander of the Allied Powers, signed the surrender document flanked by Lieutenant-General Jonathan Wainwright, who had surrendered Corregidor, and Lieutenant-General A.E. Percival who had surrendered Singapore.

Unfortunately, the loss of Singapore and British prestige could not be undone by an American general accepting Japanese surrender upon an American ship, certainly not with the unfortunate Percival, so lately a prisoner of the Japanese, hovering in the background. What message would a commemoration of 2 September send to Chinese, Malays and Indians? Even if Britain had, in the wake of Singapore's Fall, promised to guide its colonies towards self-government, it still assumed this process would take decades, and end in respectful partnership between Britain and its former colonies. Prestige was, in 1945, an important issue.[30]

So when the British army and colonial authorities returned unopposed to Singapore from 5 September 1945, they needed their own surrender. An official spokesman from the Southeast Asia Command (SEAC) told the media that, regarding the surrender of Japanese forces, 'a section has now been formed in the Command with the task of considering ways and means of bring home their defeat to them'.[31] The Japanese must surrender locally, to a victorious British commander. Fortunately Singapore was now the headquarters for SEAC with its quarter of a million troops (albeit mainly Indian troops). Consequently, local Japanese commanders were made to surrender again, this time to SEAC's Supreme Allied Commander, Admiral Lord Louis Mountbatten.

SEAC at first considered, according to one of its spokesmen, having a surrender ceremony 're-enacting in reverse at Singapore the humiliations endured by Lt-Gen Sir [sic] Arthur Percival in the surrender to Lt-Gen Yamashita here in the middle of February 1942'. However, this was rejected by 'higher levels', and a ceremony consisting of Lord Mountbatten accepting the swords of high ranking Japanese commanders was substituted instead.[32] The British chose 12 September as the date, and the imposing City Hall overlooking the *padang* and the sea beyond as the location.[f] This allowed for the parading of troops and a very visible arrival and departure of the surrendering Japanese. Some of the crowd jeered the Japanese, crying *bako daro!*, 'you fools'. For extra

---

f The Japanese liked City Hall too. For the Emperor's birthday, 29 April 2602, they had local schoolchildren converge on the *padang* holding Japanese flags. Rank upon rank sang *Aikoku Koshin Kyoko* 'Look at the dawn over the eastern seas', before shouting *Banzai* three times. Yamashita was moved to tears, saying, 'Just like Japanese children, aren't they?' Mamoru Shinozaki, *Syonan – My Story* (Singapore: Times Books, 1982 edition), pp. 42–3.

measure, Japanese prisoners were set about repairing the *padang* itself, and prominent local figures were invited to witness the event. These included not only leaders, but Elizabeth Choy, a victim of wartime torture by the Japanese military police, its *kempeitai*.[33]

This new surrender gave the British a far more satisfying date to commemorate, 12 September. This was allocated for remembering the war in Malaya and Singapore, being described as 'Malaya's own V-J Day'. On 12 September 1946, the first anniversary, the room at City Hall where the Japanese surrendered to Mountbatten was rearranged to represent the scene on the same day in 1945. Pictures of the event were hung from the chamber walls. Subsequently 12 September became an unofficial holiday in Singapore in the immediate postwar years, with many people taking the day off.[34]

The 12 September was, however, a time for celebration rather than commemoration. This still left the problem of when to honour the war dead. The 15 February was the most obvious date, but for equally obvious reasons unacceptable to the colonial regime.

The solution settled upon was to use a specifically European date. The colonial authorities chose 11 November, Remembrance Day, which marked the armistice at the end of the First World War. The dead were to be remembered on the closest Sunday to Remembrance Day each year. In Singapore and Malaya, 'men of two world wars, men who fought in the Malaya, and men who were in the resistance movement during the occupation' would line up in front of the existing cenotaphs, on which were inscribed mainly the names of Europeans who died in the two World Wars.[35] Thus remembering the war dead from the Fall of Singapore would be symbolically lost among all the wars of the British Empire: victorious wars.

The enthusiasm of the British colonial authorities for marking 12 September and 11 November was in stark contrast to their antagonism to 15 February. The supreme body of the trade unions in Malaya and Singapore, the Pan-Malayan Federation of Trade Unions, wanted to commemorate this as a day of mourning in 1946. How far the federation was influenced by a genuine desire to commemorate the Fall and the *Sook Ching* which had followed soon afterwards, how far its communist-influenced leaders hoped to embarrass the British, is not clear. What is clear is that it set up a first clash over what should be remembered, and how.

The British colonial authorities adamantly refused a permit for a procession.[36] The procession went ahead anyway. Scuffles followed between the police and what the press called 'The Fall of Singapore demonstrators' on a field outside St Joseph's Institution (the current Art Museum) on Bras Basah Road. During the ensuing mayhem the police shot dead one man and nineteen other demonstrators were injured.[37] Reporters described seeing 'crowds of excited Chinese youths and a few girls and women', while 'banners bearing pictures and Chinese characters were gathered by the police'. The police arrested twenty-four demonstrators, with ten of these later being banished from Singapore and Malaya without trial. Among the demonstrators and those arrested were a considerable number from the Ex-Service Comrade Association, men who had fought against the Japanese in the communist-led Malayan Peoples' Anti-Japanese Army (MPAJA).

The first round had gone to the British, and it was now clear British antipathy to marking 15 February was too great to be overcome. Lord Mountbatten captured the spirit of British objections when he described the demonstration as 'an attempt to organise a public holiday' to mark the 'anniversary of the subjection of Singapore by the Japanese'.[38] The editor of the pro-colonial *Straits Times* called for 15 February to be given over to private contemplation:

> Four years ago today Singapore fell to the Japanese. For the next three years those who held Malaya in bondage celebrated their triumph by declaring February 15 a public holiday. Today there is no organised observance of a historic date, nor is such a thing desirable. Rather is the occasion one for individual reflection, for something in the nature of a mental stock-taking and rededication to the task of restoring to Malaya the tranquillity which she enjoyed for so long and now misses so acutely.'[39]

The truth was that the British establishment recognised that the Fall of Singapore was seen by many as much more than an ordinary defeat. It was seen as a result of miscalculation and neglect, as a symbol of decline, and even as a siren call to decolonisation.

In the House of Commons in April 1942, Commander Robert Bower, Member of Parliament (MP) for Cleveland, had asked the government whether it was 'aware that ... this greatest of all military disasters ... would appear, as far as the public can see, to be largely due to the worst strategy since Ethelred the Unready'.[40] Lord Davies told the House of Lords that:

> This is one of the greatest disasters, if not the greatest in our military annals. Compared with the disaster at Singapore, the disasters in the past, especially our failures in the Dardenelles and in Mesopotamia during the last war all sink into insignificance. There is a consensus of opinion in regard to this point.[41]

But public opinion went beyond blaming Churchill and his military advisers, to question the performance of the whole colonial and defensive set-up in the East. Confidential reports compiled weekly by the British Ministry of Information revealed:

> A feeling ... which, though not applying in the case of those who have relatives among the Forces or the residents in the East, appears to be characteristic of the attitude of many people to the situation in the Far East as a whole. They are said to 'dissociate themselves entirely from it,

and take the line that "it serves them right", meaning by this that the white men, and our administration out there'. With the Fall of Singapore, the 'more thoughtful' are said to realise that 'the unchallenged prestige of the white man in the East has gone for ever'.[42]

This image of the Singapore campaign soon affected veterans in Britain as well as opinion in Australia. While other British failures became focused around symbols of defiance, such as the evacuation from Dunkirk in June 1940, the defeat in Singapore was recognised for what it was: a disaster.

As a result, the feelings of many veterans in the postwar years included resentment at seeming tainted by this. W.S. Kent-Hughes, Quarter Master General of the Australian Imperial Force in Malaya in 1941–2, wrote to the London *Times* in July 1947 that: 'I was astounded, when I was in England last December to find that a dark cloud of suspicion still enveloped the survivors of Singapore'. He remarked on the feeling that veterans of the Malayan campaign were not accorded the recognition for their bravery that veterans of equally disastrous campaigns had been given by the British public. The only difference between the heroes of Dunkirk, and the victims at Singapore, he felt, was that in Singapore men fought longer, in harder conditions.[43]

He therefore argued that blame seemed to attach to the defenders partly because 'Singapore had been advertised for so long as an "impregnable fortress" that the uninitiated believed it was'. By implication, its disastrously rapid fall must have been due, at least in part, to the incompetence of its defenders.[44]

British veterans of the campaign continued to feel that this cast a pall over their reputation.[45] On the twenty-fifth anniversary of the Fall of Singapore in 1967, Lieutenant-Colonel Denis Russell-Roberts tearfully explained to television cameras that:

> ... the vast majority of us felt that the campaign in Malaya had been bearable. The imprisonment of 3.5 years under the Japanese had also been bearable. But we felt that what was unbearable was the odium that was thrown in our faces by far too many people in this country when we came back at the end of it all ... .[46]

These feelings persisted even fifty years after the Fall, only to be inflamed again in 1992 by an outburst by Paul Keating, then Prime Minister of Australia. When, on 27 February 1992, Keating told the Australian parliament that Britain had 'decided not to defend the Malaysian peninsula, not to worry about Singapore', it was British veterans who seemed most upset.[g]

---

g Keating's comments came in for heavy criticism from British newspapers, including the *Sun*'s epithet that he was 'The Lizard of Oz'. These also came after Mrs Keating declined to curtsey to the visiting Queen earlier in February, and her husband had put his arm around the monarch to guide her through a crowded function room. The British press had then used the headline: 'Hands off Cobber!'.

Keating had been attempting to re-stoke the fires of Australian nationalism over the Fall of Singapore.[47] The next day Keating explained that he made his comments to demonstrate that 'we have to be aggressively Australian, wholeheartedly Australian, proud of it', and not 'some sort of cultural derivative of Britain. It's finished. It's over'. He made it clear that he was attacking, not the British veterans, but 'just the throw-backs who still inhabit some of the cracks and crevices of the British ...' and the Anglophile Australians who still 'tug the forelock to the British establishment'.[48]

Keating's outburst should be placed the context of British failure to provide the ships or aircraft Malaya had needed, this despite Australia regarding Malaya as its forward defence.[49]

Whatever the assumptions behind Keating's rhetoric, his statements stirred up emotions. Ex-servicemen such as Ken Joyce regarded them as 'an insult to the memories of the thousands of British servicemen who along with Australian and Dutch forces, were killed or suffered as POWs during the Malayan campaign in 1941–42'. Cyril Entwistle, an eighty-year-old former Grenadier Guard who was vice-patron of the British Ex-Services Club in Sydney, said that 'thousands of British servicemen fought in the Asian theatre of operation and for Mr Keating to say they abandoned Australia was simply not true'. He added, that 'for him to say otherwise insults the memories of those British servicemen who died or were captured and suffered at the hands of the Japanese'.[50]

British veterans may have felt they were being blamed all over again when, in early 1993, the British Public Record Office released secret reports on the Fall of Singapore. Reports by military commanders such as Sir Archibald Wavell, Commander-in-Chief, South West Pacific and Sir Geoffrey Layton, Commander-in-Chief of the Eastern Fleet. These had been kept back fifty years, rather than the customary thirty, precisely because their frank criticisms of all involved were judged sensitive.

Layton's summary contained the hurtful comment that 'man for man, our men were inferior to the Japanese in training and in the moral qualities of audacity, tenacity, discipline and devotion'. Harold Payne, President of the Far Eastern Prisoner of War Association, spoke for many veterans when he said that they had been through this type of post mortem before. Payne commented that 'there are some who feel bitter and they are entitled to feel bitter. And I would be a liar if I said I wasn't suffering today – in one way we all are. But there we are. It was just a chapter of accidents'.[51]

The 'great betrayal' of Australia

For Australian veterans, there was at least the possibility of deflecting blame onto the 'mother country', and continuing the Gallipoli model of contrasting Australian élan, an irreverent sense of independence, and the belief 'that Jack is not only as good as his master but better' with British bumbling, class-ridden structures, and spit and polish.[52]

More than this, however, the notion that Britain had let Australia down fuelled Australian nationalism. In 1942, confidential British reports revealed a widespread belief that the Fall of Singapore might lead Australia to leave the British Empire.[53] British colonial officials in Australia wrote to London 'warning of the possible boost to Australian nationalism caused by Britain's failure to defend the Dominion'.

Then came hints from Britain, in January 1942, that reinforcements might be directed away from Singapore and towards areas such as Burma. This set alarm bells ringing in Australia. The Australian government cabled Churchill on 23 January 1942 with a stark message: any failure to defend Singapore to the end would be seen as 'an inexcusable betrayal'.[54]

Partly as a result of Australia's position, more men were pumped into Singapore. When the Island fell despite this, Australia's popular poet Dame Mary Gilmore (1865–1962) captured the mood of many Australians in her poem 'Singapore'. The title Dame Mary Gilmore had intended, 'General Bennett and his True Men', better captured its sense of national heroism, and of the bitterness of the Australians' fate:[55]

> They grouped together about their chief,
> And each one looked at his mate
> Ashamed to think that Australian men
> Should meet such a bitter fate!
> And black was the wrath in each hot heart
> And savage oaths they swore
> As they thought of how they had all been ditched
> By 'Impregnable' Singapore!

Mary Gilmore was particularly caustic on the British establishment:

> Whose was the fault she betrayed our troops?
> Whose was the fault she failed?
> Ask it of those who slaughtered the flag
> That once to the mast was nailed.
> Tell them we'll raise it on Anzac soil
> With hearts that are steeled to the core
> We swear by our dead and captive sons
> Revenge for Singapore![56]

Even after the editor's intervention, leading to the addition of that last, heroic and hopeful stanza, the tone of bitterness lingered. Nor was it confined to the pages of journals. John Curtin told a visiting journalist that the ashtrays of the Prime Minister's office were made from the HMAS *Australia*, the only battleship the country ever had.[57] The Australian government had sunk HMAS *Australia* off Sydney Heads on 12 April 1924, in compliance with the Washington Naval

Conference limitations on British warships (the Australian Navy then being judged a part of the British fleet).[58] In fact, the decision to mothball HMAS *Australia* had been taken just before, partly because it was slow, but that failed to rob the story of its power.[59] As late as the 1980s, the University of Queensland history lecturer Charles Grimshaw, himself a Second World War veteran, would recall HMAS *Australia* to undergraduates, as a symbol of Australia's commitment to supporting British strategies.

Whether Britain had betrayed Australia by sending Antipodean forces to the Middle East, and not sending the promised fleet to Singapore in return, or Australia had betrayed itself by over-reliance on the mother country, and on strategies it knew to be fatally flawed, the moral remained the same. Australia needed to be more assertive of its separate identity and interests.[60]

In this context, it is not surprising that initial thoughts that all troops must have performed badly at Singapore, in order to lose an 'impregnable fortress', were soon replaced by an emphasis on Australian difference. War stories presented to the Australian public increasingly came to conform to the pre-existing Anzac myth, the notion formed in the First World War that Australian soldiers were better than their counterparts fighting at Gallipoli. They were held to have been superior in physique, character and fighting qualities, partly because of a 'rugged' character formed in the Australian climate, partly because their very 'colonial' nature made them less respectful of pointless authority. This image was now applied to Singapore, and there gradually arose an understanding that Australians in particular, if not quite Australian soldiers alone, had put up effective resistance to the Japanese in 1942.

First, however, this version had to displace earlier misgivings that perhaps all the soldiers must have done a poor job in losing an 'impregnable fortress'. One Australian serving on a British corvette, HMS *Aster*, wrote in his diary on 1 March 1942 that he had: 'Heard about Singapore and the daffodils (nice but yellow!) as they call those who made a discreet bolt before the Japs got too close'.[61]

As late as August 1942, an article by Keith Murdoch in the Melbourne *Herald*, while praising the vast majority of Australian soldiers, warned that hard lessons had to be learnt. Chief amongst these was that the 'distorted tradition of the last war, that discipline is not necessary to attain high fighting value', had to be abandoned. The article argued that:

> Our own [Australian] part was marred by a constant jarring and belittling of our British and Indian comrades, by inadequate discipline, and, finally, by the percentage of weak and undisciplined soldiers breaking down under the strain of battle.[62]

The Murdoch article had considerable impact within Australia. David Sissons, then a schoolboy in Melbourne, and later a fellow studying Japan–Australian relations at the Australian National University, recalls sixty years after the Fall of Singapore: 'I remember our History teacher discussing it with us in class on the Monday morning following. Murdoch was then, I think, Chairman of Directors of the *Herald* and it was only on rare occasions that he filed an article'.[63]

Even before Murdoch's article, veterans were writing in their defence. Gilbert Mant, an Australian soldier and later a journalist in the Malayan campaign, started the ball rolling. He had himself escaped from Singapore before it fell, and published *Grim Glory* in July 1942. Mant concentrated not so much on the fall of the island, as on Australian troops' successful performance on the Malayan mainland, in Johore. He highlighted the Australians' retreat from Muar, culminating with their tenacious breakout from Japanese encirclement at Parit Sulong.[h] Others concentrated on the ambush of the Japanese at Gemencheh (just north of Gemas). These stories were designed to counter the impression then abroad in Australia, as well as in Britain, that the troops defending Singapore had not 'put up a fight'.[64]

Lieutenant-General H. Gordon Bennett, the commander of the Australian 8th Division in the Malayan campaign, also contributed to this trend. Bennett was a controversial figure. Though his men had fought well in Johore, and were ordered by him to stand fast at the surrender, he himself slipped quietly out of Singapore on the night of 15 to 16 February, without authorisation from above. Returning to Australia that same month, he publicly criticised Indian and British soldiers, as well as their leaders, in often caustic remarks.[65]

This 'Grim Glory' version was further cemented by the postwar accounts of Australian authors who had been Malayan POWs. One such work was a book by Russell Braddon, which appeared on the tenth anniversary of the Fall of Singapore, in February 1952. In 1952 Braddon took Churchill's expression that Singapore was 'a naked island' and invested it with Australian sarcasm and humour, calling his book, *The Naked Island*. The book's title phrase had been used the year before by Churchill, in Volume 4 of his *The Second World War*, entitled the *Hinge of Fate*. Braddon's work soon became a best seller in Australia as well as Britain.

Many British commentators were not amused. One review in Singapore's pro-colonial newspaper, the *Straits Times* replied with its own brand of sarcasm:

> Discussing the Malayan campaign, Mr. Braddon disparages nearly everybody who was in a position of authority and, with that wisdom that comes after the event creates the impression that it would have been better for the security of Malaya if 20-year-old Gunner Braddon had had General Gordon Bennett's command.[66]

---

h The remants of two Australian battalions and some Indian troops met Japanese blocking a bridge at Parit Sulong, on the retreat from Muar. After all attempts to break through failed, they dispersed through the jungle on 22 January, many making it to Singapore to fight again. The wounded who were left behind, more than 140, were massacred in retaliation for the heavy toll the Japanese had suffered.

Whatever the merits of Braddon's book, it is a good example of how some Australians came to see themselves as the victims of a British disaster, and as having been surrounded by the incompetent and the ineffective. Braddon went so far as to portray Indian soldiers as not just hopelessly young and untrained, but cowardly too.[67] He seemed to have forgotten that every nation had its heroes as well as its villains, with determined Indian and British defence at places such as Kampar.

Braddon thus continued the emerging Australian tradition of emphasising their stand in Johore, as opposed to previous British and Indian failures. The heroics of the successful ambush at Gemencheh, of Australian anti-tank gunners taking out several tanks a time in successive engagements at Gemas and on the retreat from Muar, and of the breakout from Japanese encirclement at Parit Sulong, continued to provide the emotional focus for Australian accounts. In 1957, the official Australian war history, by Lionel Wigmore, confirmed this trend with its descriptions of the retreat from Muar. Wigmore did not avoid sensitive topics, even devoting a moderate amount of space to the issue of deserters and stragglers at Singapore. But when he came to describe the Johore battles, the old journalist in him (in 1941-42 he had also covered the Malayan campaign for the Australian Army) waxed lyrical.[68]

Wigmore described how, when a Japanese roadblock halted the retreat from Muar on 20 January, at a point just beyond Bakri:

> [Lieutenant-Colonel] Anderson[i] there decided that a rapid and spirited assault was necessary to gain space, and he ordered [Lieutenant F.G.] Beverley to lead his men singing into the struggle. This he did, and these were the words they sang:
>
>> 'Once a jolly swagman camped by a billabong
>> Under the shade of a coolibah tree ...'
>
> 'Waltzing Matilda', never sung by Australians with more enthusiasm than when they meet in surroundings strange to them, had become a battle song.[69]

In this way, Australians were presented with a campaign about which they had much to be proud, and little to be ashamed.[70]

Thus armed, Australians could remember their part in the battle, and the resulting three and a half years of captivity, with less of the ambivalence experienced by British veterans. Theirs could be a story of 'grim glory' in battle, followed by 'mateship' in captivity.[71]

Perhaps this is one reason why Australians began to commemorate 15 February in public soon after the war. Veterans gathered every year, on

---

i Lt-Col Charles Anderson, commanding the Australian 2/19 Battalion, was leading remants of the 2/29 bn, 2/19 bn, and Indians. He came to Australia from Cape Town in 1934, having served in the Kings African Rifles in the First World War, and having led big game hunting afterwards. He was awarded a Victoria Cross for his part in the Parit Sulong breakout. Beverley was leading A Company of the 2/19 battalion, Warren, *Singapore 1942*, pp. 166 and 168.

15 February, at the Cenotaph in Martin Place, Sydney. Soon the participants at these services swelled to several hundred, complete with an army band marching off to the strains of 'Waltzing Matilda'.[72]

Then a few veterans began to commemorate their experiences by revisiting Singapore as well, with the 15 February anniversary again becoming a favoured date. In time, some of these trips began to take the form of organised tours. On the twenty-fifth anniversary in 1967, veterans and wives returned, revisiting local people who had helped them during the war.[73] Larger groups made the journey in the 1970s and 1980s. At the fiftieth anniversary in 1992, Australian veterans were by far the largest contingent at ceremonies marking the Fall of Singapore. Over 1,000 Australian veterans returned on 15 February, while there were just 500 Singaporean veterans and 300 British. Veterans' relatives starting making similar journeys too, often culminating at the Commonwealth war memorial at Kranji, or at Changi.[74]

On the fiftieth anniversary in 1992, the editor of the *Australian* summed up continuing Australian feelings when he wrote:

> The fall of Singapore marked a pivotal moment in our history. It signalled the effective end of British imperial power in Asia and the eventual emergence of Asian nationhood. The debacle irrevocably altered our ties with Britain and placed us on the path to independence. Its consequences would change the very face of our nation.[75]

The following year, in 1993, this Australian view of their role as victims of British failure, and of this helping to sever the umbilical cord to the 'mother' country, received a momentary setback. The cause of this jolt was the release, by the British Public Record Office, of a secret report which had been made in 1942, under Wavell's name. The report contained the sort of retrospective opinions from survivors that one might have expected a commander to forward to his superiors. Unfortunately, much of the opinion made for uncomfortable reading in Canberra and Melbourne. In comments that appeared to reveal the dark other side of the Australian self-image as individualistic diggers, who disdained pointless authority, it evoked a picture of indiscipline, desertion and even rape. One summary of 'common views' concluded that, 'For the Fall of Singapore itself, the Australians are held responsible'. Elphick's book, *Singapore: The Pregnable Fortress* then developed this into the argument that the Australians were largely responsible for the final collapse of morale.[j]

---

[j] This quotation, and other criticisms, appear in Elphick, *Singapore: The Impregnable Fortress*, pp. 437–51, 464–71. But Elphick makes it appear as if Wavell himself believed that 'There can only be one deduction. ... For the Fall of Singapore itself, the Australians are held responsible'. In fact the most damaging phrases come from an appendix on 'Some common criticisms', first collated in a May 1942 report. The report added that, 'In justice ... it must be recognised that they were subjected ... to a bombardment which, judged by the standards of any theatre of war ... [was] very heavy'.

The Australian response came in two forms. On an academic level, scholars pointed out that the Australian troops concerned included several thousand barely trained reinforcements. As for the rest, they had been very badly served by the top command, subjected to some of the heaviest bombardment on the island, and found themselves heavily outnumbered by the initial Japanese attack on Singapore.

Far from turning tail and running at, or even before, first contact, they also suffered disproportionately high casualties. The Australian 8th Division suffered 1,789 killed, almost 10 per cent of slightly less than 18,500 men. Four of the Australian battalions suffered casualties at a level similar to the most active and effective of British units: the 2nd Argyll and Sutherland Highlanders.[76]

It is not unusual for a proportion of troops put under such pressure to turn into stragglers and even deserters, and this happened to British troops too. The defence was, in sum, that the Australians had been better in Johore and no worse than anyone else on Singapore, where desertion was a consequence not a cause of defeat.[77]

The second form of response was more robust. It was hinted that perhaps the release of the British documents was retaliation for the Australian Prime Minister Paul Keating's comments of February 1992, when Keating had claimed that Britain had decided, in 1942, 'not to defend the Malaysian peninsula, not to worry about Singapore and not to give us our troops back'.[78] We have already seen how controversial these comments were even in Australia. Political opponents retorted that Keating had 'gone off his rocker'. The President of the Returned Services League, Alf Garland, said 'He's just flipped his lid'. But for a few at least Keating's accusations still smacked of the truth, and for these the British release of documents so soon afterwards, in 1993 looked like retaliation.[79] In 1994 Ray Connolly and Bob Wilson, veterans of the Australian 8th Division, gave full vent to the anger and dismay some felt as a result, when they published their book:

Cruel Britannia
Britannia Waives the Rules 1941–42
Singapore Betrayed
Australia Abandoned
(Wavell's Bogus Report Debunked)[80]

The controversy then died down a little, in the media at any rate. But as ever with the Fall of Singapore, it only needed another key anniversary to reawaken the issues, and this turned out to be the sixtieth anniversary of the Fall of Singapore, in February 2002.

Newspapers inevitably marked the occasion with reflective articles. The Brisbane *Courier-Mail* featured a piece by military historian Peter Charlton. He led with the subtitle: 'Despite the valour of an Australian officer and his men, in 1942 Singapore fell to the Japanese'.[81] Television also got in on the act, with the

Plate 6.1 An Australian flag flutters by one of the gravestones at the Kranji War Memorial, Singapore, 15 February 2002.

Source: The Kranji Memorial stands close to the sites in the north and northwest where two Brigades of Australians faced the Japanese onslaught on 8 to 9 February 1942.

Australian current affairs television series *Four Corners*, choosing to re-examine Elphick's claims.

Had there had been large-scale Australian desertion in Singapore, which might undermine claims of Australian exceptionalism in the campaign? The programme, called *No Prisoners*, opened with shots of British veterans talking about Australian desertion, even saying that Australians had scrambled to get on boats ahead of women and children. But it went on to suggest that the main allegations were those of one English historian (Peter Elphick), who had not checked his facts properly. His principal sin appeared to be that he had named Australian 'deserters', without attempting to check their version of events. As a parting shot, it showed one escapee from Singapore selling flowers for charity, and veterans in front of their homes. It was wrong, claimed the programme, to blame the individuals for the sins of their leaders.[82]

Australian responses to the programme at its website forum clearly indicated that it had struck a chord. Many respondents could not accept that Australian soldiers would desert in numbers, although they acknowledged that British and Indians did. One respondent even relabelled someone who had left Singapore on 12 February 'a true Aussie hero' for his later acts and suffering.[83]

Perhaps this reflected a belief that 'desertion' is by definition cowardly – rather than a technical matter of deliberately going absent without leave in battle. Perhaps it also reflected a feeling that choosing to leave a Singapore doomed by 'the downright incompetence of political and military leaders', especially British who had withheld vital equipment, could be a brave and nationalistic attempt to live to fight another day. Why sacrifice good men 'on the altar of stupidity and inefficiency [?]' ...[84] Or perhaps the Anzac myth was still at work for some Australians, playing a role at the core of their definition of Australian nationhood.

There were a few respondents who suggested a different interpretation, that perhaps Australians had been no worse, but also no better, than other nationalities. After all, even the 8th Australian Division's Provost Company reported that, by 12 February 'Soldiers [in the town] ... are so numerous that it is very difficult to collect and return them', though it also noted that there were at least as many British and Indians. For 13 February it confirmed that Australian soldiers were 'very reluctant to return to the line' complaining there was no organisation there. A senior Australian officer later estimated of his countrymen that 'only two-thirds at most of those fit to fight were manning the final perimeter'.[85] More to the point, many of the British who criticised the Australians did so with an air of puzzlement, not vitriol. One Malayan businessman who criticised them said they had been 'far superior' when he fought with them in the last war.[86]

A balanced conclusion would probably be that such desertion was a cause rather than a consequence of defeat, and afflicted all forces, but that the Australians may have been amongst the worst offenders, if only because they were hit first and hardest by the Japanese assault on Singapore. Whether, as Murdoch's 1942 article seemed to hint, the Anzac myth itself, with its stress on egalitarianism and disrespect for authority as well as its innate scepticism of British command, contributed to the final scenes, remains a far more difficult question.[87]

Against this background, one participant in the Internet discussion which followed the *Four Corners* programme suggested the whole debate was outmoded, and that Australia should have outgrown the Anzac myth and its use of events such as the Fall of Singapore for nationalist purposes:

> The Anzac legend was promoted in the early 1900s to give us some sort of identity that we could project to the world to give us some status ...

I think we have progressed past just this legend to being well regarded in other areas too. Along with Anzac we now have our indigenous culture and multiculturalism and women and kids. We also had/have our bush image too. The reflecting of history has moved away from it all being about hero images to now also telling the stories too of 'ordinary people' ... in sometimes extraordinary situations.[88]

But this remained a minority view, aired without being embraced. For most Australians, including both veterans and the general public, the Fall of Singapore continued to be seen as a story of 'Grim Glory' in the face of British failure, the departure point for a growing sense of independence, and the location for the acting out of 'Anzac' exceptionalism in Malaya.

Removing the symbols of the impregnable fortress

The Australian understanding that the debacle at Singapore was not their fault, that they were brave victims, even that the event reaffirmed their uniqueness and national character, all made commemoration a less painful process. The Australians even sought to secure relics which would keep alive the memory of 15 February 1942. In 1946 the Australians acquired, and had sent back to Canberra, the table at which Percival surrendered to Yamashita at the Ford Motor Factory in the Bukit Timah area of Singapore. It has remained ever since in the Australian War Memorial. For some reason, the Australians forgot the chairs that went with it. Even then, however, the British showed little interest. Instead, these chairs now form part of Singapore's own waxworks exhibition of the 1942 surrender, housed at the 'Images of Singapore' exhibition on Sentosa.

This contrast in attitude to the remains of the day is telling, and extended to the relics of the 'impregnable fortress' itself. The colonial authorities seemed only too happy to have these removed from the landscape.

Despite their undoubted historic value, all the 15 inch guns, Singapore's largest coastal defence pieces, were allowed to vanish. Their fate contrasted with that of guns which remain untainted by Singapore's infamy. Two naval 15 inch guns, from ships which had fought at Normandy and in the Mediterranean, were placed outside London's Imperial War Museum, which they still guard today.

In the case of Singapore, however, the massive 15 inch guns had become symbols of failure. Again, images of 'impregnable' Singapore, hawked about in the final days before December 1941, came back to haunt British authorities and veterans. Before the war, the 15 inch guns had been labelled by the British press as 'monster guns': 'the greatest artillery pieces in the world'.[89] After the war, the equally false myth that 'they were pointed the wrong way' had spread so widely that their ruins became an embarrassment.

Initially, a postwar report recommended restoring many of the 6 inch guns and even a 9.2 inch battery at Blakang Mati.[90] But little came of this. Anyway, the age of the battleship was over, so there was little hope of the 15 inch guns being resurrected. In July and August 1948 the barrel of the only surviving 15 inch gun at Changi was cut up for scrap metal. A concrete underground bunker of one of the 15 inch guns was also destroyed, making way for a new runway for the Changi Royal Air Force Base. The Singapore colonial press reported this under the title 'Changi Gun Aids UK Recovery: Scrap Metal Goes to Britain':

> Working on cutting up the gun took over a month. It yielded two hundred tons of metal. The Japanese having previously removed a hundred tons by hand-cutting burners. ...
>
> The gun ... was cut into pieces by oxy-acetylene burners and loaded into the freighter *Atreus* at the Naval Base, now an important outpost in Britain's scrap metal campaign.[91]

This 15 inch gun had belonged to the Johore Battery, and was one of the last to remain *in situ*.[92] In 1951 what remained of the Buona Vista Battery was also sent to the United Kingdom, to share its predecessor's fate as scrap metal.[93]

The Changi murals: 'fortitude in a time of adversity'

For the British, the guns, and their association with the myth of British ordnance and commanders facing the wrong way, were best forgotten. When the British sought for relics which would allow them to remember, they needed sites which spoke of sorrow, and of triumph over adversity. This they found in graves and in prisons.

It was prisoner of war camps, Changi in particular, which caught the British imagination. This was hardly surprising, since for most allied troops their main experience had been not the campaign, which lasted a mere seventy days, but being prisoners of the Japanese. Books and war diaries written by troops frequently devoted just a few pages or chapters to the battles, but many more on their captivity.[94] Changi, and the much worse conditions on the Burma–Siam railway, made famous by the film 'The Bridge over the River Kwai', dominated public imagination. Returning POWs also took to revisiting Changi prison, and soon a new chapel there, first opened for convicts in 1953, came to be used by veterans and ex-internees to mark their respects. By 1956 this postwar chapel had been designated a memorial to the wartime prisoners.[95]

This need to channel wartime memories and events was not lost on one of the biggest groups in Singapore who needed a way of remembering without losing face: the British armed forces. Singapore was restored as a British main base after the Second World War, with the numbers of British servicemen swelling to tens of thousands for the Malayan Emergency (1948–60) and the Confrontation with Indonesia (1963–7). British servicemen and their families, whether based in Singapore or in Britain, needed an emotional focus for 1942.

Plate 6.2 Changi chapel. A replica in the style of the original outdoor, wooden chapels which prisoners built at Changi POW camp.

Source: Hack and Blackburn.

The solution the armed forces settled on was to remember the Fall of Singapore as a time of adversity. Adversity through which, by 'fortitude' and ingenuity, British men and women had come through. On the first postwar anniversary of the Fall of Singapore the editor of Singapore's *Straits Times* wrote that: 'in retrospect, the gloom of February 15 is pierced by the shining light of those countless examples of one of the finest of human qualities, fortitude in the face of adversity'.[96]

This need to create a positive story meant that, while the military hardware which had failed was cut up or neglected, the British armed forces looked instead for relics which could produce pride rather than pathos. They were not to be disappointed.

Plate 6.3 Changi prison.
Source: Hack and Blackburn.

Most of the Second World War chapels constructed by POWs at Changi, some very crude structures, had been destroyed in the clean-up after the war. Only one had been saved, when an Australian asked if he could arrange for it to be removed. That one went back to Australia, where for many years it languished in a basement, before finally being resurrected and reassembled at the Military College in Duntroon in the 1980s.

It seemed as if the British forces had totally destroyed this part of Changi's heritage. But, unknown to most people, one chapel still stood. This was the Chapel of St Luke, housed in the old Roberts Army Barracks. In it were the remains of five life-size murals, paintings of scenes from the New Testament. These had been painted in 1942–3, on the walls of Block 151, which was then serving as a dysentery wing.

Their painter was one Stanley Warren: Bombardier in the Field Artillery and at the time a POW in the sprawling complex that was Changi prisoner of war camp. This was the same Stanley Warren who the Japanese had put to work building access roads for their own *Syonan Chureito* in 1942. Stanley Warren began to paint the murals in the same year and, struggling against dysentery, just managed to complete the Nativity scene in time for Christmas. The rest of the murals may even have saved his life, since he was kept on to finish them while others went to the more deadly Burma–Siam railway.

The spirit of the murals soared above the circumstances of their creation. For Stanley Warren, surrounded by death in the hospital block, painted them to

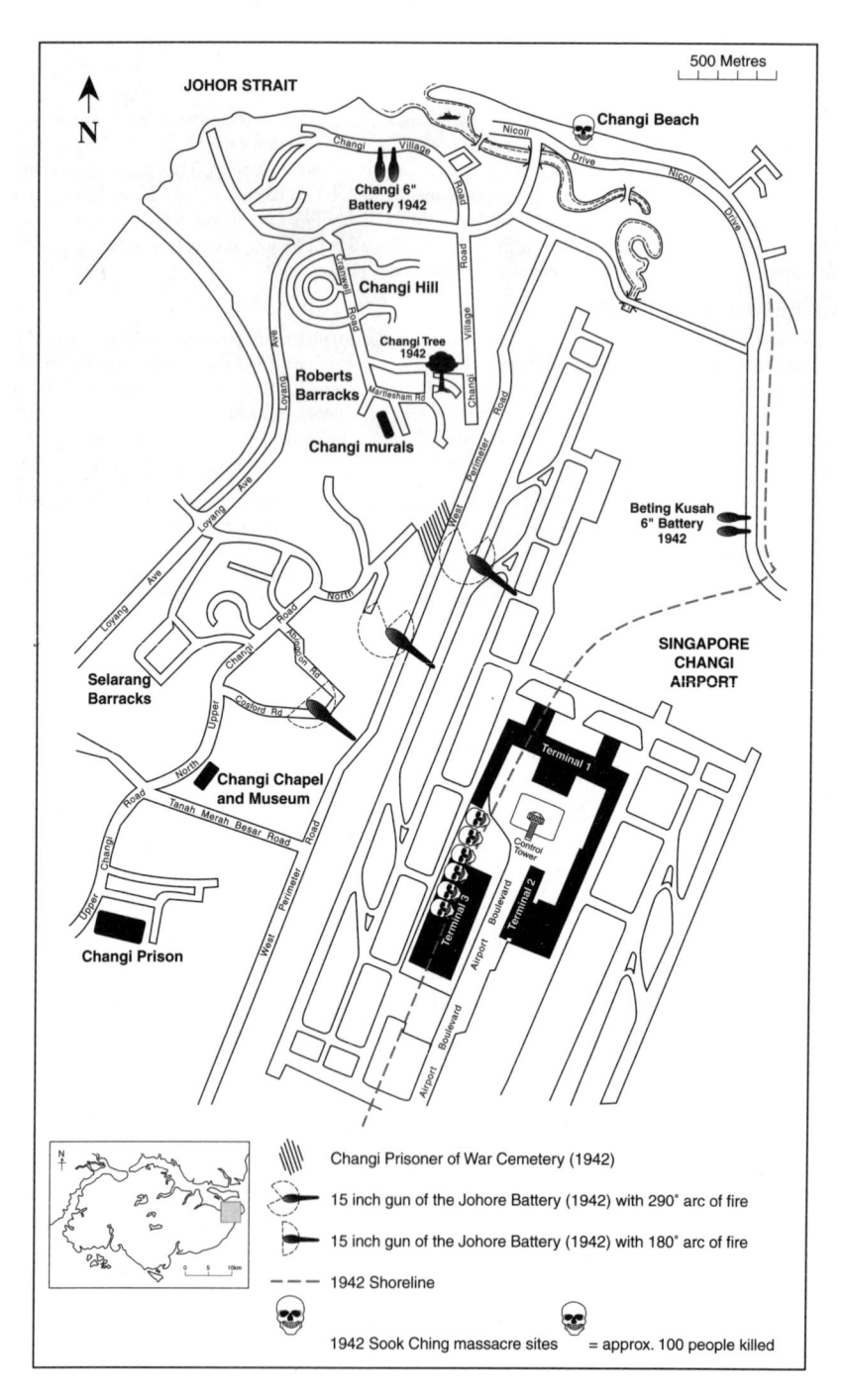

Map 6.1 The Changi historic area.

Map 6.1 Notes

The big guns
All that remains of Johore Battery's three 15 inch guns is the underground ammunition bunker of one. Ironically, the gun at this site was the only one of the three that could not fire landward. This gun had a seaward firing arc of 180. The other two guns were on naval-type mountings. They could and did fire at the Japanese. Johore Battery was supported by smaller 6 inch gun batteries near Changi Village and at Beting Kusah. All these batteries were directed by Changi Fire Command, which was on top of Changi Hill. In February 2002, the Singapore Tourism Board built a same-size replica of Singapore's 15 inch guns above the ruins of the remaining ammunition bunker.

The Changi tree
Near these guns stood the 'Changi tree'. At 76 metres tall, this *Sindora* (Sepitir) tree towered above the surrounding landscape, and was even marked on maps.[97] In February 1942 the British blew the top off it, in order to deprive the Japanese of a landmark. In February 2001, the Singapore Tourism Board planted a small sapling at the opening of the new Changi Chapel and Museum, a new 'Changi tree'. This new tree was of the *Chengai* (Balanocarpus) species, which gave its name to the area.

The Sook Ching
There are two documented *Sook Ching* massacre sites in the Changi Historic Area. On the evening of 20 February 1942 Japanese troops took about seventy Chinese men out to Changi Beach and shot them at the water's edge. Four survived because they were thought to be dead, and were able to flee later. When POWs from Changi were ordered to dispose of the bodies the next day, they found another Chinese man alive and smuggled him out of the area.

At Tanah Merah Besar Beach, on which Changi Airport is built, Chua Choon Guan and Cheng Kwang Yu have described between 400 to 600 Chinese being machine gunned by the Japanese at low tide on the evening of 22 February 1942. These survivors testified at 1947 war crimes trials that they had survived because there were too many victims for the Japanese to be able to bayonet all, in order to check that they were dead. The Japanese are rumoured to have returned every evening for next three days to machine gun more Chinese.

The prison and POWs
Changi Prison was built in 1936 to hold 600 prisoners. From 1942 to 1944, about 3,000 civilian internees were housed there. The POWs were held nearby, in former barracks. The Australian POWs were stationed in Selarang Barracks and the British in Roberts Barracks, both now used by the Singapore Armed Forces. Only in May 1944 would the POWs move into Changi prison, and even then they were also housed in huts outside the prison walls. The old Changi prison is scheduled to be demolished, to make way by 2008 for new, high-rise buildings able to hold 23,000 prisoners.

The POW cemetery
In 1942, a POW cemetery was created between Selarang and Roberts Barracks. After the war, it was moved to Kranji, due to the building of Changi RAF airport. It is now part of the Kranji War Memorial.

The murals
The British POW Stanley Warren painted the Changi murals between 1942 and 1943, in an indoor chapel in the hospital wing of Roberts Barracks. These depictions of New Testament images were restored by Warren when he visited Singapore in 1963, 1982, and 1988.

The chapels
There were also outdoor chapels created by the POWs, but all were destroyed or removed after the war. Instead, a postwar chapel in the prison came to be used by returning veterans and their families from the 1950s. When visits inside a maximum security prison were deemed impractical, the Singapore Tourism Board built a representation of the wartime wooden chapels and a small museum. These were placed just outside the gates of Changi prison in February 1988. The Changi chapel and museum moved to a new location in February 2001, because of commencement of work for the new Changi prison.

illustrate a common sense of humanity. One he felt shared by all, including his Japanese captors.

The Changi murals were now set to become a part of the military heritage of the British armed forces. In the late 1940s, when the room was being used as a store and the pictures had been partly whitewashed over, they were known to a limited number. Even then, some new arrivals were told their moral was 'the triumph of good over evil'. James Lowe, a young airman, who arrived at Changi base in December 1948, recalled that, 'we were told the wartime history ... and never to forget the terrible happenings there, we were then shown the murals, by which I was really moved'.[98]

In the late 1950s the British armed forces 'rediscovered' the murals. Recognising the power of the images, they sought to restore the Chapel of St Luke. They tracked Warren down in Britain, and brought him back to Singapore to restore them. In December 1963 he restored three scenes: the Ascension; the Last Supper; and the Crucifixion, in what was to be the first of several trips back to Singapore, stretching into the 1980s.[99]

A pamphlet was written in the late 1960s, to be given to visitors to the restored pictures. This emphasised the 'sacred' nature of the restored images, but in contrast to Stanley Warren's original purpose, it also drew a contrast between British fortitude and Japanese persecution:

> The Murals, now restored are visited by many who come to Changi. Some see them and recapture the grim days of the occupation when they were themselves prisoners at Changi. Others see them as a reminder of the faith and courage, which overcame evil and enabled them to survive it. For all who take the opportunity to see the Murals there is one enduring message of the victory of the powers of light over those of darkness.[100]

Whether young servicemen of the era fully understood Warren's wider message, of the existence of a common humanity, is not clear. Hopefully today's visitors, whether to the originals, or to the copies in the new Changi Museum and replica Chapel (opened in 2001) may notice the message in Warren's detail. His three wise men, who offer gifts in the Nativity scene, represent three racial groups: European, Middle Eastern, and Oriental. His crucifixion scene bears the telling caption, 'Father forgive them. They know not what they do.'[101]

Kranji: the British Empire's memorial to the fallen

The Changi murals continue to inspire, but their impact is individual, almost personal between painting and observer. As time went on and Singapore became convulsed with strikes and nationalist ferment in the 1950s, the British needed something on a bigger scale, a new location to remember their fallen. The old cenotaph was not ideal for this. It was located near the mouth of the

Plate 6.4 The Changi murals: 'Father forgive them'.
Source: Hack and Blackburn.

Plate 6.5 The Changi murals: 'Peace on earth'.
Source: Hack and Blackburn.

Singapore River, the *Padang*, and so also close to Chinatown and to the 'Middle Road' headquarters of radical unions. In the new circumstances of the 1950s this would hardly do for large, and predominantly European, ceremonies. Nor was it a suitable place to inter the remains of large numbers of soldiers.

The preferred site for remembering the Fall of Singapore became instead the Kranji War Memorial. This was a cemetery in the northwest of Singapore, close to where the Japanese Imperial Guards had come ashore on 9 February 1942, to be met by Australian troops.

The war memorial there had humble origins. It originally hosted a small war cemetery, principally containing of the graves of 600 prisoners of war who had died in Changi and been buried in a cemetery nearby. As with the guns, however, progress overtook history. The construction of a new RAF runway at Changi in 1946 caused the cemetery to be moved to Kranji.

At first, makeshift wooden crosses were used to mark the new graves, but British officials worried that Christian crosses might one day become targets for anti-colonial sentiment. The Imperial War Graves officers therefore used square stone slabs on which the cross was imbedded, making it less noticeable.[102] They also had a main war memorial built, and inscribed it with the names of soldiers of the British Empire who had died in the war against Japan.

The British decided to solve the problem of embarrassing anniversaries by unveiling this memorial on a neutral date. On 2 March 1957, the Kranji War Memorial was dedicated before a crowd of 3,000 members of the armed services and relatives of the war dead.[k][103]

The Kranji memorial has since retained its force as a place for veterans to commemorate their fallen comrades, with ceremonies each 11 November. But in March 1957 things did not go entirely to script.

Large numbers of Chinese attended the dedication of the Kranji War Memorial, hoping to find the names of members of the Overseas Chinese Volunteers (Dalforce to the British) or of other local volunteers. The *Straits Times*' reported this, in a piece entitled '3 women weep – sentry faints'. It noted that 'while Chinese crowds searched the granite columns for the names of those who died in the Singapore Volunteer Corps, these three old women began a mournful wailing for their dead sons'.

Above all, the solemn ceremony at the Kranji War Memorial was upstaged by a lone Chinese woman. Madam Cheng Seang Ho. Madam Cheng, 81 years old, 'in a worn samfoo broke the ranks of the huge outdoor congregation in the middle of the Kranji War Memorial unveiling ceremony' and 'stumbled up to the Cross of Remembrance'. In front of twelve distinguished military and civilian officials of the British Empire, who were about to lay their official wreaths, Madam Cheng began to wail in memory of her dead husband.[104]

---

k Included were several hundred Australians, making what they called a 'pilgrimage' under Lt-Gen Gordon Bennett. Perhaps as a symbol of separate Australian identity, this group conducted their own ceremony at the same site the next day, in addition to the main event.

Madam Cheng and her husband had fought with the wartime Chinese volunteer unit: Dalforce. She had received a commendation for her bravery in the fight for Bukit Timah. Madam Cheng and her husband were described as being 'with the Chinese volunteer force in the last stand at Bukit Timah heights, firing their last shots at the enemy from behind shell-torn tree stumps'. The report added that 'with a handful of survivors [she] escaped through the jungle' while 'her husband slipped back into Singapore city'.[105] The Japanese later tracked down her husband. He became one of the many to die at the hands of the Japanese military police, the *Kempeitai*, one of those who, in Singaporean eyes, paid the 'The price of peace'.[106]

Now, in front of the crowd, 'she sobbed loudly and rocked her head in her hands'. It was reported that 'two men tried to draw her aside but it was not until Major-General J.F.D. Steedman, Director of the Imperial War Graves Commission, gently put his around her shoulder that she stopped weeping'.[107]

Between two empires: the people of Singapore remember 15 February 1942

The hungry ghosts of February 1942

Servicemen, or at least those who had fought in or with the armies of the British Empire, and including local people who had fought in the Malay States and Straits Settlements Volunteers, now had both monuments and days for commemoration.[1]

But the opening of the Kranji War Memorial in 1957 had emphasised that many of Singapore's population still did not have a focus for their grief. Yet far more civilians had perished at the hands of the Japanese in the first few weeks after Singapore's fall, than allied soldiers in the entire military campaign. The Japanese had lost around 3,500 killed, British imperial forces a little over 8,000. Sad as these figures were, they were but a semblance of local suffering.

The Japanese *Sook Ching*, the screening out of supposedly anti-Japanese male Chinese, had been ordered within three days of the Fall of Singapore. It commenced on 18 February, and did not end until March. Chinese sources have consistently claimed that 30,000 Chinese males living in Singapore were executed, and that if those executed 'up country' in Malaya are added 50,000 were slaughtered.[108]

---

1 The British theme of fortitude continues. On 15 Jan. 2002 Far East POW veterans helped unload sleepers from the Burma–Thailand railway in England. A month later, on 15 Feb. 2002 (the 60th Anniversary of the Fall) veterans' children helped to lay four rails onto these sleepers. So 30 metres of track now stands at the National Memorial Arboretum, Alrewas, in Staffordshire. Ex-POW Mr Roy Blackler told reporters: 'They say a man died for each sleeper. When I look back on those years, I don't thinks of the sleepers. I think of each man and friend who laid them ...' *Tamworth Herald News*, 17 Feb. 2002. The children and families of the Far East POWs (COFEPOW) started an appeal to erect a memorial building nearby.

For the Chinese of Singapore and Malaya, then, 15 February 1942 had a different emotional resonance. For them it marked not so much the fall of a fortress, the end of empire, or even the beginning of nationalism, as the beginning of suffering.

The victims' families must have hoped that they would achieve justice against the perpetrators, and with justice some small relief from their anguish. But the massacre trials which started in March 1947 and ended in April were to prove horribly inadequate to this need.

Just seven Japanese officers were tried, on the basis that they held most direct responsibility for the way 'screening' or the *Sook Ching* was executed, rather than merely 'following orders'. Of these, only two received the death sentence: two lives to balance at least 30,000 by Chinese reckoning, and 5,000 according to the prosecution's cautious accusation. Yet three Japanese had been sentenced to death the year before for the lesser crime of maltreating civilian internees in the war, and another twenty-one *Kempeitai for* torture. By comparison, the massacre trial seemed to deliver too little, to pay for the lives of too many. Lee Pei Ching, of the Chinese Women's Federation, demanded: 'We want a life for a life'.[109]

The need for catharsis remained. Almost immediately after the war, Chinese literature such as Miao Xiu's *Huolang* (Waves of fire) reflected the resulting feelings of loss, anger at Japanese cruelty, and concern with resistance and revenge.[110] At the same time, there was a need to mark the Fall of Singapore more publicly, to give a focus for remembering this pain and loss. Thus, at a time when the British authorities still looked askance at commemorating 15 February, some Chinese began to quietly mark the Fall and the *Sook Ching* through their own rituals.

For some at least, this need to mark the loss of disappeared relatives was given an extra edge by Taoist traditions. There has long existed a belief amongst adherents to Taoism concerning those who die violently, and do not receive ritual offerings of food at their graves from time to time. These people become 'hungry ghosts', who are released from hell during the month of the 'Feast of the Hungry Ghosts'.

These beliefs, however symbolically or literally held, help to explain the impetus behind one of the earliest instances of public commemoration. This occurred at one of the massacre sites, in the Siglap area of eastern Singapore, in January to February 1947. The next year, these feelings fuelled an even bigger display of public mourning in the same area.[111]

In 1948, rumours spread that massacre victims' relatives had heard ghostly wails from unmarked graves all over the island. Taoist priests, according to Sit Yin Fong, a Chinese journalist, 'peered into the underworld and were thoroughly alarmed by what they saw – thousands of naked hungry and discontented ghosts roaming about the earth, their wrath threatening calamity to the land'. The Taoist priests said that 'these forgotten, tortured souls had to be appeased, and driven away from the earth to wherever they should go'.

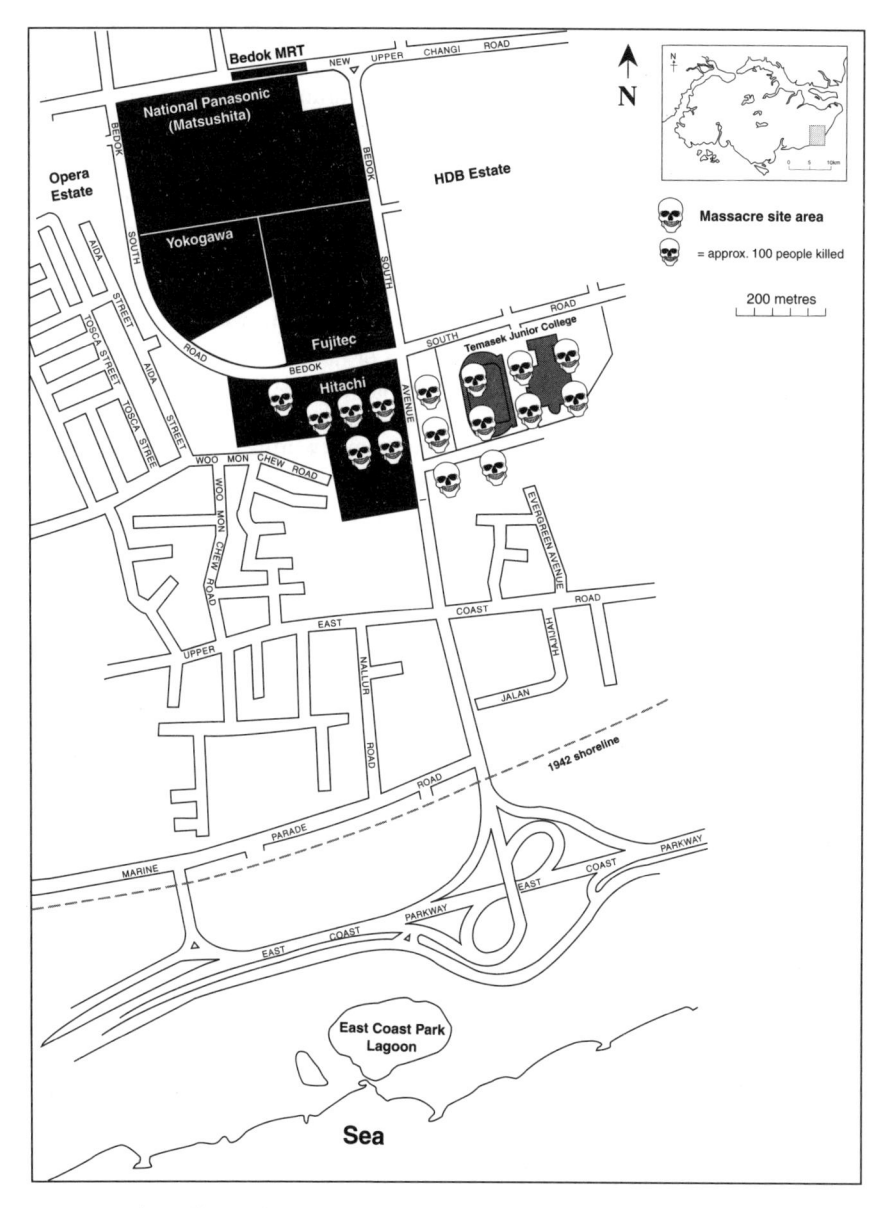

Map 6.2 The valley of death: the *Sook Ching* massacre site at Siglap – 1942 to 2002.

This idea, or fear, demanded a response. High Priestess Miaw Chin was given the task of 'screening' the ghosts of the dead, and deciding whether they should go to heaven or hell at a ceremony at the largest known *Sook Ching* massacre site, in the Siglap area. The Taoist priests of Singapore claimed that Miaw Chin had been appointed to do this by 'Hood Chor' (Kuan Yin), the Chinese goddess of mercy.[112]

The soul-raising ceremony at the Siglap massacre site was attended by thousands of relatives. Miaw Chin invited all the spirits of the dead to come and be fed and clothed. The three days climaxed on '*Tung-Chek*' Day, the traditional family reunion time soon after Chinese New Year. 'For three days and nights great piles of food, paper clothing and paper money were offered in sacrifice', burnt for the dead, and 'a thousand women asked: "How did the spirits of our men-folk fare after death?"' Miaw Chin fell into a trance, and assumed the voices of several of the victims who were identified by their relatives in the crowd. Punishment for the Japanese was not forgotten. Some relatives built paper models of naked Japanese soldiers being disemboweled by horse-faced devils in the court of Eam Lo Ong, the king of hell.[113]

But this was still not enough. Too many had disappeared on the beaches, or had been pushed from boats off the coast of Singapore and shot. The need for a more permanent way of remembering the dead and of restoring them to their relatives remained. By a twist of fate, Siglap again became a focus for grief. In February 1962 sandwashing operations in the Siglap area revealed five mass war graves, and the Chinese Chamber of Commerce began to supervise exhumation in what was soon dubbed the 'Valley of Death'. The Chamber called for people with information about other mass war graves to come forward.

This was the beginning of the exhumation of one hundred sites over four years, which recovered enough remains to fill 600 large funeral urns, each housing the remains of about thirty victims: up to 20,000 in total. Those from Siglap alone suggested 2,000 people had been killed there.[114]

The Chinese Chamber of Commerce now began a campaign to have a monument created in memory of these civilian victims of the war.[115] A campaign which gathered state support. A site was chosen for a memorial on Beach Road, between Raffles Hotel on one side and the *Padang* on the other. Work on reinterring the victims here began on 1 November 1966, with a solemn wreath-laying ceremony, a three-minute silence, and tears and memories for the crowd of witnesses who had lost husbands, fathers and sons.

On 15 February 1967 Singapore's Civilian War Memorial was finally unveiled on this spot, in the heart of Singapore. Its four pillars, soaring 67.4 metres into the air and colloquially known as 'the chopsticks', were said to represent the collective suffering of the four major ethnic groups: Chinese, Malay, Indian, and Eurasian. The merging of the four pillars at the base was further intended as a metaphor for these groups' unity. Every year since, on the anniversary of the Fall, the Chinese Chamber of Commerce which was so instrumental in its construction organises a ceremony early in the morning.[116]

The time the white man ran

While British imperialism had required a certain amnesia about 15 February, local people and politicians alike had good reason to remember the date. Quite apart from the suffering endured in the Japanese occupation, the Fall of

Plate 6.6 The Civilian War Memorial (Singapore). Below lie the remains of victims of the *Sook Ching*. Pan Shou wrote a never-used epitaph, which included the lament: 'Everywhere tears flowed. Everywhere blood flowed. And everywhere terror reigned'. It ended with the verse:

> Tears stained with flower crimson like,
> And blood tainted with the blue ocean,
> Ye wandering souls who rise with the tide,
> Shall guard this young nation.[m]

Source: Hack and Blackburn.

---

m Pan Shou (1911–99). Born in Quanzhou, China, he came to Singapore in 1929 aged 19. He was Singapore's foremost Chinese classical poet and calligrapher, a prolific artist, helped with the opening of the Chinese-speaking Nanyang University, and was a keen observer of contemporary society. The existing memorial merely dedicates itself to civilian victims of the war.

Singapore itself seemed to have been a crucial turning point in the rise of modern Singapore. The fall of the 'impregnable fortress' to the Japanese was viewed as ushering in the nationalist struggles of the postwar period, and pointing the way towards independence.

Lee Kuan Yew recalled as early as 1961 that he and his contemporaries in the struggle for independence were from 'that generation of young men who went through the Second World War and emerged determined that no one – neither the Japanese nor the British – had the right to push and kick us around'.[117]

Even earlier, in 1947, Tan Cheng Lock, then a prominent leader of Malayan Chinese, had written that:

> The prestige of the white man *per se* has gone. He can now be natural and himself, for he is seen to be a human being, who can be defeated, who can make mistakes, who is often arrogant and crude and yet who has his points ... Asia has awakened to its shame and arisen to take its destiny into its own hands ... In the new era there will be an end of Empire ...[118]

The image of the Fall as the moment that smashed the myth of white superiority took root.[119]

For the generation who experienced the Fall, and the occupation, all this was a living reality. But as time went on it meant much less to new generations. This inevitably led to a desire to preserve memories in writing, and to make the Fall concrete for those who did not have parents, or perhaps even grandparents, who could tell them about the Fall and the Japanese occupation.

The Civilian War Memorial went some way towards this, but memorials and books can seem artificial and constructed. There was also a need for images and for relics, for remnants with the power to make people feel a direct connection with the war period. And here, at least as far as military remains were concerned, there was a problem.

By the time Singapore gained internal self-government in 1959, there was little left of the coastal batteries beyond old tunnels and ruined emplacements. The housing and amenities of 'Fortress Singapore' had, however, fared much better, so that on independence on 9 August 1965 – when Singapore left Malaysia – there were still fine barracks in places such as Changi and Blakang Mati. These were inherited by the new island republic, along with the rest of Britain's military facilities, as the latter's withdrawal from East of Suez accelerated after 1968.

So as new remains of the Fortress were discovered, such as two of Fort Connaught's old 9.2 inch barrels in 1970, it fell to independent Singapore to decide what to do with them.[120] The rediscovery of the barrels came at an ideal time, as Blakang Mati was then being transformed into Sentosa, as it was called from 1972, changing it from military stronghold into Singapore's weekend playground. As part of this development, Fort Siloso was redeveloped as a 'guns of Singapore museum', opening on 8 February 1975. The rediscovered barrels were mounted at Fort Siloso in time for the opening.[121] Since the 1970s new finds have gone to increase fort Siloso's stocks, until the Fort now bristles with guns ranging from Malay cannon, through nineteenth-century muzzle-loading guns, to Japanese artillery from the Second World War.

There was, however, a desire for something more human than military hardware and ruins, something which could evoke the drama of wartime events for visitors to Sentosa. A step in this direction was taken as early as 1980, when it was announced that a waxworks exhibition would be created, featuring Percival surrendering to the Yamashita on 15 February 1942. This was to be placed on Sentosa. It was meant as an addition to an existing display of the Japanese surrendering to Mountbatten on 12 September 1945. This 1945 'Surrender Chamber' which opened in 1974 at the City Hall, was now also moved to Sentosa.[122] There, the two surrender waxworks became part of the ever-increasing collection of life-size dioramas at the 'Images of Singapore' exhibition.

At the opening of the new, combined 'Surrender Chamber' on Sentosa, on 1 August 1981, Chen Men Sheng, (then General Manager of Sentosa Development Corporation) stressed it was important for Singapore as an independent nation to mark such watersheds in its history: 'we want to show that part of World War II relating to Singapore so that our children will know what happened during this period of our history'.

When questioned by the British over the exhibition, the Singaporean reply was that this was, 'part of our history, a fact which no one can deny'. Aware that official British opinion was still hostile to marking their surrender, Chen believed that this should not stop Singaporeans marking an important event in their nation's history. He had noted that 'The Americans commemorate the Boston Tea Party . . . .', a point which was more true than it was comforting to British observers.[123]

In addition, the 'Images of Singapore' collection soon became popular with tourists, and by the 1980s boosting tourism was itself a major government aim. This became an additional motive for developing war sites. In 1987, the Singapore Tourism Board launched a project called 'The Battle of Singapore'. This involved the creation of a replica POW chapel at the 'Changi Prison Chapel and Museum' in 1988, and improving the Changi murals site as well.[124] There was, and still is, a steady stream of foreign visitors making their way through the Changi area, as well as Sentosa. In the early 1980s Australians were the largest group of visitors, excluding the Malaysian and Indonesian neighbours. For Australians, particularly those with relatives who served in the Malayan campaign, visiting sites such as Changi had considerable emotional resonance.[125]

Tourists were, however, gradually outstripped in importance by another group. By the 1990s, most visitors to Singapore's Second World War historic sites were local schoolchildren, on field trips to learn about the war and Japanese occupation.

These children became a main target audience, as the government sought to give the Fall of Singapore enhanced significance in the early the 1990s. As early as 1988 a government sponsored report on heritage stated that 'the time may now be right for an objective account of the War to be presented to young Singaporeans who have no personal memories of the traumas ...' The report further noted that 'as the trauma fades away, the lessons of the War are a valuable source of experience for Singaporeans. This experience should demonstrate for younger generations the vulnerability of Singapore and the dangers of blinkered planning'.[126]

That the government wanted to use the Fall of Singapore to emphasise the importance of the Singaporeans defending themselves is hardly surprising. Since 1967, Singapore has required all males to complete over two years of national service, and then to come back regularly for further military training. To deter any potential future enemy, Singapore claims that it can bring a quarter of a million well-trained men under arms in twenty-four hours. This is seen as necessary for a small island republic, surrounded by much larger neighbours.[127] History and Social Studies textbooks were soon making an explicit link between the Fall of Singapore and national service.[128]

The fiftieth anniversary commemorations of the surrender of Singapore gave a further impetus to this trend of harnessing past events for current purposes. There was a perceived need to find a common message for such a public event. Kwa Chong Guan, then Director of Singapore's National Museum, helped organise the museum's 1992 exhibition on the Fall and occupation. It was called 'When Singapore was *Syonan-To*'.[129] When opening the National Museum exhibit, Prime Minister Goh Chok Tong simply stated that: 'If we want peace, we must work for it, and if necessary, fight and die for it'.[130]

This message went on to be restated each time a new Second World War site was opened in the 1990s. Ong Chit Chung, a government member of parliament and historian, also organised a ten part series, 'The War Years', in Singapore's *Straits Times* for the fiftieth commemoration of the Fall of Singapore. He remarked in April 1992 that:

> It is important that this generation learns from the war. We must learn the importance of defence, learn not to take the wealth around us now for granted and, more importantly, bear in mind that Singapore must never fall again.[131]

Nor was commemoration limited to the anniversary of the beginning of the war. The end of the war served just as well. In August 1995, on the fiftieth anniversary of the end of the war, historical markers were opened at sites such as the Battle of Bukit Timah.[132] Just days later, on 12 September 1995, yet another anniversary presented itself. This was the fiftieth anniversary of the formal surrender of the Japanese to the British. At a ceremony at the Kranji War Memorial to mark the occasion, Rear Admiral (National Service) Teo Chee Hean, then Senior Minister of State for Defence, affirmed that: 'We should remember never again to be unprepared to defend our own country, our families and our way of life. We should remember that the price of peace is eternal vigilance'.[133]

These major anniversaries provided excellent foci for drawing out lessons from the war, but by their very nature they were too infrequent for a government intent on socialising successive generations. So the government also chose to upgrade the annual observance of 15 February.

In 1992 the government designated 15 February as Heritage Day. But the emphasis was not only to be a narrow one on British surrender, but a wider one on the role of the war in creating a new nation. Chua Mui Hoong, writing for the *Straits Times*, wrote at the time that the 'real heritage that we want to preserve is not only the memory of one day, February 15, 1942 ... [but] ... the legacy of the entire war, which saw the beginning of an attachment to this land as different peoples on the island banded together ... [who] forgot their differences and fought to defend the land from the intruder'.[134] He also quoted Lee Kuan Yew's speech when opening the Civilian War Memorial back in 1967:

> [It] commemorates an experience which, in spite of its horrors, served as a catalyst in building a nation out of the young and unestablished community of diverse immigrants.[135]

By now, in addition to tourism, the Fall of Singapore was increasingly being used to focus on two sets of themes: the need for self-reliance and self-defence in a small country which relies upon national service; and the beginnings of a common identity in shared suffering.

For the fiftieth anniversary commemorations of 1942, this was further reinforced by a television documentary on the Japanese occupation, *Between Empires* (February 1992). As the title suggests, this made the point that the Singaporeans owed their allegiance to neither the British nor Japanese, but to making their own destiny.[136] The producer, S. Chandra Mohan, commented that 'in the past the history of the war tended to be based on published accounts of European authors', while '*Between Empires* moves away from this and adds a Singaporean perspective'. Brigadier-General George Yeo, as Minister for Information and the Arts, suggested the history of the war might bring about a process in which 'heritage can be a catalyst in stirring patriotism', using 'history books, schools excursions, and commemorative events and exhibitions'.[137]

Since 1995, this iconic status of the Fall of Singapore has been increasingly entrenched in the public arena. In 1998, the 15 February was redesignated as Total Defence Day, on which children were to be reminded that peace should not be taken for granted. Total Defence was defined as including not just military readiness, but psychological, social, economic and civil defence as well.

That year schools marked the day with a huge range of activities, including student plays on related themes, water rationing exercises, cadet students coming to school in uniform, re-enactments of emergencies, and relatives brought in to recall the occupation.[138]

Since 1998, the media has continued to reinforce more formal education, with television showing such major drama serials as *The Price of Peace* (1996) and *A War Diary* (2002). The latter, while using one Chinese family as the focus, managed to cram in almost all the stock images on the Fall: illusory and unshakeable confidence in the British and the impregnable fortress; heroic fighting by the Malay Regiment at Pasir Panjang; Chinese resistance after the Fall; the Changi murals; the *Sook Ching*; Japanese torture; rape and comfort women; and above all, a persistent theme of disappointed faith in others, in the British, ever being able to defend Singapore.

Despite this more pervasive approach to the memory of the war, anniversaries have continued to provide opportunities for an extra intensity of media attention, and for formal, almost theatrical openings of exhibitions and sites. New sites opened on the sixtieth anniversary of the surrender, on 15 February 2002, included the Johore Battery site near Changi airport, and Bukit Chandu.

The latter site also shows a desire to ensure that the memory of war serves as a unifier for all communities alike. Bukit Chandu does this by incorporating Malay heroes as central to the war story, alongside the more usual cast of civilian victims and Chinese volunteers. On 15 February 2002 Tony Tan, as Deputy Prime Minister, opened the new museum at 'Bukit Chandu'. It is located in a converted colonial bungalow, which is believed to have been used in a support role by the Malay Regiment in February 1942. The newly opened centre, perched on a hill, and with glorious views over the southwest Singaporean coastline, was entitled 'Reflections at Bukit Chandu'.

Here was a heritage location self-consciously constructed to encourage reflection on the war in general, and on self-sacrifice and heroism in specific. Above all, Bukit Chandu's story centres on the Malay Regiment's heroic stand at Pasir Panjang Ridge on 13 to 14 February 1942, when some units, notably C Company under Lieutenant Adnan Saidi, fought almost to the last man.[139]

The project was supervised by the National Archives and National Heritage Board. The Singapore government, meanwhile, had already begun using school textbooks to emphasise that the Malay Regiment had been defending Singapore as a place, rather than its Malay and regimental honour alone.[140] Trade and Industry Minister George Yeo specifically made this point. He said that when visiting the centre:

> I was told the museum had become a cultural shrine to many Malay Singaporeans. Lt Adnan and the men of C Company sacrificed themselves not for the Malay race, but as soldiers of the British Army fighting brutal invaders. Like volunteers of other races who fought the

Japanese, including pro-communists operating in the Malayan jungle, these Malay heroes helped to create modern Singapore.[141]

Here was an attempt to bring all groups – even the wartime communist resistance – into one, unified story and interpretation of the Fall and occupation. It was an attempt to present a unified history in order to shape a common present, and to find inspiration for the future. A bronze plaque, placed next to a group of statues depicting a Malay mortar group, also quotes a previous speech given by George Yeo on the need to commemorate heroism as well as suffering:

> If we do not remember our heroes, we will produce no heroes. If we do not record their sacrifices, their sacrifices would have been in vain ... The greatest strength we have as a people is our common memories of the past and our common hopes for the future ... For without those memories the next generation will not have the fighting spirit to carry on.

In this way, 15 February has become the primary date associated with the Malayan campaign, and a central component in Singapore's project of 'National Education': education on issues the government has identified as crucial to nation-building.[142] In Singapore it is now possible to revisit 15 February again and again, and again. It is represented by mannequins of British officers surrendering in the 'Images of Singapore' exhibition on Sentosa. It is represented again in the 'Battlebox', a recreation of Percival's underground command bunker at Fort Canning, on a hill in the heart of Singapore. It is also one of the first events impressed upon visitors to the 'Discovery Centre', which emphasises the need for Singaporeans to defend themselves. Since 1998, as 'Total Defence Day', it has been observed by schools throughout the country each year, as well as by a solemn ceremony at the Civilian War Memorial.

For schools in particular mere words or visits to static displays are not enough, as they attempt to conjure up the past, to make children, many of whom live in air-conditioned comfort, comprehend the full magnitude of 1942. Plays, visits to sites such as Fort Canning, with its graves and old military buildings, and even 're-enactments' are used. Sentosa's Fort Siloso hosted one of the largest such re-enactments in November 2001. Hundreds of primary schoolchildren enlisted as 'recruits' at 'Siloso Live'. Each group toured the site, with actors standing in as sergeants, soldiers' families, and dhobymen (laundrymen). Then the experience culminated in an 'air-raid'. Hustled into gun bunkers, students crouched underground amidst smoke and gunfire, before 'Japanese' soldiers burst in, and herded them into captivity.[143]

This dramatic, indeed dramatised, use of the Fall illustrates just how central '15 February' has become for the 'Singapore Story', the way the island's history is presented for public consumption. It has achieved an iconic status in Singapore as well as internationally, fixing eyes upon the issue of the Fall rather than the campaign, of how and why a supposedly 'impregnable' fortress could have

Plate 6.7 Siloso Live! (November 2001) Actors recreate the Fall of Singapore for schoolchildren. The location is Fort Siloso on Sentosa Island (formerly called Pulau Blakang Mati). In the background are old 9.2 inch gun barrels on static display mounts.

Source: Hack and Blackburn.

surrendered so quickly, and of what the consequences were for Britain, and for awakening nationalism. So central has 15 February become in popular imagination, that we sometimes need to remind ourselves that it was, for a long time, not at all obvious that the campaign would be remembered on 15 February at all, rather than on some other date: 15 August and 12 September being prime candidates. Nor was it obvious what would be remembered, or how.

Clearly, the public history of the Fall of Singapore, of both the event and its consequences, has been subject to repeated reinterpretation. Different groups have remembered both the Fall, and the sacrifices of their war dead in different ways, each according to their own rituals and needs. It has served the interests of nation-building in more than one country, as well as tourism and the media. In this sense there are, and will continue to be, 'many Falls of Singapore', many attempts to remember, forget and reshape 15 February 1942. This much is evident even without the many perspectives we have been forced to leave out.

These many interpretations could only be given their due by a new book, or books, of their own. In the meanwhile, even a glimpse of the public life of '15 February' serves to warn us how difficult it is to impose any one account, any one answer, to the questions 'What was Fortress Singapore' and 'Did Singapore have to Fall on 15 February 1942?'

7

CONCLUSION

That the fall of Singapore in February 1942 was a catastrophic defeat for Britain is beyond dispute. That it was a departure point towards the future independence of Malaysia and Singapore seems equally clear, however winding the subsequent road to independence. But the scale of the event, and the sheer number of parties involved – Australian, British, Chinese, Indian, Malay and Japanese – has made it difficult to agree on the main causes of the calamity.

The difficulties of arriving at a final conclusion, both practical and political, were considered immediately after the end of the war. In January 1946 there were calls for an inquiry, for a definitive report to clear the air, after Churchill published his speech to a secret session of the House of Commons of 23 April 1942. In that speech, Churchill had suggested that 100,000 defenders might have surrendered Singapore to a much smaller Japanese force of 30,000, and that there did not seem to have been much bloodshed (or at least not enough in his eyes to salvage the honour of race and empire). The red rag to the bull, however, was the speech's suggestion that Australian accounts of the campaign reflected badly on Indian troops, while other credible witnesses reflected badly on the Australians.

Churchill's secret speech of 1942 had been intended to show that an inquiry then, in the midst of war, would cause more harm than good. As if to prove this point, Churchill's statements were now picked up on in Australia, where some people demanded a full inquiry, in the hope of deflecting blame away from individuals and nationalities. These included Lieutenant-General Gordon Bennett (the wartime commander of the Australian 8th Division in Singapore), and Australia's 'Returned Soldiers League'. The Australian government cabled London for their views.[1]

In London, Clement Attee's Labour government referred the matter to their military advisers, who gave the iciest of responses. The Vice Chiefs of Staff and the Joint Planning Staff warned that everyone already agreed that the campaign had been 'a military disaster'. In such a case, an inquiry would encourage mudslinging, further tension with Australia and India over the collapse of morale in Singapore and their troops' part in this, tend to blacken the name of the colonial administration and the commanders, and require investigation of the whole question of defence preparation from the interwar years on. It would also necessitate calling people of the highest rank, including Churchill himself.

The military's final advice was that the government should prevaricate. They should say that the official despatches of the commanders – documents which could be more easily limited or even sanitised – should be published first. Only after this had been done could any question of a full inquiry be properly entertained. In the worst case scenario, the planners feared public pressure for an inquiry could become irresistible. In that case, they suggested granting the most limited inquiry possible, focusing only on the period in February 1942 when Singapore itself was besieged.[2]

Britain's Joint Planning Staff thus gave the bleakest of warnings of just how difficult it was to decide why Singapore fell when it did, and how it did. Their words of warning on the scale of the problem bear repeating, for the benefit of any historian who believes they may be able to arrive at a final, definitive answer. To explain why Singapore fell, the Joint Planners said that: 'there would be no part of our war strategy or our man-power and production policy, either during or previous to the war with Germany and Italy, which might not come under examination'. They went on to list a formidable battery of questions:

(a) Whether we over-insured in other theatres at the expense of the Far East.
(b) Whether the decision to rely on air power was correct in view of existing shortages.
(c) Whether all possible steps were taken to provide the aircraft necessary.
(d) Whether until the necessary aircraft could be provided, we made satisfactory interim arrangements for the defence of the Far East.

The Joint Planning Staff continued that: 'The discussion of these problems ... must involve a wide-spread review of the overall situation in all theatres during 1941, of the deployment of aircraft through the world, and of the progress of production programmes'.[3]

The point about production is important in judging Churchill's role. It is also one of the most neglected issues. Churchill has usually been defended, or criticised, according to the more limited criteria of how he disposed of limited forces in 1941. To contemporaries, and to historians stretching from Callahan in the 1970s to Farrell in 2002, Churchill made the right call given the hand he was dealt, and the stakes he was playing for. Resources allocated to Middle East and Russian theatres had some chance of affecting a global conflict. Those allocated to Singapore were less significant. Ultimately, Britain would win or lose in the East according to whether the United States came down on its side, not according to any marginal changes to force levels in Malaya.

For others, such as Singaporean historian Ong Chit Chung, the exact opposite conclusion is reached. For them, Churchill made the wrong allocation, sending many aircraft to areas where they would be a mere drop in the ocean, but virtually no modern aircraft, and no tanks at all, to Singapore, where a small quantity might have made a large difference.

In both cases, final judgement would depend on the additional considerations, such as what scale of changes Britain could realistically have made; and how the Japanese could or would have responded to such changes in British forces, given their resources, aims and intelligence.

In so far as the debate is about Churchill and 'Fortress Singapore', however, the Joint Planning Staff study of 1946 implies that the debate about how Churchill played a poor hand, the forces available in 1941, is only half the story. One also has to look above that level to his role in war production. What was Churchill's role in dealing the hand he had to play, by setting the overall pattern for strategy and for war production? In addition, there is the level below grand strategy, the level at which Churchill and his commanders handled the unfolding tragedy in Malaya. Why did Churchill allow so many men to be committed, without the requisite equipment? Was he right to permit reinforcements in January 1942, in the face of Australian calls not to abandon Singapore, when it was becoming obvious that little could be done to save the island?

The issue of the reinforcements which landed in Singapore in January 1942 deserves closer scrutiny. The 1946 Joint Planners' report on whether to hold an inquiry suggested that Wavell, as Supreme Commander in the South West Pacific from that month, could be criticised for the way in which he failed to direct these reinforcements away from Singapore. Churchill or Wavell could have directed more of these reinforcements to the Netherlands East Indies or, even more usefully, to Burma. Instead they allowed men and machines to be sent to a futile end in Singapore.

Churchill compounded matters by his handling of the last couple of weeks. Not only did he allow more men to be fed into an increasingly open-ended hole, but he then called for them to fight to the last in the crowded streets of a colonial city, for reasons that seemed to have more to do with race and empire prestige, than with any military advantage that could be gained. The results of a final storming of the city, had he not relented at the very last moment, do not bear contemplation.

Any analysis of Churchill's role demands an examination, then, from many different angles, namely: his role in war production; his role in the allocation of resources produced between different theatres; his role, if any, in reinforcing the wrong interpretation of Japanese intentions in relation to intelligence; his part in the final few weeks and days; and his failure to insist on strategic coherence, in so far as he allowed commanders to plan for *Matador* and a fighting retreat, while denying the equipment necessary to make such plans work.

The questions involved are formidably wide-ranging, but we can, at the least, say that Churchill's strategic direction was at fault. He himself clearly thought of Singapore, when combined with Johore, as 'Fortress Singapore', an area to be screened if necessary, but without compromising the final defence of the naval base and its surrounding area. The gap between this conception of Malaya's defence, and his commanders – between 'Fortress Singapore' and *Matador* – played a significant part in the scale of the final tragedy.

The debate on Churchill will roll on. But in itself, it will remain part of a much wider debate, one in which reasons given for the Singapore disaster range from Britain's long-term imperial overstretch, through deficiencies in training or even in national characteristics, to matters of intelligence and leadership.

As the planners foresaw in 1946, it has proved virtually impossible for any one report, or book, to adequately draw together so many different considerations. This has been all the more true because the whole debate has become intertwined with issues of individual, academic and national reputation. For British academics and their readers, the issue reflects on Churchill's iconic reputation as a war leader, as the man who took hold of a floundering country, and led it to victory, or at least avoided defeat, in a good war against European and Asian 'fascism'. For Australians, the issue has become entwined with the notion of a separate Australian nationalism, and Australian military exceptionalism from Gallipoli onwards. It is further complicated by a division in Australia between those who have retained a sympathetic or even warm view of historic links with Britain, and those who have felt Australia needed to assert its separate interests and identity earlier. In Singapore itself, the Fall has taken a central place in national memory, in 'nation building', and in 'national education'.

The overall effect of these competing agendas is that the history seems to have been driven as much by the need for simplifying myths, as by the facts. This is almost as true for the academics, each one in need of a focus which will allow a great deal to be left out, and requiring a thesis in order to claim novelty, as it is for the journalists and nationalists. Hence the succession of simplifying devices, or myths: the 'impregnable fortress'; the 'guns pointing the wrong way'; the idea of a 'Singapore Strategy' centred on naval reinforcement; *Matador* as the solution, if only the resources had been supplied; the argument that there was a 'close-run' finale; and the related suggestion that a last-gasp collapse of morale played a vital role. Each device has acted as a 'myth' in trying to simplify events around one central, most important concern.

The truth, however, is that a better understanding of the Fall of Singapore will probably come not by focusing on one myth, but on the tensions between them. It is the tension between the 'Fortress Singapore' and *Matador* approaches which allow us to see how Singapore ended up with a plan for forward defence, but without either the requisite resources or a backup option. It is the tension between the Australian 'Grim Glory' version of their fighting in Malaya, and criticisms of Australian performance in Singapore, which allow us to see the way recurrent defeat, leadership failings, and being constantly outnumbered and outflanked at the local level, caused a near-collapse in morale in some units, of whatever nationality. Again, it is not the pro- or anti-Churchill accounts which are most helpful in allowing us to understand the scale of the disaster at Singapore: it is the creative tension between them. This is what gives us a window into Churchill's strengths, his willingness to take the strategic gamble and see the big picture, but also his weaknesses, his pumping of resources into pet projects such as the bomber offensive at the expense of more balanced production, and the tendency for his almost medieval rhetoric of fortresses, heroism, and blood and empire honour to shape his military pronouncements.

These dialectics are the key to a better understanding of one of the twentieth century's most catastrophic military defeats, an event that had a pivotal place in the end of Britain's empire. It is partly for that reason that this book has brought together so many different views, and has tried to avoid creating its own, simplifying myth. In the end a better understanding comes not from trying to reduce the arguments to one 'Fall of Singapore', but from understanding why and how so many different explanations for the Fall have been generated. It comes from a realisation that there was not one Fall, but from understanding the origin of, and the tensions between, the 'Many Falls' of Singapore.

Appendix A

BRITISH FORCES IN DECEMBER 1941, AND REINFORCEMENTS

Force numbers vary according to the source. The following are some of the most reputable estimates.

British imperial forces as of 7 December 1941

Source: Brooke-Popham and Layton's Report on the campaign, as found in the Supplement to the *London Gazette*, 22 January 1948.

Army strength in Malaya, 7 December 1941

Infantry battalions	Total 47
Regular battalions	31 (6 British, 18 Indian, 6 Australian, 1 Malay)
Volunteer battalions	10
Johore military forces	1
Indian state forces	5
Artillery regiments	Total 10 + 2 batteries
Field regiments	7 (approximately 152 guns)
Mountain regiments	1 (24 guns)
Anti-tank regiments	2 (84 guns)
Anti-tank batteries	2 (14 guns)
Total strength – regulars	Total 76,343
British	19,391
Australian	15,279
Indian	37,191 (includes Gurkhas)
Asiatic	4,482
Total strength – volunteers	Total 10,552
British	2,430
Indian	727
Asiatic	7,395
Grand Total	86,895

APPENDIX A

Notes for army strength in Malaya, 7 December 1941

1 *Volunteers*: The volunteers were part-trained and efficient mainly for static or local duties.

2 *Malay Regiment*: A second battalion of the Malay Regiment was raised. The First Battalion fought well around Pasir Panjang, in southern Singapore, in mid-February 1942.

3 *'Dalforce'*: This is the British name for Chinese led by Colonel Dalley, the Federated Malay States police officer put in charge of volunteers who were raised from December 1941. On the Chinese side, it was called the 'Volunteer Army' or 'The Chinese Overseas Volunteer Army'. It comprised over a thousand Chinese volunteers, many raised with the help of the Malayan Communist Party and Kuomintang, but also including ordinary *towkay*'s (towkay: old Malayan term for Chinese business man or merchant) sons and rickshaw pullers. There was initially British reluctance to raise such Chinese volunteers, partly because the most ardent anti-Japanese organisers, the local Kuomintang and communists, were seen as alien and disruptive forces. Another reason for British reluctance was that their prewar diplomacy sought to avoid antagonising the Japanese. Yet the Chinese in Malaya organised considerable anti-Japanese assistance for China, as well as boycotts of Japanese goods.

This fear was only overcome in December 1941, after the Japanese invasion, and so far too late to prepare such a force properly. Volunteer Army members sometimes wore a blue uniform, or at least a piece of red cloth round their right arm and yellow cloth round their head. Proper uniforms were in short supply, and they were given old weapons, including hunting rifles. These men and women, some with only a few days training, fought in small detachments around Kranji, Bukit Timah and other areas during the battle for Singapore. Dispersed and used as auxiliaries, such raw and lightly armed soldiers could make little difference to the outcome, however brave, and however desperate to protect their families from the fate visited on captured cities in China.

Dalforce (Overseas Chinese Volunteer Army) initial dispositions
A Company   West of the Causeway.
B Company   Kranji.
C Company   Jurong.
D Company   between Serangoon and Pasir Ris.[1]

Other local volunteers trained at 101 Special Training School and were sent up-country as stay-behind groups, originally with the rather depressing title of 'left-behind' parties. For accounts based on oral history, see a book compiled and edited by Foong Choon Hon (calling himself an 'eyewitness' to

APPENDIX A

the war), entitled *The Price of Peace: True Accounts of the Japanese Occupation* (Singapore: Asiapac, 1997).

4 *Disputed Numbers*: Warren, *Singapore 1942*, page 300, explains that most people's numbers do not add up. He argues Kirby originally overestimated British forces, eventually correcting the total Allied casualties and POWs as 130,246 (not 138,708). This means that after about 7,500 were killed, just over 120,000 must have been captured. Of these, many locally enlisted personnel were soon released.

British forces in Malaya on 7 December 1941 according to Kirby, *The Loss of Singapore*, pp. 163–4

Kirby gives a slightly higher figure for British forces in December 1941 than Percival, of 88,600. The difference seems to lie partly in his higher figure for total locally enlisted staff, at 16,800. He summarises these forces as 31 battalions, or the equivalent of three and a half divisions.

British and imperial reinforcements between 8 December 1941–15 February 1942

3 January	First British reinforcements arrive. 45th Indian Brigade Group Badly 'milked' for men to seed other units, many officers being straight from England, many men recent recruits. It is badly mauled at Muar on 15 January.
13 January	53rd British Infantry Brigade (part of the British 18th Division). Two light anti-aircraft regiments. One anti-tank regiment. 51 crated Hurricane fighter aircraft of 232 Squadron, with pilots.
22 January	44th Indian Infantry Brigade and several thousand raw Indian replacements arrive. This brigade is in a similar condition to the 45th.
24 January	Australian 2/4 Machine-Gun Battalion and around 1,900 untrained reinforcements: 'some had sailed within a fortnight of their enlistment'.[2]
29 January	Most of remaining British 18th Indian Division arrives. Churchill had instinctively wondered if this, aircraft and armour should be diverted to Burma. A 23 January telegram from the Australian government, warning the evacuation of Singapore would be an 'inexcusable betrayal', undermined such thoughts.

APPENDIX A

5 February 1942	Last of British 18th Division arrives. Some Indian vehicles and troops. Reinforcement ship, *Empress of Asia*, is sunk. Most men are saved by small boats such as the *tongkang Florence Nightingale*, manned by a medical team from Blakang Mati, and by HMAS *Yarra*. But most equipment is lost.
February 1942	No more reinforcements arrive. Two Australian divisions, one the 7th Australian Armoured Division, had been on their way east. The latter are re-routed to Burma.
12 February	From reinforcement to selective evacuation. Shore-based naval personnel, airforce ground technicians and some military officers leave. Most are sunk en route to Java.
13/14 February	Last major convoy out, taking civilians and selective military personnel. Hereafter, it was left to individuals to use small craft.

Appendix B

JAPANESE FORCES IN DECEMBER 1941

Japanese imperial forces as of 7 December 1941

Total 25th Army available to Lieutenant-General Yamashita according to Tsuji[1]

- Imperial Guards (Lt-General Nishimura) 13,000
- 5th Division (Lt-General Matsui) 16,000
- 18th division (Lt-General Mutaguchi) 13,000
- 56th Division (transferred to 15th Army for Burma)
- 3rd Tank Brigade 80 tanks
- Artillery
- Supporting arms.

Total Japanese strength deployed according to Tsuji

- 60,000 men
- 400 guns
- 120 tanks and armoured cars.

Japanese divisions in Manchuria were typically about 18,000 strong. A division initially comprised two brigades, each of two infantry regiments. By 1941, however, most brigades had changed over to just having three regiments, not four. One Japanese Regiment held three battalions, divided into three or four companies.

Total Japanese strength according to Kirby, The Loss of Singapore, pp. 522–3

- Fighting units (excluding the 56th Division, available but not used): 88,689
- Supporting (communications, HQ, land, construction, ordnance, medical): 36,719
- Total: 125,408

APPENDIX B

- Tanks (after 2nd Tank Regiment was transferred to the 16th Army in January): 79 medium tanks, 100 light tanks (1st, 6th and 14th Tank Regiments)
- Kirby adds, however, that actual numbers in Malaya, 'fell far short of these figures'
- Warren, *Singapore 1942*, p. 302 argues three understrength divisions and support cannot have contained so many men.

Japanese Forces available for the siege of Singapore (8 February 1942) according to Kirby, The Loss of Singapore, p. 527

- Combat troops: 67,660
- Service troops: 33,000
- Air and air service: 10,000
- Total: 110,660
- Tanks: 150
- Artillery 168 pieces

Japanese casualties according to Akashi[2]

- For the campaign: 5,240 dead, 9,528 injured
- In Singapore, 1,713 dead, 3,378 injured.

According to *Senshi Sōsho Vol 1. Maré Shinkō Sakusen*, p. 626, Japanese casualties for the campaign were 3,507 dead and 6,150 injured. Its figures for Singapore are the same as those of Akashi.

Appendix C

ORGANISATION AND DISPOSITION OF MALAYA COMMAND, 7 DECEMBER 1941

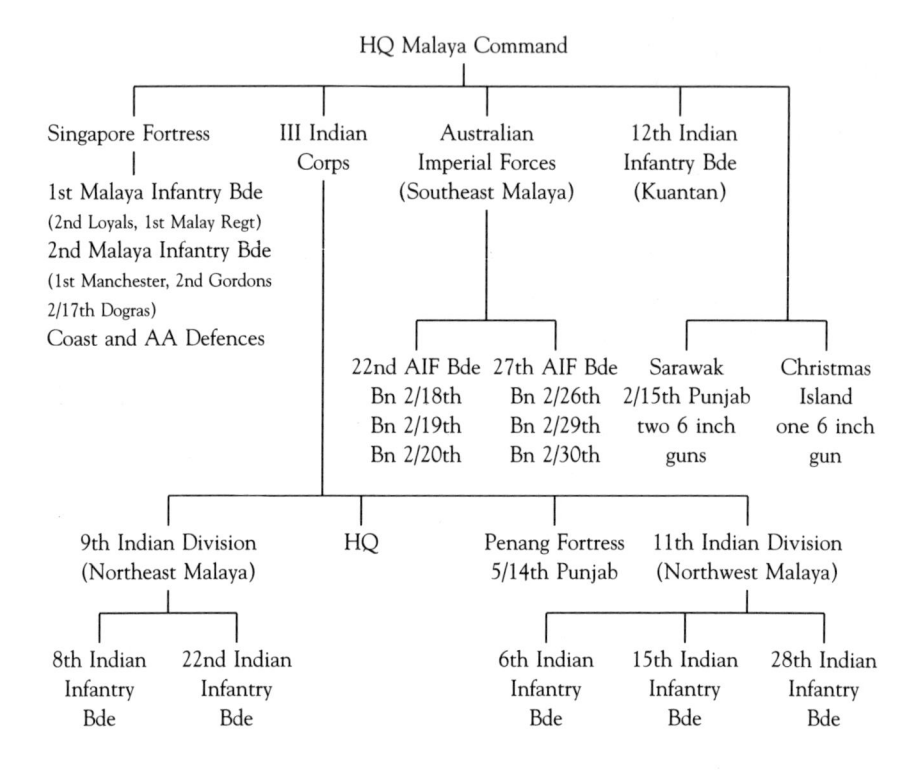

```
                            HQ Malaya Command
    ┌───────────────────┬─────────────────┬──────────────────┐
Singapore Fortress   III Indian       Australian          12th Indian
    │                  Corps       Imperial Forces      Infantry Bde
1st Malaya Infantry Bde          (Southeast Malaya)      (Kuantan)
(2nd Loyals, 1st Malay Regt)
2nd Malaya Infantry Bde
(1st Manchester, 2nd Gordons
2/17th Dogras)
Coast and AA Defences
                           ┌──────────┬──────────┬──────────┐
                      22nd AIF Bde  27th AIF Bde  Sarawak   Christmas
                      Bn 2/18th     Bn 2/26th   2/15th Punjab  Island
                      Bn 2/19th     Bn 2/29th   two 6 inch  one 6 inch
                      Bn 2/20th     Bn 2/30th     guns        gun

       ┌──────────────────┬──────────┬──────────────────┐
   9th Indian Division    HQ    Penang Fortress    11th Indian Division
   (Northeast Malaya)           5/14th Punjab      (Northwest Malaya)
      ┌─────────┐                          ┌──────────┬──────────┐
  8th Indian  22nd Indian              6th Indian  15th Indian  28th Indian
  Infantry    Infantry                 Infantry    Infantry     Infantry
  Bde         Bde                      Bde         Bde          Bde
```

Notes:
1 AIF Units shown here formed part of the 8th Australian Division
2 Far Eastern Forces further afield:
   Burma (the Burma Rifles forming the backbone of about 34 battalions)
   Hong Kong (14,564 including British, Canadian, Indian and local personnel)

Appendix D

AIRCRAFT IN THE FAR EAST AND THEIR DISPOSITION, 7 DECEMBER 1941

The standard figures given for British airpower in the Far East

Source: Air Chief Marshal Brooke-Popham, 'Operations in the Far East', *Supplement to the London Gazette*, (London, 22 January 1948), pp. 573–5.

Defending air forces in Malaya on 7 December, 1941

158 frontline + 88 maintenance or reserve. Roughly a quarter of the latter being temporarily out of action due to engine problems.

Breakdown of defending aircraft available in Malaya, 7 December 1941

24 Wildebeeste (obsolete torpedo bombers)
60 Buffalo (fighters)
31 Blenheim I, 16 Blenheim IV (Light bombers)
24 Hudson (general reconnaissance/bombers)
 3 Catalina (flying boats)
Total 158 (88) = 246

Defending air forces in Burma (20), Ceylon (2) and Hong Kong (5) were sparser.

Burma 4 Blenheim I, 16 Buffalo
Ceylon 2 Catalina
Hong Kong 3 Wildebeeste, 2 Walrus amphibian aircraft.
Burma and Ceylon total 22 (plus 16 reserves)
Far East total 185 (plus 104 reserves) = 289

Dutch reinforcements: The Dutch also sent 22 bombers and 9 fighters to Singapore.

From December 8–31: the number of frontline available aircraft available in Malaya varied between 108 and 158.

APPENDIX D

Revised figures for British airpower in the Far East

Source: Air Commodore Henry Probert, *The Forgotten Air Force: The Royal Air Force in the War Against Japan, 1941–1945* (London: Brassey's, 1995), Appendix A, p. 311. He cites AHQ Far East signal Q497, dated 9 December 1941.

Though Probert's figures at first look different from Brooke-Popham's, they are in fact not very far apart. This is because Brooke-Popham's figure of 158 serviceable, frontline aircraft for 7 December excluded serviceable machines in the maintainence unit (14), and some immediate reserves. Adding the maintenance unit alone would give approximately 172 serviceable aircraft, as opposed to Probert's 181.

It is possible that Probert gives the best approximation of total serviceable aircraft, and Brooke-Popham the closest approxination for total serviceable aircraft which were also classified as frontline.

Defending Airforces in Malaya on 9 December, 1941[1]

167 frontline + 14 serviceable aircraft in a maintenance unit gives 181 serviceable aircraft. There were an additional 84 unserviceable aircraft, plus 1 Beaufort, a few Fleet Air Arm Swordfish, and a few light aircraft of the Malayan Volunteer Air Force.

Breakdown of defending aircraft available in Malaya, 7 December 1941

Aircraft	Unit	Location	Serviceable	u/s	Totals
Wildebeeste	36 Sqn	Gong Kedah/Seletar	15	3	
Wildebeeste	100 Sqn	Seletar	16	2	36
Hudson	1 Sqn RAAF	Kota Bharu	8	6	
Hudson	8 Sqn RAAF	Kuantan	8	5	
Hudson	MU		2	2	31
Catalina	205 Sqn	Seletar	3	2	5
Blenheim I	27 Sqn	Sungei Patani	8	4	
Blenheim I	60 Sqn	Kuntan	9	4	
Blenheim I	62 Sqn	Alor Star	12	1	
Blenheim I	MU		5	43	
Blenheim IV	34 Sqn	Alor Star	21	2	
Blenheim IV	MU		1	24	
Buffalo	243 Sqn	Kallang/Kota Bharu	11	12	
Buffalo	453 Sqn	Sembawang	19	5	
Buffalo	488 Sqn	Kallang	14	3	
Buffalo	21 Sqn RAAF	Sungei Patani	23		
Buffalo	MU		12	27	126
Total			181	84	265

APPENDIX D

Requirements for the Far East

Estimated British Requirements The COS estimate for Malayan requirements in January 1941 was 336 frontline aircraft. Local commanders had estimated 566 in October 1940. Intelligence estimates for a Japanese attack ranged up to 600 or more. Such estimates would have normally be accompanied by 50 per cent reserves.

British and Japanese aircraft performance compared

The Dogfight: the Buffalo versus the Zero Theoretically the two were nearly equal at 20,000 feet, but the Zero climbed far faster, and had greater speed, below that. Even the late-arriving Hurricanes proved inferior to the Zero at altitudes of less than 20,000 feet. In reality, however, the Japanese used relatively few Navy 'Zeros', as opposed to the less impressive army version, the *Nakajima* Ki-43 fighter.[2]

	Zero fighter	Buffalo
Rate of climb to 13,000 feet	4.3 minutes	6.1 minutes
Speed at 10,000 feet	315 mph	270 mph (aprox)
Speed at 20,000 feet	295 mph	292 mph*

* proved unattainable in practice in Malaya

The twin-engined Blenheim Mk. I could reach over 280 mph at 15,000 feet if operating as a fighter. But as a bigger aircraft (it was originally used as a small passenger plane) did not have the manoeuverability for dogfights.

British intelligence on the Zero was available, but seems to have been neglected by sceptical senior RAF officers, and so not passed on to pilots. More to the point, British pilots were generally less experienced.[3]

Japanese airpower in the Far East

Japanese aircraft available for the Malayan campaign:[4]

Tsuji:	Army aircraft 459	Naval aircraft 158	Total: 617
Kirby:	Army aircraft 354	Naval aircraft 180 (+30)[5]	Total: 564

Appendix E
WAR DIARIES

The following War Diaries are compiled from the wartime War Diaries of Faber Command, Changi Command, and the overall Brigadier Commanding Fixed Defences, A.D. Curtis.

These were handwritten, some parts in Changi, by artillery officers who had been made prisoners of War. They seem to have been written in the weeks immediately after the Fall, culminating with A.D. Curtis's overall War Diary being assembled by August of that year.

They appear to draw on the testimony of a range of men, and are in places very detailed. This suggests a range of sources and a great effort to produce accuracy.

On the other hand, it seems likely that not all these men had access to detailed written documentation, as some of this at least had been destroyed on orders, or lost. Some officers were also missing, either as casualties, or because they had been evacuated, or had escaped Singapore between the 14 and 27 February, taking to small boats. On 27 February this avenue closed, as the last of the British and Indian gunners were evacuated from Blakang Mati.

Some of those who escaped wrote their accounts in Ceylon or India, and they can be found in War Office files compiled on the Fall of Singapore in 1942 itself. Others, such as Major (later Lt-Colonel) Macleod-Carey, wrote their accounts in postwar journals, especially *The Gunner*.

The following War Diaries have been compiled by cross-referencing the War Diaries.

APPENDIX E

War Diary for Johore Battery

Date	Event	Remarks
5.2.42	First mention of Johore Battery specifies 2 guns only fired on West Johore Bahru and mainland N of Punggol Point	Reported Effective
7.2.42	Engaged hostile railway gun on mainland	Neutralisation
8.2.42	Engaged mainland enemy troop concentration NW of Punggol Point.	Harassing fire
9.2.42	Engaged mainland targets N of Punggol Point to Johore Bahru.[1]	
	Johore Fort bombed.	
10.2.42	Engaged village W of Pasir Panjang.	Neutralising enemy tanks.
	Engaged mainland Johore N of Punggol Point to Johore Bahru.	Harassing enemy line of communication
	Johore Fort bombed.	
11.2.42	Engaged Bukit Timah Road.	Harassing fire and neutralising enemy battery
	Engaged West of Pasir Panjang Village.	
	Engaged mainland Johore N of Punggol Point to Johore Bahru.	
	Johore Fort bombed.	
12.2.42	Engaged Bukit Timah and Pasir Panjang Rd in the morning.	Harassing fire[2]
1300	Order for Changi Fire Command guns to be prepared for demolition by 1830 hours. Johore and Changi Fort to fire away all ammunition possible.	
1530	Fortress Plotter destroyed.	
Afternoon	Engaged NW portion of naval base.	Harassing fire
1630	Demolition cancelled.	
1845	Demolition ordered.	
2045	Johore Fort destroyed.	
2300	9th Coast Rgt went to Balastier recreation ground.	
13.2.42	9th Coast Rgt reorganized as infantry battalion of four companies at 0630. Tasks:	
	1 A–C coys covered 3000 yds Arthur Bridge to S Whampoe.	
14.2.42	2 A and C coys sent N.E. of Kallang aerodrome.	
	3 D coy sent from Balastier to Geylang in reserve role.	
15.2.42	News of surrender reached 9th Coast Rgt at 1830.	

Before its destruction, Johore Fort fired 194 rounds of 250, all AP [armour piercing]. Together with the two batteries of 9.2 inch guns, this makes it one of most active coastal batteries.

APPENDIX E

War Diary for Connaught Battery

Date	Event	Remarks
11.2.42	Concentration on Jurong and Ulu Pandan village and Jurong Road begins after noon.	Area Shoots
12.2.42	Connaught puts down three concentrations on Tengah aerodrome starting just after midnight.	
0130	First concentration	
0330	Second	
0630	Third	
Afternoon	Bukit Timah and Jurong Road.	Harassing fire
Night	Further three concentrations on Tengah.	
13.2.42		
1100	Bukit Timah area.	
14.2.42	0730 following guns destroyed.	Magazine hoists out of action. Shells have to be brought up manually.
	Personnel from other forts concentrating at Connaught for defence.	
18–26.2.42	Gunners and Federated Malay States Volunteer forces (FMSVF) at Connaught and other locations witness the machine-gunning of Chinese pushed off boats. Some of the victims are buried on Blakang Mati.	
27.2.42	Final evacuation of personnel to Changi and Farrer Park.	

According to the War Diaries, Connaught Battery used all 75 HE, and 217 of its AP, shells over its three days of firing. According to the postwar comments of Battery Commander, J.W. Hipkin, it even hit targets north of the Causeway. However, the 1942 War Diary entry does not mention this. Other accounts contradict it, and this would have been at extreme range, if possible at all. The War Diaries also state that Tekong Battery's three 9.2 inch used 75 HE and 200 AP.[3]

APPENDIX E

War Diary for Labrador Battery

Date	Event	Remarks
10.2.42	Intermittent shelling near Labrador. Anti-aircraft guns and positions around Keppel Golf course appearing to be the targets.	
11.2.42	Air bombing and shelling in vicinity of Labrador and northern slopes of Faber Ridge fairly constant throughout the day.	One enemy battery of 5.9 inch guns near Bukit Timah, another between Jurong River and Jurong Road. Sunk.
1200	Labrador and Siloso engaged enemy concentrations at the west end of West Coast road and at Jurong river position.	
2000	Labrador engaged stationary two-masted junk lying NE of Nine Islands. Mainly to stimulate morale of HKSRA gunners.	
12.2.42	About 16 Australian stragglers arrive by sea at 0700.	
Morning	Labrador shelled together with Keppel and Mount Faber. Blakang Mati being bombed.	
Afternoon	Engaged targets on West Coast Road with Siloso.	
2100	Engaged unidentified craft drifting slowly from W to E between P. Sebarok and St Johns West inside No. 2 minefield. Together with Siloso. Despite having a similar silhouette to a Japanese landing craft, later concluded to be a *tongkang* carrying oil drums.	About 180 degrees bearing and 6000 yards distance. Sunk.
13.2.42	Dive bombing and shelling intensified, especially around AA positions on Keppel golf course.	
1100	Engaged targets on West Coast Road with Siloso.	Harassing fire
1300	Fired on Japanese troops advancing on Pasir Panjang using map. These troops were about to launch the major attack on the Malay Regiment and Pasir Panjang from about 1400 hours.	
1400	Shelled by enemy 5.9 inch battery located near Jurong River. Concrete cover to No. 2 gun hit and gun damaged. Magazine hit twice. Shell splinters penetrate the steel door: three killed, several wounded. Indian other ranks left and took cover in old magazines to the E. of Labrador fort. Captain Kinlock got an Indian officer (Jemadar Lal Khan) and enough men to man one gun. Remaining gun fired at West Coast Road target, attracting further enemy fire. As a result all Indian other ranks left the fort for good.	
1830	Demolished. Cannot bear closer than Pasir Panjang village due to a 310 degree arc, itself caused by overhead cover against bombing.	

APPENDIX E

Date	Event	Remarks

14–15.2.42   Remaining 26 (including 16 Australians) redeployed as an infantry platoon, part of a larger force under Major Macleod-Carey. Sent to the Morse road-Pender-Keppel dockyard area. They formed the reserve behind Bukit Chermin from 1800. Came under attack from mortar, machine-gun and air strafing that evening and next day. Constant changes in organisation.

16.2.42   Japanese marched personnel to Gillman Barracks, detaining them there for five days with just flour and water. They then marched independently to Changi POW camp.

Faber Command's 6 inch guns fired 240 HE [high explosive] and 54 'CPBC' [common pointed ballistics cap] over three days.
Changi Command's 6 inch guns fired 600 HE and 150 'CPBC' over a longer period. This is a fraction of the 10,700 shells (590 per gun) available.[4]

APPENDIX E

War Diary for Siloso Battery

Date	Event	Remarks
11.2.42		
1200	Labrador and Siloso engaged enemy concentrations at the west end of West Coast Road and at Jurong river position.	
12.2.42		
Afternoon	Engaged targets on West Coast Road with Labrador. Fired on Oil Tanks at Pulau Bukom.	At least two set on fire.
	HKSRA crew morale by now shaken by air raids here and at Labrador.	
2100	Engaged unidentified craft drifting slowly from W to E between P. Sebarok and St Johns West inside No. 2 minefield together with Siloso.	Sunk. Originally said to be a landing craft, probably a *tongkang* carrying oil drums.
13.2.42		
1100	Engaged targets on West Coast Road with Labrador.	Harassing fire
2115	Craft spotted approaching harbour entrance and sunk with two shells. Sole wounded survivor reports it was carrying Australian stragglers.	
2130	Ordered to expend as much ammunition on land targets as possible, as the enemy was now reported on the line of Alexandra Road.	
14.2.42		
0200	Visibility from Siloso observation posts down to about 2,000 yards, due to oil fires at Pulau Bukom and Normanton.	
0415	Ordered to prepare for demolition.	
0500	Following false rumours of landings, guns demolished with 40 lbs of gelignite per gun.	
0630	Personnel retired to Fort Connaught, where the guns were also destroyed. Manned the fort for defence.	

Appendix F

GUN STATISTICS

The 15 inch batteries

Main sources

1 WO252/1362: Inter-Service Topographical Department, 'Supplement on Defences to I.S.T.D (S.E.A.C) Docket on Singapore and Southern Johore', 29 May 1945. Reference to the gun manuals shows this to be approximately reliable. We prefer a source which follows the manuals more closely, and gives more details: John Campbell, 'British Heavy Coast-Defence Guns in World War Two', in John Roberts (ed.), *Warship 1995* (London: Conway Maritime Press, 1995), pp. 79–86.
2 Ian Buxton, *Big Gun Monitors* (Tynemouth: Trident, 1978), and *Naval Weapons of World War Two* (London: Conway, 1985).
3 War Diaries in the WO172 series, and gun logs from Priddy's Hard (Gosport) consulted at Winchester County Archives. It is possible the latter may eventually be housed at the new naval artillery museum at Gosport, called 'Explosion'.
4 The gun manual for 15 inch Mk. II mounting, and correspondence between Donald Carmichael and Commander C.B. Robbins on the guns' installation.

Warning

Gun statistics vary. The 240 degree traverse with gun stops in, and 290 degree traverse with them removed is, however, confirmed by the gun manuals. These give the limiting factor as hydraulic cables. Campbell is the most detailed source, and is consistent with the gun manuals and one of the officers who installed the weapons. The guns on Mk. II mountings may have been able to traverse almost 360 degrees if power was foregone, but their operation would then be difficult, and their efficiency against ships impaired.[1]

APPENDIX F

Context

For most British bases, the most powerful weapons were 9.2 inch guns. There were just seven 15 inch guns based on land in the British Empire. The only ones outside of Singapore were two at Wanstone, near Dover, from 1942–59, covering the English Channel. They were assisted by radar for target tracking.[2] By comparison, Spain had at least sixteen 15 inch guns in Vickers-Armstrong built turrets (similar to Singapore Mk. II mountings) from the 1930s.[3] The US had 16 inch guns around its coast, and at Panama and Hawaii.

Gun history

Designed in 1911, with Churchill authorising production in 1912, the 15 inch naval gun saw action on warships from 1915. It was on battleships such as *Barham* (Johore Battery No. 3 – Registered No. 88) and *Valiant* (Johore Battery No. 2 – No. 54) at the Battle of Jutland.[4] Buxton states that it was 'probably the most successful tactically and strategically of any of the world's navies' big guns', being the mainstay of British capital ships in the two World Wars. 58 turrets and 186 guns (produced between 1912 and 1918) served on 22 ships (16 capital ships and six monitors) until withdrawal from sea service in 1954.

The life-cycle of a gun

To appreciate the idea of 'HMS *Singapore*', the island as equivalent to a stationary battleship, it helps if we understand the life of the guns. A gun barrel was constructed from several rings. The innermost ring received rifling, that is, a spiral or 'corkscrew'. The purpose of this was to rotate the shell when the firing charge propelled the shell outwards, so making it more stable in flight. But every time a shell was fired the burning gases from the propellant charge eroded the rifling. In effect, a gun could fire about 200–300 rounds at full charge before its barrel needed relining. Ian Buxton's *Big Monitor Guns* (London: World Ship Society, 1978), p. 177 explains this as follows:

> the longer body and greater longitudinal inertia of the HE could result in unsteady flight if the rifling was too worn to give sufficient spin for stabilisation. The life of a gun was determined by the extent of erosion in the bore, caused mainly by the burning gases of the propellant charge ... A gun was generally condemned when wear reached about 0.74 in at one inch from the commencement of rifling ... . After removal from its mounting, a gun in good condition otherwise could be relined by replacing the inner A-tube at a cost of £5,000. Guns could thus have been fitted in several ships during their overall life-span.

Hence some of Singapore's guns had been rotated off battleships around 1930 to 1932, and sent eastwards.

APPENDIX F

Statistics for the 15 inch gun batteries

Pieces	Buona Vista Battery		Johore Battery		
	No. 1 Gun	No. 2 Gun	No. 1 Gun Right	No. 2 Gun Centre	No. 3 Gun Left
Map Ref.[5]	75621272	76051243	009181	013185	016190
Shell size	15 inch (381mm)	15 inch	15 inch	15 inch	15 inch
Mark	I	I	I	I	I
Max. Elevation	45 degrees	45 degrees	55 degrees	45 degrees	45 degrees
Registered No.	146	174	78	54	88
Manufacturer and date of manufacture[6]	Elswick 1918	Vickers 1918	Vickers 1915	Woolwich 1915	Beardmore 1915
Date supplied from RN sources	1932	1932	1930	1932	1932
Gun installation	1938–39	1938	1936–37	1938–39	1938–39
Previous History	No Vessel given	No vessel given	No Vessel given. Started as an experimental 14 inch and rebored	HMS Valiant 1915 until refitting	HMS Barham 1915 until refitting
Max range (yds) (a)	36900	36900	36900	36900	36900
Rounds fired in Singapore	0	0	0	116[7]	78[8]
Max. Depression (deg)	2	2	5	2	2
Shell weight	1938 lbs (879 kg)	1938 lbs	1938 lbs	1938 lbs	1938 lbs
Gun weight (90 ton barrel and 10 ton breech)	100 tons (101,605 kg)	100 tons	100 tons	100 tons	100 tons
Length	650.4 in	650.4 in	650.4 in	650.4 in	650.4 in
Rate of fire (r.p.m.)	1–2	1–2	1–2	1–2	1–2
Arc of fire (degrees clockwise when true north is zero)					
Buffers in place	61–301	61–301	67.5–247.5	60–300	75.5–315.5
Buffers removed	36–326	36–326	not applicable	35–325	50.5–340.5
Hydraulic power disconnected	360	360	not applicable	360	360
Speed of elevation	5 degrees/sec	360	not applicable	360	360
Speed of traverse	3 degrees/sec	360	not applicable	360	360

Direction

Targets were observed from hills. There was a 100 foot stereoscopic rangefinder. This and a depression range finder fed information to the fire control post. There a fire direction table translated the information into range and bearing allowing for target direction and speed. This data was fed to the gun by electrical induction, by means of Magslip cables.

Mountings					
Mark	II	II	I	II	II

Destroyed

Date	From 0600 11 February (b)		2045 hours 12 February (d)		
Method for gun	250 lbs gelignite		350 lbs	350lbs	350lbs
Result	One gun intact, but only with manual operation		Destroyed	Destroyed	Destroyed

APPENDIX F

Notes for the 15 inch gun battery statistics

a) The Wanstone Battery of two 15 inch guns, the only other land-based 15 inch guns in the British Empire, had a maximum range of 42,000 yards or more if 'supercharge' was used. This supercharge was not available in Singapore. However, we should note that the maximum range for hitting another ship in action was held by HMS *Warspite*, which hit the Italian *Giulio Cesare* at 26,200 yards in July 1940.

b) All the 15 inch guns were demolished, except one at Buona Vista. Australian POWs stated the Japanese got this one gun working, with manual operation. Royal Engineers destroyed Johore Battery including workshops, the railway crane and magazines. The latter were blown up with timed explosive pencils on a one hour delay. The Japanese also got two 6 inch guns working.

c) Changi Hill housed the Fort observation and command post. It also housed the Johore Battery's observation post, with its 100 foot 'Barr and Stroud' Rangefinder. Beneath 'in solid rock' were battery and fortress plotting rooms. Faber Command's command post was at Mount Faber.

d) When Johore Battery guns were demolished by 350 lbs of gelignite in the breach, with a fuse, reports stated that 'the whole area was an inferno, and ... the jungle which ran for miles was set ablaze'.[9]

e) Weight: gun 90 tons; gun and breech 100 tons; total gun in action, 373 tons.[10] Barrel length: about 16.5 metres or 54.2 feet.[11]

f) HMS *Terror*. HMS *Terror* was a monitor ship with 15 inch guns. It was stationed at Singapore from January 1934 to January 1940, to provide cover while the more permanent heavy guns were being installed and finished. With two 15 inch guns (30 degree elevation – range 33,550 yards or 30,680 metres) it would have been stationed just southeast of the naval base in war, and integrated into the fire control system.[12]

g) The crew of a 15 inch gun was considerable. For a typical naval style turret mounting two guns, it came to 95, broken down to:
- Gunhouse 17 (officer, gunlayers, gun crew, sightsetters)
- Working Chamber 6
- Magazine 7
- Shell-room 22
- Control, direction, transmitting, ordnance artificers 31[13]

h) The Mk. II mounting resembled a battleship 'turret' in many ways, but lacked heavy armour. Its shield was as thin as 2 inches in places.

The smaller guns[14]

Main source: Public Record Office, London
WO252/1362: Inter-Service Topographical Department, 'Supplement on Defences to I.S.T.D (S.E.A.C) Docket on Singapore and Southern Johore, Amendment No. 1', 29 May 1945.

APPENDIX F

Statistics for the smaller guns[15]

Gun type	Range (yards)'	Shell weight
6 inch Mk. 7	14,100 (8 miles)	100 lbs
6 inch Mk. 24	24,500 (14 miles)	102 lbs
9.2 inch	31,300 (18 miles)	380 lbs
9.2 inch	26,900 (15 miles)	380 lbs

The 9.2 inch gun range given is for Tekong. This document gives a shorter range for Connaught's 9.2 inch guns: 29,600 yards (15 miles).
Older models of 6 inch guns had been a principal armament in coast defence since 1882, as '80 pdrs'.

Anti motor torpedo boat (AMTB/close defence guns)

One 18 pdr, four 12 pdr, and a number of twin-barreled 6 pdrs, all for close defence.

High explosive (HE) and armour piercing (AP) ammunition available in 1942, compared to field artillery[16]

Coastal artillery (excluding 6, 12 and 18 pdrs)

	No.	HE per gun	AP per gun	Total HE/AP
15 inch	5	None	250	0/1200
9.2 inch	6	25	300	75/1800
6 inch	18	50	590	10700

Field artillery (excluding 2 pdrs, 3.7 and 4.5 inch Howitzers and 75mm)

	No.	HE per gun	AP per gun	Total HE/AP
18 pdr	59	2,800	112	470400/18600
25 pdr	166	2,327	22	137300/1300

There were almost a million rounds of HE for the combined field guns and mortars, in addition to their AP and smoke shells.

Appendix G
THE FIRE COMMANDS[1]

The following are breakdowns of guns by Fire Command. For the modern guns this is precise. For close defence guns it is an approximation, due to the inadequacy of the sources. Where the relevant Royal Artillery war diaries describe a battery, this is the preferred source.

Faber Fire Command

Modern guns installed in the 1930s

Battery	Guns	Location	Personnel	Comments
Buona Vista	2 – 15 inch	South Coast	31 Coast RA	Did not fire
Pasir Laba	2 – 6 inch	West coast	HKSRA	One gun fired
Labrador	2 – 6 inch	South coast	HKSRA	Fired sea and land
Siloso	2 – 6 inch	W Blakang Mati	HKSRA	Fired sea and land
Serapong Spur	2 – 6 inch	NE Blakang Mati	HKSRA	Did not fire
Connaught	3 – 9.2 inch	SE Blakang Mati	RA	Fired landward only
Silingsing	2 – 6 inch	E Pulau Brani	HKSRA	Did not fire

AMTB (anti motor torpedo boat and close harbour defence)

Battery	Guns	Location	Personel	Comments
Berlayer Point	2 – 12 pdrs	Near Labrador	RA	See endnote[2]
Pulau Hantu	1 – 18 pdr	Pulau Hantu	RA	
Oso, Siloso Pt	1 – 12 pdr	Blakang Mati	HKSRA	
Berala Reping No.	2 – twin 6 pdr	NE Blakang Mati	RA	
Teregah	2 – dummies	Blakang Mati	None	Wooden 6 pdr decoys
Loudon	1 – 6 pdr[3]			

Notes for Faber Command

- Blakang Mati ('behind death' in Malay). Now Sentosa (Isle of Tranquillity). In 1941 it housed several batteries. About 2¼ miles by ¾ mile, it lies ½ mile

APPENDIX G

south of Singapore. Explanations of the name include the dangerous reefs which originally lay at the western entry to Keppel Harbour.
- Berlayer Point, Pulau Hantu and Siloso Point together were intended to stop any enemy entering Keppel Harbour from the West
- AMTB guns had traverses of less than 180 degrees, and were generally not sited to fire landwards, e.g. Berlayer not at all, Pulau Hantu only towards Berlayer Point. Many sources suggest the 6 inch guns could fire all-round. In fact the traverse varied greatly. Only a few, such as the 9.2 inch guns in naval-style turret mountings, and the 6 inch guns on Tekong, had a traverse at least close to 360 degrees.
- Where guns were manned by HKSRA, engine rooms and lights were operated by British personnel. There was a British Officer Commanding and section officer, and also volunteers on searchlights.

Changi Fire Command

Modern guns installed in the 1930s

Battery	Guns	Location	Personnel	Comments
Johore Battery	3 – 15 inch	Changi*	7 Coast RA	Fired Johore, Singapore
Changi	2 – 6 inch	Changi	HKSRA	Fired Johore, P.Ubin
Beting Kusah	2 – 6 inch	Changi	HKSRA	No record found
Tekong	3 – 9.2 inch	W Tekong	RA	Fired on Johore, P.Ubin
Sphinx	2 – 6 inch	W Tekong	HKSRA	Fired on Johore, P.Ubin
Pengerang	2 – 6 inch	S Johore coast		Fired at junk 11.2.42

AMTB (anti motor torpedo boat and close harbour defence)

Battery	Guns	Location	Comments
Calder Harbour	2 – twin 6 pdrs	Calder Harbour	
Pulau Sajahat	2 – twin 6 pdr	2 miles N Changi Pt	Small island
Palm	2 – twin 6 pdr	Changi Outer	
School	2 – twin 6 pdrs	Changi Inner	
Pulau Ubin	2 – twin 6 pdrs	Pulau Ubin	Emplacement only. No guns.
Ladang	1 – 12 pdr	Tekong	Fired at P.Ubin 2100 on 13.2.42

Demolition

12.2.42 Johore, Changi, Beting Kusa, Palm
14.2.42 Sajahat, Ladang, Calder, Sphinx, Tekong, Pengerang

GLOSSARY

Adat	Malay custom.
Attap	Thatch constructed from the *nipa* palm.
Battery	A group of guns controlled as one unit, though they might be placed some distance, even several hundred feet, apart.
Breech	The rear of a gun barrel.
Digger	Slang for Australian soldier
Gingkos	An ornamental tree.
Godown	A warehouse.
Kampong	A Malay village, often of houses built on stilts and roofed with palm thatch.
Padang	An open green or recreational space.
Padi	Dry rice fields.
Pulau	Island.
Regiment	A unit of troops. Japanese infantry regiments normally comprised three infantry battalions (about 2,600 to 3,500 men).
Sook Ching	Purification through purging. The Japanese screening of Chinese males to identify and eliminate 'anti-Japanese' elements. Since most survivors experienced only the screening, it is also remembered as the 'selection'.
Tongkang	A Chinese junk or sailing boat of moderate size.
Torii	Japanese word for a gate, usually with a flat cross-beam, and associated with the entrance to a shrine.
Traverse	The horizontal rotation or swing of a gun.

NOTES

PREFACE

1 For instance Public Record Office, Kew Gardens, England (henceforth all documents are from this source, unless otherwise indicated), WO172/176, containing a report on coast defences by A.D. Curtis. See also WO172/180, which has a detailed report on Faber fire command. Both appear to have been drawn up in Changi in 1942. By contrast, other artillery officers escaped to India and Ceylon, where they wrote reports. Both lacked the original documents, which had been ordered destroyed. As the report in WO172/176 warns 'all written records existing prior to 15 February have been destroyed'.

1 INTRODUCTION

1 For the impact on decolonisation, see Karl Hack, *Defence and Decolonisation in Southeast Asia: Britain, Malaya and Singapore 1941–1968* (Richmond, Surrey: Curzon, 2001), pp. 35–55.
2 Roosevelt's War Message to Congress of 8 Dec. 1941, as cited in Oscar Theodore Barck, Jr, *America in the World: Twentieth Century History in Documents* (New York: Meridian, 1961), pp. 333–4. Roosevelt's precise words were 'Yesterday, December 7, 1941 a date which will live in infamy the United States of America was suddenly and deliberately attacked by naval and air forces of the Empire of Japan'. Whether Japan's surprise attack was the real infamy, or Britain and America's breath-takingly inadequate state of readiness for Japanese actions which intelligence warned them were possible, if not likely, is a moot point.
3 *Matador* is emphasised to some extent by Dr Ong Chit Chung (see below in Chapter 1), and even more so in Andrew Gilchrist, *Malaya 1941: The Fall of an Empire* (London: Hale, 1991). The latter seems to suggest it could have disrupted Japanese plans, whereas its cancellation dispirited the defenders, and left them with no adequate back-up plans.
4 C.M. Turnbull, *A History of Singapore, 1819–1988* (Oxford: Oxford University Press, 1989), p. 183; Brian Farrell, Appendix 3, in Murfett *et al.*, *Between Two Oceans: A Military History of Singapore* (Singapore: Oxford University Press, 1999), pp. 341–64.
5 This point is not emphasised enough in much of the Malayan campaign literature, but can be corrected by reading works with a wider Pacific focus. See for instance H.P. Willmott, *Empires in the Balance: Japanese and Allied Pacific Strategies to April 1942* (London: Orbis, 1982), pp. 93–4, 168–70.
6 Ian Morrison, *Malayan Postscript* (Kuala Lumpur: S Abdul Majeed, 1993 edition), first published as *Malayan Postscript* (London: Faber, 1942). For an introduction to the rest

of the '1942' literature, see Catherine Porter, 'Autopsies on the Southeast Asia Debacle: A Review Article', *Pacific Affairs* 16, 2 (June 1943), 206–15. The books reviewed, written by reporters, included George Weller, *Singapore is Silent* (New York: Harcourt Weller, 1942); Cecil Brown, *Suez to Singapore* (New York: Random House, 1942); and O.D. Gallagher, *Action in the East* (New York: Doubleday, 1942).

7 For this debate, see also one of the very best accounts of events, Louis Allen, *Singapore 1941–1942* (London: Frank Cass, 1993 edition), pp. 202–46. For civilian woes, see CO967/77.

8 Actually, told this way the story misses out the important postwar reports of the campaign commanders. The ones published at this time include Lt-General A.E. Percival's 'Operations of Malaya Command from 8 December 1941 to 15 February 1942', in the Second Supplement to the *London Gazette* of 20 Feb. 1948, published 26 February 1948; and Air Chief Marshal Sir Robert Brooke-Popham, Commander-in-Chief, Far East, 'Operations in the Far East from 17 October 1940 to 27 December 1941', in the Supplement to the *London Gazette* of 20 January 1948, published on 22 January 1948. Of the two, Brooke-Popham's, complete with appendices, was the more informative. But, unlike Kirby's works, these remained better known to specialists than to a wider public and academia.

9 S. Woodburn Kirby, *The War Against Japan: The Loss of Singapore* (London, 1957).

10 Kirby, Major-General Stanley Woodburn: born 1895; 2nd Lt Royal Engineers 1914 serving Europe and Mesopotamia and Military Cross; Singapore 1923–6; variously Staff College, War Office and Imperial Defence College in the 1930s; India 1940-3, rising to D.C.G.S; War Office 1943–4; Deputy Chief of Staff, Control Commission for Germany, 1945; retired 1947; military historian, 1950. In late 1935, as a Lt-Colonel and General Staff Officer II in the War Office dealing with Singapore, Kirby was brought to the Imperial Defence College, and wrote an unofficial report entitled 'Notes on Singapore'. These suggested that, with the imminent completion of the Fortress defences, the Japanese would not attempt to attack Singapore directly, as previously anticipated. He recommended mobile columns to fan out from Singapore, in order to counter landings on the east coast of the mainland, in Johore. He was thus one of the earliest proponents of a switch in emphasis from 'Fortress' to mainland defence. In 1935–6, Dobbie and Percival then added the idea that the Japanese might land in northern Malaya, and in southern Thailand too. So Kirby's own, early ideas were transitional between the 'Fortress Singapore' and 'Forward Defence' approaches. See Ong Chit Chung, *Operation Matador: Britain's War Plans against the Japanese, 1918–1941* (Singapore: Times Academic Press, 1997), pp. 41–3 (and footnotes 132ff.), 61. See also WO106/5698; CAB122/25; and Imperial War Museum, P21/41, Percival Papers, Col. Thomas Hutton to Lt.-Col. Percival, 13 Jan. 1936, with enclosed 'Notes on Singapore'.

11 S. Woodburn Kirby, *Singapore: The Chain of Disaster* (London: Cassell, 1971).

12 To take but a couple of quotations even from Kirby's tamer book, *The Loss of Singapore*: 'the disasters which befell the British Commonwealth forces in the Far East had their origins in events which took place between the First and Second World Wars (p. 451), and (when talking of Wavell, who he admired), 'nor could any one man in the short space of six weeks have been able to rectify the failures of the previous twenty years' (p. 468).

13 C.N. Parkinson, *Britain in the Far East: The Singapore Naval Base* (Singapore: Donald Moore, 1955), chapter I, 'The Tide of Empire', pp. 1–5, says there were 14 British gunboats on the Yangtze, but by Second World War, just one. For him, the tide of empire turned with the decisions of a Liberal Government, in 1908, to favour using public money to redistribute wealth and offer welfare payments, meaning an increasing reluctance to fund the nodal points and ships on which empire relied. This

sounds suspiciously like the Tory interpretation of history, in which welfare and attention to the unwashed masses caused decline in what really mattered, Britain's reputation and power abroad. The decision to withdraw capital ships from the East was actually taken in 1905, having more to do with strategic overstretch when faced with increased German naval power, rather than with welfare, egalitarianism or Liberalism. Indeed, there were still twenty gunboats on the Yangtze in September 1939. The final dispersal began that October, following Japanese expansion in southern China and Japanese suggestions their removal would minimise the chance of incidents. The majority went to Singapore and were refitted as minesweepers.

14 W.D. MacIntyre, *The Rise and Fall of the Singapore Naval Base, 1919–1942* (London: Macmillan, 1979); James Neidpath, *The Singapore Naval Base and the Defence of Britain's Far Eastern Empire, 1919–1941* (Oxford: Clarendon Press, 1981). A full list of this wave of books would be long indeed, including the likes of Hamill, Marder and more. For a review of the school, see Malcolm Murfett, 'Living in the Past: A Critical Re-examination of the Singapore Naval Strategy, 1918–1941', *War and Society*, 11, 1 (May 1993), 73–103. It is, of course, a matter of emphasis, each 'school' stressing one or more aspects, despite usually acknowledging most of the full range of issues.

15 G.C. Peden, 'A Matter of Timing: The Economic Background to British Foreign Policy, 1937–1939', *History* 69 (February 1984), 15–28.

16 Key examples of this school include Ritchie Ovendale, '*Appeasement*' *and the English-Speaking World: Britain, the United States, the Dominions, and the Policy of 'Appeasement', 1937–1939* (Cardiff: University of Wales, 1975); W.R. Louis, *British Strategy in the Far East, 1919–1939* (Oxford: Oxford University Press, 1977); Peter Lowe, *Great Britain and the Origins of the Pacific War* (Oxford: Clarendon Press, 1977); and, more recently, E.M. Andrews, *The Writing on the Wall: The British Commonwealth and Aggression in the Far East* (Sydney: Allen and Unwin, 1987). Nicholas Tarling's *Britain and the Onset of the Pacific War* (Cambridge: Cambridge University Press, 1996) will certainly not be the last in this genre, but it may well remain the book with the most comprehensive regional coverage. Then there are studies of Britain's relations with specific countries, especially Thailand (so important for *Matador*, the British plan for a pre-emptive seizure of southern Thai ports). For the latter, see Nigel Brailey, *Thailand and the Fall of Singapore: A Frustrated Revolution* (Boulder, Colorado and London: Westview, 1986); Richard Aldrich, *The Key to the South: Britain, the United States and Thailand during the Approach to the Pacific War, 1929–1942* (Kuala Lumpur: Oxford University Press, 1993); and E. Bruce Reynolds, *Thailand and Japan's Southern Advance, 1940–1945* (New York: St. Martin's Press, 1994). These show how diplomatic complications, the need not to alienate Thailand, or be the first to abrogate its neutrality, complicated *Matador*.

17 Indeed, even growing US–British partnership in 1940–1 did not guarantee a higher priority for the East, since the two decided to take a defensive stance in the East, and deal with Hitler first. Also, when, how and even if a United States President could turn financial and logistical support into a full war were still very real questions. For the background, see Malcolm Murfett, *Fool-Proof Relations: The Search for Anglo-American Naval Cooperation During the Chamberlain Years, 1937–1940* (Singapore: Singapore University Press, 1984).

18 Raymond Callahan's *The Worst Disaster: The Fall of Singapore* (Singapore: Cultured Lotus, 2001, first published in 1977). See also his 'Churchill and Singapore', in Brian P. Farrell and Sandy Hunter (eds), *Sixty Years On: The Fall of Singapore Revisited* (Singapore: Eastern Universities Press, 2002) pp. 156–72.

19 Brian Farrell made this point well in his '1941 An Overview', paper presented at the 'Sixty Years On: The Fall of Singapore Revisited', conference, National University of

Singapore, 15–17 Feb. 2002. This has now been published under the same name, Farrell and Sandy Hunter (eds), *Sixty Years On*, pp. 173–82.

20 Brian Farrell, *The Basis and Making of British Grand Strategy, 1940–1943: was there a plan?* (Lewiston, New York: E. Mellen Press, 1998), 2 volumes.

21 Again, Brian Farrell made this point well in his '1941 An Overview', paper presented at the 'Sixty Years On: The Fall of Singapore Revisited', conference, National University of Singapore, 15–17 Feb. 2002.

22 Harrow was Churchill's school. Ethelred II (born 968, reigned 978–1016) was dubbed *Unread* at the time, or with bad counsel, interpreted by later generations as unready. His defensive strategy was to ward off the Danish invaders by paying them increasingly large amounts of money, called Danegeld, when they threatened English shores. But for some reason they kept coming back. Ethelred II was eventually deposed by the Danes. Soon after, Canute became the first Danish king of England.

23 Ong, *Operation Matador*. But this position was stated in even clearer terms in reviews and in letters appearing in the *Straits Times*, see for instance letter from Ong Chit Chung to the, *Straits Times* 30 April 1997, p. 30; *Straits Times*, 5 April 1997, p. 4; *Sunday Times* (Singapore), p. 8; and *Straits Times*, 16 Feb. 1992. Ong Chit Chung has been teaching military history in Singapore since the 1970s, see *New Nation*, 14 June 1979, p. 11.

24 In Aug. 1940 Churchill promised Russia 200 aircraft (on top of 40 already sent), and the diversion of 200 American aircraft. The opinion that these aircraft could have arrived in time comes from a British author, Air Commodore Sir Henry Probert, in his *The Forgotten Air Force: The Royal Air Force in the War Against Japan, 1941–1945* (London: Brassey's, 1995), p. 35.

25 Earle Page, *Truant Surgeon* (Sydney, 1963), pp. 310–16, as cited in Glen St John Barclay, 'Singapore Strategy: the Role of the United States in Imperial Defense', *Military Affairs* 39, 2 (April 1975), 54–9.

26 For a short introduction to the British–Australian spat, see Richard Wilkinson, 'Ashes to ashes', *History Today* 52, 2 (February 2002), pp. 36–42. See also: *Guardian*, 29 Feb. 1992; and *Independent*, 29 Feb. 1992.

27 Brian Farrell, Appendix 3, in Murfett *et al.*, *Between Two Oceans*, pp. 341–64.

28 Wigmore was a representative of the Australian Department of Information in Singapore during the campaign. He was given the job of writing the volume on the loss of Singapore by Gavin Long, who was the overall editor of the 22-volume Australian official war history of Second World War. Long himself was a journalist, who had been appointed on the recommendation of C.E.W. Bean, another journalist and writer of the Australian official war history of First World War. Bean had helped create the myth of the Anzac legend of the Australian soldiers being rugged bushman going off to war bound together by the common bonds of mateship. Long, too, believed, as he wrote in the last volume of the World War Two series, that, 'Armies are not created in a social vacuum and derive their characteristics from the community from which they spring'. See John Murphy, 'The New Official History', *Australian Historical Studies*, 26, 102 (1994), 119–24; and A. B. Lodge, *The Fall of General Gordon Bennett* Sydney: Allen and Unwin, 1986), pp. 65–6, 296–306. For more on Wigmore's volume and its relationship to the Anzac myth and Australian historiography, see Chapter 6 below, p. 157.

29 For a bizarre early example Curtin proposing reliance on airships rather than sea ships, see David Day, *John Curtin: A Life* (New York: HarperCollins, 1999), pp. 347–8.

30 The relationship between politics and historical interpretation (let alone historians as individuals) is tendentious. Nevertheless, broadly speaking critics of empire and British strategy have been more likely to come from, or sympathise with, the Australian Labor Party. The Labor Party, in turn, has had strong union and Irish

Catholic support. Those Australians less critical of British strategies, and of close Australian alignment with them, have been more likely to come from, or sympathise with, the opinions of, the more Anglophone Liberal and National Parties and their conservative predecessors. See for instance *Weekend Australian* 29 Feb. to 1 March 1992, on Keating's Feb. remarks. It said 'three respected military historians' (including David Day and Gregory Pemberton) 'supported the thrust of Mr Keating's assessment'. Day called it 'a perfectly accurate representation of Britain's attitude to Australia. We have to look at the world through Australian eyes, not British eyes'.

31 David Day, *John Curtin*, pp. 446–57. The units concerned were the Australian 6th and 7th Divisions (64,000 troops), and the dates for the main dispute, from 15 Feb. (the first Australian suggestions these divisions should go directly home) to 22 Feb., when a Curtin telegram was sent rebuffing Churchill and Roosevelt's pleas, and Churchill's ruse of saying the ships had been routed in anticipation of Australian agreement, and might not have the fuel to reach Australia direct. For a more popular rendition of this, and other Singapore Fall stories, see Gregory Pemberton, 'Out of crisis a new-found sovereignty', *Weekend Australian*, Special Edition, 15–16 Feb. 2002.

32 David Day, *The Great Betrayal: Britain, Australia and the Pacific War* (London: Oxford University Press, 1988): David Day, *Reluctant Nation: Australia and the allied defeat of Japan 1942–45* (Melbourne: Oxford University Press, 1992). John McCarthy, 'Singapore and Australian Defence, 1921–1942', *Australian Outlook*, 25, 2 (August 1971), 165–80; John McCarthy, 'The "Great Betrayal" Reconsidered: An Australian Perspective', *Australian Journal of International Affairs* 48, 1 (May 1994), 53–60; and also his *Australia and Imperial Defence, 1918–39* (St Lucia: University of Queensland Press, 1976). Peter Dennis, 'Australia and the Singapore Strategy', in Farrell and Hunter (eds), *Sixty Years On*, also suggests Australia failed to rigorously analyse assumptions in the 1920s–30s. He only does this by looking at debates within the Australian defence establishment of the time.

33 Brian Farrell was still completing his campaign study, *The Defence and Fall of Singapore*, at the time of writing, with the germ of his ideas available in his chapters in Murfett *et al.*, *Between Two Oceans*, pp. 175–247, 336–64. For other key examples of these genres, see: A.E. Percival, *The War in Malaya* (London: Eyre and Spottiswoode, 1949); Clifford Kinvig, *Scapegoat: General Percival of Singapore* (London: Brassey's, 1996), and 'General Percival and the Fall of Singapore', in Farrell and Hunter (eds), *Sixty Years On*, pp. 240–61; Gordon Bennett, *Why Singapore Fell* (Sydney: Angus & Robertson, 1944); and A.B. Lodge, *The Fall of General Gordon Bennett* (Sydney, 1986). For works by and about successful field officers, see Ian Stewart, *History of the Argyll and Sutherland Highlanders 2nd Battalion (The Thin Red Line) Malayan Campaign, 1941–42* (London, 1947); and Stan Arneil, *Black Jack: The Life and Times of Brigadier Sir Frederick Galleghan* (Melbourne, 1983). Warren, *Singapore 1942*, pp. 345–53, is a good source for further battalion and regimental histories. Then there are more anecdotal histories, such as Jonathan Moffatt and Audrey Holmes McCormick, *Moon over Malaya: A Tale of Argylls and Marines* (Stroud: Tempus, 2001).

34 The 'race war' and nationalism school of thought permeates, or at least informs, several works from 1945, through Allen, to present day, notably: Morrison, *Malayan Postscript*; Christopher Thorne, *The Issue of War: Societies and the Far Eastern War of 1941–45* (London: Hamish Hamilton, 1985), pp. 185ff.; Elphick, *The Pregnable Fortress*, *passim*, at least in the sense of nationalism undermining Asian assistance of the empire and reliability of troops; and at the Pacific level, John Dower, *War Without Mercy: Race and Power in the Pacific War* (London: Faber and Faber, 1986). British colonial authorities also took the lesson that old trusteeship attitudes to race and colonies were deficient for modern war, see Hack, *Defence and Decolonisation*, pp. 43–9.

35 Elphick: *Singapore: The Pregnable Fortress* (London: Hodder, 1995); Elphick and

Smith *Odd Man Out: The Story of the Singapore Traitor* (London: Hodder and Stoughton, 1993).
36 Fujiwara Iwaichi, F. *Kikan: Japanese Army Intelligence Operations in Southeast Asia during World War II* (Singapore: Heinemann Asia, 1983).
37 All these authors (except Elphick) have published articles and reviews in the journal *Intelligence and National Security* (*INS*). But see especially Anthony Best, *British Intelligence and the Japanese Challenge in Asia* (London: Macmillan, 2002), as well as his 'Constructing an Image: British Intelligence and Whitehall's Perception of Japan, 1931–1939', *INS* 11, 3 (1996), 403–23, and '"This Probably Over-Valued Military Power": British Intelligence and Whitehall's Perception of Japan, 1939–41', *INS*, 12, 3 (1997), 67–94; Peter Elphick, *Far Eastern File: The Intelligence War in the Far East, 1930–1945* (London: Hodder and Stoughton, 1997); Richard Aldrich, *Intelligence and the War Against Japan: Britain, America and the Politics of Secret Service* (Cambridge: Cambridge University Press, 2000), and John Ferris, '"Worthy of Some Better Enemy?": The British Estimate of the Imperial Japanese Army, 1919–41', *Canadian Journal of History*, 28 (1993), 223–56. For a more Singapore-based perspective on the same theme, there is Ban Kah Choon, *Absent History: The Untold Story of Special Branch Operations in Singapore, 1915–42* (Singapore: Raffles, 2000). Finally, for the 'conspiracy' branch of this school, see James Rusbridger and Eric Nave, *Betrayal at Pearl Harbor* (London: Michael O'Mara, 1991), and a critique of it in Richard Aldrich, review of *Betrayal at Pearl Harbor*, in *INS*, 7, 3 (1992), 335–6.
38 John Ferris, '"Worthy of Some Better Enemy?"'; John Ferris, 'Student and Master: The United Kingdom, Japan, Airpower, and the Fall of Singapore, 1920–1941', in Farrell and Hunter (eds), *Sixty Years On*, pp. 94–121; 223–56; and Probert, *The Forgotten Air Force*, pp. 25–7.
39 Aldrich, *Intelligence and the War Against Japan*, pp. 60–6.
40 Two works in particular touch on airpower. Air Commodore Henry Probert's *The Forgotten Air Force* asks if the *Prince of Wales* could have been saved but for the ship's radio silence, and revises figures slightly, for instance saying there were 181 serviceable aircraft, not 158, in December 1941. A. D. Harvey, 'Army Air Force and Navy Air Force: Japanese Aviation and the Opening Phase of the War in the Far East", *War in History* 6, 2 (1999), pp. 174–204 argues that Japanese technical superiority (especially the numbers of Navy Zeros) has been exaggerated, even if its numbers have not.
41 James Leasor, *Singapore, The Battle that Changed the World: The Enthralling Story of the Rise and Fall of a Magical City* (London: House of Stratus, 2001). Noel Barber, *Sinister Twilight: The Fall of Singapore* (London: Arrow, 1988, first published in 1968). Another book in this genre has been republished more recently, namely: Frank Owen, *The Fall of Singapore* (London: Penguin, 2002). First published in 1960.
42 For instance, Ong Chit Chung cites Imperial War Museum, London, AL: Japanese Accounts of Strategy, Plans and Campaigns, 1941–1952. These were written by Japanese officers for the Historical Records Section of the First (Army) and Second (Navy) Demobilization Bureaus after the war, and translated. A full set is available at the Office of the Chief of Military History in Washington. See for instance *Malay Operations Record, November 1941-March 1942: The Records of the Malayan Operations of the 25th Army* (Monograph No. 54). For a more comprehensive list of Japanese sources as of 1977, see Allen, *Singapore 1941–1942*, bibliography, pp. 327, 331–4; and Allen, 'Notes on Japanese Historiography: World War Two', *Military Affairs* 35, 4 (December 1971), 133–8.
43 Masanobu Tsuji, *Shingapōru Ummei no tenki* [Singapore The Hinge of Fate] (Tokyo: Tōnanseihoku Shahan, 1952).

44 First published in English as Masanobu Tsuji (translated by Margaret Lake, introduction by Lt-Gen. Gordon Bennett), *Singapore: The Japanese Version*, (London: Constable, 1960). Now available under several titles, including, Masanobu Tsuji, *Singapore 1941–1942: The Japanese Version* (Singapore: Oxford University Press, 1988).

45 For Tsuji's political resurgence, see Robert Guillain, 'The Resurgence of Military Elements in Japan', *Pacific Affairs* 15, 3 (September 1952), 211–25.

46 Akashi Yoji, 'General Yamashita Tomoyuki', in Farrell and Hunter (eds), *Sixty Years On*, p. 193. Louis Allen also dubs Tsuji 'that notorious egotist', in his 'The Surrender of Singapore: The Official Japanese Version', *The Durham University Journal* 29, 1 (1967), 2. Tsuji temporarily withdrew himself from the General Staff when Yamashita refused reinforcement to troops hard-pressed at Kampar in late Dec. 1941 to early Jan. 1942, on the grounds that it was to be outflanked by sea. Yamashita valued Tsuji, but confided his frustration to his diary entry for 3 Jan. 1942. Those who see British command tensions as significant would do well to pay equal attention to frictions inside the Japanese command.

47 Presumably part of the attraction for Bennett was that both men had escaped without authorisation, and both claimed they did so to preserve their talents for later rebuilding, whether military or civil. The most helpful English-language details so far appear in Ian Ward's rather sensationalist, *The Killer They Called a God* (Singapore: Media Times, 1992), the 'god' in the title referring to the idea of a 'strategic god'. See especially pp. 110–13, 188–9, 298 and 302 for Japan's intelligence chief on Singapore, Lt-Colonel Sugita, blaming the *Sook Ching* on Tsuji. Ward was Southeast Asia correspondent for the *Daily Telegraph* from 1962–87. Tsuji's book on Malaya was his third in three years (starting with *Senkō Sanzenri* [3000 League Odyssey] in 1950, published in English as *Underground Escape* in 1952) leading up to his election to the House of Representatives in Oct. that year. In 1961 he went to Vientiane to meet the *Pathet Lao*, and subsequently disappeared. Information on Tsuji was also confirmed by a paper by Ishiku Tomoyuki, 'Colonel Tsuji and the Conduct of the Malaya/ Singapore Campaign', presented at the 'Sixty Years On: The Fall of Singapore Revisited', conference, National University of Singapore, 15–17 Feb. 2002. But other accounts seem to make Yamashita and Suzuki, his Chief of Staff, the primary causes of an 18 Feb. 1942 order for *genju shobun* (severe disposal, meaning execution without trial in military parlance) of hostile Chinese. See Akashi Yoji, 'General Yamashita Tomoyuki: commander of the Twenty-Fifth Army', in Farrell and Hunter (eds), *Sixty Years On*, p. 199.

48 All Japanese sources were provided and translated by David Sissons unless noted otherwise. *Senshi Sōsho* [War History Series], Volume 1, *Marē Shinkō Sakusen* [The Malayan Campaign] (Tokyo: Asagumo, 1966). This series, of over a hundred volumes, was the Japanese equivalent to the Australian and British official histories of the Second World War. It was produced by researchers in the Office of Military History in the National Defence College of the Defence Agency. There was an ad hoc committee for each work, with regular officers as the main authors. Its sources included papers from armed service ministries, diaries of participants, and interviews. For this and more Japanese sources, see Louis Allen, 'The Surrender of Singapore: The Official Japanese Version', 1–2. Other readily available Japanese-language works on the Malayan campaign are also seldom cited, such as the meticulously detailed work found in Yoshiki Saito's 1972 book, *Mōshin – Marē Shingapōru* [Determined Offensive: Malaya and Singapore] (Tokyo: Gakken, 1972). This was part of a paperback series aimed at the mass market, though with good access to the sources. Then there is Shigetaka Onda's *Marē-sen* [The Malayan Campaign] (Tokyo, 1977). Onda, a specialist author on military history, used the archives, and interviews of 5th

NOTES

Infantry Division men. His other books covered Guadacanal, New Guinea, Nomonhan, Mindanao, and the sinking of the *Yamato*.

49 Henry Frei was working on a book on the Japanese perspective at the time of his death in 2002. For a taste of his work, see, 'The Island Battle: Japanese Soldiers Remember the Conquest of Singapore', in Farrell and Hunter (eds), *Sixty Years On*, pp. 218–39. The book Frei was writing at the time of his death, the nearest we have to a Japanese soldier's-eye view (in English at any rate), is *Guns of February: Ordinary Japanese Soldiers' Views of the Malayan Campaign in 1941* (Singapore: Singapore University Press, 2003). See also Kazuo Tamayama and John Nunneley, *Tales by Japanese Soldiers of the Burma Campaign, 1942–1945* (London: Cassell Military, 2000). Also of relevance here are Henry Frei, *Japan's Southward Advance and Australia: From the Sixteenth Century to World War II* (Melbourne: Melbourne University Press, 1991), which was a pioneering work in presenting Japanese-language perspectives to an English-language readership; and his 'Japan Remembers the Malaya Campaign', in Paul Kratoska (ed.), *Malaya and Singapore During the Japanese Occupation* (Singapore: JSEAS Special Edition No. 3, 1995), pp. 148–68.

50 See for instance Akashi Yoji, 'General Yamashita Tomoyuki: commander of the Twenty-Fifth Army', in Farrell and Hunter (eds), *Sixty Years On*, pp. 183–207. Yamashita was the overall Japanese commander in the Malayan campaign.

51 This work is particularly useful for the perspective of the Japanese 5th Division (a Division raised in the Chūgoku, the Hiroshima district), which played a central role on Singapore itself.

52 Some documents, such as the War Diaries, have been used, but only in the most cursory fashion. Others, such as WO252/1259, containing maps and pictures, and WO252/1362, containing a 1945 Southeast Asia Command report on the guns and their fate after the Fall, we had not seen cited anywhere else at the time of writing.

53 Participation-observation at 'Fort Siloso Live', 7–10, 12–13 November 2001. At this event students were told they are 'recruits', before flag-raising, hauling a replica gun up a hill, talking to a 'Mrs Cooper' and *dhoby* (laundry) man, and then undergoing air-raid drill in one of the Fort's darkened, 'smoke'-filled tunnels. Finally, they were 'captured', marched off, and interrogated by 'Japanese' soldiers. The target audience was students within the range of nine to eleven years old. The event was repeated in Oct.-Nov. 2002.

2 SINGAPORE IN 1941

1 Tsuji, *Singapore 1941–1942*, p. 216.
2 For a very personal account of the feel of 1920s Singapore, see George Peet, *Rickshaw Reporter* (Singapore: Eastern Universities, 1985). A reporter on the *Straits Times*, Peet arrived in 1923, just in time to witness the completion of the causeway and the rapid rise of the motor car in the 1930s.
3 Leonore Manderson, *Sickness and the State: health and illness in colonial Malaya, 1870–1940* (Cambridge: Cambridge University Press, 1996).
4 In 1931 the population was 557,745, though by its fall in 1942 it had been swollen by refugees. By 1947, it had grown to 938,144. Saw Swee-Hock, 'Population Growth and Control', in Ernest Chew and Edwin Lee (eds), *A History of Singapore* (Singapore: Oxford University Press, 1991), p. 221.
5 R.B. Smith, 'Some Contrasts Between Burma and Malaya in British Policy in South-East Asia, 1942–1946', in R.B. Smith and A.J. Stockwell, *British Policy and the Transfer of Power in Asia: Documentary Perspectives* (London: SOAS, 1988), p. 31 gives an estimate of 5,278,866 for 1938.

6 For Chinatown in the 1950s, see Barrington Kaye, *Upper Nankin Street Singapore* (Singapore: University of Malaya Press, 1960), pp. 1–2, *passim*. In 1822 Raffles suggested the area southwest of the river be allocated to the Chinese.

7 *Straits Times*, Monday 16 April 2001, p. 19, Braema Mathi, 'Revive drop-off scheme for abandoned babies'. By contrast, between 1993 and 2000 just 41 babies were abandoned. Peter Dunlop, *Street Names of Singapore* (Singapore: Who's Who Publishing, 2000), p. 49. The Convent of the Holy Infant Jesus was opened in 1854 by Father Beurel, a French Jesuit priest who also founded St Joseph's Institution nearby (in premises now occupied by the Singapore Art Museum). Babies might be abandoned at the 'Gate of Hope' at the Bras Brasah-Victoria Street corner. The nuns moved from Victoria Street to Tao Payoh in 1983. The Victoria Street premises are now refurbished as the entertainment centre *Chijmes*.

8 E.M. Glover, *In Seventy Days: The Story of the Japanese Campaign in British Malaya* (London: Frederick Muller, 1946), p. 39.

9 Kirby, *The Loss of Singapore*, p. 183. There has been much debate on the lights. The moon would have been enough anyway, and Singapore's gas lamps would have taken time to extinguish.

10 Glover, *In Seventy Days*, pp. 157–8. Ivan Simson *Singapore, Too Little, Too Late: The Failure of Malaya's defences in 1942* (Singapore: Donald Moore for Asia-Pacific Press, 1970), p. 93. Simson suggests about 400 to 500 deaths a day (p. 96), and up to 2000 casualties and missing all-told. Large concrete pipes, up to 6 feet long, were also provided as shelters, and later on slit trenches too.

11 Leasor, *Singapore: The Battle That Changed the World*, p. 177 and 245–6. Noel Barber, *Sinister Twilight: The Fall of Singapore* (London: Collins, 1968), pp. 88–9 gives an account of one woman saved because three other people who were killed fell on top of her. Page 126 describes shells hitting Orchard Road. On page 245 Leasor quotes an 'eye-witness' thus: 'eight decapitated bodies in one street ... I looked at the drains on each side of the narrow street. They were full of water, bloody water'. Compare this to Lavinia Warner and John Sandilands, *Women Beyond the Wire: The True Story of Japan's P.O.W.s That Inspired the Motion Picture Paradise Road* (London: Arrow, 1997), pp. 27, 34, 41. As for the air raids, Singaporean author Goh Sin Tub has captured the same moment:

> 'We walk that eerie road,
> Devastated Singapore,
> Burning, billowing black,
> Bodies rushing on the road,
> Bodies still on the road
> (except that body, that part of body, in the drain
> minus arm, minus leg and don't know what ...
> pain everywhere.
> .... Is this real?

Goh Sin Tub, 'Remember that December?', from Robbie B. H. Goh (ed.), *Memories and Desires: A Poetic History of Singapore* (Singapore: Unipress, 1998), p. 27.

12 James Francis Warren, *Ah Ku and Karayuki-San: Prostitution in Singapore 1870–1940* (Singapore: Oxford University Press, 1993). Singapore was not so obviously 'Singalore', but the sin was there all the same, with sly prostitutes, and even 'rickshaw parades'.

13 The classic account for opium is Carl Trocki's *Opium and Empire: Chinese Society in Colonial Singapore, 1800–1910* (Ithaca and London: Cornell University Press, 1990).

NOTES

14 The Ma-Zu-Po (Tian Shang Sheng Mu) statue was imported from China in 1840. Thian Hock Keng temple in Telok Ayer Street has a particular importance, as the location of an early joss house (circa 1821–2) where immigrants burnt incense to the Goddess of the Sea after safe arrival.

15 The situation changed in 1941 of course, with United States entry against any Japanese move south looking more likely from July and August. British 'appeasement' and diplomacy in the East is a well worn theme. For a recent and comprehensive survey, see Nicholas Tarling, *Britain and the Onset of the Pacific War* (Cambridge: Cambridge University Press, 1996).

16 For the long Asian war of the Chinese, see Yen Ching-hwang, 'The Overseas Chinese and the Second Sino-Japanese War, 1937–1945, *Journal of the South Seas Society* 52 (August 1998), 150–9. It is easy to forget just how rigid this sense of racial hierarchy was, with very limited mixing, separate clubs, and different common rooms in some schools for Asian and European masters. John Butcher, *The British in Malaya, 1880–1941: A Social History of a European Community in Colonial South-East Asia* (Kuala Lumpur: Oxford University Press, 1979), pp. 167–92

17 E.M. Glover, quoted in Chan Heng Chee, *A Sensation of Independence: A Political Biography of David Marshall* (Singapore: Times, 1985), pp. 34–5. Also Glover, *In Seventy Days*, passim.

18 Dunlop, *Street Names of Singapore*, p. 33. Another explanation for the name is that it is a mispronunciation of *temak*, the Malay name for a species of tall tree.

19 WO32/3628, document 6A, 24 February 1934, mentions the need for Singapore to withstand Japanese bombardment and raiding parties, and mentioning 20 days as the period for a fleet to arrive from the Mediterranean, or 28 days from the Atlantic.

20 C.N. Parkinson, *Britain in the Far East: The Singapore Naval Base* (Donald Moore: Singapore, 1955), Chapter 1, 'The Tide of Empire', pp. 1–5, gives a brilliant and succinct view of Singapore's place in imperial changing communications. But for his less sure-footed interpretation of British decline, blaming it on domestic governments preference for welfare over guns, see the Introduction above, p. 213, note 13.

21 Singapore Correspondent, 'Opening of the Dock', passim, in *The Times Weekly Edition*, Thursday 3 March 1938, p. 34 (reprinted Singapore: Singapore History Consultants, 2001).

22 Leasor, *Singapore: The Battle That Changed the World*, pp. 123–4. Tsuji, *Singapore 1941–1942*, p. 218.

23 Turnbull, *A History of Singapore*, p. 137. Kallang opened in 1937.

24 See the next note for the Gillman Commission's views, and for the 'Kreta Ayer Incident' see Tanjong Pagar Constituency, *Tanjong Pagar: Singapore's Cradle of Development* (Singapore: Landmark Books for Tanjong Pagar Citizens' Consultative Committee, 1989), pp. 101–3. For the full background of rising strikes, communism and Kuomintang sentiment, see C.F. Yong, *The Origins of Malayan Communism* (Singapore: South Seas Society, 1997), pp. 74–8, passim.

25 See Major-General R.P. Pakenham-Walsh, *History of the Corps of the Royal Engineers 1938–1948 Volume 9*, (Chatham: Institution of Royal Engineers, 1958).

26 James McCrane, 'The Influence of the Royal Engineers in Singapore', *The Veteran* 7 (August 2001), 51–61 has good photographs and detail. He is writing a book on the Royal Engineers in Singapore.

27 Squadron Leader H. A. Probert, *History of Changi* (Score: Changi Prison, 1988). First printed by Prison Industries, 1965. The quotation on the barracks is from p. 34. Colonel L.N. Malan, 'Singapore: The Founding of the New Defences', *Royal Engineers Journal* Volume LIII (June 1938), pp. 213–35. The quotation on the junk is from p. 221.

28 For more detail on the RAF in the East, and Changi, see Probert, *The History of Changi* and Air Chief Marshal Sir David Lee, *Eastward: A History of the Royal Air Force in the Far East, 1945–1972* (London: HMSO, 1984). For the wider context of British defence and Singapore from 1941, see Hack, *Defence and Decolonisation*. After Kallang, Paya Leba was the next civil airport. Changi was originally handed over to the Singapore military, only taking over as the main civilian airport comparatively recently, in 1981. The postwar decision for the RAF to further develop Changi paralleled that of the 1920s to develop Sembawang. Basically, Tengah was fully occupied by tactical aircraft, so there was no runway capable of taking aircraft over 65,000 pounds without deteriorating. See WO203/6242.

29 For a good account of the empire peaking in the interwar period, see John Darwin. 'Imperialism in Decline? Tendencies in British Imperial Policy Between the Wars', *Historical Journal*, xxiii, 3 (1980), 657–79.

30 For the flavour of the time for Europeans, see Margaret Shennan, *Out in the Midday Sun: The British in Malaya, 1880–1939* (London: John Murray, 2000) and John Butcher, *The British in Malaya*.

31 The Colonial Office frowned on this practice when it involved its own staff from 1909 on, see Butcher, *The British in Malaya*, Chapter 8, 'European Men and Asian Women', pp. 193–222.

32 Turnbull, *A History of Singapore*, p. 136.

33 *Ibid.* Malayan Breweries has metamorphosed into Asia-Pacific Breweries, but it still produces Tiger Beer. In 1933 a German brewery was established too.

34 See Braddon *The Naked Island*, p. 60–1.

35 See for instance, Warner and Sandilands, *Women Beyond the Wire*, pp. 16, 23 following.

36 Warner and Sandilands *Women Beyond the Wire*, p. 22; E.M. Glover, *In Seventy Days*. Glover was managing editor of the Tribune Group of Malayan newspapers, and offered 'a newspaperman's viewpoint', in a script largely written in 1942, though published after the war. See pp. 8 and 47 for air-conditioning.

37 *Straits Times*, Monday 29 December 1941: 'Some folks these days walk around with long gloomy faces ... There are others who carry on with a smile and "Whistle while they Work". We are in the latter category. ...'

38 Barber, *Sinister Twilight*, front page, cites Churchill's *The Second World War*, Vol. 4, *The Hinge of Fate*, as follows: 'I confess that in my mind the whole Japanese menace lay in a sinister twilight ... If, on the other hand, Japanese aggression drew in America, I would be content to have it'.

39 Warner and Sandilands *Women Beyond the Wire*, p. 23. Some Australians were less lucky, Russell Braddon being served 'hot meat and vegetable stew for seventeen consecutive meals' until his gunner friends resorted to buying eggs fried by local cooks in the NAAFI canteen, Braddon *The Naked Island*, p. 56–7. For many the likes of Lavender Street became a welcome respite for their food if not for the ladies of the night. Indeed, they could seem almost unavoidable, given rickshaw pullers' propensity to go to take other ranks to such places regardless. For Lavender Street and resentment at the lack even of 'civility' by many civilians, see also pp. 51–2 and 58–9.

40 See WO106/2441, Bond telegram of 12 Dec. 1940, for the effect of this on the volunteers.

41 Ivan Simson, *Singapore, Too Little, Too Late*, p. 20, uses the phrase 'a fool's paradise'.

42 Russell Braddon, *The Naked Island*, p. 51, describes the first drive through Singapore of Australian troops, fresh off their transports from Sydney 'young and full of hope' (pp. 50–1).

3 THE FATAL DECISIONS

1 Brooke-Popham to Ismay, October 29, 1941, Kings College London: Liddell Hart Centre for Military Archives, Brooke-Popham Papers v/1/19; Brooke-Popham, 'Most Secret. Aggressive Action Against Japan' 30 August 1941; Brooke-Popham Papers v/4/29. Cited in Raymond Callahan, *The Worst Disaster*, p. 109, and footnote 96.
2 For an early, bold statement of this, see Parkinson, *Britain in the Far East*, Chapter 1, 'The Tide of Empire', pp. 1–5, and note 31 above. The naval approach (though perhaps not such a simplistic conclusion) continued in a long series of works, through to MacIntyre, *The Rise and Fall of the Singapore Naval Base* and Neidpath, *The Singapore Naval Base*. Not until Ong's *Operation Matador* did the message finally sink home that the ultimate decisions were mainly about land and air forces.
3 Nadzon Haron, 'Colonial Defence and the British Approach to the Problems of Malaya', in MAS, 24, 2 May 1990), 275–95. The most comprehensive work is Murfett et al., *Between Two Oceans*.
4 Ong, *Operation Matador*, p. 11. John Keegan, ed., *The Times Atlas of the Second World War* (London and New York: Times Books, 1989), p. 67. The United States had about three carriers in the Pacific, about seven in total, if those still not fully operational, or converted to seaplane carriers, were excluded.
5 CAB21/893 contains correspondence for the period 1939–40.
6 Parkinson, *Britain in the Far East*, p. 33. The force was projected to include ten cruisers and twenty-four cruisers.
7 Neidpath, *The Singapore Naval Base*, p. 55. Murfett et al., *Between Two Oceans*, Chapter 6, pp. 145–74.
8 See the following note for detail. But there is also a good summary in Kirby, *The Loss of Singapore*, pp. 7–14. The 1928 recommendations followed a 1927 visit to Singapore by a committee headed by Sir Webb Gillman. It recommended a first stage of three heavy guns, plus all the medium and close defence weapons. There could then be further investigation of the guns versus air issue, before deciding the final number of the biggest guns. When the COS accepted the Gillman committee report in March 1928, they suggested phase one be completed in five years, phase two postponed for the time being. The Labour Government of 1929–31 then tried to build on the Kellogg-Briand Pact of 1928, suspending all Singapore work pending a 1930 Naval Disarmament conference. The resulting London Naval Treaty of April 1930 found agreement on suspending battleship replacement, fixed cruiser ratios at 10:10:6½, and gave US, Britain and Japan destroyer and submarine parity. Then came the Japanese invasion of Manchuria of September 1931, the League of Nations' call for withdrawal a year later, the establishment of the puppet state of Manchukuo, and the Japanese pressure on and around Shanghai (outside of the international settlement) from January to May 1932, following a riot there. It is not surprising, therefore, that the Committee of Imperial Defence (CID) advised a resumption of work in Singapore come March 1932. A Sub-Committee of the CID, under Stanley Baldwin, had since December 1931 been discussing the still unresolved air-gun controversy. In May 1932 it agreed to rely on guns, but base defence on inter-service cooperation, air power being involved in fighter defence, offence against ships, etc. Cabinet endorsed the recommendations and accelerated Stage One of the fixed defences. Following events simply confirmed the urgency, namely: the League condemnation of Japan in March 1933; Germany's repudiation of Versailles disarmament clauses in 1934, Japan's repudiation of the Washington Treaty in December 1934 (as she was entitled to on two year's notice). Stage One of the defences was now due to be completed in 1936–7. In July 1935 the British government authorised work begin on Stage Two, that is, two additional 15 inch guns and more work on two more airfields (including

Tengah). A late 1935 naval conference failed to resurrect naval limitation, so the work then proceeded to completion in 1939, when there was merely a little work remaining on the already emplaced 15-inch guns. Around 1938–41, many of the guns were also given added overhead concrete cover, supported by back walls, as a defence against bombing. This was in sharp contrast to the pre-1930s when, far from being casemated, many British guns were more or less open, with just a protective shield at the front.

9 These debates are well covered in all the standard books, such as Murfett *et al.*, *Between Two Oceans*, Chapters 6–7, and those by Neidpath, MacIntyre and others.
10 See Neidpath, *Singapore Naval Base*, pp. 81ff.; MacIntyre, *The Rise and Fall of the Singapore Naval Base*, pp. 69 ff.; and Murfett *et al.*, *Between Two Oceans*, p. 149.
11 The best existing account is Ong Chit Chung, *The Landward Defence of Singapore, 1919–1938* (Singapore: Heinemann Asia Centre for Advanced Studies, Faculty of Arts and Social Sciences, NUS, 1988). See also his *Operation Matador*, pp. 19–54; and Ian Hogg, *British and American Artillery of World War Two* (London: Arms and Armour Press, 1978), p. 183.
12 Hack, *Defence and Decolonisation*, pp. 110–13; Dol Ramli, 'History of the Malay Regiment', *JMBRAS*, 38, 1 (1965), 199–243; Haron, Nadzon. 'Colonial Defence and the British Approach to the Problems of Malaya', *MAS*, 24, 2 (May 1990), 275–95.
13 Malcolm Murfett, 'Living in the Past: A Critical Re-examination of the Singapore Naval Strategy, 1918–1941', *War and Society*, 11, 1 (May 1993), 73–103. For 6,500 km of roads, 1,600 km of railway, see Ong, *Operation Matador*, p. 61.
14 Callahan, *The Worst Disaster*, p. 260, citing Churchill, *The Second World War*, Vol. 4, *The Hinge of Fate*, pp. 68–9. Three days later, Churchill was to win a vote of confidence 464 to 1.
15 Ong, *Operation Matador*, pp. 55–87.
16 Dobbie as cited in Lt-General A.E. Percival, 'Operations of Malaya Command, From 8 December, 1941 to 15 February, 1942', Second Supplement to *The London Gazette* of Friday, 20 February, 1948, dated Thursday, 26 February, 1948, p. 1250.
17 See various Dobbie correspondence in WO106/2441.
18 Ong, *Operation Matador*, pp. 100–2. Percival, 'Operations of Malaya Command', pp. 1250–1.
19 Ong, *Operation Matador*, p. 104, citing to COS, 10 September 1940.
20 The 16th October 1940 Tactical Appreciation was submitted to the COS by the three service commanders at Singapore: Vice-Admiral Layton for the Royal Navy; Lieutenant-General Bond for the Army; and Air Vice-Marshal Babington for the RAF. The late October 1940 Commanders' Far East defence conference included the same three, plus representatives of Australia, New Zealand, India and Burma. It was intended to be followed by meetings with the Dutch. Percival, 'Operations of Malaya Command, pp. 1250–1. Ong, *Operation Matador*, pp. 123–5, 163. Kirby, *The Loss of Singapore*, pp. 48–9.
21 James Leasor, *Singapore: The Battle That Changed the World*, p. 160.
22 Percival, 'Operations of Malaya Command, p. 1253.
23 Ong Chit Chung, 'Major-General Dobbie and the Defence of Malaya, 1935–38', *JSEAS*, 5, 2 (1986), 282–306; and Ong, *Operation Matador*. Serious planning began in March, and was endorsed by a somewhat reluctant Churchill on 10 April 1941.
24 Percival, 'Operations of Malaya Command', p. 1252–3.
25 Adapted from, Air Chief Marshal Brooke-Popham, 'Operations in the Far East', *Supplement to the London Gazette*, (London, 22 Jan. 1948), p. 537. For the Songkhla position, see the map on p. ix.
26 Ong, *Operation Matador*, p. 143–5.
27 Ong, *Operation Matador*, p. 165, citing Dill to Churchill on 15th May, *passim*.

28 Churchill, *The Second World War*, Vol. 4: *The Hinge of Fate*, p. 61.
29 Another MP, Mr Wedderburn (Renfrew, Western) summed up the dilemma Churchill saw in his comments to the House on 20 May: 'The hard truth is that if Russia is victorious, it will be very easy to recover those parts of the Empire which we have lost, while if Russia is defeated, we shall lose a great deal more of the Empire ...' 380 H.C. Deb., 5s, 20 May 1942, col.309.
30 WO106/2528, 'Note on Minute from Prime Minister to General Ismay dated 19 January 1942', 21 January 1942. For Churchill's August 1940 views on delaying the despatch of a fleet, even after Japan might have attacked, see Raymond Callahan, *The Worst Disaster*, p. 52: Churchill to Menzies, 11 August 1940,

> The Eastern Mediterranean Fleet ... could, of course, at any time be sent through the Canal into the Indian Ocean, or to relieve Singapore. We do not want to do this, even if Japan declares war, until it is found to be vital to your safety. Such a transference would entail the complete loss of the Middle East, and all prospect of beating Italy ... We hope, ... to keep the Eastern Mediterranean Fleet at Alexandria during the first phase of an Anglo-Japanese war ...

On the other hand, if white Australia were threatened, Churchill said 'we should then cut our losses in the Mediterranean.'
31 See for instance Callahan, *The Worst Disaster*, p. 195, citing Churchill, *The Second World War*, Vol. 3, *The Grand Alliance* (Boston: Houghton Mifflin, 1950), p. 608.
32 WO106/2528, 'Note on Minute from Prime Minister to General Ismay dated 19 January 1942', 21 January 1942, *passim*. See also Churchill, *History of the Second World War*, Vol. 4: *The Hinge of Fate*, pp. 42-4; the important minute Churchill reproduces in his memoirs in No. D4/2, 19 Jan. 1942, CAB120/615; and related material in WO106/2583A. See also Hack, *Defence and Decolonisation*, p. 39.
33 Ong, *Operation Matador*, p. 163
34 Murfett et al., *Between Two Oceans*, p. 166. See also WO106/2441 for Dobbie discussing this with a reluctant War Office, and saying that the northeast monsoon clearly did not stop landings, as had 'been proved by the landing of 5,000 smuggled coolies near Mersing in that period'.
35 Kennedy, Paul, *The Rise and Fall of the Great Powers: Economic Change and Military Conflict from 1500 to 2000* (London: Fontana, 1989), pp. 453-6; John Keegan (ed.), *The Times Atlas of the Second World War* (New York: Harper and Row, 1989), pp. 66-7.
36 377 H.C. Deb., 5s, 8 January 1942, cols. 132-4. He was not the only person to question the bombing strategy the time, see also Mr Richard Stokes (MP for Ipswich) 380 H.C. Deb., 5s, 19 May 1942, col.178: 'I believe the major strategical error in the war ... was made when the Prime Minister decided in 1940 that the way to win this war was by bombing ...'
37 Probert, *The Forgotten Air Force*, pp. 17-20, 28-35, 311. The latter included 79 Buffalo fighters.
38 Ong, *Operation Matador*, p. 170. Callahan, *The Worst Disaster*, p. 150-4, adds that this was still not enough to replace loss and wastage and build up a reserve equal to plans for 'Crusader', Auchinleck's planned offensive in North Africa.
39 In many ways, the 1942 debates in the House of Commons set out the context as well as any historian has managed since. For the quotation here, again from Richard Stokes (MP for Ipswich), see 380 H.C. Deb., 5s, 19 May 1942, col. 176.
40 Brooke-Popham, 'Operations in the Far East', *Supplement to the London Gazette* (22 Jan. 1948), p. 551. When fifty-one Hurricanes arrived late in the day, they came with just 24 pilots, Wigmore, *The Japanese Thrust*, p. 221.

41 380 H.C. Deb., 5s, 19 May 1942, col. 198.
42 380 H.C. Deb., 5s, 20 May 1942, col. 309.
43 Braddon, *The Naked Island*, p. 66.
44 Catherine Porter, 'Autopsies on the Southeast Asia Debate', *Pacific Affairs* 16, 2 (June 1943), p. 212. The author is here drawing on O.D. Gallagher, *Action in the East* (New York: Doubleday, 1942).
45 Callahan, *The Worst Disaster*, p. 259.
46 The North African campaigns yo-yoed back and forth, and numbers changed rapidly. For a short, sharp impression, see Keegan (ed.), *The Times Atlas of the Second World War*, pp. 78–81. Callahan, *The Worst Disaster*, p. 43, cites a July 1942 Oil Control Board paper for Cabinet, saying loss of the Middle East would necessitate an extra 270 oil tankers for the American run: '... the Oil control Board conclude that the loss of Abadan and Bahrein would ... force a drastic reduction in our total war capacity and probably abandonment of some of our present fields of action'. Callahan also cites fears it would lessen Germany's economic problems, and that loss in Britain's one remaining land front against Axis powers would hit Britain's credibility in American eyes. See also *op. cit.*, pp. 154–5.
47 One could speculate that the COS thought Japan might still attack the Soviet Union after June precisely because this would have been the right thing for Japan to do. Soviet defeat might have created a huge Axis block and shifted the global balance of power.
48 Hack, *Defence and Decolonisation*, p. 39, and p. 51, footnote 16. British intelligence is a crucial issue here, and a growing area. Most sources suggest intelligence machinery, coordinated by the Admiralty-controlled 'Far Eastern Combined Bureau' was inadequate in scale, and also that the Japanese were underestimated due to some combination of stereotyping, or (Ferris) ethnocentrism whereby it was assumed Asian theatres and Japanese performance there could not be taken as indicative of potential against a first-rate European power. At its most extreme, it is also suggested that Churchill, imbued with a tendency towards racial or national stereotyping not exactly atypical of his generation, completely misjudged the capabilities of given nationalities. These included the Turks in 1915 and the Japanese in 1941. To give any of these issues the room they deserve would totally disrupt an overview, so the interested reader must pursue the topic independently. See Elphick, *Far Eastern File*; Aldrich, *Intelligence and the War Against Japan*; two articles by A. Best, 'Constructing an Image: British Intelligence and Whitehall's Perception of Japan, 1931–1939, *INS* 11, 3 (1996), pp. 403–23, and '"This Probably Over-Valued Military Power": British Intelligence and Whitehall's Perception of Japan, 1939–41', *INS*, 12, 3 (1997), 67–94; as well as J. Ferris, '"Worthy of Some Better Enemy?" The British Estimate of the Imperial Japanese Army 1919–41, and the Fall of Singapore', *Canadian Journal of History* 28 (1993), 223–56. For a work which touches on Churchill's views on race, see Clive Ponting's *Churchill* (London: Sinclair-Stevenson, 1994).
49 Ong, *Operation Matador*, p. 189; Aldrich, *Intelligence and the War Against Japan*, p. 52. Kirby, *The Loss of Singapore*, p. 459. Aldrich notes that the JIC anticipated the general nature of an attack, but this was hardly surprising. The real issue was how likely it thought an attack on Malaya was, compared to Japan's other issues.
50 The possibility of a German victory in Barbarossa is briefly and brilliantly summarised in Michael Burleigh, 'What if Nazi Germany had defeated the Soviet Union?' in Niall Ferguson (ed.), *Virtual History* (London: Picador, 1997), pp. 321–47. Perhaps Britain's intervention in the Balkans and North Africa were not crucial in delaying, and weakening, Barbarossa. Perhaps they were. But which was the right approach in the situation? To put everything into the active conflicts on which world history, the competition between totalitarianism and a pathetic remnant of European

NOTES

democracy, depended? Or to garrison each peaceful outpost and by-station securely, hoping to cover every option? For once, perhaps, Churchill's infamous impatience and desire to find new battles (a new Straits of Constantinople, Gallipoli, or Norway) may have had some value.

51 Raymond A. Esthus, 'President Roosevelt's Commitment to Britain to Intervene in a Pacific War', *The Mississippi Valley Historical Review*, 50, 1. (June 1963), pp. 28–38. This article shows it was not just a matter of words, either, as the United States followed up with requests for cooperation in building airbases in the region.
52 Ong, *Operation Matador*, p. 196.
53 Ong, *Operation Matador*, p. 164, for Churchill's directive to the COS on 28 April 1941, prioritising the Middle East.
54 Kirby, *The Loss of Singapore*, p. 83.
55 Ong, *Operation Matador*, p. 226.

4 THE CAMPAIGN: FROM SINGAPORE TO SYONAN

1 The phrase 'invading army's drunken rampage through Chinese cities' is Turnbull's, from her *History of Singapore*, p. 181. It is too good a phrase not to use, but quotation marks here might mislead the reader into thinking the words were the Governor's. The policeman is quoted in Peter Elphick and Peter Smith, *Odd Man Out*, p. 254, note 16. See also Leasor, *Singapore: The Battle That Changed the World*, p. 249.
2 The Kuomintang (Guomindang in the modern pinyin form) government had abandoned it for Chungking (Chongqing). Though details are disputed, it is clear the Japanese killed and raped on a huge scale. Singapore was to have its own, more cold-blooded nemesis, in the Sook Ching operations. Joshua A. Fogel (ed.), and Charles S. Maier, *The Nanjing Massacre in History and Historiography* (University of California Press, 2000); Katsuichi Honda, Frank Gribney, Karen Sandness, Honda Katsuichi, Frank B. Gibney (eds), *The Nanjing Massacre: A Japanese Journalist Confronts Japan's National Shame (Studies of the Pacific Basin Institute)* (M.E. Sharpe, 1999). For Glover destroying his stocks, see his *In Seventy Days*, pp. 199–200.
3 PREM3/168/7A, Churchill to Wavell, 19 January 1942.
4 Churchill on 10 Feb, as cited in Murfett *et al.*, *Between Two Oceans*, p. 233.
5 Murfett *et al.*, *Between Two Oceans*, p. 236, and note 109, p. 246.
6 By 1931 the Malays formed 49 per cent of the population of the Malayan peninsula (excluding Singapore), Chinese 34 per cent, Indians up to 15 per cent. If Singapore was added into the equation the Chinese became over 39 per cent. See CO537/1478, FE(0)(46)52, 'British Foreign Policy in the FE', 16 April 1948, para. 59, for the 1931 census; and Werner Vennewald, *Chinesen in Malaysia: Politische Kultur und Strategisches Handeln* (Hamburg, 1990), p. 116. With Singapore included, Malays made up 44.4 per cent of the Malayan peninsula's population of 5,849,000, Chinese 39.2, Indians 14.3, 'others' 2.1. See also, A. Stockwell, *British Policy and Malay Politics During the Malayan Union Experiment* (Kuala Lumpur, 1979), p. 85, note 1.
7 WO106/2550A, 'Brilliant 7-Day Drive of Imperial Forces Down Malay Peninsula to Singapore Told', *Japan Times and Advertiser*, 8 April 1942, almost certainly by Tsuji (e.g. by 'Chief Staff Officer Who planned Bold Campaign'.
8 Leasor, *Singapore: The Battle That Changed the World*, p. 170.
9 Akashi Yoji, 'General Yamashita Tomoyuki', in Farrell and Hunter (eds), *Sixty Years On*, p. 190. This gives the combat figure for the first waves as 17,230.
10 In fact, the idea of a huge British advantage in men may be one of the more persistent myths (see also the appendices, and related footnotes just below). The two sides seem not to have been greatly mismatched in manpower, if the British official history is to be believed. Kirby suggests a paper total (admitting in reality actual

227

figures landed were lower) of 88,689 Japanese, including infantry, artillery, engineers, anti-tank, air defence, river crossing and signals and railway troops. To this he adds 36,719 HQ, communications, land service, construction, ordnance and medical personnel, to make a total of 125,408. In Public Affairs Department Ministry of Defence *Oriente Primus: First in the East: Singapore Artillery 100th Anniversary* (Singapore: Singapore Artillery and Public Affairs Department, MOD, 1988), p. 43–44, suggests a total of 123,300 Japanese. The latter also says 228 tanks (probably the figure before the 3rd Tank Regiment was reassigned elsewhere), Kirby 179, Tsuji just 120 (including armoured cars). In short, the Japanese probably had fewer men, but were not the dramatically shrunken numbers one sometimes imagines when reading accounts of the fall. In aircraft and tanks, meanwhile, the advantage lay overwhelmingly on their side. Comparing figures, it does seem likely Tsuji conveniently added only some of the units into his totals. This because where Kirby and Tsuji both give figures for the same unit, Tsuji's figure is often only marginally lower, e.g. 5th Division 15,342 (Kirby) versus 16,000 (Tsuji), 18th Division 22,206 (Kirby) versus 13,000 (Tsuji), Imperial Guards 12,649 (Kirby) versus 13,000 (Tsuji). See Kirby, *The Loss of Singapore*, pp. 522–3, and Tsuji, *Singapore 1941–1942*, p. 36.

11 Tsuji, *Singapore: The Japanese Version* (London: Constable, 1962), pp. 35–6. See also Kirby, *The Loss of Singapore*, pp. 521–3; and In *Oriente Primus: First in the East: Singapore Artillery 100th Anniversary* (Singapore: Singapore Artillery and Public Affairs Department, MOD, 1988), p. 43–4. This gives a clear breakdown, though unfortunately with no source cited. Again, no two sources really make sense when read together:

	In Oriente	Kirby	Tsuji
25th Army: Guard Division	18,400	12,649	13,000
5th Division	25,200	15,342	16,000
18th Division	17,300	22,206	13,000
Artillery, support, administration	62,200	36,719	Not specified
Total	123,300	125,408	60,000
Tanks	228	179 (from Jan.)	80
Artillery	188	Not specified	400

The gap between Kirby and Tsuji is further narrowed when one considers both that the former is listing the whole 25th Army, parts of which deployed elsewhere, and his statement that 'The numbers in Malaya fell far short of these figures'.

12 Andrew Gilchrist, *Malaya 1941: The Fall of an Empire* (London: Hale, 1991), pp. 11, 106 ff., argues that *Matador* could have prevented catastrophe, so avoiding a defeat which led, 'directly to the impotence of Britain ... in the post-war World'. Gilchrist served as a Foreign Office Counsellor in the Commissioner-General's Office in the 1950s. Yet see also PREM3/168/3, General Wavell's report (Wavell arrived in Singapore as Supreme commander in the Far East on 7 Jan. 1942), 'Operations in Malaya and Singapore', 8 Sept. 1942. This concluded that Matador, 'without denying the enemy in any appreciable degree ... [gave] every possibility of losing an entire brigade'. Gilchrist's *Malaya 1941* is an example of the opposite conclusion coming to predominate.

13 Elphick, *Singapore: The Pregnable Fortress*, pp. 521–2, cites General Heath, commanding officer in the north, criticising Brooke-Popham for not standing down *Matador* earlier. There is a major historiographical debate, between those who think *Matador* should have been launched, and those who feel a Songkhla position would have been cut off by Japanese landings north and south. In which case, a line further

NOTES

south, in Kedah's plains, or mid-Malaya, or in Johore, should have been chosen. This, however, would have meant abandoning then northern aerodromes.

14 Brooke-Popham, 'Operations in the Far East'. For *Operation Matador*, see pp. 545–6, 553–4.
15 Percival, 'Operations of Malaya Command', pp. 1252–3.
16 See Wavell's 1942 report, in PREM3/168/3.
17 Kirby, *Singapore: Chain of Disaster*, p. 126.
18 Kirby, *The Loss of Singapore*, p. 461–2 was scathing, '"Matador" was a contributory cause of the initial disaster ... The timing however was bound up with political and diplomatic considerations which lay outside the competence of military commanders ... In the circumstances the plan was fundamentally impracticable and should never have been accepted'. See also Ivan Simson, *Singapore, Too Little, Too Late: The Failure of Malaya's Defences in 1942* (Singapore: Donald Moore for Asiapacific Press, 1970), p. 48: 'It was probably better that Matador was called off. If carried through it would have dispersed our weak forces over a still wider area'.
19 See various reports on the Singapore campaign by Lt-Col Stewart in WO106/2550A, drawn up in India and dated around July 1942.
20 WO106/2550A, telegram from Ceylon of 5 May 1942, containing the views of Mr Seabridge, editor of the *Straits Times*, these being dated 28 Feb. 1942. For a balanced view of the Indian Army as having performed unevenly, in line with other nationalities, see Alan Warren, 'The Indian Army and the Fall of Singapore', in Farrell and Hunter (eds), *Sixty Years On*, pp. 199, 270–89.
21 Richard Aldrich, *Intelligence and the War Against Japan: Britain, America and the Politics of Secret Service* (Cambridge: Cambridge University Press, 2000) p. 42. See also Elphick, *Pregnable Fortress*.
22 Source: Brooke-Popham and Layton, 'Operations in the Far East, from 17th October 1940 to 27th December 1941', in a Supplement to the *London Gazette*, 22 January 1948; and for a considered analysis of why Indian troops (often illiterate, of many languages) suffered more from the effects of 'milking', Kirby, *The Loss of Singapore*, pp. 513–15, 528.
23 Tsuji, *Singapore 1941–1942*, p. 49.
24 Mr Chelliah Thuraijah Retnam, Oral History Interview 000579/04, Singapore National Archives. Mr Chelliah Thuraijah Retnam was served with the Blakang Mati Medical Station, and later observed Japanese in Thailand able to survive on very little, whereas British troops seemed unable to.
25 WO106/2528, D.D.M.I Far East to War Office, 5 January 1942.
26 'Read This Alone – and the War can be Won', taken in translated form from Tsuji, *Singapore 1941–1942*, Appendix 1, pp. 295–349.
27 Perhaps, however, sergeants and medical staff always tell their troops that the locals are VD-ridden? Russell Braddon reports Australian gunners being told local women were 96 per cent affected, later upgraded to 99.9 per cent for effect, and also being solicited even in rural Malaya, see Braddon *The Naked Island*, pp. 55 and 67. At least for Singapore, contagious diseases had indeed been on the increase in the 1930s, since the closing of brothels which had been more easily influenced by the government to control disease than the 'sly' prostitution that replaced them. Warren, *Ah Ku and Karayuki-san*, pp. 175–6.
28 For accounts of Southeast Asian women, see Maria Rosa Henson, *Comfort Woman: A Filipina's Story of Prostitution and Slavery under the Japanese Military* (Oxford: Rowman and Littlefield, 1999); and the account and photograph of 'Madam X' in George Hicks, *The Comfort Women: Sex Slaves of the Japanese Imperial Forces* (Singapore: Heinemann Asia, 1995), p. xi and photographs. See also Keith Howard (ed.), *True Stories of the Korean Comfort Women* (London: Cassell, 1995); and *positions east asia*

cultures critique 5, 1 (Spring 1997), a special edition on comfort women. George Hicks includes a dramatic account of a young Chinese girl, the then 15-year-old Chinese 'Madam X', being raped in front of her family, and then trucked off to join dance hostesses in Kuala Lumpur who had been rounded up and forced into prostitution (pp. xii-xiii).

29 Toh Boon Ho, book review of *Raising Churchill's Army: The British Army and the War Against Germany, 1919–1945* (Oxford: Oxford University Press, 2000), in *Pointer* 28, 2 (April-June 2002), 141–5. This point was made to Karl Hack by Toh Boon Ho and Toh Boon Kwan.

30 Tsuji, *Singapore 1941–1942*, p. 40, and p. 179 for the quotation.

31 Yoji Akashi, 'Lai Tek', *Journal of the South Seas Society* 49 (1994), 67. Special Training School 101 did the training. Britain realised that it was arming one enemy (the communists) to fight another. So 1941 is the best starting date for the origins of the postwar emergency, as it is for decolonisation.

32 For the quotation and figures, see 'Operations in the Far East', *Supplement to the London Gazette* (22 Jan. 1948), Order of the Day by Brooke-Popham and Layton of 8 Dec. 1941; and Appendix M, pp. 575–6, 569–74. The core of regular Asians was the one (later two) battalion(s) of the Malay Regiment. See also the comments on race in, Morrison, *Malayan Postscript*, p. 39; and Allen, *Singapore*, pp. 247–63.

33 WO106/2550A, 'Brilliant 7-Day Drive of Imperial Forces Down Malay Peninsula to Singapore Told', *Japan Times and Advertiser*, 8 April 1942, almost certainly by Tsuji (e.g. by 'Chief Staff Officer Who planned Bold Campaign').

34 WO106/2550A, 'Brilliant 7-Day Drive of Imperial Forces Down Malay Peninsula to Singapore Told', *Japan Times and Advertiser*, 8 April 1942.

35 Such myths seem utterly ineradicable, see for instance Yee Hwee Joo, *Impact: History of Southeast Asia* (Oxford: Oxford University Press, 2000), p. 83, 'The British had expected a sea attack on Singapore from the south. Consequently, they concentrated their defences in Singapore ... Unfortunately ... the Japanese invasion was launched from the north of Malaya ...' The author, like many others, is presumably thinking of the lack of fixed defences in north Singapore. But the implication of British surprise still misleads the unwary.

36 Intelligence showed attack imminent, but not whether Malaya would be targeted early. Brooke-Popham knew he was to be replaced, and a 29 Nov. intercept showed pro-Japanese Thai ministers hoped preemptive UK attack would justify calling Japan for help, Elphick, *Far Eastern File*, pp. 308–26.

37 Elphick, *Far Eastern File*, pp. 308–26.

38 Cited in Hack, *Defence and Decolonisation*, p. 39.

39 Brooke-Popham, 'Operations in the Far East', p. 575. At 10,000 feet the speeds of the Zero and of the defenders 60 Buffalo frontline fighters (52 reserves, 21 temporarily out of action due to engine trouble) were 315 and 270 miles per hour respectively. They were more comparable at 20,000 feet, but the rate of climb of the Buffalo was much slower. I have based my aircraft figures on Brooke-Popham's report, which shows 158 frontline and 88 reserve, with operational aircraft ranging between 108 and 158 in December. Dutch numbers can be found in Callahan, *The Worst Disaster*, p. 164.

40 A.D. Harvey, 'Army, Air Force and Navy Air Force: Japanese Aviation and the Opening Phase of the War in the Far East', *War in History* 6, 2 (1999), 174–204. Harvey notes the Ki–43, though with good aerobatic ability, lacked armour and self-sealing tanks, and was under-armed. But the Brewster Buffaloes in Malaya also seem to have drastically underperformed in speed and climb. Harvey notes the Japanese force included 27 A6M2 Navy Zeros, 59 Ki–43 fighters, and 87 out-dated Ki–27 with fixed undercarrraiges, as well as 70 Army recce and cooperation planes. This to

NOTES

oppose 60 Brewster Buffalo fighters. See also Probert, *The Forgotten Air Force*, p. 29, which notes the lack of a proper Operational Training Unit, with only a makeshift one from Sept. 1941.

41 For the first quotation, see Oxford, Rhodes House, Granada 'End of Empire' series, Malaya, Vol. 4, p. 129, comments by Lt Harold Payne, made during 1980s interviews. For the Singaporean view, see Maurice Baker, *A Time of Fireflies and Wild Guavas* (Singapore: Federal Publications, 1995), p. 87. For Stewart, see WO106/2550A, 'Comments by Lieutenant-Colonel I.M. Stewart', 12 July 1942. For 'Flying coffins', see Leasor, *Singapore: The Battle That Changed the World*, p. 167. For the Zero performance of 325 mph at 10,000 feet (295 at 20,000 feet), and a climb to 10,000 feet in 4.2 minutes (versus the Buffalo taking 6.1 minutes), see Brooke-Popham, 'Operations in the Far East', p. 575. For the Hurricanes, see Tsuji, *Singapore 1941–1942*, pp. 197–8.

42 Singapore even concluded the monsoon might postpone any attack until Feb. 1942, despite Percival (GOC Malaya) having argued as early as 1938 that it did *not* rule out operations. Allen, *Singapore: 1941–1942*, pp. 50–1; Ong, *Operation Matador*, p. 167; Murfett et al., *Between Two Oceans*, p. 185.

43 Warren, *Singapore 1942*, pp. 66–71.

44 Kirby, *The Loss of Singapore*, p. 194–96. The Japanese had two battleships (*Kongo*, *Haruna*) and all the associated support lurking off Indochina, ready to intervene, with air support mainly from land bases rather than carriers.

45 The COS had preferred to send a total of 6 capital ships (four obsolescent and then occupied with Atlantic convoy duties), to force the Japanese to divide their forces. Churchill had insisted on a modern deterrent force of 2 modern capital ships and an aircraft carrier. Kirby, *The Loss of Singapore*, pp. 75, 84–5.

46 Tsuji claimed the invasion fleet had 1 cruiser, 10 destroyers and a handful of submarines available, *Singapore 1941–1942*, p. 37. But other sources suggest a battleship, 8 cruisers and support were in the area or nearby. See Callahan, *The Worst Disaster*, p. 182; and Kirby, *The Loss of Singapore*, pp. 490–2. The bigger problem is that Japan could have varied this force right up until the last week or two, so we do not know what Japan would have committed if *Indomitable* had arrived.

47 Marder, *Old Friends, New Enemies: The Royal Navy and the Imperial Japanese Navy 1936–41* (Oxford: Oxford University Press, 1981), Vol. I, pp. 414–17, 431–8, 454–6.

48 Keegan, *Times Atlas of World War II*, p. 67. A.J. Marder, *Old Friends, New Enemies*, Vol. 1, pp. 296–333. Kirby, *The Loss of Singapore*, pp. 58–9. Ultimately, however, we have relied upon the official history, Kirby, *The Loss of Singapore*, pp. 490–2. This gives Japan's main fleet as of 8 December 1941 as:

- 10 battleships (two 16 inch, eight 14 inch, an additional two 18.1 inch battleships were added later, the *Yamato* becoming operational within days of the outbreak of the war)
- 6 fleet carriers
- 4 light fleet carriers
- 18 heavy cruisers
- 21 light cruisers
- 112 destroyers
- 65 submarines

49 See above notes, but in March the Japanese concentrated no less than 4 carriers south of Java, in support of the battle for Java. These included *Akagi*, *Kaga*, *Soryu* and *Hiryu*, and a naval air fleet of about 150 aircraft. Kirby, *The Loss of Singapore*, p. 538.

50 Japanese carriers, like the British, varied widely in their capacity. But several of the best could carry 70 or more aircraft (two *Shokaku* class carriers carried over 80 a piece). For more details on British carriers, see A.J. Marder, *Old Friends, New Enemies*, pp. 231–3. Marder lists a total of nine British carriers, but that seems to include the auxiliary *Audacity*, with just 6 aircraft, as one of four older carriers. For a comparison of carriers, see Kirby, *The Loss of Singapore*, pp. 490 and 501, which suggests 'about twenty four aircraft' for Japanese light carriers against 12 for the British *Hermes* class; and about 63 aircraft for Japanese fleet carriers against 45 for the *Indomitable* class, and 33 for *Formidable*. Comparable figures from one source are useful, since no two sources ever seem to agree. Deck capacity could be varied for some tasks, by 'as much of fifty per cent', Kirby, *The Loss of Singapore*, p. 501.

51 Callahan, *The Worst Disaster*, pp. 144, 158–9. Of the three older carriers, *Eagle* was on standby for 'Pilgrim', an operation to seize Spanish and Portuguese Atlantic islands should Hitler attack their metropolitan power. Otherwise German aircraft might further throttle Britain's Atlantic umbilical cord to the United States. A second, HMS *Furious*, was ferrying aircraft to the Middle East via West Africa. HMS *Hermes*, as noted, was eventually sent to the Indian Ocean. The Indian Ocean Fleet of April 1942 included 5 battleships, 4 'R' class, 3 aircraft carriers, 7 cruisers, and 14 destroyers.

52 The Japanese lost 4 fleet carriers to the United States loss of 1. But Japan still had more carriers in the Pacific.

53 Tsuji, *Singapore 1941–1942*, p. 101.

54 For Yamashita and *Kirimomi Sakusen*, see Akashi Yoji, 'General Yamashita Tomoyuki', in Farrell and Hunter (eds), *Sixty Years On*, pp. 190–3.

55 Kirby, *The Loss of Singapore*, pp. 186–7.

56 It is here, in the detail that the sheer absurdity of British preparations really comes out. See Lt Col. E. L. Sawyer, 'Prisoner of War in Changi', *Journal of the Royal Artillery* 124 (Spring 1997), p. 53. The Battery had four 3.5 inch howitzers, and had formerly trained with the 1/14 Punjab. The situation gets Worse too, as the regiment was given several different types of equipment: howitzers, anti-tank guns captured from the Italians in Africa, and 'two 18-pounder guns which had been saluting guns'.

57 Kirby, *Singapore: The Chain of Disaster*, pp. 136–7, 142. Kirby, *The Loss of Singapore*, pp. 170, 186–8.

58 Percival, 'Operations of Malaya Command, pp. 1253. Further north there was too much malaria.

59 Sawyer, 'Prisoner of War in Changi', p. 53.

60 Akashi Yoji, 'General Yamashita Tomoyuki', in Farrell and Hunter (eds), *Sixty Years On*, p. 191. Warren, *Singapore 1942*, pp. 79–95. The two Brigades were the 6th and 15th Indian Brigades, both under the command of the 11th Indian Division.

61 The positions were 6 Brigade (henceforth Bde) left, 15 Bde right, and 26 Bde in reserve, on a fairly wide front. Even the official history's bland language cannot disguise the scale of disaster, admitting that the Japanese used just 'a strength equivalent to two battalions supported by light tanks' to defeat two Brigades to the front, one in reserve. Kirby, *The Loss of Singapore*, p. 210–11

62 Kirby, *The Loss of Singapore*, p. 215–17. The Gurun position lay across the road and railway about 3 miles north of Gurun, flanked by jungle-covered slops of Kedah Peak (4,000 feet high) on the West and jungle to the east. It was to be held by three depleted Brigades, one (15th) down to 600 men after Jitra.

63 For more detail on the Malayan campaign, see Allen, *Singapore 1941–1942*, Chapter VIII, 'The Campaign', pp. 121–84 (p. 123 for Jitra); and Elphick, *Singapore: The Pregnable Fortress*, Chapter 10, 'The Loss of Northern Malaya', pp. 315–434.

64 Akashi Yoji, 'General Yamashita Tomoyuki', in Farrell and Hunter (eds), *Sixty Years On*, p. 193.

NOTES

65 Allen, *Singapore 1941–1942*, pp. 131–5. Warren, *Singapore 1942*, pp. 120–4.
66 Eyewitness, 'The Gunners of the 11th Indian Division in Malaya', *The Gunner*, May 1946, 32–3; Allen, *Singapore 1941–1942*, pp. 146–51. For the glow-worm, see the irreverent Braddon's *The Naked Island*, p. 56.
67 Murfett at al, *Between Two Oceans*, pp. 202–4. Allen, *Singapore 1941–1942*, p. 132. Kirby, *The Loss of Singapore*, p. 231–2.
68 Kirby, *The Loss of Singapore*, pp. 277–8.
69 In this instance a blown bridge would certainly have delayed the attack and saved many casualties and losses. But in general Japanese infantry could take their bicycles and wade across shallow rivers, while the engineers soon found the sawmills in each newly conquered area, so replenishing their supply of bridge timbers. Tsuji, *Singapore 1941–1942*, p. 181, 183–5. Kirby, *The Loss of Singapore*, p. 281, states the Japanese used one tank company, and one infantry battalion (42nd Infantry Regiment) in motor transport and engineers. The remaining tanks and infantry were available for outflanking if necessary.
70 Eyewitness, 'The Gunners of the 11th Indian Division in Malaya', pp. 33.
71 WO106/2550A, 'Brilliant 7-Day Drive of Imperial Forces Down Malay Peninsula to Singapore Told', *Japan Times and Advertiser*, 8 April 1942.
72 Simson, *Singapore, Too Little, Too Late*, p. 65. Simson points out that War Office anti-tank pamphlets were left undistributed till the last minute, and he was not allowed to put into effect anti-tank training.
73 WO106/2550A, 'Brilliant 7-Day Drive of Imperial Forces Down Malay Peninsula to Singapore Told', *Japan Times and Advertiser*, 8 April 1942.
74 For this and the details of the subsequent narrative see Allen, *Singapore 1941–1942*, pp. 151–9; Elphick, *Singapore: The Pregnable Fortress*, pp. 377–434
75 Allen, *Singapore 1941–1942*, pp. 155–6; Kirby, *The Loss of Singapore*, pp. 302–3. Typically, however, the communications lines were not adequately concealed or protected, so they were cut, and artillery support never came.
76 Wigmore, *The Japanese Thrust*, pp. 210–21.
77 The Australians including some gunners, and the 2/19 and 2/20 battalions.
78 Braddon *The Naked Island*, p. 101–2. Braddon's book is a classic Australian castigation of what he sees as denial of the necessary equipment and stupidity by high-ups of all kinds. His unit manned 25 pounder guns at the Battle for Muar. Of 45 Indian Brigade's recruits he continues:

> the greater part of the Brigade was composed of young natives who had been in the Army only a few months (most of that spent traveling from India to Malaya) ... The more amenable to instruction learnt how to discharge a rifle – which they did without any discrimination at all, in no particular direction ... but most of them remained in a state of profound ignorance.

79 Elphick, *Singapore: The Pregnable Fortress*, pp. 381–9; Allen, *Singapore 1941–1942*, pp. 156–7.
80 Allen, *Singapore 1941–1942*, pp. 157–8.
81 WO106/2550A,'The Evacuation of the Imperial Forces in Malaya into Singapore island', Lt J.O.C. Hayes, Royal Navy (Navy Liaison Officer with III Corps).
82 See (quotation) Morrison, *Malayan Postscript*, (London, 1942), pp. 187–8; Macintyre, *Rise and Fall of the Singapore Base*, pp. 195–6; PREM3/168/3, 'Wavell's Report on Operations in Malaya', Sept. 1942: and Murfett et al., *Between Two Oceans*, p. 193.
83 CAB120/615, Prime Minister to General Ismay, for COS Committee, 16 December 1941. Callahan, *Worst Disaster*, p. 223 dates this 15th, but in London it was dated as received on 16th.

84 CAB120/615, Prime Minister for Lord Privy Seal. General Ismay for COS Committee, 19 Dec. 1941. Charmley, *Churchill, The End of Glory*, pp. 479–80.
85 WO106/2550A, 'Brilliant 7-Day Drive of Imperial Forces Down Malay Peninsula to Singapore Told', *Japan Times and Advertiser*, 8 April 1942.
86 Allen, *Singapore 1941–1942*, p. 149.
87 WO106/2550A, 'Brilliant 7-Day Drive of Imperial Forces Down Malay Peninsula to Singapore Told', *Japan Times and Advertiser*, 8 April 1942. See also Stewart's appreciations, written around July 1942 when in India, in WO106/2550A; and Tsuji, *Singapore 1941–1942*, p. 177.
88 Tsuji, *Singapore 1941–1942*, p. 183–5: 'A division was equipped with roughly five hundred motor vehicles and six thousand bicycles'.
89 WO106/2550A, 'Brilliant 7-Day Drive of Imperial Forces Down Malay Peninsula to Singapore Told', *Japan Times and Advertiser*, 8 April 1942. See also Stewart's appreciations, written around July 1942 when in India, in WO106/2550A; and Tsuji, *Singapore 1941–1942*, p. 177 and 195. The last records the Japanese abandoning a detour around the Gemas position, and through jungle, 'because of the difficult terrain and obstinate resistance there'.
90 WO106/2550A, 'Brilliant 7-Day Drive of Imperial Forces Down Malay Peninsula to Singapore Told', *Japan Times and Advertiser*, 8 April 1942, almost certainly by Tsuji (e.g. by 'Chief Staff Officer Who planned Bold Campaign').
91 See for instance the many 1942 reports in WO106/2550A, especially those by Mr Seabridge, editor of the *Straits Times*, these being dated 28 February 1942.
92 Stewart wrote a number of appreciations around July 1942, when in India. See WO106/2550A.
93 Allen, *Singapore 1941–1942*, p. 160.
94 WO106/2528, 'Note on Minute from Prime Minister to General Ismay dated 19 January 1942', 21 January 1942, *passim*.
95 Morrison, *Malayan Postscript*, p. 139. Tsuji, *Singapore 1941–1942*, p. 221, 227. The Sultan's palace was also known as the *Istana Hijau* or 'Green Palace'.
96 Kirby, *The Loss of Singapore*, p. 365–6, 397, 408, covers the scuttling of the floating dock, and denial of the naval base. See also: Rhodes House, Oxford: Mss Brit Emp 527/9, Granada End of Empire interviews, Malaya, Madoc interviews; and Morrison, *Malayan Postscript*, p. 145. Morrison calls the nearly empty base (of around 7 to 8 Feb. 1942) 'my most tragic memory of the whole Malayan campaign'. The final destruction and evacuation was carried out between 9 and 11 Feb.
97 Winston Churchill, *The Second World War*, Vol. 4: *The Hinge of Fate*, p. 82. Churchill says 85,000, 'of this total probably 70,000 were armed'. Then there were volunteers on top, about 15,000, to make 100,000, and finally headquarters and support and ancillary staffs for three services, making over 130,000 personnel all-told. Tsuji, *Singapore 1941–1942*, p. 220, says Japan's pre-conquest estimate of actual 'British' fighting strength on Singapore was 30,000, and its post-conquest estimate about 60,000. Tsuji, *Singapore 1941–1942*, p. 187, also suggests 440 Japanese guns, but there he is talking about the whole army, not just those committed at Singapore.
98 Murfett *et al.*, *Between Two Oceans*, pp. 216–18. Percival later claimed that the army forces were about 85,000 with 70,000 combatants after Medical, Pioneer and other ancillary units were deducted. But see the note above for this being 100,000 when local volunteers were added, 130,000 with ancillary staff. Against this, Percival claimed Japan might have mustered 60,000. Certainly, 3 Japanese divisions and support suggests a Japanese figure far in excess of 30,000. See Percival, 'Operations of Malaya Command', p. 1311, with its suggestion that 60,000 Japanese combat troops were used against Singapore. Special pleading or no, this figure sounds closer to the truth, once artillery and combat support is included. See also Tsuji, *Singapore*

1941–1942, pp. 35–7. Tsuji always emphasised Japanese inferiority in men, but his figures for the three divisions alone come to 42,000 (from which casualties would have to be deducted). Then there are the men for the 168 guns, for 120 tanks and armoured vehicles, and for supporting engineers and so on. That makes Percival's estimate for Japanese numbers appear not far short of the mark.

99 Allen, *Singapore 1941–1942*, pp. 160–70, deals with this in detail, and the way Wavell's explicit preference for placing the freshest troops in the northwest was rejected by Percival.
100 Tsuji, *Singapore 1941–1942*, p. 187, says there were 50 motor boats and about 100 folding boats for each division.
101 Allen, *Singapore 1941–1942*, pp. 168–70; Elphick, *Singapore: The Pregnable Fortress*, pp. 421–30; Murfett *et al.*, *Between Two Oceans*, pp. 225–9.
102 Allen, *Singapore 1941–1942*, pp. 170–1; Murfett *et al.*, *Between Two Oceans*, pp. 226–30.
103 Simson, *Singapore, Too Little, Too Late*, pp. 108–9.
104 Warren, *Singapore 1942*, pp. 193–95, 198, 232–5.
105 Allen, *Singapore 1941–1942*, pp. 170–1. Murfett *et al.*, *Between Two Oceans*, pp. 227–9. Kirby, *The Loss of Singapore*, p. 382–4.
106 Kirby, *The Loss of Singapore*, p. 380–6. This plan, issued on the night of 9–10 February, was a contingency plan for final withdrawal to the city perimeter, encompassing MacRitchie and Pierce Reservoirs.
107 Allen, *Singapore 1941–1942*, pp. 171; Murfett *et al.*, *Between Two Oceans*, pp. 228–30; Elphick, *Singapore: The Pregnable Fortress*, pp. 427–32.
108 Leasor, *Singapore: The Battle That Changed the World*, p. 246.
109 Murfett *et al.*, *Between Two Oceans*, pp. 232–3.
110 Tsuji, *Singapore 1941–1942*, p. 214, 250–51. WO106/2550A, 'Brilliant 7-Day Drive of Imperial Forces Down Malay Peninsula to Singapore Told', *Japan Times and Advertiser*, 8 April 1942.
111 Tsuji, *Singapore: The Japanese Version*, p. 252. Toh Boon Ho has suggested to the authors that Tsuji may have taken a calculated risk that Percival would surrender rather than fight hand to hand in a city, given knowledge of what had happened in China, and that he had already abandoned Penang, Ipoh and Kuala Lumpur without a fight.
112 Lim Chok Hui, Bukit Timah Resident, quoted in National Heritage Board, *The Japanese Occupation 1942–1945* (Singapore: Times, 1996), p. 47; Murfett *et al.*, *Between Two Oceans*, pp. 232–2.
113 Tsuji, *Singapore 1941–1942*, pp. 256–9.
114 Raffles College has undergone many changes, most recently being the 'National Institute of Education', and, from 2000, the 'Singapore Management University'.
115 See the map at WO106/2528. Dated 19 Jan. 1942, this shows a British estimate of 5 Japanese Divisions (5, 18, ?38, ?57, ?116) and one tank Regiment (3rd Tank Brigade). We do know Yamashita had been allocated the 56th Division. Percival's 'Operations in Malaya Command', p. 1311, goes further: 'It was estimated they probably had available for operations against Singapore a total strength of seven to eight divisions.' This was a crippling assumption.
116 Kirby, *The Loss of Singapore*, p. 398–401.
117 Eyewitness, 'The Gunners of the 11th Indian Division in Malaya', *The Gunner*, May 1946, p. 34.
118 WO106/2550A, 'Brilliant 7-Day Drive of Imperial Forces Down Malay Peninsula to Singapore Told', *Japan Times and Advertiser*, 8 April 1942, almost certainly by Tsuji.
119 WO172/191, 'Notes on matters affecting Nos 4 and 5 sections of 968 Battery, 16th Defence Regiment, RA at Singapore during the period 5 to 27 February, 1942.

120 Glen St John Barclay, 'Singapore Strategy: The Role of the United States in Imperial Defense', *Military Affairs* 39, 2 (April 1975), 57.
121 Lt-Col C.C.M. Macleod-Carey, 'Singapore Guns', in *War Monthly* 1976, pp. 34–9.
122 For Japanese sources see Allen, *Singapore 1941–1942* and Louis Allen, 'Notes on Japanese Historiography: World War II', *Military Affairs* 35, 4 (December 1971), 133–8.
123 WO106/2550A, 'Brilliant 7-Day Drive of Imperial Forces Down Malay Peninsula to Singapore Told', *Japan Times and Advertiser*, 8th April 1942 says there were 1,000 rounds a gun, 400 fired in the build-up, 400 before the morning of 15 Feb. This account, described as by 'the Chief Staff Officer who planned Bold Campaign', is almost certainly by Tsuji. Despite some inconsistencies between this and his book, many of the same phrases, issues and stories are repeated, in the same style, for instance Tsuji not wearing a helmet on 15 Feb. (compare to Tsuji, *Singapore 1941–1942*, p. 261), comparing the distance covered in Malaya to that between Tokyo and Shimonoseki, and the need to land reinforcements at Singora, not nearer Singapore, late in the campaign.
124 Tsuji, *Singapore 1941–1942*, p. 260. The *Japan Times* version says 200 shells were left on the morning of 15 Feb., the book says 100 shells left when discussing about 2 p.m. in the afternoon.
125 See for instance Allen, *Singapore 1941-1942*, p. 174; and J.D. Potter, *The Life and Death of a Japanese General* (New York: Signet Books, 1962), pp. 77–80, 85, 88–9.
126 WO106/2550A, telegram from Ceylon dated 5 May 1942, containing the views of Mr Seabridge, editor of the *Straits Times*, these being dated 28 Feb. 1942
127 Australian War Memorial 52, 18/2/21, 8 Austr Div Provost Coy War Diary, entries for 12–15 Feb.
128 Australian War Memorial 52, 18/2/21, 8 Austr Div Provost Coy War Diary, entries for 4, and 2–15 Feb.
129 See for instance: PREM3/168/3; PREM3/168/3B; and WO106/2550A. The idea of the battle as a close-run thing was told in excellent story-form by the *Daily Express* correspondent James Leasor as long ago as 1968. Leasor, *Singapore: The Battle That Changed the World*, pp. 244–58.
130 The quotation is from Louis Allen, *Singapore 1941–42* (London, 1977), pp. 174 ff. See also Turnbull, *History of Singapore*, p. 183; and Masanobu Tsuji, *Singapore: The Japanese Version* (London, 1962), pp. 260–1. Andrew Gilchrist, *Malaya 1941: The Fall of an Empire* (London, 1991), pp. 61 ff., points out Japan was also operating at its limits, given operations stretching from China to India, and Manchuria to Perth.
131 Kirby, *The Loss of Singapore*, p. 417: 'As soon as the Fall of Singapore was assured, Lieut-General Sano, commanding the division [38th Division having taken Hong Kong], was instructed to proceed with the plan for the occupation of southern Sumatra'. Leading elements left Camranh Bay on 9th February. See also pp. 419–20. By 15 Feb. the British and Dutch were abandoning Palembang, and the Japanese already controlled Malaya, Singapore, Borneo, Luzon excepting Bataan, and Celebes (Sulawesi).
132 This idea was developed in response to suggestions and papers by Richard Aldrich and Carl Bridge.
133 Japanese generals were notoriously competitive, a factor spurring Yamashita's impatience. This might have complicated reinforcements. Syonan (or Shonan – Light of the South) was the name Japan gave to Singapore. See Wilmott, *Empires in the Balance*, pp. 227–9, 234–6, 296–9, 303, 324–5, *passim*. Murfett et al. *Between Two Oceans*, Chapter 8 and Appendix 3, argue this point in more depth.
134 For spies see Elphick, *Far Eastern File*, or his shorter, more palatable book with Michael Smith, *Odd Man Out*. On Malaya having priority, Tsuji, *Singapore*

1941–1942, p. 25, says: 'It must be specially mentioned that in the selection of personnel Malaya was given priority ...'.
135 Kennedy, *The Rise and Fall of the Great Powers*, passim.
136 In Nov. 1940 a conference in the Far East, under Admiral Layton, concluded 556 aircraft would be needed. And conditions deteriorated in July 1941, when the Japanese secured bases from the French in southern Indochina.
137 Winston Churchill, *The Second World War*, Vol. 4: *The Hinge of Fate*, p. 60–1.
138 Kings College London, Liddell Hart Centre for Military Archives, Vlieland Papers. These contain Vlieland's writings from circa 1960s, as well as original documents he drew up in Singapore. In the former, he specifically says El Alamein in 1942 tied up 220,000 men, 1,600 tanks and 800 aircraft against Rommel's 120,000, 600 tanks and 300 aircraft, and asks if the outcome really justified the loss of the Far East.
139 Japanese intelligence relied not just on formal organisation, but also on a spectrum of information from societies such as *Ketsumeidan* (League of Blood) and *Dai Ajai Kyokai* (Great Asia Society). As Bah puts it, someone in 'A shop here, a farm there or a trading company'. Ban Kah Choon, *Absent History: The Untold Story of Special Branch operations in Singapore, 1915–1942* (Singapore: Raffles, 2001), p. 179.
140 See for instance, Elphick and Smith, *Odd Man Out*, Aldrich, *Intelligence and the War Against Japan*, pp. 43–8, and Elphick, *Far Eastern File* for intelligence in general. Heenan's name appears on a memorial stone at Kranji War Memorial, maintained by the Commonwealth War Graves Commission. Their policy is to list all soldiers who died in service. Unlike many others, Heenan was not discharged from the army before being shot, and therefore is listed. The War Graves Commission lists him as having died on 15 Feb. 1944, the date all those missing at the Fall were finally accepted as dead. Failed attempts by veterans' families to get Heenan's name removed after the publication of Elphick and Smith's *Odd Man Out*, were reported in the *Electronic Telegraph* (online), Monday 13 April 1998.
141 Figures from Carl Bridge, 'The Malayan Campaign, 1941–2: An International Perspective', paper given at the Institute of Commonwealth Studies (London, circa 1994–5), p. 2. For the argument that the 200 Hurricanes 'might have made all the difference', in Malaya, see Allen, *Singapore 1941–1942*, p. 50. The COS did complain to the Defence Committee that the aircraft would have paid a better dividend in Turkey, the Middle East or Malaya.
142 Aldrich, *Intelligence and the War Against Japan*, p. 46. It seems that in the chaos of war British sources failed to notice they had lost the report to Germans, and the implications. Aldrich does a brilliant job of unravelling the *Automedon* story.
143 Willmott, *Empires in the Balance*, pp. 226–7. See also Tsuji, *Singapore 1941–1942*, p. 25 and 35. Japan considered using 5 divisions, reduced it to 4, and Yamashita left even one of these in reserve 'after consideration of the fighting capacity of the British Army at the beginning of the campaign'.
144 Alec Ng Wei Kwang and Toh Boon Ho, 'Yamashita and the Assault on Singapore: Was Yamashita's success a bluff that worked or the culmination of calculated risk-taking?', *The Veteran* 8 (August 2002), 86–94.
145 His commanding officer later commended his 'initiative and example', especially on 15th. See WO172/189, 'Report of the 9th Coast Regiment: Proceedings Defence of Singapore', 22 Feb. 1942, signature unclear but apparently by commanding officer, probably Lt Col C.P Heath. The 2nd Lt was B. Griffith of 7th Battery, 9th Coast Regiment Royal Artillery, who had joined his unit in March 1941.
146 WO106/2550A, telegram from Ceylon of 5 May 1942, containing the views of Mr Seabridge, editor of the *Straits Times*, these being dated 28 February 1942. See also PREM3/168/7B, *passim*, for reports on the fall. For St Andrews Cathedral, see Barber, *Sinister Twilight*, pp. 193–4. See also Australian War Memorial 52, 18/2/21, 8

NOTES

Austr Div Provost Coy War Diary, entries for 12–15 Feb; and CAB119/208, Joint Planning Staff file on 'The Malayan Campaign – Implications of a Public Inquiry', 1946, p. 12: 'the defence of the island was badly organised ... The overwhelming fact ... is that there was a breakdown in morale'.

147 Lt-Col C.C.M. Macleod-Carey, 'Singapore Guns', in *War Monthly* 1976, pp. 34–9.

148 At Singapore – after previous deaths, captures, desertions and reinforcements – Percival was left with around 100,000 according to Allen, *Singapore 1941–1942*, pp. 270–1, and 85,000 according to Murfett et al., *Between Two Oceans*, p. 218. Allen suggests around 35,000 Japanese were used in the final assault on Singapore, still far too small for three divisions, plus artillery, tanks and support. Allen's larger figures for British forces, meanwhile, are probably due to his including 14,382 local volunteers in the count. See the notes by Captain P.J. Rivers in Mr Chelliah Thuraijah Retnam, Oral History Interview 000579/04, Singapore National Archives, appendix, p. 55 for 106,000 as the figure left in the final perimeter. Leasor, *Singapore: The Battle that Changed the World*, p. 264 also gives figures for British losses. According to Tsuji, The Japanese lost just 1,715 dead and 3,378 wounded in taking Singapore itself, a stunningly small number considering the men and weapons arrayed against them. Tsuji, *Singapore 1941–1942*, p. 271. For disputes over numbers, see also Warren, *Singapore 1942*, pp. 299–300, 302. He says 'over 100,000' passed into captivity, to which we might add around 7,500 killed (10,000 wounded), up to 10,000 taken prisoner on the mainland, a few thousand escapees, and a proportion of the 12,000 plus local Asian volunteers and regulars who were able to melt away. That accounts for most of the approximately 130,000 total of allied forces.

149 Laurence Rees, *Horror in the East* (London: BBC, 2001), gives a good introduction, including the use on occasions of live victims for bayonet practice. For Malaya, Braddon *The Naked Island*, pp. 169–70, describes Chinese heads on poles in Kuala Lumpur, and a particularly sadistic torture of a senile old man by setting him on fire, and then offering him water to douse the flames: boiling water. Training which involved violence as a common form of discipline, the frustrations of fighting an endless war in a hostile land, and the idea of fighting for God-Emperor and a superior Japanese race, came together with terrible consequences for the conquered.

150 For a Japanese account, see Akashi Yoji, 'General Yamashita Tomoyuki: commander of the Twenty-Fifth Army', in Farrell and Hunter (eds), *Sixty Years On*, p. 199. But Akashi seems to distance Yamashita from the way his orders were executed, arguing that, 'under the rules of war, a mopping-up operation was legitimate'.

151 For details on *Sook Ching* locations, see Singapore National Heritage Board, *The Japanese Occupation* (Singapore: Times, 1996), pp. 68–73. For accounts of the screening, lists of Chinese, and the quotation, see *Straits Times* 18 March 1947, pp. 1 and continuation. The witnesses the article cites from the city were mainly police, the witnesses from Blakang Mati a mix of gunners and other Europeans. The original trial affidavits are in WO235/1004, 'Defendants at the War Crimes Trials Held in Singapore'. See also WO203/6086, 6087, 6186, and 6187.

152 For details on *Sook Ching* locations, see National Heritage Board, *The Japanese Occupation*, pp. 68–73. The quotation is from 'Declaration of the Chief of the Syonan Defence Quarters of Nippon Army', *Syonan Times*, 23 Feb. 2602, as cited in Paul Kratoska, *The Japanese Occupation of Malaya, 1941–1945* (London: Allen and Unwin, 1998), pp. 97–8.

153 WOo172/180, Faber Fire Command, 'Survey of Operations', p. 582; WO172/176. The 138 Chinese were washed up on the 'S.E. Beaches of Blakan Mati' between 24 and 26 Feb., but others were washed up around the north too. For a few days, Blakang Mati [Sentosa] truly justified its Malay name: 'behind death'. It was packed

with defeated British and Indian troops, with bomb damage to building and roads, and the bodies caught in wire on the beaches could be smelt even on the hills of Fort Connaught. The quotation used in the text is a press summary of the trial affidavit given by European planter Mr Eric R.G. Bruce (on Blakang Mati at the time as a Lt with a FMSVF machine gun company) for the 'Chinese Massacre Trial' then going on in Victoria Hall. See *Straits Times* 18 March 1947, pp. 1 and continuation, and his affidavit in WO235/1004. The firing took place about 1,400 yards from his position at Fort Connaught, between Blakang Mati and St John's Island. The exercise was repeated several times. The overall victims included labourers wearing Singapore Harbour Board armlets, and a very few women. What the planters, miners and managers of the FMSVF felt as they saw the consequences of Britain's failure, is not recorded. As for the rest of the troops on Blakang Mati, most of the British gunners of Faber Fire Command had retired to join their comrades on Blakang Mati by 14 Feb., blowing up the guns there the same day. There followed looting by British, Australians, Malays and Chinese until guards were posted on barracks and messes on 16. Blakang Mati and Pulau Brani were evacuated by the Japanese as late as 27 Feb. Indeed, some men on the island only heard of the surrender as late as 0225 hrs on 16 Feb. Likewise, the Artillery War Diaries suggest the Japanese did not reach Tekong and Pengerang Batteries until 22 February, having largely bypassed eastern Singapore in the campaign. The final evacuation of Blakang Mati covered 31 British and 14 Indian officers, and 551 British and 736 Indian other ranks, though of course others had by then taken to small boats to make their escape.

5 THE GUNS OF SINGAPORE

1 Kings College London, Liddell Hart Centre for Military Archives, Vlieland Papers. Vlieland continued: 'imagine a last-ditch attempt to hold the Isle of Wight with the whole of the British Isles in enemy hands, all surrounding sea and air space at the enemy's sole disposal and the Solent strangely shrunk to the width of a sizeable river and spanned by a causeway'.
2 Tsuji also stated that, 'Britain's boast that Singapore was an impregnable fortress, and her attempted coercion of Japan by dispatching to Singapore the two great and efficient battleships, *Repulse* and *Prince of Wales*, were things that remain fresh even now in the memory of the people of Japan'. Tsuji, *Singapore 1941–1942*, p. 217; and that 'In this great fortress ... there was however an important weak point ... the rear defences in the region of Johore Province were incomplete' (p. 218).
3 This article came at a time when the British government was just resuming building on the base, and took a generally sceptical tone on its value. It also cited Sir Ian Hamilton's famous line that, 'Now I have no fears unless we ourselves fit out a halfway house and then – half-garrisoning it, as is our wont – make a present of it to the wrong people'. The article went on:

> Does not that last sentence strike at the root of the problem ...? For in the nature of things, since any war into which Britain is plunged is likely to be world-wide, she will inevitably be compelled, if not to half-garrison it with troops, at any rate to half-defend it with ships ... unless she is willing to sacrifice the command, nay even jeopardise the defence, of her home seas'. (p. 316)

Why were such warnings not heeded? Perhaps in part because of the split between internationalist, League of Nations rhetoric on one side, and Conservative defence of

NOTES

realpolitik (if half-funded) on the other. This article, for instance, criticised the base for threatening the prospects of disarmament.

4 The comparison falls flat in two respects. First, Britain enjoyed aerial and naval supremacy (as shaky as the latter was), so Tobruk could be resupplied and some troops rotated even. Second, Rommel eventually bypassed Tobruk, just as the Japanese reduced the forces in the Philippines facing Bataan. By comparison, Singapore was a major Japanese objective in itself.

5 The details of these debates have been traced in several works, not least Neidpath, *The Singapore Naval Base*, pp. 82–101, 108–21. Neidpath's appendix on the guns, pp. 221–5, was still the most reliable source available at the time of writing. Ong, *The Landward Defence of Singapore*, pp. 10–11, has as good, brief a summary.

6 Leasor, *Singapore: The Battle That Changed the World*, p. 83.

7 In 1927 the War Office appointed a commission (the Gillman Commission) of officers, who studied proposals for a gun system on site, and produced the basis for work, which began soon after. The Commission consisted of:

- Major-General Sir Webb Gillman, late of the Royal Artillery, and afterwards Master General of Ordnance (ordnance meaning artillery equipment).
- Colonel L.N. Malan, who was to be Chief Engineer Malaya, in charge of construction
- Lt-Col R.F. Lock, Royal Artillery, Secretary of the Ordnance Committee.

The Committee of Imperial Defence used these findings as the basis for a scheme of works, which initially envisaged two stages:

Stage One: to 1933
- three 15 inch guns
- four 9.2 inch guns (half in existence, requiring modernisation)
- eight 6 inch guns
- anti-aircraft guns, lights and associated equipment.

Stage Two 1933 to 1937
- completion of works.

See Pakenham-Walsh, *History of the Corps of the Royal Engineers* Vol. 9, (Chatham: Institution of Royal Engineers, 1952).

8 WO32/3626, draft letters from Downing Street to Straits Settlements, dated May 1928 and April 1929. Pakenham-Walsh, *History of the Corps of the Royal Engineers* Vol. 9. See also, MacIntyre, *The Rise and Fall of the Singapore Naval Base*, pp. 75–84. Technical arguments delayed work, the medium and heavy guns (9.2 and 15 inch respectively) from 1928 anyway. The delay followed the poor showing of existing, older 9.2-inch guns in gunnery trials in England, necessitating a technical review and gunnery trials to ascertain the best way of using heavier guns. This would also allow a further assessment of the weight of threat (what proportion of its fleet Japan could be expected to spare for Singapore), and the additional British naval and air forces that might be available at Singapore such as a possible aircraft carrier.

9 When the British Labour government called a halt in June 1929, pending a 1930 naval conference, the following had been completed, supervised by the Chief Engineer Malaya and Gillman committee member Colonel L. N. Malan:

- Anti-malarial work including clearing of swamps.
- Two piers and a wharf.

- A broad gauge railway intended to carry the largest crane in the world from the coast at Changi to the site you are standing on, in order to mount the 15-inch guns at Changi (Johore Battery). Technical arguments delayed work on the heavy and medium guns (15 and 9.5 inch respectivly) from 1928 anyway.
- A narrow 2-foot gauge line to other sites. This eventually carried a single package as heavy as 17 tons.
- A specially designed dock to receive the barges required to carry the heaviest guns
- Water supply installed and roads built.
- The site for a cantonment (a permanent camp) cleared and two 3-story barrack houses and married quarters built, complete with a recreation ground. Tree planting and landscape gardening.
- A power station.
- One battery site had been brought near to completion (a 6-inch battery at Changi).

Pakenham-Walsh, *History of the Corps of the Royal Engineers* Vol. 9. There was then a formal government decision in 1930 to halt coastal defence works until 1935. See WO32/3631, 'Note on SINGAPORE NAVAL BASE for Meeting of FIGHTING SERVICES COMMITTEE on 13th May 1930, 12th May 1930'.

10 By August 1934 at least 3 batteries, all in the east, had their guns, namely: Tekong Besar's three 9.2 inch; Sphinx's two 6 inch guns on the same island; and Changi's two 6 inch. See Col. K.W. Maurice-Jones, *The History of Coast Artillery in the British Army* (London: Royal Artillery Institution, 1959), p. 210.

11 Ong, *The Landward Defence of Singapore*, pp. 10–11. After Japan's Dec. 1934 denouncing of the Washington Treaty (which removed it from restrictions on naval building once a 2 year grace period was over), Britain's War Office responded by calling for a 1935 report on eastern coastal defences, which also recommended new 9.2 inch guns for Hong Kong and Ceylon, four 6 inch guns for Penang and 2 guns for Kilindini. Maurice-Jones, *The History of Coast Artillery*, p. 211.

12 See WO32/3632, draft letter to Governor of Straits Settlements, May 1928; and Major-General L. E. Beavis, 'The Defences of Singapore', *Stand-To* (Canberra), Vol. 8, No. 2 (March-April 1963), p. 9. Blakang Mati had had coastal guns built before 1880, and was in the 1930s still very much a military island, and the closest Singapore had to a 'fortress'. It then had four 6 inch guns (and a number of AMTB batteries) and 9.2 inch guns (3 at Connaught Battery), as well as a few close defence guns (12 pounders), and fine barracks and associated facilities. Nearby, there were more guns at the small islands of Pulau Brani and Pulau Hantu, as well as at Labrador on the mainland opposite. Developed since 1972 as a tourist and recreational facility, the island retains many of the old buildings. 'Siloso Fort' (the site of a Second World War 6 inch battery of two guns) has been turned into a heritage site, with a collection of military ordnance dating back to seventeenth-century Malay guns, some Japanese guns, and some interesting pictures and accounts from the 1930s. The site also traces Sentosa's earlier association with coastal artillery. As early as 1881 Siloso itself had three 7 inch Rifled Muzzle Loading guns and two 64-pounder guns, to help protect the edge of the harbour, which was expanding westward from Singapore City. Nor was Singapore without coastal guns before Blakang Mati's development. There were already by the 1860s coastal guns around the city, protecting the city and harbour. These were at Fort Fullerton (at the mouth of the Singapore River), Fort Canning, Mount Palmer, Mount Faber, and (a little later) Tanjong Katong. In the 1860s the guns totalled about twenty 68 pounder, twelve 8 inch breech loaders, eleven 8 inch Howitzers, and four 13 inch mortars. Fort Canning was then the most important site, being positioned in the city, about a quarter of a mile inland, and

central to the harbour, on a hill about 150 feet high. It had seven 68 pounders, eight 8 inch Breech Loaders, five 8 inch Howitzers and two 13 inch mortars in 1863. Its grand magazine could hold about 2,500 barrels of powder. Percival used the buildings on Fort Canning (by then not a site for coastal guns, which had migrated out of the city, to Blakang Mati and the East) to direct the battle for Singapore. Some of Fort Canning's underground rooms are now open as the 'Battlebox'. There were also barracks for European troops at Tanglin, about 3 miles west of Singapore town, as early as the 1860s. Again, Singapore has a remarkable amount of historical continuity in its military sites, for a modern city. The Tanglin area still houses the 'Tanglin' (British) school and Singapore Armed Forces premises, as well as many bungalows and houses built for the British services. For more detail, see P.K. Yeoh, 'Fortress Singapore', *Fort* (United Kingdom: Fortress Study Group, 1979).

13 Major-General L.E. Beavis, 'The Defences of Singapore', *Stand-To* Vol. 8, No. 2 (March–April 1963), p. 9:

> The original plan ... provided for a 15-inch battery on the southern edge of Blakang Mati Island, situated south of Keppel Harbour. This appeared an unnecessarily vulnerable site, as direct fire (that is, with a view of the target) was not a requirement for heavy guns, although a requirement for the 6-inch close defence guns'.

So the site for these was moved to one 'behind a low ridge of hills, some five miles west of Singapore ... In due course the Buona Vista battery was installed there'. In fact the case against Blakang Mati was more varied, including the indivisibility of placing primary batteries on more easily attacked outlying islands, the greater difficulty of running a railway there to take very heavy ammunition and spare parts, and maintenance of communication. See WO32/3622, Lt-Col. H.R. Brancker, Commanding RA Singapore, report of 20 August 1924, p. 37.

14 WO32/3622 contains various 1924 reports which discuss the merits of the sites, including the tree cover at Bee Hoe, Changi (the approximate position of the later Johore Battery).

15 How did 'HMS *Singapore*' compare to a real ship?

'HMS *Singapore*'	Force Z
six 15-inch	HMS *Repulse* six 15-inch
six 9.2-inch	HMS *Prince of Wales* ten 14-inch
18 6-inch	HMS *Danae*, *Dragon* and *Durban* six 6-inch apiece (cruisers)
Close Defence guns	HMS *Electra*, *Express*, *Tenedos*, RAN *Vampire*
	Gunboats *Dragonfly*, *Grasshopper*, *Scorpion*
	One Armed Merchant Cruiser (another at Penang).

16 See Appendix F on gun statistics, and John Campbell, 'British Heavy Coast-Defence Guns in World War Two', in John Roberts (ed.), *Warship 1995* (London: Conway Maritime Press, 1995), pp. 79–86, especially pp. 82–3.

17 SEAC report on the guns dated 29 May 1945, and found in WO252/1362, p. 57, has one 18 pounder at Pulau Hantu. This is the only time an 18-pounder is mentioned. See also Denis Rollo, *The Guns and Gunners of Hong Kong* (Hong Kong: The Gunners Roll of Hong Kong, after 1991), p. 114.

18 For the twin barrelled 6 pounders, see Maurice-Jones, *History of Coast Artillery in the British Army*, pp. 216–17. Macleod-Carey, 'Singapore Guns', p. 39; SEAC report on the guns dated 29 May 1945, and found in WO12/1362. Typically for the guns, the sources disagree on numbers and types. Macleod-Carey says twenty 6 pounders and

seven 12 pounders, to make 27. Added to the 29 modern guns that makes 56. But Macleod-Carey gets many details wrong, and is again contradicted by the War Diaries as well as the SEAC report of 1945, drawn up with a view to allied attacks. The latter says Faber had five AMTB batteries (presumably about 10 guns) and Changi four (about 7 guns as at least one was a single) making around 17. The latter would imply around 46 coastal guns in total. For the War Diaries confirming the Pulau Hantu 18 pounder, which Macleod-Carey's list omits, see WO12/180, summary entry for Pulau Hantu, 13 February 1942.

19 Squadron-Leader J. Clements, 'Blakang Mati – Island Fortress of Singapore', *Royal Artillery Journal* 108 (1981), 135–9.
20 Page was a former leader of a conservative government in Australia. See *Straits Times* (Singapore), 28 November 1941, p. 8, and 'Pacific Defences Impregnable', *Straits Times*, 26 November 1941. See also *Straits Times*, 26 November 1941, p. 8: 'Miniature Fortresses Surround Singapore: Powerful Guns On Islands'; and *Straits Times*, 17 Nov. 1941, p. 9, which has Mr J. L. Garvin stating in the *Sunday Observer* that 'No more formidable stronghold has been known than Singapore today. Malaya, as she is now fortified and manned, is a bristling and terrible obstacle'. Unfortunately this last had equal nonsense to proclaim on Hong Kong as another 'Malta', which rather lessens the effect. More interestingly, the papers show how anxious people then were that war was imminent.
21 Winston Churchill, *The Second World War*, Vol. 4: *The Hinge of Fate*, pp. 41–3.
22 Unfortunately, only a small land force was allocated to deal with coastal forts and gun batteries which might interfere with the naval operation. The attack began 19 Feb., but minefields and shore-based artillery inflicted heavy casualties. Another attack in mid-March by 18 battleships resulted in a third of its ships being put out of action. Finally, Allied forces tried securing the straits by landing at Gallipoli in April, only to find themselves pinned to the beaches until their final evacuation in December. For an entertaining read on the Dardanelles episode, see John Charmley, *Churchill: The End of Glory*, pp. 105–25, 131–2.
23 Hogg, *British and American Coast Artillery*, pp. 198–200. The guns were from the reserve stock for King George V class battleships. The first gun was emplaced by 3 August 1940, the second in Feb. 1941. S.C.G. Gale, 'The Guns of Dover 1939–1956', *The Gunner* 11 (November 2000), 28–9. But see also comments on this article, and further information on the Dover guns, in *The Gunner* 12 (2000), p. 43, and 1 (January 2001), 34.
24 Tsuji, *Singapore, 1941–1942*, pp. 8–9.
25 Winston Churchill, *The Second World War*, Vol. 4: *The Hinge of Fate*, pp. 41–3.
26 WO106/2550,'Report on the Surrender of Singapore', no date, by a member of the volunteer forces on Singapore, serving on searchlights at Fort Berlayer. The third battery mentioned here is Serapong, but the War Diaries state this did not fire. By contrast, we know Siloso, opposite the witnesses' position at Berlayer, did. So 'Serapong' is almost certainly a mental slip for Siloso, which the author may well have seen firing.
27 Cited from Morrison, *Malayan Postscript*, p. 150. In the original 1942 version, this quotation occurs on p. 143. See Murfett et al., *Between Two Oceans*, p. 244, footnote 74.
28 Glover, *In Seventy Days*, pp. 11–12. Ong, *The Landward Defence of Singapore*, p. 2.
29 Catherine Porter, 'Autopsies on the Southeast Asia Debacle', *Pacific Affairs* 16, 2 (June 1943), p. 207. By March 1941 actual expenditure was £4 million, estimated total expenditure £5 million. This was extended to cover landward defences, but subject to detailed approval of the War Office until 11 Dec. 1941, when the War Office gave the GOC Malaya 'a free hand with regard to such expenditure'. Yet again, a general atmosphere of parsimony created an environment, a mentality,

which stifled preparations. Lt-General A.E. Percival, 'Operations of Malaya Command, From 8 Dec. 1941 to 15 Feb. 1942', Second Supplement to *The London Gazette* of Friday, the 20 Feb., 1948, dated Thursday, 26th February, 1948, p. 1248.

30 Lt-Col. Alfred H. Burne, 'The Truth About the Singapore Guns', *The Gunner* (April 1945), p. 6, says: 'General E.O. Lewin wrote an article refuting the libel which appeared in THE GUNNER for November last'. As early as 1943 the myth had entered the historiography, see Catherine Porter, 'Autopsies on the Southeast Asia Debacle: A Review Article', *Pacific Affairs* 16, 2 (June 1943), p. 207: 'Singapore's much-touted defenses – for what they were worth – were for attack by sea. Its 15-inch guns could not be turned to fire upon an enemy approaching down the peninsula. The Japanese, Weller says, never bothered to attack those gun emplacements'. The books being reviewed by Porter included George Weller, *Singapore is Silent* (New York: Harcourt Weller, 1942); Cecil Brown, *Suez to Singapore* (New York: Random House, 1942); and O.D. Gallagher, *Action in the East* (New York: Doubleday, 1942).

31 Lt-Col. Alfred H. Burne, 'The Truth About the Singapore Guns', *The Gunner* (April 1945), p. 6. Burne suggested the myth might have been popularised by a parliamentary speech: 'I suspect the myth arose in civilian minds: the first reference to it in print I saw was a speech in the House of Lords by, I fancy, Lord Addison.'

32 Ong, *The Landward Defence of Singapore*, p. 3. Evidence that Churchill was misinterpreted as saying the guns 'could only fire out to sea' can be found in Major-General L.E. Beavis, 'The Defences of Singapore', *Stand-To* (Canberra), Vol. 8, No. 2 (March–April 1963), p. 8. Beavis then adds his own layer of myth by stating that four of five 15-inch guns had an arc of fire of 360 degrees, and one of 35 degrees. Both statements are incorrect.

33 C. Northcote Parkinson, 'The Pre–1942 Singapore Naval Base', *U.S. Naval Institute Proceedings* (September 1956), (Annapolis, MD: U.S. Naval Institute, 1956), p. 942, *passim*. It not impossible that Parkinson did not write the description, that is not unknown with journals, though the style looks consistent. Either way, the unsuspecting reader would most probably attribute the authority of the author to the caption.

34 As late as 1989 Peter Calvocoressi, Guy Wint and John Pritchard could still emphasise the guns facing the wrong way and a British 'delusion' that Singapore was 'impregnable' to land attack. This despite being well aware that British plans in 1941 centred on an air-land defence of the Kra in the north. Peter Calvocoressi, Guy Wint and John Pritchard's *Total War: The Causes and Courses of the Second World War* (Revised Edition, Harmondsworth, 1989), pp. 986–98, 991. Ong, *Operation Matador*, gives a good commentary on the myth, see pp. 19–21 for Ong noting the repetition of the myth in British papers and television in the 1970s and 1980s.

35 *The Guns of Navarone*, the 1961 film based on Alastair MacLean's 1957 novel. Unfortunately, Singapore's guns were not important enough to require the sort of heroics Gregory Peck and David Niven demonstrate to destroy just 2 guns, overlooking a vital maritime channel near the island of 'Kheros'. The film is, even now, widely available in Singapore and elsewhere on CD and DVD.

36 For the American guns, including a good picture of a gun peering from a fairly restrictive 'window' of a massive concrete casemate, see the Fort MacArthur Museum site (Los Angeles, USA) at http://www.ftmac.org/. Some American guns, however, were on open concrete pits, relying on dispersal for protection. Fort Siloso, on Sentosa (Blakang Mati) in Singapore, now houses a range of Second World War and pre-Second World War guns, information and veterans' memories of the 1930s. (http://www.fort.com/). The website is informative and visually rich. As of 2001, however, it inevitably still included some of the errors and simplifications of the

NOTES

literature existing at the time. Such as dating Connaught's destruction to 15 Feb., rather than 14 Feb., or having 3 Johore Battery guns firing at Johore Bahru, rather than two.

37 Good examples of this view can be found in Simson, *Singapore, Too Little, Too Late*, Glover, *In Seventy Days*, and Barber, *Sinister Twilight*.
38 Ian Graeme, 'Singapore 1939–1942', *The Journal of the Royal Artillery*, 103 (1976), p. 21. Ian Graeme was Subaltern, Adjutant Battery Commander 3rd Heavy Anti-aircraft Regiment Royal Artillery in 1941. The mess referred to was shared with the 7th Coast Regiment, Royal Artillery.
39 Mr Chelliah Thuraijah Retnam, Oral History Interview 000579/04, Singapore National Archives, appendix on background. As with other Indian units, officers and some NCOs were British, but other ranks were mainly Sikhs and Punjabi Muslims recruited in India or, for a few, in Hong Kong. From the 1890s their companies were commanded by a Subedar, assisted by a Jemadar, rather than just being seen as assisting European gunners. For the HKSRA's genealogy, starting with the raising of Gun Lascars in 1847, through changes of name to Asiatic Artillery, then Hong Kong Royal Artillery Companies and Singapore Royal Artillery Company (1893), see Denis Rollo, *The Guns and Gunners of Hong Kong*, pp. 12–17, 66, 102–3. In 1893 there were 5 of these companies, just one of them in Singapore (soon to be 2), where it was called the 'Singapore Company, Royal Artillery'. In 1898 they were grouped into a battalion (*ibid*, p. 69) called the Hong Kong-Singapore Battalion Royal Artillery, paralleled by the Ceylon-Mauritius Battalion, Royal Artillery until the latter was disbanded.
40 Headquarters, USAFFE and Eighth US Army (Rear), *Report on Installations and captured weapons, Java and Singapore 1942* (Washington DC: Office of Military History, Department of the Army, 1958). An American publication of 'a report made by Lt-Col Tadataka Namaguchi of Army Technical Headquarters and Maj Akiyama of Army Heavy Artillery School of an inspection tour of Singapore and Java between March and May 1942'.
41 *Report on Installations and captured weapons, Java and Singapore 1942*, p. 17.
42 Brigadier W.H.H. Wilberforce, 'Hong Kong Singapore Brigade Royal Artillery: A Subaltern in pre-War Singapore', *Royal Artillery Journal* 122 (September 1995). Normally in Singapore cabarets, men paid for a ticket, which bought the right to dance with one of the 'taxi-dancers'. Many, if not most, taxi-dancers seem to have been dancers pure and simple, though a girl would sometimes be booked out for an evening, and sometimes more might be involved than dinner at a local restaurant or open-air food-hall. See also Braddon *The Naked Island*, p. 70, for other ranks having to ration themselves, at the grand price of 25 cents a ticket.
43 Ian Graeme, 'Singapore 1939–1942', *Royal Artillery Journal* 103 (1976), 20–6. Ian Graeme was Adjutant to the Battery Commander, 3rd Heavy Anti-aircraft Regiment RA, in Singapore; Wilberforce, 'Hong Kong Singapore Brigade Royal Artillery: A Subaltern in pre-War Singapore', p. 31.
44 Lt-Col A.H. Burne, letter to the editor of the *Daily Telegraph*, 16 Oct. 1950.
45 Winston Churchill, *The Second World War*, Vol. 4: *The Hinge of Fate*, p. 82: 'Those of the heavy guns of the coast defences which could fire northwards were not of much use, with their limited ammunition, against the jungle-covered country in which the Japanese were gathering'. See also pp. 47–8.
46 Churchill, *Second World War*, Vol. 4, *The Hinge of Fate*, pp. 42–3. Lt-Col Alfred H. Burne, 'The Truth About the Singapore Guns', *The Gunner* (April 1945), p. 6 He said that: 'At the time of the siege all the guns of the main armament possessed all-round traverse, and could shoot over the land as well as over the sea'.
47 Kirby, *Singapore: The Chain of Disaster*, pp. 28–30.

48 See WO32/3622, Lt-Col H.R. Brancker, Commanding RA Singapore, report of 20 August 1924, p. 37.
49 Lt-Col A.A. Tawney, *The Gunner*, (February 1951), p. 51. Neidpath later suggested four guns could fire landward as well, see Neidpath, *The Singapore Naval Base*, pp. 223–5. This is Neidpath's appendix on 'The Guns of Singapore', which traced the myth partly to Churchill's postwar history of the war, and partly to Glover's *Seventy Days*.
50 Ong, *The Landward Defence of Singapore*, p. 13, footnote 47 says three fired. He cites Macleod-Carey as evidence for all the Johore Battery (3 guns) firing towards Johore, and all the Buona Vista Battery (2 guns) not doing so. He also refers to a 1941map which shows a 180 degree arc for Buona Vista's guns. But this neglects the fact that one of Johore Battery's guns (on the Mk. I emplacement) could turn only 180 degrees facing southeast, that is almost entirely seaward. Neidpath in 1981 said 'at least two' guns *did* fire landward, while four *could*. That is, all the Mk. II turret-style guns could have targeted Japanese troops if modified (the Buona Vista ones otherwise only reached Johore south of Japanese troops), while the Mk. I could not. See Neidpath, *The Singapore Naval Base*, p. 225. Neidpath is thus still the nearest to the mark, but unfortunately few people read to appendices on page 225 of a such specialist book.
51 See Ong, *The Landward Defence of Singapore*, and *Operation Matador*, pp. 19–54. See also Murfett et al., *Between Two Oceans*, p. 244, footnote 74 for Stanley Falk, *Seventy Days to Singapore: The Malayan Campaign 1941–1942* (London: Robert Hale, 1975), pp. 202–4, and the official history, Kirby, *The Loss of Singapore*, p. 361.
52 Ong, *The Landward Defence of Singapore*, p. 15: 'All of the six 9.2" guns and eighteen 6" guns could traverse 360 degrees and could fire landward'.
53 See *Coast Artillery* Drills, Part III, Pamphlet No. 2, *Gun Drill – B. L. 15-inch Mk I Gun on Mk III mounting (Land Service)* (London: War Office, 1943), p. 97 ff (Ch. II, 'Mounting, 15-inch, Mark II). The walking cables are also described for a naval turret mounted gun in *Turret Gun Drill for 15 Inch Twin Mark I/N R. P. Mountings* (London: 1948).
54 According to a Faber Fire Command War Diary of 27 July 1942, 'the 15 inch equipments at BUONA VISTA could not bear further NORTH than 301 degrees (i.e. Sungai PENDAS on the southern Johore Coast West of P. Laba). The enemy landing was well north of this . . .'. Based on other sources for calculating traverse, the 301 degrees is probably calculated from true north. The guns themselves faced south.
55 See for instance John Campbell, 'British Heavy Coast-Defence Guns in World War Two', in John Roberts (ed.), *Warship 1995* (London: Conway Maritime Press, 1995), 79–86.
56 Tsuji, *Singapore 1941–1942*, pp. 253–4. First published as Masanobu Tsuji, *Singapore: The Japanese Version* trans. Margaret E. Lake (London: Constable, 1960).
57 See the related appendices for more. In brief, the 1942 War Diaries show Connaught Battery's bombarded Tengah extensively after midnight on the night of 11 to 12 February 1942. But they make no mention of Johore Battery's 15 inch guns firing at Tengah, which was almost as far from Johore Battery as any Singapore target could be. The only other 15 inch guns, at Buona Vista, did not fire. Nor is it likely that the fairly detailed War Diaries would have omitted mention of firing so many shells at so important a target as Tengah. More likely, Tsuji chose to believe he was under fire from the biggest guns (he loved a good story) and Macleod-Carey in the 1970s simply quoted Tsuji. Since everyone wrongly assumed the latter was a good source, as a contemporary commander at Faber Fire Command, many people replicated the error. See for instance Maj. J.C. Aviet, 'The Big Guns of Singapore', *The Pointer* 4, 3 (January 1979), pp. 32–50. Yet it now seems Macleod-Carey may have made errors concerning dates, targets and cables.

NOTES

58 For 4 guns firing landward, see MacIntyre, *The Rise and Fall of the Singapore Naval Base*, pp. 121–2. He states of the guns: 'four of these had an arc of fire of 360 degrees, and subterranean magazines', apparently basing this on the account of an Australian officer, L.E. Beavis, involved in ordering the guns in the early 1930s. Beavis says 'the 9.2 inch guns had an arc of fire of almost 360 degrees, and four of the five 15-inch guns, on naval type turret mountings, had an arc of fire of 360 degrees. The fifth 15-inch gun had an arc of fire of only about 35 degrees'. The latter is almost certainly a simple error, replacing the traverse with the elevation, as even the Mk.I had a traverse of nearer 180 degrees. L.E. Beavis, 'The Defences of Singapore', *Stand-To* 8, 2 (Canberra, 1963), 7–9. This suggests many authors err in following Beavis for the guns' traverse. Some information coming from artillery sources may also inadvertently given the impression that most or all the 15 inch guns could fire landward, e.g. 'The 15-inch guns ... since they possessed only A.P. shell they obviously could not have much practical effect against land targets. Since, however, they seem linked in the popular mind with the land defence of the island it should be added that they had all-round traverse, though adjustments had to be made and power-loading abandoned if fire was to be applied in *all* directions.' From: Editorial Notes, *The Gunner*, XXXIX, No. 7, October 1947. As for others saying all the 15 inch could fire landwards, this myth probably derived from their discovering the Mk. II's had the potential for all-round traverse, without knowing that there was a single Mk. I as well, or that the Mk. II emplacements had gunstops and cables which restricted movement. More recent statements favour three 15 inch guns having all-round traverse. In this they accept Macleod-Carey's statement that the 2 at Buona Vista could not fire because of cables and gun-stops. It hardly seems likely Macleod-Carey, who helped command these guns, could be mistaken on this. Lt-Colonel Macleod-Carey, 'Singapore Guns', *War Monthly* (1976), p. 38. Hence Ong suggests that, 'except for two 15" guns, they had all-round traverse and could aim at landward targets. And these guns did fire at Japanese targets in Johore and Singapore', and 'the three at Johore Battery had all-round traverse'. Ong, *The Landward Defence of Singapore*, pp. 12, 16. Murfett et al., *Between Two Oceans*, p. 223–4 also has 'three of the 15" guns, all of the 9.2" guns, and six of the eighteen 6" guns' being 'brought to bear'. Elphick, *Singapore: The Pregnable Fortress*, pp. 303–5 also suggests three 15 inch guns fired. The problem with this is, first, that detailed plans and the war diaries both suggest one Johore Battery gun could not and did not fire to the rear, being on a Mk. I emplacement with traverse not possible beyond 180 degrees, due to fixed obstructions Second, that Macleod-Carey is unreliable on several issues, such as getting the wrong date for a ship being sunk, and suggesting it was a landing ship, when his commanders at the time concluded it was a *tongkang*.

59 The report occurs in WO172/176. The author is given as 'Brigadier ... Commander Fixed Defences Malaya'.

60 When the War Diary first mentions Johore Battery firing towards Malaya, it confirms only two guns fired. Subsequently the War Diary seems to use 'Johore Battery' for shorthand, without specifying how many guns. When Macleod-Carey said 'the three 15in guns' of Johore Battery he was probably using this as another way of saying 'Johore Battery'. Since he had already used the term 'Johore Battery' in a previous sentence, it may have been an attempt to avoid repetition. In other words, an attempt at good English may have resulted in inaccurate history. Lt-Col Macleod-Carey, 'Singapore Guns', *War Monthly* (1976), p. 38.

61 Ong, *The Landward Defence of Singapore*, p. 11. See also CAB21/402, sheet 447, *passim*. A detail about the sultan ceremonially firing the first shot from the guns occurs in Richard Holmes and Anthony Kemp, *The Bitter End* (Chichester: Strettington House, 1982), p. 23, but without the citation of a source.

62 P.K. Yeoh, 'Fortress Singapore', *Fort* Vol. 7 (1979) uses layout plans from WO78/4389 to conclude that (p. 34): 'An arc-of-fire of about 180 degrees facing approximately due south was indicated. The gun pit itself was not symmetrical and the vertical stop wall at the front of the pit broke the circular sweep of the rest of the pit. Two stanchions for the crane pads are shown, located in the centre of this wall'. See also John Campbell, 'British Heavy Coast-Defence Guns in World War Two', in John Roberts (ed.), *Warship 1995*, 79–86; and correspondence between Colonel Donald Carmichael (an RAOC officer involved with installation of the guns) and Commander C.B. Robbins. This correspondence was based on, Firepower, Woolwich, James Clavell Library: Military Documents 2252, Carmichael Papers, 'Johore Battery', 28 Oct. 1938, *passim*. This contains precise, contemporary figures on the traverse of each of the Johore Battery's three guns.

63 Philip Sims, in his 'The Harbor Defenses of Singapore: Facing the Wrong Way?', *Coast Defense Journal* (Feb. 2001), p. 5. See also Campbell, 'British Heavy Coast-Defence Guns in World War Two', pp. 79–86. This is confirmed by Lt-Col A.A. Tawney, who was commanding his own regiment of anti-aircraft artillery at the time. Commenting on 'The Singapore Myth', he wrote that, 'most batteries could fire on an all-round traverse. The big exception was one 15-in. gun which was on an original mounting which gave only a 180-degree arc'. For the 50–230 degree traverse, see WO252/1362, Inter-Service Topographical Department, 'Supplement on Defences to I.S.T.D (S.E.A.C) Docket on Singapore and Southern Johore, Amendment No. 1', 29 May 1945. The latter gives the Buona Vista traverse as 050 to 320 degrees from due north (that is, from a line pointing almost directly to the rear of the gun, towards Malaya). This compares to the 050–340 arc it suggests for Johore Battery. See also Firepower, Woolwich, James Clavell Library: Military Documents 2252, Carmichael Papers, various papers on Singapore's Guns dating from the 1930s.

64 He wrongly assumed four 15 inch guns could traverse all-round, but it is clear that the one he identifies as not able to must be the Mk. I. Lt-Col A.A. Tawney, *The Gunner*, (February 1951), p. 51. The 50 to 230 degree traverse is given in a SEAC report on the guns dated 29 May 1945, and found in WO252/1362.

65 For confirmation that the Buona Vista guns were 15 inch Mk II Mtgs, see the War Diary of Faber Fire Command in WO172/180.

66 Compare the account of Lt-Col Tawney, *The Gunner* (February 1951), p. 51 with that found in *Senshi Sōsho* [War History Series], Volume 1, *Marē Shinkō Sakusen* [The Malayan Campaign], p. 547, describing how a dug-out of the observation post of a heavy artillery battalion of the 18th Division received a direct hit in which a medical officer and seven others were killed or wounded. From reading the sources, David Sissons suggests that perhaps this could be the site that Tawney was shown by the Japanese.

67 J. Hodder, Diary entry for 11 Feb. 1942, Mss. Ind. Ocn. s. 52, Rhodes House, Oxford. His diary is mainly concerned with his experiences during the Japanese invasion of Singapore and as a prisoner-of-war afterwards. He had been an engineer installing a generator in the Maternity Hospital.

68 Lt-Col A.A. Tawney, *The Gunner*, (February 1951), p. 51. He commanded a nearby Heavy Anti-Aircraft Regiment.

69 Combine WO172/176, 'Fixed Defences Singapore' War Diary, pp. 270–2, saying Johore fired at the Bukit Timah area on the morning of the 12 Feb., with Kirby, *The Loss of Singapore*, p. 398, on Massey-Beresford's retreat, 'covered by fire from the fixed coast defence btys', and Percival, 'Operations of Malaya Command, pp. 1320–1.

70 As ever, the sources are full of contradictions. WO172/176, 'Fixed Defences Singapore' War Diary, pp. 270–2, says Johore only fired at the Bukit Timah area on the morning of the 12 Feb. There is no mention, there of coastal artillery assisting

NOTES

Tomforce's counter-attack towards Bukit Timah early on 11 Feb. (that seems to have been supported by field artillery as 'what appeared to be several thousand shells rained down', from *Senshi Sōsho* [War History Series], Vol 1, *Marē Shinkō Sakusen* [The Malayan Campaign], p. 585. Nor does the War Diary mention any bombardment of Bukit Timah that night, though Japanese sources mention cratering (*op. cit.*, p. 591) which indicates coastal guns firing AP, and Lionel Wigmore, *The Japanese Thrust* (Canberra: Australian War Memorial, 1967), p. 362 mentions 'information was received' that fortress guns had fired into Bukit Timah on the night of 11 to 12. The nearest we can get to a reconciliation is that Australian forces requested Fortress guns assist their own artillery on the night of 11 to 12 Feb., which the guns did early on 12 Feb. This firing, perhaps as late as dawn on 12 Feb., left the area around Bukit Timah Rifle Range (today's Rifle Range Road) heavily cratered.

71 Lt-Col Macleod-Carey, 'Singapore Guns', *War Monthly* (1976). Macleod-Carey, then a Major, was second in charge at Faber Fire Command, in 1941–42. He was still in Singapore on 14 Feb., when he was put in charge of a rifle company newly formed from miscellaneous gunners and Australian stragglers. This took up a reserve position behind the 2nd Malay Regiment (later relieved by RAOC) at 'Bukit Chermin' on a section of the front at Pender – Morse Road – Keppel Dockyard West by 1800 hours, remaining there until the surrender. Macleod-Carey was reported missing presumed escaped from the night of 15 Feb., with the remainder of the platoon marched off to the nearby Gillman Barracks next day. He made good his escape to Ceylon. So Macleod-Carey should be a good witness. But his article contains a number of probable errors of the type common in oral history, for instance simply saying 'Johore Battery' and its 'three guns' fired at Johore, when it was really two, and giving the wrong date for firing on one ship. He is therefore a useful general source for Faber Fire Command, and for the feel of events, but only when vigorously cross-checked. For details contradicting Macleod-Carey's account, see WO172/180, Faber Fire Command, 'Survey of Operations', Diary, 14.2.1942, Faber.

72 Serapong is almost certainly a mistake for Siloso. From Berlayer (adjacent to Labrador on the mainland opposite), the witness would have been able to see Fort Siloso on Blakang Mati firing. The searchlights at Berlayer may even have helped light one or more *tongkangs* for the Labrador guns to fire on. So he probably means Siloso. Especially as no War Diary located mentions Serapong firing, and the traverse of Serapong seems to have been limited to the southeast, where we know no targets presented themselves.

73 WO106/2550,'Report on the Surrender of Singapore', no date, by a member of the volunteer forces on Singapore, serving on searchlights at Fort Berlayer. This corresponds to various entries in WO172/180, Faber Fire Command, 'Survey of Operations', Diary and Reports on individual batteries. These repeatedly note guns unable to traverse fully because of concrete protection, the Berlayer report simply stating that 'The 12 pdrs [2] could not be fired landwards'.

74 WO172/180, Faber Fire Command, 'Survey of Operations', Buona Vista report.

75 Compare for instance the comments in P.K. Yeoh, 'Fortress Singapore', *Fort* Vol. 7 (1979); WO78/4389; Campbell, 'British Heavy Coast Defence guns in World War II', p. 81; and WO252/1362, Inter-Service Topographical Department, 'Supplement on Defences to I.S.T.D (S.E.A.C) Docket on Singapore and Southern Johore, Amendment No. 1', 29 May 1945. The latter gives the Buona Vista traverse as 050 to 320 degrees from due north (that is, from a line pointing almost directly to the rear of the gun, towards Malaya). This compares to the 050–340 arc it suggests for Johore Battery. The Fixed Coastal Defences War Diary's suggestion that Buona Vista could only fire to 301 degrees makes it likely its gun-stops (designed to protect hydraulic and possibly other cables) had not been removed (see also the next note). Consider the similar Johore's

NOTES

Mk. II mountings on Battery guns 2 and 3. These could only reach 300 and 315 degrees respectively with gun-stops in place, but upped to 325 and 340 degrees once removed (Firepower, Woolwich, James Clavell Library: Military Documents 2252, Carmichael Papers, 'Johore Battery', 28 Oct. 1938, *passim*). Combined with Macleod-Carey's desire to defend the preservation of Faber's guns in case of sea attack (he says cables for fire control fitted in 1938 were what limited traverse, and insists the guns had to be conserved in case a fleet appeared) and considering at least one volunteer's statement that requests to alter some guns were refused, it seems very likely there was a conscious decision not to adjust Buona Vista. Of course, we still cannot be sure. See also Macleod-Carey *War Monthly* (1976), p. 38; WO172/176, entries in the War Diary; the text above; and Faber Fire Command War Diary of July 1942 in WO172/180 for this, and Buona Vista's guns being 15 inch C.B Mk.II Mtgs.

76 See the gun manual as cited in the note above.

77 We calculate the initial traverse by starting from 301 degrees (since we take the War Diary, written by the men making the decisions in 1942, as the most accurate available source) and subtracting the maximum traverse with gun stops in place according to the relevant gun manual, and as confirmed by Col Carmichael, who helped install the 15 inch guns. That means 301 − 240 = 61. This gives an arc of 61–301 degrees with gunstops in place. We also know, from the gun manuals, that removing the stops added 50 degrees traverse (290 with stops − 240 without = 50). We then arive at the arc with gunstops removed by borrowing an assumption from Campbell, 'British Heavy Coast Defence Guns in World War II', p. 83. When he looks at Johore Battery, he assumes for its guns that the extra traverse gained by removing gun stops (50 degrees) was distributed equally, adding 25 degrees of traverse to both sides. This seems a reasonable assumption until disproved, since if a margin of safety was desired, it would presumably be similar for each direction. Also, Campbell is a naval historian, gives the most precise figures, and where his sources can be checked against the Carmichael papers in Firepower, James Clavell Library, Woolwich, they are unerringly accurate. We prefer his figures whenever possible. Hence we have distributed the 50 degrees of turn gained by removing stops equally. That gives an arc of 36–326 degrees. We have assumed that, by comparison, the SEAC report of 1945 was likely to be reasonably, but not totally, accurate. This is because it gives a maximum arc of 50–320 degrees. Though this is about right, we can guess that it is likely to be slightly out, since it adds up to 270 degrees. That is, it is slightly short of the 290 degrees maximum arc specified by the gun manual for a gun with stops removed. If all this looks like the work of slightly deranged alchemists, then we plead that this informed guesswork is at least transparent, and an improvement on previous accounts, which have tended to accept one source from many without stating why. See: WO172/180, Faber Fire Command, 'Survey of Operations', Buona Vista report; WO252/1362, Inter-Service Topographical Department, 'Supplement on Defences to I.S.T.D (S.E.A.C) Docket on Singapore and Southern Johore, Amendment No. 1', 29 May 1945; O172/176; *Coast Artillery* Drills, Part III, Pamphlet No. 2, *Gun Drill* − B. L. *15-inch Mk I Gun on Mk III mounting (Land Service)* (London: War Office, 1943), p. 97 ff. (Chapter II, 'Mounting, 15-inch, Mark II'); and correspondence between Col Carmichael and C.B. Robbins, copied to the authors.

78 They were at the end of Ulu Pandan Road, close to where it joins Clementi Road.

79 WO172/180, Faber Fire Command, 'Survey of Operations', Buona Vista report.

80 Dol Ramli, 'History of the Malay Regiment 1933–1942', *Journal of the Malaysian Branch of the Royal Asiatic Society* 38 (1965), p. 230. The 2nd Battalion Malay Regiment had deployed thinly on a line from the West Coast Road up the Pandan River, with A Company 'near the Mortar Range about 200 yards to the left of the 15" gun battery'. Ramli draws on statements by men of the Malay Regiment.

NOTES

81 See the Faber Fire Command War Diary of July 1942 in WO172/180 for this, and the guns being 15 inch C.B Mk. II Mtgs'. Later rumours caused by the confusion included the following: 'at one time the battery commander was locked in a gun turret with Japs beating on the armoured doors'. See WO252/1362, Inter-Service Topographical Department, 'Supplement on Defences to I.S.T.D (S.E.A.C) Docket on Singapore and Southern Johore, Amendment No. 1', 29 May 1945, p. 59. By contrast, the War Diary simply records firing all around the guns, the belief at Buona Vista that it was surrounded at about 0555. It suggests changes among allied units caused the confusion, and notes that after the guns were blown the Australians established firm positions west of the guns, allowing the remaining gunners to retreat along the railway line after 1300.

82 WO172/180, 'Summary of Operations Feb. 8 to Feb. 15 1942, Faber Fire Command, Diary, 'No 2 gun could not bear NE up Johore Straits'. See also the Pasir Laba Battery report. Even No. 1 gun had to have some overhead cover removed before firing.

83 WO172/180, 'Summary of Operations Feb. 8 to Feb. 15 1942, Faber Fire Command, Pasir Laba report. The guns were manned by the HKSRA.

84 WO172/180, 'Summary of Operations Feb. 8 to Feb. 15 1942, p. 511 and 566. The Diary and Siloso accounts have both Siloso and Labrador opening up on the far end of the West Coast Road from 11 Feb. But the Labrador report does not mention these targets until later. What is clear is that these guns had silently registered land targets on the coast previously, and now fired using a 1/25,000 map. Siloso fired at the West Coast Road at 1200 hours 11 Feb., and again on 12 Feb. Siloso also helped destroy oil tanks on Pulau Bukum at 1600 hours 12 Feb.

85 Lt-Col J. W. Hipkin, letter to the *Daily Telegraph*, 10 Feb. 1982, p. 16, column 6. Hipkin stated this in his capacity as the wartime commander of Connaught Battery, though the War Diaries do not confirm it. There are also reports that this would have been at extreme range, if possible at all.

86 Barrels were 'rifled'. That is, they had spiral grooves on the inside, which by rotating the shell spun it in flight, helping to keep it stable and accurate. Once the barrel was worn smooth, it would either have to be replaced, or less accuracy accepted. For firing north of the causeway, see Lt-Col J.W.N. Hipkin, letter to *Daily Telegraph*, 10 Feb. 1982, p. 16, column 6.

87 Mr Chelliah Thuraijah Retnam, Oral History Interview 000579/04, Singapore National Archives, pp. 9–10, 15. Mr Chelliah Thuraijah Retnam was served with the Blakang Mati Medical Station.

88 WO172/180, 'Faber Fire Command, Survey of Operations, Feb. 8th to Feb 15th 1942', by Lt-Col Cardew, commanding 7th Coast Regiment Royal Artillery, 15 August 1942, sub-section on Fort Connaught, p. 578. 36 HE rounds were used. According to the diary, the guns had 75 HE (25 per gun), according to Macleod-Carey, 30 per gun (Macleod-Carey, 'Singapore Guns', p. 39). The Connaught report 'recommended that for Coast Fortresses liable to be attacked by land the proportion of HE landwards firing shall be considerably augmented in the future'.

89 WO172/180, 'Faber Fire Command, Survey of Operations, Feb. 8 to Feb 15 1942', p. 578, it put another three concentrations, and another 63 rounds, onto Tengah on the night of the 12 to 13 Feb. Tsuji claims to have been shelled at Tengah at a time that looks like early on 11th February, but we deduce this is an error in timing (or construction) on his part, as Connaught was the only heavy gun battery to shell Tengah, and did not fire at all until the afternoon of 11th according to the War Diaries. See Appendix G for a full explanation.

90 WO172/176, 'War Diary', p. 274, and the entry for Connaught Battery in WO172/180, pp. 578–79. This reports about 70 rounds AP fired towards 'Bukit Timah area' where enemy tanks reported massing.

NOTES

91   Yoshiki Saito, *Mōshin Marē Shingapōru*, p. 183.
92   Shigetaka Onda, *Marē-Sen* [The Malayan Campaign], Vol. 2, p. 198.
93   This is all confirmed by another "Eyewitness", in *The Gunner*, (April 1948), p. 9: 'On the nights of the 10, 11 and 12 February, the 9.2-inch Gun Battery firing from Blakan Mati [sic] fired three groups of harassing fire on to Tengah aerodrome, then occupied by the Japanese. It is believed that heavy casualties were caused'.
94   WO172/180, 'Faber Fire Command, Survey of Operations, Feb. 8 to Feb 15 1942', by Lt-Col Cardew, commanding 7th Coast Regiment Royal Artillery, 15 August 1942, sub-section on Fort Connaught, p. 579–80.
95   WO172/180, Faber Fire Command, 'Survey of Operations', 13.2.42, 'Labrador' Report, p. 550.
96   As at Bukit Timah, Japanese soldiers then sought vengeance by killing some of those who surrendered, and also by hanging the bayoneted Malay Regiment's Lieutenant Adnan upside down from a tree. For details, see Dol Ramli, 'History of the Malay Regiment 1933–1942', *Journal of the Malaysian Branch of the Royal Asiatic Society* 38 (1965), 235–40; and Lim Choo Hoon, 'The Battle of Pasir Panjang Revisited', *Pointer* 28, 1 (2002), http://www.mindef.gov.sg/safti/pointer/Vol28_1/1.htm. Lt Adnan had been shot and bayoneted as part of close fighting by 'C' Company on a hill. For the guns involved see WO172/176, 'War Diary', pp. 274–5.
97   Mr Chelliah Thuraijah Retnam, Oral History Interview 000579/04, Singapore National Archives, appendix, p. 58. WO172/180, 'Faber Fire Command, Survey of Operations, Feb. 8th to Feb 15th 1942', by Lt-Col Cardew, commanding 7th Coast Regiment Royal Artillery, 15 August 1942, sub-section on Fort Connaught, p. 577. On 18 January a bombing raid killed a number of men on Blakang Mati, with splinters penetrating the armoured turret of No. 2 Gun Connaught, killing one and injuring one there and necessitating the complete replacement of the gun.
98   Rollo, *The Guns and Gunners of Hong Kong*, p. 112.
99   Maurice-Jones, *History of Coast Artillery in the British Army*, p. 212. According to this history 'local Asiatics' were considered for recruitment, but 'Straits Settlements Chinese and Tamils were completely unsuitable to perform the duties of "higher gun numbers", were graded as Category III Personnel, only fit for manual labour!' So recruitment was extended to 'Punjabi Mussalmans and Sikhs of inferior quality, and … Jats and other Hindu classes'. It would be interesting to know why local recruitment failed, whether because of prejudice or preference on either side, low wages, or even low education of applicants due to colonial education policy (or rather the lack of one). Maurice-Jones served with the HKSRA himself, see Rollo, *The Guns and Gunners of Hong Kong*, p. 116.
100 WO172/180, Faber Fire Command, 'Survey of Operations', Diary, 13.2.42, 'Labrador', and the separate 'Labrador Report' appended, p. 553: 'The continuous dive bombing attacks in the vicinity of the Fort, the high level attack generally, *total absence of a definite sea attack* … all assisted in producing in my opinion this state of demoralisation'.
101 The time given is 2000 hours. The report on Labrador also suggests the guns could not bear on targets too close since: 'the concrete dive bombing cover erected over the guns at Labrador Fort, precluded their use landwards beyond 310 degrees bearing, which for all practical purposes was at most Pasir Panjang Village'. WO172/180, Faber Fire Command, 'Survey of Operations', Diary, 13.2.42, 'Labrador', and the separate 'Labrador Report' appended, p. 555.
102 WO172/180, Faber Fire Command, 'Survey of Operations', Berlayer Report, p. 561–2. Captain Pickard, OC Berlayer, continued to Pulau Hantu. On the night of 13 to 14 Feb. the Berlayer group took up defensive positions, then moving to Berala Reping next morning.

NOTES

103 WO172/180, Faber Fire Command, 'Survey of Operations', p. 566, for Siloso Battery's two 6 inch guns firing about 40 rounds, to set fire to Pulau Bukom oil tanks and drums at 1600 hours on 12 February. The fires were also from oil tanks inland, at Normanton, see p. 567. The lowest figure for visibility at 0200 on 14 Feb. is 1,000 yards (p. 570).
104 Mr Chelliah Thuraijah Retnam, Oral History Interview 000579/04, Singapore National Archives, pp. 11. WO172/180, Faber Fire Command, 'Survey of Operations', Connaught Report. Gunner Minshull was injured while blowing one of the Serapong magazines.
105 WO172/180, Faber Fire Command, 'Survey of Operations', Diary, 14.2.42, and entries in the various battery reports. Other Faber batteries destroyed on 14 Feb. included Silingsing's 6 inch guns, and the older batteries at Berala Reping and Loudon. Siloso's guns had their breeches blown off by 40lbs gelignite each, and observation post instruments, wireless and other equipment was smashed. Additional reasons for demolition were the absence of infantry defence except for one company of Federated Malay States Volunteer Force, the water supply had broken down; and at Connaught the gun barrels were all but worn smooth and one lift out of action.
106 Mr Iskandar Mydin, 'Laying a Ghost to Rest: "The Guns which Faced the Wrong Way", Blakang Mati, 1942', *Royal Artillery Journal* 116 (1989), p. 71.
107 This was the reason give by Lt-Col W.M. Hipkin, letter to the *Daily Telegraph*, 10 Feb. 1982, as cited in Iskandar Mydin, 'Laying a Ghost to Rest', pp. 72, 74 note 5.
108 'Editorial Notes' in *The Gunner* XXIX, No. 7, October 1947.
109 For the 200 shell limit, see CAB16/105, Adm Sir F. Field to Coast Defence Committee, 3rd meeting, 3 March 1932.
110 Lt-Col C.C.M. Macleod-Carey, *War Monthly* (1976), p. 34. Macleod-Carey's account of firing on a ship around midnight on 14 February. In fact Connaught's guns were demolished early on 14. The date given in Faber Command War Diary for this event (in WO172/180) was around 2100 hours on 12 Feb. This also suggested the ship concerned was probably a *tongkang* carrying oil, not a Japanese landing ship, as thought at the time. It even identified the ship as likely to be one previously tied to a wharf at Pulau Sebarok (Middle Island), but cut lose when denial of oil tanks there was carried out. See for instance p. 567. The main benefit, the report for Siloso suggested, was to boost HKSRA morale, which had been 'badly shaken' by air raids. A further complication is that Macleod-Carey says 'six guns' opened up supposedly including Serapong, but figures for traverse and the absence of any mention of Serapong firing in the War Diaries suggest this is probably an error. Indeed, the war diaries specifically mention Labrador and Siloso firing, but not Serapong. See WO172/176, p. 274; and WO172/180, p. 587: 'No Sea targets appeared in the Battery zone and no ammunition was expended on Land Targets. The Guns could bear as far as the Civilian Airport ...'
111 WO172/176, various entries in the War Diary. See also WO172/180, 'Summary of Operations Feb. 8 to Feb. 15 1942, Faber Fire Command, Labrador report, which places the sinking of what Macleod-Carey had confirmed as a Japanese landing ship at just after 2100 on 12 Feb. Macleod-Carey dates it later, which is probably the effect of oral history. Labrador also helped sink an abandoned *tongkang* on 11th, as practice and 'to stimulate morale amongst the H.K.S.R.A'. The boat which was carrying Australian stragglers was sunk at 2115 hours on 13 Feb., the one wounded Australian being despatched to hospital, the rest presumed drowned. The subsequent vessel was spotted at 0100 on 14 Feb., and landed ten men and an officer (see p. 570 of the source cited).
112 Lt-Col Alfred H. Burne, 'The Truth About the Singapore Guns', *The Gunner* (April 1945), p. 6.

113 Cited from Ian Morrison, *Malayan Postscript* (Kuala Lumpur: S. Abdul Majeed edition, 1993) p. 150. In the original 1942 version, this quotation occurs on p. 143. See Murfett et al., p. 244, footnote 74.
114 See for instance the SEAC report on the guns dated 29 May 1945 in WO252/1362, pp. 3–4. This lists Connaught's traverse as 058 to 295 degrees ('now probably all round'), Serapong Battery's as 020 to 270 degrees, Labrador as 225 to 270 degrees, and so on. It only lists two batteries (Tekong, three 9.2 inch; Sphinx, two 6 inch on the same island) as having all-round traverse. Hence, for instance, this would make it difficult for Labrador to bear on land targets, except those coming directly along the coast towards it.
115 The report on Labrador also suggests the guns could not bear on targets too close since: 'the concrete dive bombing cover erected over the guns at Labrador Fort, precluded their use landwards beyond 310 degrees bearing, which for all practical purposes was at most Pasir Panjang Village'. WO172/180, Faber Fire Command, 'Survey of Operations', Diary, 13.2.42, 'Labrador', and the separate 'Labrador Report' appended, p. 555.
116 Rollo, *The Guns and Gunners of Hong Kong*, p. 145, has an excellent picture of one of these structures, the 6 inch barrel poking out of its rather dumpy encasement.
117 Lt-Col R. McCraig, 'The Second World War – The Far East: Part 2 – The Gunners in Hong Kong, Singapore and Burma', *Royal Artillery Journal* 122 (Spring 1995), p. 12: 'My great friend John Munro was Brigade Major there and according to him by far the most, effective support in breaking up the numerous Jap attacks was given by the 9.2 guns at Stanley.
118 Murfett et al., *Between Two Oceans*, pp. 223–4 also has 'three of the 15" guns, all of the 9.2" guns, and six of the eighteen 6" guns' being 'brought to bear". The figure for the 6 inch guns is probably slightly wrong, as almost every figure concerning these guns tends to be. See the War Diary in WO172/176, which lists the guns of Labrador, Sphinx, and Pasir Laba (just one could bear) as firing, making 5 in total. But Changi Battery also fired landward, albeit only very briefly, making 7. It would be rash, given the fate of previous statements, to treat this as more than a pretty good estimate.
119 Approximately 15 out of 29 guns, see the previous note. For example seven 6 inch (2 only very briefly), six 9.2 inch and two 15 inch. But with the normal caveat, that this is our guess given incomplete and contradictory sources.
120 The five 6 inch are one Pasir Laba, plus pairs at Changi (at the very end only), and Sphinx. Macleod-Carey mentions the three Connaught 9.2 inch guns firing at Johore as well, writing that:

> Connaught Battery ... Targets which I know were engaged included Johore Bahru, right across Singapore Island, where the Japanese had their HQ, possible landing places on the south bank of the Johore Strait, a tank attack on the Bukit Timah road, Tengah airfield, Jurong road and the Japanese artillery spotter already mentioned.

The commander of Connaught confirms this. But none of the various War Diaries mention Connaught firing at Johore, and Johore Bahru would have been about 15–16 miles away, at the very limit of the gun's range. That is, various sources suggest ranges of between 26,900 (15 miles) and 29,200 yards (16 1/2 miles) for these guns. Only one source suggest a greater range, and that specifically suggests Tekong's guns had greater range, while opting for just 26,900 yards for Connaught. Given Macleod-Carey's other slips, for instance saying all three Johore Battery guns fired at Johore Bahru, and citing Tsuji's account of coming under fire from the same,

NOTES

this could be another. Another witness on Blakang Mati corroborates the War Diary's omission of Jurong as a target. Mr Chelliah Thuraijah Retnam, Oral History Interview 000579/04, Singapore National Archives, pp. 9–10, 15. Mr Chelliah Thuraijah Retnam served with the Blakang Mati Medical Station, and talked with the gunners and officers at Connaught, to which he seems to have been attached at one point. Though a medical dresser not a gunner, he is explicit that hitting the Causeway was considered, but that officers said it could not be reached. He is also broadly reliable for most other facts, though not for dates. He says: 'it wouldn't reach the Causeway. So it must have fallen somewhere near Kranji, Jurong...'. See also the notes to the Appendix giving the War Diary for Connaught Battery. Perhaps the guns were fired at maximum range, but with the commanders concluding this was ineffective or fell short. See also, WO172/180, 'Faber Fire Command, Survey of Operations, Feb. 8 to Feb 15 1942', by Lt-Col Cardew, commanding 7th Coast Regiment Royal Artillery, 15 Aug. 1942, *passim*, especially the sections on Connaught; and WO172/176.

121 For defensive Works, see Murfett et al., *Between Two Oceans*, pp. 188–9 (for War Office wages for labour being set too low), 221–22. This states: 'Percival did order Work on defences to begin, but no great activity ensued'. See also Kirby, *The Loss of Singapore*, pp. 360–61.

122 Simson, *Singapore, Too Little, Too Late*, p. 36–8. Simson cites Kirby's official history (p. 16) as saying these fortifications, in the jungle near Kota Tinggi, were started by Dobbie in 1939 and abandoned shortly after. He suggests only £23,000 out of £60,000 allocated was spent.

123 Winston Churchill, *The Second World War*, Vol. 4: *The Hinge of Fate*, p. 41–2.

124 Ong, *The Landward Defence of Singapore*, pp. 3, citing Churchill, *The Second World War* Vol. 4: *The Hinge of Fate*, p. 43.

125 Percival, 'Operations of Malaya Command, pp. 1308:

> The Beach Defences were designed to protect the Islands of Singapore and Blakang Mati, Pulau Brani and the Pengerang area in South Johore from a seaborne attack. On Singapore island they extended along the South Coast from Pasir Panjang to Changi: a distance of 20 miles ... The material defences comprised anti-boat, anti-tank and anti-personnel defences. They included timber-scaffolding tank obstacles, mines and barbed wire'. Together with the coastal guns, the front-door was doubly bolted.

See also p. 1309. We do not know why the line of fortifications began in Johore in the 1930s was abandoned. Kirby, *The Loss of Singapore*, p. 360–1.

126 Again, Tsuji's analysis is spot on. The point was not just that Singapore had not been prepared, but that Johore had been neglected: 'In this great fortress ... there was however an important weak point ... the rear defences in the region of Johore Province were incomplete' (Tsuji, *Singapore 1941–1942*, p. 218).

127 WO106/2528, 'Note on Minute from Prime Minister to General Ismay dated 19 January 1942', 21 January 1942.

128 Ong, *The Landward Defence of Singapore*, pp. 3, citing Churchill, *The Second World War* Vol. 4, *The Hinge of* Fate (London: Cassell, 1951), p. 44. The minute Churchill reproduces here is No. D4/2, 19 Jan. 1942, Cab120/615. Also in WO106/2583A and others.

129 CAB120/615: Prime Minister's personal minute, No. D4/2, 19 Jan. 1942, personally signed.

130 Ong, *The Landward Defence of Singapore*, pp. 3, citing Churchill, *The Second World War* Vol. 4: *The Hinge of Fate*, p. 43.

131 Churchill, *The Second World War*, Vol. 4: *The Hinge of Fate*, pp. 43–4.
132 WO106/2528, 'Defence of Malaya', Note on Minute from Prime Minister to General Ismay dated 19 Jan. 1942, itself dated 21 Jan. 1942.
133 WO106/2550A, telegram from Ceylon dated 5 May 1942, containing the views of Mr Seabridge, editor of the *Straits Times*, these being dated 28 Feb. 1942. By the time higher rates were agreed, increased danger made still higher rates necessary. The whole process is indicative of what Stewart called 'a nation of Theorists' falling to more practical Japanese. What was needed was local authority to set rates as needed once war was likely. Having to refer back to London for pay rates was, in the circumstances, a ridiculous procedure.
134 Tsuji, *Singapore 1941–1942*, p. 221.
135 Churchill, *The Second World War* Vol. 4: *The Hinge of Fate*, pp. 43–5.
136 Ivan Simson, *Singapore, Too Little, Too Late*, p. 36, *passim*. Simson's book does give the impression of a man perhaps not as sensitive as possible to the position and jealousies of the GOC (Malaya), Percival, and formation commanders to an outsider telling them what to do. See pages 44 to 46. But the GOC at least should have been attempting to distil useful ideas, for instance on anti-tank defences, and to have been at least mildly aware that a man having come from two years' involvement in British defences, Britain then fearing invasion, might have something worth using. The rejection of Simson's idea for a practice invasion of the East Coast, if true, corroborates Stewart's complaints that realistic, all-unit training was badly neglected. The attitude of the upper echelon of civil service and military in Malaya seems to have lacked a sense of reality and urgency, and openness to practical innovation.
137 Simson, *Singapore, Too Little, Too Late*, p. 44.
138 Simson, *Singapore, Too Little, Too Late*, p. 68. Simson, however, makes no mention of Percival's later justifications, that the terrain was unsuitable, and his men better concentrated for counter-attacks.
139 Percival, 'Operations of Malaya Command', p. 1309.
140 Percival, 'Operations of Malaya Command', pp. 1309–10.
141 Tsuji, *Singapore 1941–1942*, p. 221.
142 Barber, *Sinister Twilight*, p. 119 gives a succinct summary, based on Simson. Kirby, *The Loss of Singapore*, p. 374.
143 Simson, *Singapore, Too Little, Too Late*, p. 33.
144 WO106/2528, 'Note on Minute from Prime Minister to General Ismay dated 19 January 1942', 21 January 1942.
145 CAB120/615, Prime Minister to General Ismay, for COS Committee, 16 Dec. 1941.
146 CAB120/615, Prime Minister for Lord Privy Seal. General Ismay for COS Committee, 19 Dec. 1941.
147 Winston Churchill, *The Second World War*, Vol. 4: *The Hinge of Fate*, p. 10.
148 Tsuji, *Singapore 1941–1942*, p. 151. But see also p. 219. The problem with Tsuji is twofold. First, he loves a good story. Second, he read British accounts, notably Churchill. It is the old complaint that a tribal chief, when expecting to be interviewed by an anthropologist, may go out and read anthropological works first. Tsuji is clearly engaging with Churchill in his work, as well as trying to uphold Japanese honour and propagandise its position, hence comments on all human nature being the same. So is this an unadulterated Japanese view, or the integration of Churchill's account with Tsuji's? So for instance p. 219:

> According to Mr Churchill's memoirs, Singapore's rear defences (the Johore front) were believed to be in readiness ... On the morning of 19 Jan., from a telegram from General Wavell, Mr Churchill for the first time heard not only

NOTES

that there were no permanent fortifications for the rear of Singapore ... In the circumstances Mr Churchill's rebuke was quite proper ... This however was ... the unexpected good fortune of the Japanese Army.

As with so much of the history of Singapore's fall, it seems almost to be a self-referential exercise of one text talking to another.
149 Winston Churchill, *The Second World War*, Vol. 4: *The Hinge of Fate*, pp. 37–8.
150 Tsuji, *Singapore 1941–1942*, p. 151.
151 Ong, *Operation Matador*, is excellent in giving the feel for how momentum built behind the idea of a defence of Malaya to be mounted in the north, first in Malaya, and then extending late on to the COS. in London.
152 General Lionel Bond was GOC Malaya after Dobbie. In June 1940 he argued that, with just 8 battalions at the time, dispersal for all-Malayan defence was unsound, much to the annoyance of the Air Officer Commanding, Air Marshal Babington. The latter wanted his aerodromes in the north, newly built, defended. Bond proposed to concentrate almost all his garrison of 8 battalions on Singapore and south Johore, leaving one battalion and volunteers for the mainland airfields. Of course, massive infantry reinforcements followed, but Bond's insight about dispersal versus accepting a limited defence (and so some damage to the naval base) still has a resonance for 1941–42. Kirby, *The Loss of Singapore*, p. 33.
153 Winston Churchill, *The Second World War*, Vol. 4: *The Hinge of Fate*, pp. 43–4.

6 AFTER THE BATTLE

1 For the House of Commons, see pp. 46, 49-50. See also Braddon, *The Naked Island*, pp. 184–5, on POWs in Pudu gaol (Kuala Lumpur) around late Jan. to early Feb. 1942: 'We huddled in the sun against the hot wall and threshed it out. Threshed out how we'd had no air support but that, provided we'd held the little bastards up for as long as possible, we'd done all we could ask'. According to him the conclusion that they had signed up for it come what may was arrived 'after four days of fierce and continuous wrangling'. But they still hoped Singapore would not fall at that point. Braddon was a voluntary recruit to the Australian Imperial Force, in which he served as a gunner. He was with the Australians on the retreat from Muar, when they were outflanked and surrounded at Parit Sulong. After the remaining men split and sought to escape in small groups, he was eventually captured and sent first to Kuala Lumpur, then Singapore, and then to the Siam–Burma railway. His book takes a self-conscious 'Australian digger' stance, seeing most officers and authorities as useless, and wearing a level of individuality and resistance to pointless orders as a badge of pride. The heads mentioned were probably those of looters.
2 This chapter does not in any way claim to present a final or comprehensive account of memory and 1939–45. It merely offers readers an insight into the history of '15 February' as a date. It entirely omits, for instance, Indian memories. This theme awaits further research to make possible a book on the 'Many Falls of Singapore' as experienced and remembered by all the different groups. In the meantime, interested readers will find a fuller account, both of facts and of the historiography, in P. Lim Pui Huen and Diana Wong, (eds) *War and Memory in Malaysia and Singapore* (Singapore: Institute of Southeast Asian Studies, 2000). See also various articles in Paul Kratoska (ed.), *Malaya and Singapore During the Japanese Occupation* (Singapore: Special Edition of the *Journal of Southeast Asian Studies*, 1995).
3 Where possible, the romanisation of Japanese that was used in Singapore during the 1940s has been kept. This has been done to prevent rewriting the commonly accepted names in the history of Singapore under the Japanese Occupation. Using

consistently the modern Hepburn romanisation would mean rewriting 'Syonan' as 'Shonan'. Also, throughout the chapter, Japanese names have been kept in the fashion that literature on the history of Singapore has used them, which often is not in the Japanese fashion, e.g. 'Mamoru Shinozaki' is used even though the Japanese fashion would dictate that 'Shinozaki Mamoru' would be more appropriate.

4 See Tsuji, *Singapore 1941–1942*, passim, for the tone; and WO106/2550A, 'Brilliant 70-Day Drive of Imperial Forces Down Malay Peninsula to Singapore Told', *Japan Times and Advertiser*, 8 April 1942. Again, there later Japanese debate is worth a book in its own right, see for instance: Henry P. Frei, 'Japan Remembers the Malaya Campaign', in Kratoska (ed.), *Malaya and Singapore During the Japanese Occupation*, pp., 148–68. The issue of Japanese war memory is far too complex to deal with here. See R.J.B. Bosworth, *Explaining Auschwitz and Hiroshima: History Writing and the Second World War* (London: Routledge, 1993); and George Hicks, *Japan's War Memories: Amnesia or Concealment* (Ashgate, 1997).

5 Cited in Donald Keene, 'The Barren Years: Japanese War Literature', *Monumenta Nipponica*, 33, 1, Spring 1978, pp. 90–1. Fumi Saito added a purification stanza to this chorus, one which betrayed both Buddhist and Christian influences:

> The flames that burn
> Purging away more than
> One hundred twenty
> Years of wickedness,
> Do not cease, night or day

6 Tsuji, *Singapore 1941–1942*, p. 25, passim, for the image of conquering an impregnable fortress. Symbolic time was important even in the campaign, with Tsuji noting the capture of Bukit Timah in time for *Kigensetsu*.

7 Braddon, *The Naked Island*, pp. 382–4, contains an intriguing example of this. An apparently friendly Japanese interpreter gives Braddon books on Japanese bushido and flower arranging, and then his own play, in which:

> British, American and Dutch prisoners-of-war had worked with Nippon on the glorious project of the Thailand railway. By completing it, they had both atoned for the accumulated sins of their forefathers in the East and had imbibed sufficient culture from their guards to raise themselves on to an altogether higher spiritual plane ... It concerned Allied P.O.W's who, after working with a noble Japanese guard on the Railway, became convinced that the Japanese way of life was quite the best and the British way of life quite the worst.

8 The British colonial authorities, upon their re-occupation of Singapore, quickly turned the clocks back to the time used before Japan had introduced Tokyo Time in 1942. Two days after the British had returned to Singapore, one of the prominent stories on the front page of the first issue of the *Straits Times* on 7 Sept. 1945 was entitled 'Malaya Finished With "Tokyo Time"'. The story announced: '"Japanese Time will never be used in Malaya again," declared the British Military Administration's broadcasting station, Singapore, last night, when it was announced that the time to be used in future will be the time in use in this country before 17 February 1942. This will be $7^{1/2}$ hours ahead of Greenwich mean time'.

9 Times are taken from the those used in the Tokyo War Crimes Trials cited in Arnold C. Brackman, *The Other Nuremberg: The Untold Story of the Tokyo War Crimes Trials* (New York: William Morrow, 1987), p. 237.

NOTES

10 Akashi Yoji, 'General Yamashita Tomoyuki: commander of the Twenty-Fifth Army', in Farrell and Hunter (eds), *Sixty Years On*, p. 198.
11 Kevin Blackburn and Edmund Lim, 'The Japanese war memorials of Singapore: monuments of commemoration and symbols of Japanese imperial ideology', in *South East Asia Research*, 7, 3 (1999), 321–40.
12 For a feel of Yasukuni, and the difficulties in reconciling its role in making the spirits of those who died, *Kami*, objects worthy of respect and worship, with Japan's war crimes, see http://www.yasukuni.or.jp/english/index.html. The site contained at the time of writing attempts to undermine the significance of 'comfort women' and an emphasis on heroism when talking of The Second World War. Included in its *kami* (spirits) were, it asserted: 'also 1,068 "Martyrs of Showa" who were cruelly and unjustly tried as war criminals by a sham-like tribunal of the Allied forces (United States, England, the Netherlands, China and others). These martyrs are also the kami of Yasukuni Jinja.' They include the actual physical remains of 14 Class A war criminals.
13 *Straits Times* 17 Aug. 2001, p. 22. This comment suggested there was a real dilemma, since Japan's wartime victims could not accept commemoration at a shrine where war criminals had been deified in 1978, and Japanese could hardly banish from their minds the spiritual significance of the place. It suggested two alternatives: remove the war criminals' remains; or focus memory on *Chidorigafuchi*, the Tomb of the Unknown soldier, opened in 1959 and containing the ashes of 348,000 soldiers. Koizumi had promised to visit on 15 Aug., so some Japanese newspapers, such as *Sankei Shimbun*, found his change of the date 'regrettable': Japanese Foreign Press Centre online site. http: www.fpcj.jp/e/shiryo/jb/0138.html. See also *Japan Times* 20 Aug. 2001 for Lee Kuan Yew's critical view of Yasukuni.
14 Helen Hardacre, *Shinto and the State, 1868–1988* (New Jersey: Princeton University Press, 1989), p. 95.
15 See Kevin Blackburn and Edmund Lim, 'The Japanese war memorials of Singapore: monuments of commemoration and symbols of Japanese imperial ideology', in *South East Asia Research*, 7 (3): 321–40, 1999; and Edmund Lim, 'Japanese War Memorials in Singapore: Monuments of Commemoration or tools of Propaganda', (BA Honours Academic Exercise, National Institute of Education, Nanyang Technological University, 1999).
16 The builder of the *Syonan Jinja*, Major Yasuji Tamura, boasted in November 1942 that it was planned that 'within 30 to 50 years' it should be 'second only to Tokyo's world famous *Meizi Zinzya*' (*Meiji Jinja*). *Syonan Times*, 13 November 2062 (1942). The *Syonan Times*, which underwent several name changes during the Japanese Occupation, was always published in the lingua franca of Singapore – English. However, there was a Japanese edition for Japanese troops and civilians in Singapore. Also, *Meizi Zinzya* was written according to the romanisation of Japanese during the 1940s. Throughout the chapter, the 1940s romanisations have remained within quotation marks. The modern romanisation is outside the quotation marks, e.g.: *Meiji Jinja*. The *Meiji Jinja* itself, or shrine built in honour of the Meiji emperor, was the first Shinto shrine to be conceived and funded as a truly national project rather than built by local devotees, as other major Shinto shrines had been in the past. The Meiji Shrine, completed in 1920, symbolised the rise of Shinto as a state religion, which was manipulated by the state in order for it to indoctrinate loyalty and unify the populace. Hardacre, *Shinto and the State*, p. 38, p. 80, and pp. 93–4. Tamura's claim suggests the Singapore Shinto shrine was of considerable importance to the Japanese military, but it cannot be taken at face value as it was published in the prime means of disseminating printed propaganda in Singapore, the *Syonan Times*.
17 *Syonan Times*, 23 July 2602 (1942).

NOTES

18 *Syonan Times*, 8 May 2602 (1942).
19 P. Lim Pui Huen and Diana Wong, (eds) *War and Memory in Malaysia and Singapore*, p. 1, and Lim, 'War and Ambivalence: Monuments and Memorials in Johor', 139–59 in *ibid*.
20 *Syonan Times*, 8 May 2602 (1942). The road Stanley Warren worked on, now called Lorong Sesuai still exists, along with the stairs.
21 Edmund Lim, 'Japanese War Memorials in Singapore: Monuments of Commemoration or tools of Propaganda', pp. 25–6, 30–2; *Syonan Sinbun*, 9 Dec. 2602.
22 *Syonan Sinbun (Times)* 9 December 2602 (1942).
23 Edmund Lim, 'Japanese War Memorials in Singapore', p. 30–1. WO106/2550A, 'Copy of Extract from "Japan Times and Advertiser" of April 8 1942, by 'Chief Staff Officer Who Planned Bold Campaign Against Eastern Base of Britain'.
24 Mamoru Shinozaki, *Syonan – My Story: The Japanese Occupation of Singapore* (Singapore: Times, 1982), p. 118. Most Eurasians, as well as a significant minority of the Chinese, were Christians.
25 The controlled local press trumpeted that the *Syonan Jinja*'s proposed stadiums and exhibition pavilions 'would be utilized as institutions for the teaching of Nippon's Greatest Works in the World forever' and 'will reveal the lofty ideals of Nippon as leader of East Asia, add a bright touch of colour to Syonan-to and portray the sacred work of the Syowa era forever'. *Syonan Times*, 23 July 2602 (1942).
26 Tamura most likely did envisage a grandiose structure that would be a memorial to his army's achievements. He had played a crucial part in the Malayan campaign. Tamura was Officer-in-Command of the Japanese 5th Division's Engineers Regiment, which had enabled the Japanese armed forces to make successful early landings on the Malayan peninsula and then facilitated the attack on Singapore itself, as well as assisting the rapid advance of the Japanese forces down the peninsula. The people of Singapore were told by Tamura that the *Syonan Jinja*, with its envisaged 15 square kilometres of surrounding recreational park area and sporting facilities, was to be 'the locale for the Greater East Asiatic Olympics in the post-war days of peace'. *Syonan Sinbun (Times)*, 16 February 2603 (1943).
27 Chin Kee Onn, *Malaya Upside Down* (Kuala Lumpur: Federal Publishers, 1976). First published in 1946.
28 The destruction of a shrine by fire in accordance with Shinto rites is not an act of desecration but a traditional part of a purification process. Shinto shrines are supposed to be regularly destroyed by fire and rebuilt in order to be purified. However, this is only strictly adhered to by the Ise Grand Shrine, which is burnt and rebuilt at intervals of every 20 years. The Ise Grand Shrine was the Shinto shrine that the *Syonan Jinja* was modelled after, Shinozaki, *Syonan – My Story*, p. 118. Hardacre, *Shinto and the State*, p. 96, p. 166 and p. 190.
29 Dixon to Singapore Tourist Promotion Board, 1989, in The Battle for Singapore, Changi Prison Chapel & Museum, serial number 61, file reference number PD/PRJ/45/87, Vol. 8 (MFL AJ024), in the Records of the Singapore Tourist Promotion Board (National Archives of Singapore); *The Statesman*, 11 Sept. 1945; and *Straits Times*, 9 Nov. 1945
30 For British decolonisation policy in general, and its relationship with defence policy and prestige, see Hack, *Defence and Decolonisation*, passim.
31 *The Statesman*, 12 Sept. 1945.
32 *The Statesman*, 7 Sept. 1945.
33 Phan Ming Yen, 'The day Singaporeans called their Japanese occupiers fools', based partly on the memory of Mr Lionel de Rosario, a survivor of the notorious Burma–Siam 'Death' Railway, where a beating had left his hearing impaired. He also recalled seeing the Japanese working on the *padang* that morning. Life Section, *Straits Times*

12 Sept. 1995, pp. 1–2. Photographs of Japanese at work can be seen in Singapore's National Archives.
34 *Indian Daily Mail*, 13 Sept. 1946.
35 *Straits Times*, 10 and 11 Nov. 1947.
36 See CO537/1579, 'Strikes and Demonstrations'.
37 *Straits Times*, 16 Feb. 1945. Turnbull, *A History of Singapore*, p. 224.
38 *Straits Times*, 18 Feb. 1946.
39 *Straits Times*, 15 Feb. 1946.
40 379 H.C. Deb., 5s, 16 April 1942, col. 334.
41 122 H.L. Deb., 5s, 19 May 1942, col. 1029.
42 INF 1/2921: Ministry of Information. Home Intelligence Division Weekly Report No. 78, 18 February 1942.
43 *Times*, 30 July, 1947.
44 *Times*, 30 July, 1947.
45 *Times*, 9 Aug. 1947.
46 *Eastern Sun*, 15 Feb. 1967.
47 For a full discussion, see McCarthy, 'The "Great Betrayal" Reconsidered', pp. 53–60.
48 *Courier-Mail*, 29 Feb. 1992.
49 For this sort of debate, see Day, *The Great Betrayal*. See also McCarthy's lucid summary in 'The "Great Betrayal" Reconsidered', pp. 53–60.
50 *Weekend Australian*, 29 Feb.–1 March 1992.
51 *Independent*, 26 Jan. 1993.
52 The atmosphere and writings in Australia in 1942 about the fall of Singapore recalled the mythology of the Anzac legend that was created from the experience of Australians in the equally disastrous Gallipoli campaign during the First World War, in which the British establishment was also held to blame. Australian soldiers were seen as displaying national values in battle, such as 'ruggedness', mateship, and egalitarianism, that transcended the military failure. The creation of this myth of an Anzac legend out of the military failure at Gallipoli has been well documented in works, such as D.A. Kent, 'The *Anzac Book* and the Anzac Legend: C.E.W. Bean as Editor and Image-Maker', *Historical Studies* (*Australian Historical Studies*) 21, 84, (1985), 376–90; Alistair Thomson, *Anzac Memories: Living with the Legend* (Melbourne: Oxford University Press, 1994); and K.S. Inglis, *Anzac Remembered: Selected Writings of K.S. Inglis* (History Department: University of Melbourne, 1998). The quotation is from Russel Ward, *The Australian Legend* (Melbourne: Oxford University Press, 1958), p. 2.
53 INF 1/2921: Ministry of Information. Home Intelligence Division Weekly Report No. 78, 25 March 1942.
54 The 23 January cable was sent under Prime Minister Curtin's name, but Curtin was absent at the time. It was probably written by his pugnacious Minister for External Affairs, Dr. H.V. Evatt. Day, *The Great Betrayal*, pp. 248–9 and pp. 263–4. For the cable see also Day, *John Curtin: A Life*, pp. 444–5.
55 W.H. Wilde, *Three Radicals* (Melbourne: Oxford University Press, 1969), p. 7.
56 See the use of the poem in Ray Connolly and Bob Wilson, *Cruel Britannia: Britannia Waives the Rules, 1941–42* (Broadmeadows, New South Wales: Ray Connolly Bob Wilson, 1994), p.ix. When originally published in the *Australian Women's Weekly* in 1942, however, it had a slightly different form than Mary Gilmore originally intended. Its original last stanza read, 'Ask it of those who boasted her [Singapore] power – Braggarts and fools to the core, Who flung to the wind a nation's pride, In the Ruins of Singapore'. The editors and censors had softened her original poem's references to patriotism blotted out by greed, profiteers, power seekers and the 'craven' at home. And that last, hopeful stanza had been added. The first attempt submitted on 1 March 1942 had also been entitled 'Major-General Bennett and his

true Men'. Dame Mary Gilmore had published war poems as far back as 1918, and was a frequent contributor to debates in newspapers. See W.H. Wilde, 'Mary Gilmore and 1942', *The Bulletin*, 22 July 1980, 77–81; W.H. Wilde and T. Inglis Moore (eds.) *Letters of Mary Gilmore* (Melbourne: Melbourne University Press, 1980), pp. 177–85; and W.H. Wilde, *Courage a Grace: A Biography of Dame Mary Gilmore* (Melbourne: Melbourne University Press, 1988), pp. 356–63.

57 *Argus*, 14 January 1924.
58 Brown, *Suez to Singapore*, p. 521.
59 Ian Hamill, *The Strategic Illusion: The Singapore Strategy and the Defence of Australia and New Zealand* (Singapore University Press, 1981), p. 43.
60 For the idea that the Australian elite knew full well the inadequacies of the British policies they backed, but perhaps lacked the independence, or the willingness to pay extra costs, which alternatives might have involved, see for instance McCarthy, 'The "Great Betrayal" Reconsidered', pp. 53–60.
61 M.I. Bird, *Outside: The Life of C. T. J. Adamson* (Adelaide: Crawfurd House, forthcoming), Chapter 20. HMS *Aster* was then serving in the Indian Ocean, and expecting any minute to meet the Japanese fleet sent eastwards after Singapore's fall. Adamson's father was of long-standing Australian stock, his mother Scottish, but his education was British public school.
62 *Herald* (Melbourne), 15 August 1942, pp. 4–7.
63 Personal communication with David Sissons, 5 July 2002.
64 Gilbert Mant, *The Singapore Surrender* (Kuala Lumpur: Synergy Books International, 1991), p. 8.
65 Lodge, *The Fall of General Gordon Bennett*, pp. 212; and Gordon Bennett, *Why Singapore Fell* (Sydney: Angus and Robertson, 1944).
66 *Straits Times*, 18 February 1952.
67 Braddon, *The Naked Island*.
68 Wigmore, *The Japanese Thrust*, p. 387. By 2002, it was not possible to avoid a longer discussion of this issue, see also Warren, *Singapore 1942*, pp. 262–3, 268–9.
69 Wigmore, *The Japanese Thrust*, p. 237.
70 Wigmore quotes Anderson: 'The well-trained Australian units showed a complete moral ascendancy of the enemy. They outmatched the Japs in bushcraft and fire control' demonstrating 'superior spirit and training' in hand to hand combat. Wigmore, *The Japanese Thrust*, p. 246. See also p. 248 for enemy losses around Muar of 'a company of tanks and the equivalent of a battalion of men'.
71 The classic account of Australian mateship is given in Russel Ward, *The Australian Legend* (Melbourne: Oxford University Press, 1958). Ward examines how mateship emerged out of the uniqueness of the Australian landscape. According to the mythology, the harshness of the Australian environment not only created a 'rugged' character but forged bonds between the males working in the Australian outback. In the 1890s, magazines, such as the *Bulletin*, promoted this bush myth as a unique form of Australian nationalism. Ward argued that the bush ethos went off to war in 1914. C.E.W. Bean, the official Australian war historian for the First World War, fashioned the Anzac legend out of the notion that Australian troops represented in battle this bush ethos and its values of ruggedness, egalitarianism, looking after your mates or fellowmen, and being disrespectful of authority figures. There are various manifestations of the mateship and the Anzac legend. Russell Braddon's writings, although upholding parts of the tradition of mateship, such as disrespect for authority, also illustrate tension within the tradition of 'sticking with your mates'. However, many Australians who became POWs have attributed their survival rates being better than those of British soldiers under similar conditions to the myth of the 'rugged' Australian bush character, and of not pursuing individual goals at the

NOTES

expense of their 'mates'. A.J. Sweeting adopts this mythology in his section on the Australians as POWs in Wigmore, *The Japanese Thrust*, p. 581. This emphasis on Australian mateship helping men endure the harshness of captivity comes to the fore again in the 1980s in Hank Nelson, *Prisoners of War: Australians Under Nippon* (Sydney: ABC Books, 1985).

72 Australian services seem to have started in a small way in the late 1940s, and gradually ballooned. By 1948 Lt-General Gordon Bennett could lead a march of 180 men in the Sydney service. On 15 Feb. 1949 there was a service at St Andrews Cathedral. As the strains of 'O Valiant Hearts' died away, a wreath was laid at the altar on behalf of the Pacific Prisoners of War Association. More than 800 Australian 8th Division veterans publicly marched to the Cenotaph that year. *Sydney Morning Herald*, 16 Feb. 1949, p. 3–4. Thereafter it seems services involving a few hundred were common. By the 1990s the veterans were dwindling, but the State Governor and senior officers still attended, with a good crowd. It is very much a public event, still, including the recital of the ode, and the playing of the National Anthem, as well as *The Last Post*. Information by email from Lynette Silver to Kevin Blackburn, dated 24 Sept. 2002.

73 *Straits Times*, 15 Feb. 1967 and *Eastern Sun*, 16 Feb. 1967.

74 *Straits Times*, 8 Feb. 1972. *Straits Times*, 16 Feb. 1982. *Weekend Australian*, 15–16 Feb. 1992.

75 *Weekend Australian*, 15–16 Feb. 1992.

76 For an excellent summary, see Farrell's Appendix 3 in Murfett et al., *Between Two Oceans*, pp. 341–64. For a balanced Australian summary, there is David Horner's 'It was a bugger's muddle', *The Weekend Australian*, 16–17 January 1993, p. 17. For Australian figures, and unit breakdowns which show just how badly Australian units suffered compared to many other nationalities, see Warren, *Singapore 1942*, pp. 302–6. According to his figures, no less than three battalions (2/18th 2/19th 2/20th) suffered greater casualties than the most active and successful British battalion (the 2nd Argyll and Sutherland Highlanders), another coming close. The 2/19th (which was at Parit Sulong and opposed the first Japanese landings in Singapore) suffered at least 335 dead and 197 wounded, over 50 per cent.

77 See the previous note. See also David James, *The Rise and Fall of the Japanese Empire* (London: Allen and Unwin, 1951), p. 233, *passim*, for Australians 'streaming down Bukit Timah Road' early on 9 February, and saying, 'Chum, to Hell with Malaya and Singapore. Navy let us down, airforce let us down. If the bungs (natives) won't fight for their bloody country, why pick on me'. James, a British officer seconded to HQ, 8th Australian Division, went on, however, to stress British stragglers too. For the most recent Australian summary, there is Warren, *Singapore 1942*, pp. 262–3.

78 See 'Poor British Generalship' in *The Australian*, 13 Jan. 1993, p. 5, citing Senator Chris Schacht for the retaliation line.

79 There really is no substitute for reading the original press debate. See for instance, articles and letters on this in *Guardian*, 29 Feb. 1992; and *Independent*, 28 Feb. 1992. Britain's *Sun* newspaper dubbed Keating 'The Lizard of Oz'. The 'off his rocker' comment was by opposition leader John Howard. In 1999, Australians rejected becoming a republic in a referendum, though this was as much due to distrusting politicians over the alternatives, as it was to continuing support for the monarchy.

80 Connolly and Wilson, *Cruel Britannia*.

81 *Courier-Mail*, 15 February 2002.

82 Military records in the Australian War Memorial for example, available throughout much of the postwar period, contain much evidence that Australian soldiers deserted. See AWM 54 553/6/2 and Ref ABDACOM OPX 1428 17/2 for a list of one group of deserters compiled by Australian military authorities.

83 The programme focused especially on Roy Cornford, who left Singapore on the SS *Empire Star* on 12 Feb. 1942. Thus, rather than focus on the real core issue of how many men 'deserted' on Singapore (the vast majority of these remaining stuck on the island), it focused on the marginal and 'soft' issue of the minority who 'escaped'. Cornford appeared on *No Prisoners*, and, when asked if he considered himself a deserter, said no – he had been on a boat, rowing back towards his own lines when he saw and boarded the *Empire Star*. He added that he did not think there were deserters on the ship. In the subsequent online forum, he seemed to some to become almost a hero, on the grounds he said he helped defend the ship, volunteered to stay and fight in Java, and was later on a ship that was torpedoed, before spending time as a POW. In this way he was, by implication, integrated into the more normal discourse of Australian mateship in captivity. See 'Emma' re Roy Cornford, 11/03/2002 21:40:43, 'You're a true Aussie Hero', in http://www.abc.net.au/4corners/specials/noprisoners/. The problem with this kind of approach, apart from the fact that it focuses on a minority category of 'escapees', is that Military Police were desperately trying to round up stragglers and return men, and reported increasing resistance. More specifically, it is unfortunate that Cornford's name (NX44955 PTE Cornford R.C.) seems to appear in a list of 95 Australian troops (at least 75 also named as Singapore and Malaya deserters) in Java. This was sent 'to prevent any of them being confused with genuine escapees' should their early return (to get them out of the way) become possible. The note alleged this was not just because they had left Singapore early, but because of a supposed lack of cooperation in Java. Some had run away from aerodrome protection duty at the first sound of the alarm, and alleged comments included 'The Japs are better than us and it is no good trying to fight them'. Interestingly, Cornford's television interview and the message overlap in detail, but differ in interpretation. It is also notable, however, that Cornford (and many like him) was newly recruited (in September 1941 in his case) and only half-trained. He was also put with the 2/19th battalion, whose tales of near annihilation in Johore might not have helped morale. Clearly, there can be extenuating circumstances for 'escaping' early, or for 'desertion' by those who never left the island. But equally it is vital that language should mean something, lest discussion degenerate into posturing. See, 'Note for Prime Minister', citing reports from Brigadier Blackburn in Java, and with the list of soldiers incorporated, Australian National Archives: A5954, Item 527/9, *passim*; *Four Corners, No Prisoners*; and AWM 54 553/6/2, Ref ABDACOM OPX 1428 17/2, 2 March 1942, *passim*.

84 Even a British report of May 1942, pleaded that not only had the Australian troops received the heaviest shelling, but that 'they were near home and that home was under imminent threat of invasion'. See CAB119/208, 'Malaya and Singapore', Report drawn up by Major H.P. Thomas, 30 May 1942, pp. 17,24. The quotations are from Hector Chalmers, a Lieutenant in the Australian Army Corps. He did not abscond, but he recalls a similar feeling on 12 Feb. when told his Provost men might have to join the fight: 'I don't remember being unduly elated by this idea, and was certainly, by that time, not very keen on sacrificing either myself or my troops on the altar of stupidity and inefficiency ... owing to the downright incompetence of political and military leaders', Hector Chalmers, 'This Now', Chapter XIII, pp. 145–80 (Changi: unpublished, 1945), in AWM PR84/252.

85 AWM 52, 18/2/21, 'War Diary, From 1 Feb. 42 to 15 Feb. 42, 8 Aust Div Provost Coy AIF', see especially entries for 12–15 Feb., and a 4 Feb. entry suggesting early reports of Australian misbehaviour were sometimes ill-directed, because 'Nearly all British troops are wearing Aust. Style slouch hats'. See also Hector Chalmers, 'This Now', Chapter XIII, pp. 145–80 (Changi: unpublished, 1945), in AWM PR84/252, for 'an infinitely larger number of Indians' in the city; and Warren, *Singapore 1942*,

pp. 262–3, 268–9, citing (p. 262) Lt-Col. Thyer, Australian 18th Division GSO 1, for the quotation.
86 WO106/2550A, Notes on Interview with Mr Raymond Thomas, Malayan Business Man, 3 June 1942. A British Major claimed at least 80 per cent of those thronging the waterfront by 11 February were Australians, with 30 out of 45 deserters on one ship out being Australian, the balance British, but this contradicts other accounts which show a more balanced affair. WO106/2550A, Report by Major J. C. Westall.
87 This is more or less the position of the Canadian historian Brian Farrell, who presented himself on *No Prisoners* almost as the neutral and slightly puzzled referee, arbitrating in a squabble between his 'imperial cousins'. See also his excellent 'Controversies surrounding the Surrender of Singapore, February 1942', Appendix 3, pp. 341–64, in Murfett et al., *Between Two Oceans*. For the most recent Australian summary, see Warren, *Singapore 1942*, p. 262–3.
88 'Emma' re History v Propaganda 11/03/2002 23:01:45 in http://www.abc.net.au/4corners/specials/noprisoners/
89 *Daily Herald*, 22 May 1934.
90 WO203/6034: 'Singapore and Penang Coast Artillery', report by Col F. W. Price, Changi, February 1946. Price reported that 'there are, from the gunnery point of view, no defences whatsoever remaining in either base ... Every gun of the original twenty four batteries in SINGAPORE and three in PENANG is out of action'. Even Buona Vista No. 2 gun, the sole 15 inch survivor, was crippled by lack of parts. He recommended restoring: Sphinx 6-inch 45 degree battery, Beting Kusa 6-inch 45 degree battery, Connaught 9.2-inch 45 degree battery, Silingsing 6-inch 45 degree battery, and 5 AMTB batteries. Ultimately 7 AMTB batteries involving 11 guns were agreed. However, for the lack of progress by the end of 1947 (by when the War Office had knocked down his recommendation of 11 batteries to 3), see WO203/6242.
91 *Sunday Times* (Singapore), 22 Aug. 1948.
92 C. Northcote Parkinson, 'The Pre-1942 Singapore Naval Base' *U.S. Naval Institute Proceedings*, 82, 9 (September 1956), p. 942, and *New Nation*, 24 July 1976.
93 Eric R. Alfred, 'The Famous "Wrong Way" Guns of Singapore, where are they now?, *Pointer*, 12, 1 (October–November 1985), p. 99.
94 See R.P.W. Havers, *Reassessing the Japanese Prisoner of War Experience: the Changi POW camp, Singapore 1942–5* (London: RoutledgeCurzon 2003); and his 'The Changi POW Camp and the Burma–Thai Railway', in Philip Towle, Margaret Kosuge and Yoichi Kibata, (eds), *Japanese Prisoners of War* (London: Hambledon, 2000), pp. 17–35. The relative independence, under their own officers, and sprawling nature of the barracks and grounds used, made Changi seem a release compared to the far more deadly Siam–Burma Railway. But vitamin deficiencies, working parties and brutal reprisal for transgression were still ever-present.
95 Most people probably get their impression of the Burma–Siam Railway from the 'The Bridge over the River Kwai', the 1957 film of Pierre Boulle's novel. No matter that the 'Kwai' was a tributary of the river involved, that there were two bridges, that these survived until 1945, nor that the majority of forced labourers (c.270,000) were Asian rather than western (c.60,000). The film leaves an indelible image of whites POWs working on the bridge, only for it to be destroyed by 'Force 316' (Boulle's version of Force 136) upon completion. Boulle's novel was fiction based on fact, and on knowledge gained as a Malayan rubber planter, French secret agent, British Special operations force member, and prisoner of Vichyite Indochina. For a short introduction to the 412 km 'Death Railway' from an Asian perspective, see Goh Chor Boon, *Living Hell: Story of a WWII Survivor at the Death Railway* [Tan Choon Keng] (Singapore: Asiapac, 1999).
96 *Straits Times*, 15 February 1946.

97 Probert, *History of Changi*, p. 7, suggests the tree was 150 feet high. But we prefer more detailed, botanical sources, namely: J. A. Reid and W. T. Quaife, 'More about the Changi Tree', letter to the Editor, *Malayan Nature Journal*, 23 (1970), p. 177. Reid and Quaife were ex-POWs, who gave a vivid, detailed description of the tree's fate. They estimate the tree's dimensions to have been 250 feet (the top 100 feet being blown off, still leaving 150 feet remaining after the surrender), with an 11.5 feet (3.5 metre) diameter. See also E. J. H.Corner, *Wayside Trees of Malaya* (Singapore: Government Printing Office by W. T. Cherry, 1940), pp. 403–4.

98 Letter to Kevin Blackburn from James Lowe, Lumb Rossendale, England, 31 March 1998 (billeted at Changi 1948 to 1949).

99 The Crucifixion mural could only be restored in part, as it had had a doorway going through its lower half. At the time it appeared two more had been lost when a wall was knocked down by the Japanese. Warren used the drafts for one, the Nativity mural, to recreate it on a wallboard.

100 *The Changi Murals* (Singapore: Kok Wah Press, 1966?) – a copy sent to Kevin Blackburn in correspondence with John Gimblett, a guide to the Changi murals for the Church of England in Singapore at Changi military base (1967 to 1970), 14 August 1999.

101 Kevin Blackburn, 'The Historic Site of the Changi Murals: a place for pilgrimages and tourism', *Journal of the Australian War Memorial* 34 (2002), online at http://www.awm.gov.au/journal/j34/

102 War Memorial Singapore, General Department, original correspondence, 1950–1956, CO1032/73 (Public Record Office, London).

103 *Straits Times*, 4 March 1957.

104 *Straits Times*, 8 March 1957.

105 *Sunday Times* (Singapore), 25 July 1948. The Singapore Social Welfare Department checked her story, as she had been in her 60s even then. Upon confirmation, it secured her an allowance of $50 a month, and installed Singapore Improvement Trust flat with 6 months' free rent.

106 TCS 8, a Singaporean channel showing Chinese-language programmes, broadcast a 32-part drama serial entitled 'The Price of Peace' in 1996, and starring Jame Lye and Carole Lim. This was inspired by a book compiled and edited by Foong Choon Hon (who lived through the war and describes himself as 'an eye witness to the war'), and entitled *The Price of Peace: True Accounts of the Japanese Occupation* (Singapore: Asiapac, 1997). First published in Chinese in 1995. The theme was continued in Foong's *Eternal Vigilance: The Price of Peace* (Singapore: Chinese Chamber of Commerce and Industry, 1999). This Chinese-language sequel featured personal accounts. It originated in a SCCCI photographic exhibition of 1998, which Minister of Information George Yeo suggested be turned into a book.

107 *Sunday Times* (Singapore), 3 March 1957.

108 Further local *sook chings* followed in Malaya, in which the Chinese were killed in retaliation for alleged guerrilla activity near their towns or villages. Chua Ser Koon, 'The Japanese's View of the War Fifty Years After', in Foong, (ed.), *The Price of Peace*, pp. 322–39.

109 Yamashita was tried and executed by the Americans in the Philippines in Feb. 1946. The two sentenced to death at the Singapore massacre trial were Lt-Gen Kawamura Saburo and Lt-Col Oishi Masayuki. The quotation is from the *Singapore Free Press* of 5 April 1947, as quoted on p. 49 of Simon Smith, 'Crimes and punishment: local responses to the trial of Japanese war criminals in Malaya and Singapore, 1946–48', *Southeast Asia Research* 5, 1 (March 1997), 41–56. See also Kevin Blackburn, 'The Sook Ching Massacre', *Journal of the Malaysian Branch of the Royal Asiatic Society* 73, 2 (2000), 71–90; Terence Tan Sian Yeow, 'The War Crimes of the Japanese Officers

NOTES

involved in the *Sook Ching* Massacre' (Singapore: National Institute of Education, Nanyang Technological University, unpublished Academic Exercise, 2001); and Wai Koeng Kwok, 'Justice Done? Criminal and Moral Responsibility in the Chinese Massacres Trial, Singapore 1947', (Yale University: Genocide Studies Program Paper Paper No. 18, 2001).

110 See Yeo Song Nian and Ng Siew Ai, 'The Japanese Occupation as Reflected in Singapore–Malayan Chinese Literary works after the Japanese Occupation (1945–49)', in Paul Kratoska (ed.), *Malaya and Singapore During the Japanese Occupation* (Singapore: Special Edition of the *Journal of Southeast Asian Studies*, 1995), 106–18.
111 *Straits Times*, 3 Feb. 1947.
112 For more details and context, see Virginia Dancz, *Women and Party Politics in Peninsular Malaysia* (Singapore: Oxford University Press, 1987), pp. 46–7, which draws on Alan Elliott, *Chinese Medium Cults in Singapore* (London: London School of Economics Monograph on Social Anthropology No. 14, no date).
113 *Sunday Times* (Singapore), 25 July 1948.
114 *Eastern Sun*, 2 November 1966.
115 Memorials built to Chinese massacred by the Japanese have been seen by some as symbolically being the graves of their loved ones. Thus allowing families to make offerings to a memorial may prevent their relatives from becoming 'hungry ghosts'.
116 *Eastern Sun*, 2 Nov. 1966. The government matched civilian funds dollar for dollar. Leaders of the Chinese Chamber of Commerce, including of course its President, Mr Soon Peng Yam, were prominent in the first wreath-laying ceremony of 1 Nov. 1966.
117 Cited in Kratoska, *The Japanese Occupation of Malaya*, p. 357.
118 *Indian Daily Mail*, 15 August 1947.
119 In 1982 for instance, in its commemoration of the fortieth anniversary, the *Straits Times* highlighted a comment in a letter from D.E.S. Chelliah, that the fall of Singapore 'destroyed the myth of the superiority of the white man forever'. *Straits Times*, 22 Feb. 1982.
120 *The Gunner*, November 1986. National Archives of Singapore: Sentosa Development Corporation Records, Asset Inventory, FS 1012, File No. 464, (Microfilm BA 42 item 9).
121 They were moved in September 1974.
122 The move came in July 1975. National Archives of Singapore: Sentosa Development Corporation Records, Surrender Chamber, File No. 119 Fort Siloso SC 3009 (Microfilm BA 018 item 15).
123 *New Nation*, 3 August 1981, *Straits Times*, 3 August 1981, and National Archives of Singapore: Sentosa Development Corporation Records, Fort Siloso, File No. 176, CSE/SDC/12.11 Vol. 1 (Microfilm BA 023 item 5).
124 National Archives of Singapore: Singapore Tourist Promotion Board Records: Robertson E. Collins Project Report 8 March 1987 A Plan to Re-Design the Changi Prison Stop on the East Coast Tours, 57, PD/PRJ/45/87, Vol. 1, Changi Chapel and Museum and Changi Prison; and East Coast Tour, 67, PD/PRJ/45/88, Vol. 7, Battle for Singapore, Changi Chapel and Museum in (MFL AJ024); Kevin Blackburn, 'Changi: A Place of Personal Pilgrimages and Collective Histories', *Australian Historical Studies*, Vol. 30, No. 112, April 1999, 153–73.
125 Kevin Blackburn, 'Commodifying and Commemorating the Prisoner of War Experience in Southeast Asia: The Creation of Changi Prison Museum', *Journal of the Australian War Memorial* (2000) No. 33 http://www.awm.gov.au/journal.
126 *The Committee on Heritage, Report*, November 1988 (Singapore, 1988), pp. 31–2.
127 Tim Huxley, *Defending the Lion City: The Singapore Armed Forces* (Sydney: Allen and Unwin, 2000).

NOTES

128 Singapore Ministry of Education *Social Studies: Secondary 1*, (Singapore: Curriculum Development Institute of Singapore, 1994), p. 97. This textbook said that 'from the British defeat we learn' that 'a country must always be well-prepared for any attacks' and that 'it must not depend on others to protect its people'. Stressing the suffering of the Japanese Occupation, it stated that 'the people must be trained to defend their own country'. Thus, 'in 1967, the government started National Service' ... .
129 Personal Communication, Feb. 2002.
130 *Straits Times*, 10 Feb. 1992.
131 *Straits Times*, 4 April 1992.
132 *Straits Times*, 26 June 1995. Wang Kai Yuen, a government member of Parliament, opened one of several new historic markers for war sites. In opening the marker for the Battle of Bukit Timah, he claimed he had a good knowledge of the war years because of his mother, adding that: 'Perhaps as a result of her experience, she has always been an ardent advocate of strong government and a supporter of national service'.
133 *Straits Times*, 16 Sept. 1995.
134 *Straits Times*, 9 Feb. 1992. Chua added that: 'the war enhanced the consciousness that this land was worth fighting for. And that, for a largely immigrant population whose loyalties lay elsewhere, was a big step towards nationalism'.
135 *Straits Times*, 9 Feb. 1992. Chua also used the comments of Toh Chin Chye, Lee Kuan Yew's former Deputy Prime Minister, that 'for all of us, the war and its aftermath ignited political consciousness, as we followed the divesting of the British Empire'.
136 *Between Empires*, VHS, (Singapore Broadcasting Corporation, 1992).
137 *Straits Times*, 10 Feb. 1992. Brigadier-General George Yeo, Minister for Information and the Arts and Health, added a further gloss to these fiftieth anniversary celebrations. On the fiftieth anniversary of the surrender of the Japanese in Singapore of 12 September 1945, Yeo stated that 'the war pushed the generation of that time towards nation building, and the present day Singaporeans could share in this common spirit'. He added that the war 'was part of Singapore's history which binds all Singaporeans together, regardless of race and religion', *Straits Times*, 13 Sept. 1995. See also *Straits Times*, 12 Sept. 1995, where he suggested the history of the war might bring about a process in which 'heritage can be a catalyst in stirring patriotism'.
138 *Straits Times*, 18 May 1997.
139 For a summary, see Lim Choo Hoon, 'The Battle of Pasir Panjang Revisited', *Pointer* 28, 1 (2002), online at http://www.mindef.gov.sg/safti/pointer/Vol28_1/1.htm.
140 *History of Modern Singapore: Secondary 1* (Singapore: Curriculum Development Institute of Singapore, 1994), p. 145; *The Dark Years 4B Discovering Our World* (Singapore: Curriculum Planning and Development Division, 1999), p. 21; and *Understanding Our Past: Singapore from Colony to Nation* (Singapore: Curriculum Planning and Development Division, 1999), p. 78. For the Regiment as more specifically 'Malay' and elite, with visits by the Sultans to cement its identity, see Nadzon Haron, 'The Malay Regiment, 1933–1955: A Political and Social History', (Essex: Unpublished Ph.D, 1988). For local, colonial-era forces in general, see Karl Hack, '*Biar mati anak: Jangan mati adat* (Better your children die than your traditions)": Locally-raised forces as a barometer for Imperialism and Decolonisation in British Southeast Asia, 1874–2001', in *Southeast Asia Research* (November 2002); and M.C. Sheppard, *The Malay Regiment* (Kuala Lumpur: Public Relations Department, 1947).
141 *Straits Times*, 1 Aug. 2002, Home Section, p. 2. The quotation was from a speech at the *Berita Harian* Achiever of the Year Award ceremony, held on the night of 31 July.

142 See the brochure for the National University of Singapore's 'Sixty Year's On: The Fall of Singapore Revisited' conference of 15–17 Feb. 2002 (Singapore: NUS National Education Committee, 2002), for the example of a university presenting itself as the culmination of 'a comprehensive effort by the nation's schools, by its efforts in all five areas of Total Defence'.
143 Participation-observation at 'Fort Siloso Live', 7–10, 12–13 Nov. 2001. At this event students are told they are 'recruits', before flag-raising, hauling a replica gun up a hill, talking to a 'Mrs Cooper' and *dhoby* (laundry man), and then undergoing air-raid drill in one of the Fort's darkened, 'smoke'-filled tunnels. Finally, they are 'captured', marched off, and interrogated by Japanese in open space before 3 big gun barrels. Having been told a 'code-word', the students were then expected to refuse to reveal this. At the end the Japanese, in fact actors who nicely balance seriousness with not being too frightening for 10-year olds, had to surrender in their turn. The event finished with each cohort of students talking to a war veteran. The target audience was students within the range of 9 to 11 years old, and accompanying worksheets ask students to consider how they felt, and what they learnt about being prepared for war. The event was repeated in Oct.-Nov. 2002.

7 CONCLUSION

1 See for instance *Sydney Morning Herald*, 28 Jan. 1946, p. 1–2, for an editorial, Bennett, Earle Page (Australia's Special Representative to the War Cabinet at the time of the surrender) and many more wanting an inquiry. Phrase used in the Australian press included 'Scapegoats for Singapore' and 'Libel on the A.I.F.'
2 Cab119/208, Joint Planning Staff file on 'The Malayan Campaign – Implications of a Public Inquiry', 1946, *passim*.
3 Cab119/208, JP(46)29(Final), 5 March 1946, 'Malayan Campaign – Public Inquiry', by the Joint Planning Staff.

APPENDIX A: BRITISH FORCES IN DECEMBER 1941, AND REINFORCEMENTS

1 Imperial War Museum: papers of Major MacDonald Ian Alexander (Special Operations Executive).
2 Kirby, *The Loss of Singapore*, pp. 324–5.

APPENDIX B: JAPANESE FORCES IN DECEMBER 1941

1 From: Masanobu Tsuji, Singapore 1941–1942: The Japanese Version of the Malayan Campaign of World War II (Singapore: Oxford University Press, 1988), pp. 36–8.
2 Akashi Yoji, 'General Yamashita Tomoyuki: commander of the Twenty-Fifth Army', in Farrell and Hunter (eds), *Sixty Years On*, p. 197.

APPENDIX D: AIRCRAFT IN THE FAR EAST AND THEIR DISPOSITION, 7 DECEMBER 1941

1 Information on British aircraft from Brooke-Popham, 'Operations in the Far East', pp. 573–5.
2 Kirby, *The Loss of Singapore*, p. 324.
3 Kirby, *The Loss of Singapore*, p. 240; Elphick, *Far Eastern File*, pp. 165–7; Aldrich, *Intelligence and the War Against Japan*, p. 63. Probert, *The Forgotten Air Force*, pp. 25–7.

4 Tsuji, *Singapore 1941–1942*, p. 37. Kirby, *The Loss of Singapore*, p. 524. The latter suggests there were no less than 180 Japanese fighters available.
5 Kirby, *The Loss of Singapore* actually states these forces (the 22nd Air Flotilla and a detachment of bombers from the 21st Air Flotilla) amounted to 180, but there were a total of 30 aircraft on 3 seaplane tenders too.

APPENDIX E: WAR DIARIES

1 According to Tsuji, the Imperial Guards concentrated its artillery on Pulau Ubin, in the Johore Strait, after taking that island on the night of 7/8 February. On the 8th these guns (including 36 field guns) concentrated fire on 'the Changi fortress'. The counter-bombardment 'did extraordinarily little damage except to the innocent rubber-trees' ... there were no casualties'. Tsuji, *Singapore 1941–1942*, p. 235.
2 The bombardment of Bukit Timah Road on 11th and 12th February was against the Japanese 5th Division and Tank Brigade. The 5th Division having taken Bukit Timah heights on 10 to 11 Feb., they were pressing towards the reservoirs and down Bukit Timah Road by 12 Feb.
3 Lt-Col J.W. Hipkin, letter to the *Daily Telegraph*, 10 Feb. 1982, p. 16, column 6. But contrast this to this the War Diary entry on Fort Connaught in WO172/180.
4 CAB120/615 has an Annex on Coast Artillery as at 20 January 1942, showing shell availability.

APPENDIX F: GUN STATISTICS

1 John Campbell, 'British Heavy Coast-Defence Guns in World War Two', in John Roberts (ed.), *Warship 1995* (London: Conway Maritime Press, 1995), 79–86.
2 G.R. Cook, letter to *The Gunner* (March 2001), p. 31; Hogg, *British and American Coast Artillery*, pp. 200–2.
3 Cdr Charles B. Robbins, 'Research Note: Spanish Heavy Coast Artillery in the Modern Era', *The Coast Defense Study Group Journal* 13, 2, pp. 92–7. British guns were 15 inch 42 calibre, Spanish guns 15 inch 45 calibre. Their range with a 1951 lb projectile and muzzle velocity of 2500 fps (elevation 40 degrees) was 38,386 yards. The first four were installed at El Ferrol in 1929, their turrets with splinter-proof casings, and having a traverse of 300 degrees (similar to Singapore Mk II turrets). There were also batteries at La Coruña, Cartagena, and Port Mahon (Balearic Islands: La Mola, Llucalcri, Favaritx). In 1941 two guns were relocated at Punta Paloma, on the Spanish coat opposite Gibraltar. This was the last battery in service, at the end of the twentieth century. There were also many smaller guns, including 12 inch guns from battleships. Smaller efforts were made by Japan and Italy (15 inch guns), and in Germany's 'Atlantic Wall' programme.
4 John Campbell, 'British Heavy Coast-Defence Guns in World War Two', in John Roberts (ed.), *Warship 1995* (London: Conway Maritime Press, 1995), p. 85.
5 Coordinates refer to 1930s and 1940s 1:25,000 inches military maps of Singapore, as used by British, United States and Japanese forces, notably War Office, 'Johore and Singapore' (1928, 2nd edition 1939).
6 For these details, see John Campbell, 'British Heavy Coast-Defence Guns in World War Two', in John Roberts (ed.), *Warship 1995* (London: Conway Maritime Press, 1995), 81–3. The three Johore guns had been relined in 1930–1.
7 WO172/182, 'Report on Active Service of 7 Coast Bty R.A.', 'Left Section Jo Bty', no date.
8 WO172/182, 'Report on Active Service of 7 Coast Bty R.A.', 'Left Section Jo Bty', no date.

NOTES

9 WO172/180, 'Summary of Operations Feb. 8 to Feb. 15 1942, Faber Fire Command, Buona Vista Report.
10 Hogg, *British and American Artillery of World War Two*, p. 201.
11 Hogg, *British and American Artillery of World War Two*, p. 201.
12 John Campbell, 'British Heavy Coast-Defence Guns in World War Two', p. 81.
13 Buxton, *Big Gun Monitors*, p. 173.
14 Hogg, *British and American Artillery of World War Two*, p. 190–3; as well as WO252/1362.
15 For details of actual gun arrival in Singapore, including the substitution of four 12 pounders for some of the double-barrelled 6 pounders in 1940, due to the threat to the UK, see WO106/2555, *passim*.
16 We have used the War Diary in WO172/176 for the HE available. This agrees with the War Diary in WO172/180. Macleod-Carey's figures in 'Singapore Guns', p. 39, differ in giving 30 HE per gun for the 9.2 inch guns. For AP and field guns we have used the figures in CAB120/615, for ammunition available as at 21 January 1942.

APPENDIX G: THE FIRE COMMANDS

1 Additional sources for this appendix include: WO252/1362, Inter-Service Topographical Department, 'Supplement on Defences to I.S.T.D (S.E.A.C) Docket on Singapore and Southern Johore, Amendment No. 1', 29 May 1945; WO172/180; WO172/176; Karthiravelu, 'Fortifications in Singapore, 1819–1942' (University of Malaya, Unpublished Academic Exercise, 1957); and 'Major (DO) H. Norbury RA (Retired), 'An Exercise in Repository', *The Gunner* (November 1986), pp. 12–13. For instance, WO252/1362 confirms the War Diary account that Pulau Hantu had an 18 pounder, though most postwar sources assume there was one, or even two 12 pounders there. Examples of unreliable sources for gun number and type includes Colonel K. W. Maurice-Jones, *History of Coast Artillery in the British Army*.
2 There were four obsolete 12 pounders in total. These were sent around 1940, to substitute for a few of the modern twin barreled 6 pounders diverted elsewhere 'owing to the threat to the U.K' in 1940. See WO106/2550, note of 16 November 1940.
3 WO172/180, 'Faber Fire Command, Survey of Operations', p. 581, mentions this gun, describing it as on 'the boom entrance', and being disabled by being tipped into the sea.

BIBLIOGRAPHY

Useful bibliographies

Aldrich, Richard. *The Key to the South*, pages 380 to 389. A comprehensive 1993 survey of British sources on pre-1942 central defence and foreign policy making, and on Southeast Asia.

Murfett *et al.*, *Between Two Oceans: A Military History of Singapore*. The bibliography is not annotated, but it still provides one of the most up-to-date sources.

Turnbull, C. M. *A History of Singapore*, see pages 330–60, for an exhaustive summary of sources on Singapore available up to 1989. Especially useful for its annotated bibliography.

Warren, Alan. *Singapore 1942: Britain's Greatest Defeat* (Singapore: Talisman, 2002). Warren is strong on Australian sources, primary and secondary.

Primary sources unpublished

In the United Kingdom

Firepower (the Royal Artillery Museum) and the James Clavell Library (the Royal Artillery Library), Woolwich, England

Carmichael Papers MD2252: Colonel Donald Carmichael was Ordnance Mechanical Engineer in Singapore and site engineer for the Buona Vista Battery.

Hampshire County Record Office, Winchester

Priddy's Hard Collection: 109M91: The gun logs of Singapore's 15 inch guns. It is possible these may eventually be housed at the new naval artillery museum at Gosport, called 'Explosion'.

Imperial War Museum

Various papers of soldiers and of Malay Regiment officers.
Photograph and Film Archives.
Percival Papers.

BIBLIOGRAPHY

Liddell Hart Centre for Military Archives, King's College, London

Brooke-Popham Papers: Air Chief Marshal Sir Brooke-Popham, Commander-in-Chief, Far East, 1940–1.
Vlieland, C.A.: Secretary of Defence for Malaya, 1938–41.
Wort, Major Adjutant: Officer of the 1st Battalion, Malay Regiment.

National Library of Scotland, Edinburgh

Major-General Murray-Lyon: The fall of Singapore. See the enclosed work by Colonel A.M. Harrison, *History of the 11th Indian Division in Malaya* (3 volumes, typescript: no provenance or date).

Public Records Office, Kew Gardens, London

ADMIRALTY

ADM1: Admiralty. Secretariat files.

ADM195: Admiralty. Contains information on the naval base development.

AIR MINISTRY

AIR2: General Correspondence. For air views on base and coast defence development.

CABINET OFFICE

CAB5: Committee of Imperial Defence. Memoranda. Contains information on coast defence and naval base development.
CAB16: Committee of Imperial Defence. Ad hoc sub-committee papers. Information on coast defence and naval base development.
CAB 21: Cabinet Secretariat. Includes confidential papers on naval base and coastal guns planning.
CAB23: Cabinet minutes.
CAB55: Committee of Imperial Defence.
CAB79: Chiefs of Staff committee meetings.
CAB80: Chiefs of Staff committee memoranda.
CAB101: Cabinet Historical Section, official histories.
CAB105: War Cabinet telegrams.
CAB119: Joint Planning Staff Files (1939–1945).
CAB120: Ministry of Defence Secretariat Files. Includes appendices, maps, ammunition availability, some of Churchill's minutes, excerpts of telegrams, and other details.
CAB122: British Joint Staff Mission: Washington Office Files 1940–45.
CAB127: Private collections of ministers and officials, 1922–50.

BIBLIOGRAPHY

COLONIAL OFFICE

CO273: Straits Settlements Original Correspondence, 1932–46.
CO537: Colonial Office, supplementary correspondence, 1938–50.
CO967: Colonial Office. Private office papers.
CO1032: File73, War Memorial Singapore, General Department, correspondence, 1950–56.

FOREIGN OFFICE

FO371: Foreign Office general correspondence.

MAPS AND PLANS EXTRACTED FROM OTHER SERIES

MPI1: Maps of batteries and guns.

MINISTRY OF INFORMATION

INF 1: File 2921, Home Intelligence Division Weekly Reports 1942.

PRIME MINISTER'S OFFICE

PREM 3: Prime Minister's operations files.
PREM 4: Prime Minister's confidential files.

WAR OFFICE

WO32: Registered Papers, General Series, 1930s to 1945. Includes papers on the planning and building of the Fortress system.
WO33: Reports and miscellaneous.
WO78: War Cabinet Committees. Includes papers on the planning of the Fortress system.
WO106: Directorate of Military Operations and Intelligence Papers. Includes some files with post-Fall reports on Malaya and Singapore.
WO172: Southeast Asia Command, War Diaries. Includes the War Diaries for the Royal Artillery Regiments in Singapore, and related Royal Engineer units. See especially files 172, 180 and 189.
WO193: Directorate of Military Operations Papers.
WO196: Directorate of Artillery Papers.
WO203: War crimes Trials.
WO208: Directorate of Military Intelligence Papers.
WO216: Chief of Imperial General Staff Papers.
WO235: Includes documents on postwar trials of Japanese.
WO252: Topographical and Economic Surveys. SEAC. File 1362. contains a full 1945 report on Singapore's defences, with attached plans of the emplacements. WO252/1259 contains maps and pictures.
WO259: Private Office Papers, Secretary of State.

BIBLIOGRAPHY

Rhodes House, Oxford

Granada 'End of Empire' series, Malaya, Volume 4. Interviews on Malaya covering the campaign and decolonisation periods.

Thomas, Sir Shenton: Governor of the Straits Settlements from 1936 until Singapore's Fall, on the defence of Malaya and Singapore.

In Singapore

National Archives of Singapore

The Battle for Singapore, Changi Prison Chapel and Museum files (MFL AJ024), in the Records of the Singapore Tourist Promotion Board.

Fort Siloso and Surrender Chambers Files in the Sentosa Development Corporation Records.

Oral History Records for World War Two.

Microfilms of Overseas Holdings.

In Australia

Australian War Memorial

AWM 52: War Diaries.
AWM 54: Written records.
AWM 67: Gavin Long Papers.
AWM PR: Private records..

For the debate on Singapore's last days, see especially the little-used Hector Chalmers, 'This Now', Chapter XIII, (Changi: unpublished, 1945), in AWM PR84/252.

Australian National Archives

A5954:   Shedden Papers.

In Japan

Japan Centre for Asian Historical Records: http://www.jacar.go.jp.

Documents from the National Archives, Diplomatic Record Office, Foreign Ministry, and National Institute for Defence Studies. Japanese-language, with an option to search in English-language.

BIBLIOGRAPHY

Primary sources published

In the United Kingdom

Brooke Popham, Air Chief Marshal 'Operations in the Far East', *Supplement to the London Gazette*, (London, 22 Jan. 1948).
Coast Artillery Drills, Part III, Pamphlet No. 2, *Gun Drill B. L. 15-inch Mk I Gun* (London: War Office, 1943), p. 97 ff (Ch. II, 'Mounting, 15-inch, Mark II).
Maltby, Air Vice Marshal Sir Paul. 'Report on the Air Operations during Campaigns in Malaya and the Netherlands East Indies from 8 December 1941 to 12 March 1942', *Third Supplement to the London Gazette of 20 February 1948*, dated 26 February 1948.
Parliamentary Debates. House of Commons, Hansard. 1941–2.
Parliamentary Debates. House of Lords, Hansard. 1941–2.
Percival, Lt-General, Lt-Gen. A.E. 'Operations of Malaya Command, From 8th December, 1941 to 15th February, 1942', Second Supplement to *The London Gazette* of Friday, the 20th February, 1948, dated Thursday, 26th February, 1948.
Wavell, General Sir Archibald. *Despatch by the Supreme Commander of the ABDA Area to the Combined Chiefs of Staff on the Operations in the Southeast Pacific, 15 January to 25 February 1942* (London: HMSO, 1948).

In the United States

Headquarters, USAFFE and Eighth U.S. Army (Rear), *Report on Installations and captured weapons, Java and Singapore 1942* (Washington DC: Office of Military History, Department of the Army, 1958).

In Japan

The following Japanese texts contain extensive excerpts from regimental histories and diaries:.
Senshi Sōsho [War History Series] Vol. 1, *Marē Shinkō Sakusen* [The Malayan Campaign] (Tokyo: Asagumo Shimbunsha, 1966).
Saito, Yoshiki. *Mōshin – Marē Shingapōru* [Determined Offensive: Malaya and Singapore] (Tokyo: Gakken, 1972).
Onda, Shigetaka. *Marē-Sen* [The Malayan Campaign] (Tokyo, 1977).
There are also Japanese accounts drawn up under the American postwar administration of Japan, and translated:.
Malay Operations Record, November 1941-March 1942: The Records of the Malayan Operations of the 25th Army (Monograph No. 54).

Newspapers and periodicals

Australian (Sydney)
Argus (Melbourne)
Courier-Mail (Brisbane)
Daily Herald (London)
Daily Telegraph (London)

Eastern Sun (Singapore)
Guardian (Manchester)
Herald (Melbourne)
Herald News (Tamworth, England)
Independent (London)
Indian Daily Mail (Singapore)
Japan Times (Tokyo)
New Nation (Singapore)
Singapore Standard (Singapore)
Statesman (Calcutta)
Straits Times (Singapore)
Sunday Observer (London)
Sunday Times (Singapore)
Sydney Morning Herald
Syonan Times (Singapore)
Times (London)

Secondary sources: books

Aldrich, Richard (ed.). *British Intelligence, Strategy and the Cold War, 1945–51* (London: Routledge, 1992).
——. *The Key to the South: Britain, the United States and Thailand during the Approach of the Pacific War* (Singapore: Oxford University Press, 1993).
——. *Intelligence in the War Against Japan: Britain, America and the Politics of Secret Service* (Cambridge: Cambridge University Press, 2000).
Allen, Charles (ed.). *Tales From the South China Seas: Images of the British in South-East Asia in the Twentieth Century.* (London: Faber and Faber, 1983).
Allen, Louis. *Singapore, 1941–1942* (London: Davis-Poynter, 1977).
Amin, Mohamed and Caldwell, Malcolm. *Malaya: The Making of a Neo-Colony* (Nottingham: Spokesmen Books, 1977).
Andrews, E.M. *The Writing on the Wall: The British Commonwealth and Aggression in the East* (Sydney: Allen and Unwin, 1987).
Arneil, Stan. *Black Jack: The Life and Times of Brigadier Sir Frederick Galleghan* (Melbourne, 1983).
Bach, John. *The Australia Station: A History of the Royal Navy in the South West Pacific, 1821–1913* (Kensington, New South Wales: New South Wales University Press, 1985).
Ban Kah Choon. *Absent History: The Untold Story of special Branch operations in Singapore, 1915–1942* (Singapore: Raffles, 2001).
Baker, Maurice. *A Time of Fireflies and Wild Guavas* (Singapore: Federal Publications, 1995).
Barber, Noel. *Sinister Twilight: The Fall of Singapore* (London: Collins, 1968).
Barck, Oscar Theodore Jr. *America in the World: Twentieth Century History in Documents* (New York: Meridian, 1961).
Beloff, Max. *Dream of Commonwealth, 1921–42* (London: Macmillan, 1989).
Bennett, Lieutenant-General H. Gordon. *Why Singapore Fell* (Sydney: Angus and Robertson, 1944).
Best, Anthony. *British Intelligence and the Japanese Challenge in Asia* (London: Macmillan, forthcoming 2002).

Bird, Michael I. *Outside: The Life of C.T.J. Adamson* (Adelaide: Crawfurd House, forthcoming).
Blake, Christopher. *A View from Within: The Last Years of British Rule in Southeast Asia* (Charlbury: Mendip Publishing, 1990).
Bond, Brian. *British Military Policy Between the Two World Wars* (Oxford: Oxford University Press, 1980).
Bosworth, R.J.B. *Explaining Auschwitz and Hiroshima: History Writing and the Second World War* (London: Routledge, 1993).
Brackman, Arnold C. *The Other Nuremberg: The Untold Story of the Tokyo War Crimes Trials* (New York: William Morrow, 1987).
Braddon, Russell. *The Naked Island* (Leicester: Charnwood edition, 1982) First published by Laurie, 1952, and in London by Bodley Head, 1952.
Brailey, Nigel. *Thailand and the Fall of Singapore: A Frustrated Asian Revolution* (Boulder, Colorado and London: Westview, 1986).
Brown, Cecil. *Suez to Singapore* (New York: Random House, 1942).
Butcher, John. *The British in Malaya, 1880–1941: The Social History of a European Community in Colonial South-East Asia* (Oxford: Oxford University Press, 1979).
Buxton, Ian. *Big Gun Monitors* (Tynemouth: Trident, 1978).
——. *Naval Weapons of World War Two* (London: Conway, 1985).
Callahan, Raymond. *The Worst Disaster: The Fall of Singapore* (Singapore: Cultured Lotus, 2001), first published 1977.
Caldwell, Malcolm. *Malaya: The Making of a Neo-Colony* (Nottingham: Spokesman, 1977).
Calvocoressi, Peter, Guy Wint and John Pritchard. *Total War: The Causes and Consequences of the Second World War* (Second Edition, Harmondsworth: Penguin, 1989).
Chan, Heng Chee. *A Sensation of Independence: A Political Biography of David Marshall* (Singapore: Times, 1985).
Chapman, F. Spencer. *The Jungle is Neutral* (London: Chatto and Windus, 1949).
Charmley, John. *Churchill: The End of Glory, A Political Biography* (London: Sceptre, 1995 edition). First published 1993 by Hodder.
Cheah, Boon Kheng. *Masked Comrades: A Study of the Communist United Front in Malaya, 1945–48* (Singapore: Times Books International, 1979).
——. *Red Star Over Malaya: Resistance and Social Conflict During and After the Japanese Occupation of Malaya, 1941–46* (Singapore: Singapore University Press, 1983).
Chew, Ernest and Lee, Edwin (eds). *A History of Singapore, 1819–1988* (Oxford: Oxford University Press, 1991).
Chin Kee Onn, *Malaya Upside Down* (Kuala Lumpur: Federal Publishers, 1976'. First published 1946.
Churchill, Sir Winston. *The Second World War* (6 Vols, London: Cassell, 1948–54).
Clayton, Anthony. *The British Empire as Superpower 1919–1939* (London: Macmillan, 1986).
Connolly Ray and Wilson, Bob. *Cruel Britannia: Britannia Waives the Rules, 1941–42* (Broadmeadows, New South Wales: Ray Connolly and Bob Wilson, 1994).
Crosby, Josiah. *Siam: The Crossroads* (London: Hollis and Carter, 1945).
Dancz, Virginia. *Women and Party Politics in Peninsular Malaysia* (Singapore: Oxford University Press, 1987).
Day, David. *The Great Betrayal: Britain, Australia and the Pacific War, 1939–42* (London: Oxford University Press, 1988).

——. *The Reluctant Nation: Australia and the Allied Defeat of Japan, 1942–45* (Oxford: Oxford University Press, 1992).
——. *John Curtin: A Life* (Sydney: HarperCollins, 1999).
Dennis, Peter. *Troubled Days of Peace: Mountbatten and SEAC, 1945–1946* (Manchester: Manchester University Press, 1987).
Dixon, Norman. *On the Psychology of Military Incompetence* (London: Cape, 1976).
Dockrill, Saki. (ed.) *From Pearl Harbor to Hiroshima: The Second World War in Asia and the Pacific, 1941–1945* (London: Macmillan, 1994).
Donnison, F.S.V. *British Military Administration in the Far East* (London: HMSO, 1956).
Dower, John. *War Without Mercy: Race and Power in the Pacific War* (London: Faber and Faber, 1986).
Dunlop, Peter. *Street Names of Singapore* (Singapore: Who's Who Publishing, 2000).
Elliott, Alan. *Chinese Medium Cults in Singapore* (London: London School of Economics Monograph on Social Anthropology No. 14, no date).
Elphick, Peter. *Singapore: The Pregnable Fortress: A Study in Deception, Discord and Desertion* (London: Hodder and Stoughton, 1995).
——. *Far Eastern File: The Intelligence War in the Far East, 1930–1945* (London: Hodder and Stoughton, 1997).
Elphick, Peter and Smith, M. *Odd Man Out: The Story of the Singapore Traitor* (London: Hodder and Stoughton, 1993).
Elsbree, W. *Japan's Role in Southeast Asian Nationalist Movements* (Cambridge, MA: Harvard University Press, 1953).
Falk, Stanley. *Seventy Days to Singapore: The Malayan Campaign 1941–1942* (London: Robert Hale, 1975).
Farrell, Brian P. *The Basis and Making of British Grand Strategy, 1940–1943: Was there a Plan?* (Lewiston, New York: E. Mellen Press, 1998), 2 Vols.
Farrell, Brian P. and Sandy Hunter (eds.), *Sixty Years On: The Fall of Singapore Revisited* (Singapore: Eastern Universities Press, 2002).
Farwell, Bryon. *Armies of the Raj: From the Mutiny to Independence* (London: Viking, 1990).
Ferguson, Niall (ed.). *Virtual History* (London: Picador, 1997).
Fogel, Joshua A. and Charles S. Maier (eds), *The Nanjing Massacre in History and Historiography* (University of California Press, 2000).
Foong Choon Hon. *The Price of Peace: True Accounts of the Japanese Occupation* (Singapore: Asiapac, 1997). First published in Chinese in 1995.
——. *Eternal Vigilance: The Price of Freedom* (Singapore: Chinese Chamber of Commerce and Industry, 1999).
Frei, Henry. *Japan's Southward Advance and Australia* (Melbourne: Melbourne University Press, 1991).
——. *Guns of February: Ordinary Japanese Soldiers' Views of the Malayan Campaign in 1941* (Singapore: Singapore University Press, 2003).
Fujiwara, Lieutenant-General Iwaichi, F. *Kikan: Japanese Army Intelligence Operations in Southeast Asia during World War Two* (Hong Kong: Heinemann Asia, 1983).
Gallagher, O.D. *Action in the East* (New York: Doubleday, 1942).
Gilchrist, Andrew. *Malaya 1941: The Fall of an Empire* (London: Hale, 1991).
Glover, E.M. *In Seventy Days: The Story of the Japanese Campaign in Malaya* (London: Frederick Muller, 1946).

Goh Chor Boon. *Living Hell: Story of a WWII Survivor at the Death Railway* (Singapore: Asiapac, 1999).

Goh, Robbie B.H. (ed.) *Memories and Desires: A Poetic History of Singapore* (Singapore: Unipress, 1998).

Graham, G. S. *Great Britain in the Indian Ocean, 1810–1850* (Oxford: Clarendon Press, 1967).

Hack, Karl. *Defence and Decolonisation: Britain, Malaya and Singapore, 1941–1968* (Richmond, Surrey: Curzon, 2001).

Hamill, Ian. *The Strategic Illusion: The Singapore Strategy and the Defence of Australia and New Zealand, 1919–1942* (Singapore: Singapore University Press, 1981).

Hardacre, Helen. *Shinto and the State, 1868–1988* (New Jersey: Princeton University Press, 1989).

Havers, R.P.W. *Reassessing the Japanese Prisoner of War Experience: the Changi POW camp Singapore 1942–5* (London: RoutledgeCurzon 2003).

Henson, Maria Rosa. *Comfort Woman: A Filipina's Story of Prostitution and Slavery under the Japanese Military* (Oxford: Rowman and Littlesfield, 1999).

Hicks, George. *The Comfort Women* (Singapore: Heinemann Asia, 1995).

Hicks, George. *Japan's War Memories: Amnesia or Concealment* (Ashgate, 1997).

Hogg, Ian. *British and American Artillery of World War Two* (London: Arms and Armour Press, 1978).

Holland, Robert. *Britain and the Commonwealth Alliance, 1918–1939* (London: Macmillan, 1981).

Holmes, Richard and Kemp, Anthony. *The Bitter End* (Chichester: Strettington House, 1982).

Honda Katsuichi, Frank Gribney, Karen Sandness, (eds), *The Nanjing Massacre: A Japanese Journalist Confronts Japan's National Shame (Studies of the Pacific Basin Institute)* (New York: M.E. Sharpe, 1999).

Howard, Keith (ed.), *True Stories of Korean Comfort Women* (London: Cassell, 1995).

Howard, Michael. *The Continental Commitment: The Dilemma of British Defence Policy in the Era of the Two World Wars* (Harmondsworth: Penguin, 1974).

Huxley, Tim. *Defending the Lion City: The Singapore Armed Forces* (Sydney: Allen and Unwin, 2000).

Inglis, K.S. *Anzac Remembered: Selected Writings of K.S. Inglis* (History Department, University of Melbourne, 1998).

Ismay, Lord. *The Memoirs of General The Lord Ismay* (London: Heinemann, 1960).

James, David. *The Rise and Fall of the Japanese Empire* (London: Allen and Unwin, 1951).

Kaye, Barrington. *Upper Nankin Street Singapore: A Sociological Study of Chinese Households Living in a Densely Populated Area* (Singapore: University of Malaya Press, 1960).

Keay, John. *The Last Post: The End of Empire in the East* (London: John Murray, 1997).

Keegan, John (ed.), *The Times Atlas of the Second World War* (London and New York: Times Books, 1989).

Kennedy, Paul. *The Rise and Fall of the Great Powers: Economic Change and Military Conflict from 1500 to 2000* (London: Fontana, 1988).

Kinvig, Clifford. *Scapegoat: General Percival of Singapore* (London: Brassy's, 1996).

Kirby, S. Woodburn. *Singapore: The Chain of Disaster* (London: Cassell, 1971).

——. *The War Against Japan: The Loss of Singapore* (London, 1957), volume I.

Kok, Koun Chin. *History of Malaya and Singapore* (Singapore: Oxford University Press, 1997).

Kratoska, Paul. *The Japanese Occupation of Malaya, 1941–1945* (London: Allen and Unwin, 1998).

—— (ed.). *Malaya and Singapore During the Japanese Occupation* (Singapore: Special Edition of the *Journal of Southeast Asian Studies*, 1995).

—— (ed.) *Southeast Asian Minorities in the Wartime Japanese Empire* (London: RoutledgeCurzon, 2002).

Lapping, Brian. *End of Empire* (New York: St. Martin's Press, 1985).

Lau, Albert. *The Malayan Union Controversy* (Oxford: Oxford University Press, 1991).

Leasor, James. *Singapore, The Battle that Changed the World: The Enthralling Story of the Rise and Fall of a Magical City* (London: House of Stratus, 2001).

Lee, David. *Eastward: A History of the Royal Air force in the Far East, 1945–1972* (London: HMSO, 1984).

Lee Kuan Yew, *The Singapore Story: Memoirs of Lee Kuan Yew* (Singapore: Singapore Press Holdings, Times Editions, 1998).

Lim Pui Huen, P., and Diana Wong, (eds) *War and Memory in Malaysia and Singapore* (Singapore: Institute of Southeast Asian Studies, 2000).

Lodge, A.B. *The Fall of General Gordon Bennett* (Sydney: Allen and Unwin, 1986).

Louis, William Roger. *British Strategy in the Far East, 1919–1939* (Oxford: Oxford University Press, 1971).

——. *Imperialism at Bay: The United States and the Decolonisation of the British Empire, 1941–1945* (Oxford: Clarendon Press, 1977).

Lowe, Peter. *Great Britain and the Origins of the Pacific War* (Oxford: Clarendon Press, 1977).

——. *Britain and the Far East: A Survey from 1819 to Present* (London: Longman, 1985).

Lowenthal, David. *The Past is a Foreign Country* (Cambridge: Cambridge University Press, 1985).

MacCarthy, John. *Australia and Imperial Defence 1918–1939: A Study in Air and Sea-Power* (St. Lucia: University of Queensland Press, 1976).

Macleod-Carey, C.C.M. 'Singapore Guns', in *War Monthly* 1976, pp. 34–39.

McCoy, A. (ed.). *Southeast Asia under Japanese Occupation* (Yale: Yale University Press, 1980).

McGibbon, I.C. *Blue Water Rationale: The Naval Defence of New Zealand, 1914–41* (Wellington: Government Printing Office, 1981).

MacIntyre, W.D. *The Rise and Fall of the Singapore Naval Base, 1919–1942* (London: Macmillan, 1979).

Mamoru Shinozaki, *Syonan My Story: The Japanese Occupation of Singapore* (Singapore: Times Books, 1982 edition).

Manderson, Leonore. *Sickness and the State: Health and Illness in Colonial Malaya, 1870–1940* (Cambridge: Cambridge University Press, 1996).

Mant, Gilbert. *The Singapore Surrender* (Kenthurst: Kangaroo Press, 1992).

Marder, A.J. *Old Friends, New Enemies: The Royal Navy and the Imperial Japanese Navy 1936–41* (Oxford: Oxford University Press, 1981).

Mason, Philip. *A Matter of Honour: An Account of the Indian Army, its Officers and Men* (London: Cape, 1974).

Maurice-Jones, Colonel K.W. *History of Coast Artillery in the British Army* (London: Royal Artillery Institution, 1959).

Middlebrook, Martin and Patrick Mahoney. *Battleship: The Loss of the Prince of Wales and the Repulse* (London: Allen Lane 1977).
Moffatt, Jonathan and Audrey Holmes McCormick, *Moon over Malaya: A Tale of Argylls and Marines* (Stroud: Tempus, 2001).
Montgomery, Brian. *Shenton of Singapore: Governor and Prisoner of War* (London: Leo Cooper/Secker and Warburg, 1984).
Morrison, Ian. *Malayan Postscript* (London: Faber and Faber, 1942).
Murfett, Malcolm. *Fool-Proof Relations: The Search for Anglo-American Naval Cooperation During the Chamberlain Years, 1937–1940* (Singapore: Singapore University Press, 1984).
Murfett, Malcolm, John Miksic, Brian Farrell and Chiang Min Shun, *Between Two Oceans: A Military History of Singapore from First Settlement to Final British Withdrawal* (Singapore: Oxford University Press, 1999).
National Heritage Board (Singapore), *The Japanese Occupation 1942–1945* (Singapore: Times, 1996).
Nelson, Hank, *Prisoners of War: Australians Under Nippon* (Sydney: ABC Books, 1985).
Neidpath, James. *The Singapore Naval Base and the Defence of Britain's Far Eastern Empire, 1919–1941* (Oxford: Clarendon Press, 1981).
Ong Chit Chung, *Operation Matador: Britain's War Plans against the Japanese, 1918–1941* (Singapore: Singapore University Press, 1997).
——. *The Landward Defence of Singapore, 1919–1938* (Singapore: Heinemann for the National University of Singapore Centre for Advanced Studies, Occasional Paper, 1988).
Ovendale, Ritchie, *'Appeasement' and the English-Speaking World: Britain, the United States, the Dominions, and the Policy of 'Appeasement', 1937–1939* (Cardiff: University of Wales Press, 1975).
Owen, Frank. *The Fall of Singapore* (London: Penguin, 2002). First published in 1960.
Page, Sir Earle. *Truant Surgeon* (Sydney: Angus and Robertson, 1963).
Pakenham-Walsh, R.P. *History of the Corps of the Royal Engineers, 1938–1948*, Volume 9 (Chatham: Institution of Royal Engineers, 1958).
Parkinson, Northcote C. *Britain in the Far East* (Singapore: Donald Moore, 1955).
Peet, George. *Rickshaw Reporter* (Singapore: Eastern Universities, 1985).
Percival, Lieutenant-General Arthur E. *The War in Malaya* (London: Eyre & Spottiswoode, 1949).
Perry, F.W. *The Commonwealth Armies: Manpower and Organisation in Two World Wars* (Manchester: Manchester University Press, 1988).
Ponting, Clive. *Churchill* (London: Sinclair-Stevenson, 1994).
Potter, J.D. *The Life and Death of a Japanese General* (New York: Signet Books, 1962).
Probert, Squadron Leader H.A. *History of Changi* (Singapore: Score, 1988). First published by Prison Industries in 1965.
——. *The Forgotten Air Force: The Royal Air Force in the War Against Japan 1941–1945* (London: Brassey's, 1995).
Public Affairs Department, Ministry of Defence. *Oriente Primus: First in the East: Singapore Artillery 100th Anniversary* (Singapore: Singapore Artillery and Public Affairs Department, MOD, 1988).
Rees, Laurence. *Horror in the East* (London: BBC, 2001).
Reynolds, E. Bruce. *Thailand and Japan's southern advance, 1940–1945* (New York: St. Martin's Press, 1994).
Roberts, John (ed.). *Warship 1995* (London: Conway Maritime Press, 1995).

Roff, William R. *The Origins of Malay Nationalism* (Kuala Lumpur: University of Malaya Press, 1967).

Rollo, Denis. *The Guns and Gunners of Hong Kong* (Hong Kong: The Gunners' Roll of Hong Kong, no date but 1991 or after).

Rose, Saul. *Britain and Southeast Asia* (London: Chatto and Windus, 1972).

Rusbridger, James and Nave, Eric. *Betrayal at Pearl Harbor:* (London: Michael O'Mara, 1991).

Shennan, Margaret. *Out in the Midday Sun: The British in Malaya, 1880–1939* (London: John Murray, 2000).

Sheppard, M.C. *The Malay Regiment* (Kuala Lumpur: Public Relations Department, Malay Peninsula, 1947).

Shinozaki, Mamoru. *Syonan – My Story: The Japanese Occupation of Singapore* (Singapore: Times, 1982).

Shores, Christopher, Brian Cull and Yasuho Izawa. *Bloody Shambles: The Drift to War to the Fall of Singapore, the Defence of Sumatra and the Fall of Burma* (London: Grub Street, 1990), Vol. 1.

Simson, Ivan. *Singapore: Too Little, Too Late. The Failure of Malaya's Defences in 1942* (London: Leo Cooper, 1970).

Singapore Artillery. *In Oriente Primus: First in the East: Singapore Artillery 100th Anniversary* (Singapore: Singapore Artillery and Public Affairs Department, MOD, 1988).

Singapore Ministry of Education. *Social Studies: Secondary 1*, (Singapore: Curriculum Development Institute of Singapore, 1994).

Singapore National Heritage Board. *The Japanese Occupation* (Singapore: Times, 1996).

Stewart, Ian. *History of the Argyll and Sutherland Highlanders 2nd Battalion (The Thin Red Line) Malayan Campaign, 1941–42* (London: Thomas Nelson, 1947).

Stowe, Judith. *Siam Becomes Thailand: A Story of Intrigue* (London: Hurst, 1991).

Stockwell, A.J. *British Policy and Malay Politics During the Malayan Union Experiment* (Kuala Lumpur, 1979).

Tamayama Kazuo and Nunneley, John *Tales by Japanese Soldiers of the Burma Campaign, 1942–1945* (London: Cassell Military, 2000).

Tanjong Pagar Constituency, *Tanjong Pagar: Singapore's Cradle of Development* (Singapore: Landmark Books for Tanjong Pagar Citizens' Consultative Committee, 1989).

Tarling, Nicholas (ed.). *The Cambridge History of Southeast Asia: The Nineteenth and Twentieth Centuries* (Cambridge: Cambridge University Press, 1992), Vol. 2.

———. *The Decline and Fall of Imperial Britain in Southeast Asia* (Oxford: Oxford University Press, 1993).

———. *Britain and the Onset of the Pacific War* (Cambridge: Cambridge University Press, 1996).

Thomson, Alistair, *Anzac Memories: Living with the Legend* (Melbourne: Oxford University Press, 1994).

Thorne, Christopher. *Allies of a Kind: The United States, Britain and the War Against Japan, 1941–1945* (London: Hamish Hamilton, 1978).

———. *The Issue of War: States, Societies and the Far Eastern War of 1941–45* (London: Hamish Hamilton, 1985).

Trocki, Carl. *Opium and Empire: Chinese Society in Colonial Singapore, 1800–1910* (Ithaca and London: Cornell University Press, 1990).

Tsuji, Masanobu. *Singapore 1941–1942: The Japanese Version of the Malayan Campaign in World War Two* (Singapore: Oxford University Press, 1988). First published in English by Constable and Company, 1962).

Turnbull, C.M. *A History of Singapore* (2nd edition, Oxford: Oxford University Press, 1989).

Vennewald, Werner. *Chinesen in Malaysia: Politische Kultur und Strategisches Handeln* (Hamburg, 1990).

Ward, Ian. *The Killer They Called a God* (Singapore: Media Times, 1992).

Ward, Russel, *The Australian Legend* (Melbourne: Oxford University Press, 1958).

Warner, Lavinia and John, Sandilands. *Women Beyond the Wire: The True Story of Japan's P.O.W.s That Inspired the Motion Picture Paradise Road* (London: Arrow, 1997).

Warren, Alan. *Singapore 1942: Britain's Greatest Defeat* (Singapore: Talisman, 2002).

Warren, James Francis. *Ah Ku and Karayuki-san: Prostitution in Singapore, 1870–1940* (Singapore: Oxford University Press, 1993).

Weller, George. *Singapore is Silent* (New York: Harcourt Weller, 1942).

Wigmore, Lionel, *The Japanese Thrust* (Canberra: Australian War Memorial, 1957).

Wilde, W.H, *Three Radicals* (Melbourne: Oxford University Press, 1969).

——. *Courage a Grace: A Biography of Dame Mary Gilmore* (Melbourne University Press, 1988).

Wilde, W.H. and Inglis, Moore, T. (eds). *Letters of Mary Gilmore* (Melbourne University Press, 1980).

Wilmott, H.P.W. *Empires in the Balance: Japanese and Allied Pacific Strategies to April 1942* (London: Orbis, 1982).

Wohlstetter, R. *Pearl Harbor: Warning and Decision* (Stanford, California: California University Press, 1963).

Yap Siang Yong, Romen Bose and Angeline Pang, *Fortress Singapore: The Battlefield Guide* (Singapore: Times Books International, 1995). First edition 1992.

Yee Hwee Joo, *Impact: History of Southeast Asia* (Oxford: Oxford University Press, 2000).

Yong, C.F. *The Origins of Malayan Communism* (Singapore: South Seas Society, 1997).

Ziegler, Philip. *Mountbatten: The Official Biography* (London: Collins, 1985).

——. *Wilson: The Authorised Life* (London: HarperCollins edition, 1995).

Secondary sources: articles and reviews

Akashi, Yoji. 'Lai Tek', *Journal of the South Seas Society* 49 (1994), 87–95.

——. 'General Yamashita Tomoyuki: Commander of the 25th Army', in Brian Farrell and Sandy Hunter (eds), *Sixty Years On: The Fall of Singapore Revisited* (Singapore: Eastern Universities Press, 2002), pp. 183–207.

Alfred, Eric R. 'The Famous "Wrong Way" Guns of Singapore, where are they now?', *Pointer*, 12, 1 (October-November 1985), 91–100.

Aldrich, Richard. 'A Question of Expediency: Britain, the United States and Thailand, 1941–42', *JSEAS*, 19, 2 (September 1988), 209–44.

——. Review of J. Rusbridger's *Betrayal at Pearl Harbor*, in *Intelligence and National Security*, 7, 3 (1992), 335–6.

Allen, Louis. 'The Surrender of Singapore: The Official Japanese Version', *The Durham University Journal* 60 [New Series 29, 1] (December 1967), 1–7.

——. 'Notes on Japanese Historiography: World War II', *Military Affairs* 35, 4 (December 1971), 133–38.

BIBLIOGRAPHY

Aviet, Major J.C. 'The Big Guns of Singapore', *The Pointer* 4, 3 (January 1979), 32–50. This contains an excellent range of information, especially on fire control, and the sites after 1945. But it is unreliable for the guns in action, replicating errors found in Macleod-Carey and others, including the simplification that many guns had all-round traverse.

Bagoo, Abdul Karim bin. 'The Origin and Development of the Malay State Guides', *JMBRAS*, 35, 1 (1962), 51–94.

Beavis, Major-General L.E. 'The Defences of Singapore', *Stand-To* 8, 2 (March-April 1963), 7–9.

Barclay, Glen St John. 'Singapore Strategy: The Role of the United States in Imperial Defense', *Military Affairs* 39, 2 (April 1975), 54–9.

Best, Anthony. 'Constructing an Image: British Intelligence and Whitehall's Perception of Japan, 1931–1939', *Intelligence and National Security* 11, 3 (1996), 403–23.

———. '"This Probably Over-Valued Military Power": British Intellligence and Whitehall's Perception of Japan, 1939–41', *INS*, 12, 3 (1997), 67–94.

Blackburn, Kevin, 'Changi: A Place of Personal Pilgrimages and Collective Histories', *Australian Historical Studies*, 30, 112 (April 1999), 153–73.

———. 'Commodifying and Commemorating the Prisoner of War Experience in Southeast Asia: The Creation of Changi Prison Museum', *Journal of the Australian War Memorial*, 33 (2000) http://www.awm.gov.au/journal/.

———. 'The Collective Memory of the *Sook Ching* Massacre and the Creation of the Civilian War Memorial of Singapore', *Journal of the Malaysian Branch of the Royal Asiatic Society*, 73, Part 2, (December 2000), 71–90.

———. 'The Historic War Site of the Changi Murals: A Place for Pilgrimages and Tourism', *Journal of the Australian War Memorial*, 34 (2001) http://www.awm.gov.au/journal/.

———, 'Nation Building and Public Representations of History: The Japanese Occupation as a "Shared Past" in Singapore', *Public History Review*, 9 (2001), 8–22.

Blackburn, Kevin, and Lim, Edmund, 'The Japanese War Memorials of Singapore: Monuments of Commemoration and Symbols of Japanese Imperial Ideology', *South East Asia Research*, 7, 3 (November 1999), 321–40.

Buesst, Tristan. 'The Naval Base at Singapore' *Pacific Affairs* 5, 4 (April 1932), 306–18.

Brailey, Nigel. 'Thailand, Japanese Pan-Asianism and the Greater East Asia Co-Prosperity Sphere', in Saki Dockrill, *From Pearl Harbor to Hiroshima*, pp. 119–33.

Bridge, Carl. 'The Malayan Campaign, 1941–2: An International Perspective', paper given at the Institute of Commonwealth Studies (London, circa 1994–5).

Burleigh, Michael 'What if Nazi Germany had defeated the Soviet Union?', in Niall Ferguson (ed.), *Virtual History* (London: Picador, 1997), pp. 321–47.

Burne, Lt-Colonel Alfred. 'The Truth Abouth the Singapore Guns', *The Gunner* (April 1945), 6.

Callahan, Raymond. 'Churchill and Singapore', in Brian Farrell and Sandy Hunter (eds.), *Sixty Years On: The Fall of Singapore Revisited* (Singapore: Eastern Universities Press, 2002), pp. 156–72.

Campbell, John. 'British Heavy Coast-Defence Guns in World War Two', in John Roberts (ed.), *Warship 1995* (London: Conway Maritime Press, 1995), 79–86.

Clements, Squadron Leader J. 'Isle of Peace: Blakang Mati Island Fortress of Singapore', *Royal Artillery Journal* 108 (1981), 135–9.

Corner, E.J.H. *Wayside Trees of Malaya* (Singapore: Government Printing Office by W. T. Cherry, 1940).

Chua Ser Koon, 'The Japanese's View of the War Fifty Years After', in Foong Choon Hon, (ed.), *The Price of Peace* (Singapore: Asiapac, 1997), pp. 322–339.

Darwin, John. 'Imperialism in Decline? Tendencies in British Imperial Policy Between the Wars', *Historical Journal*, xxiii, 3 (1980), 657–79.

Day, David. 'Anzacs on the Run: The View from Whitehall, 1941–42', *JICH*, 14, 3 (1986), 187–202.

Editorial Notes, *The Gunner*, XXXIX, No. 7, October 1947.

Esthus, Raymond A. 'President Roosevelt's Commitment to Britain to Intervene in a Pacific War', *The Mississippi Valley Historical Review*, 50, 1. (June 1963), 28–38.

Eyewitness, 'The Gunners of the 11th Indian Division in Malaya', *The Gunner* (May 1946), 36–38.

Eyewitness, *The Gunner*, (April 1948), 9.

Farrell, Brian. '1941: An Overview', in Brian Farrell and Sandy Hunter (eds.), *Sixty Years On: The Fall of Singapore Revisited* (Singapore: Eastern Universities Press, 2002), pp. 173–82.

Ferris, J. '"Worthy of Some Better Enemy?" The British Estimate of the Imperial Japanese Army 1919–41, and the Fall of Singapore', *Canadian Journal of History* 28 (1993), 223–56.

———. 'Student and Master: The United Kingdom, Japan, Airpower, and the Fall of Singapore, 1920–1941', in Brian Farrell and Sandy Hunter (eds), *Sixty Years On: The Fall of Singapore Revisited* (Singapore: Eastern Universities Press, 2002), pp. 94–121.

Frei, Henry. 'The Island Battle: Japanese Soldiers Remember the Conquest of Singapore', in Brian Farrell and Sandy Hunter (eds.), *Sixty Years On: The Fall of Singapore Revisited* (Singapore: Eastern Universities Press, 2002), pp. 218–39.

Gale, S.C.G. 'The Guns of Dover 1939–1956', *The Gunner* 11 (November 2000), 28–9.

Graeme, Ian. 'Singapore 1939–1942', *Royal Artillery Journal* 103 (1976), pp. 20–6.

Guillain, Robert. 'The Resurgence of Military Elements in Japan', *Pacific Affairs* 15, 3 (September 1952), 211–25.

Hack, Karl. '*Biar mati anak: Jangan mati adat* (Better your children die than your traditions)': Locally-raised forces as a barometer for Imperialism and Decolonisation in British Southeast Asia, 1874–2001, in *Southeast Asia Research* (November 2002).

Haron, Nadzon. 'Colonial Defence and the British Approach to the Problems of Malaya', *Modern Asian Studies*, 24, 2 (May 1990), 275–95.

Harvey, A.D. 'Army, Air Force and Navy Air Force: Japanese Aviation and the Opening Phase of the War in the Far East', *War in History* 6, 2 (1999), 174–204.

Havers, R.P.W. 'The Changi POW Camp and the Burma–Thai Railway, in Philip Towle, Margaret Kosuge and Yoichi Kibata, (eds), *Japanese Prisoners of War* (London: Hambledon, 2000), pp. 17–35.

Iskandar Mydin. 'Laying a Ghost to Rest: "The Guns Which Faced the Wrong Way", Blakang Mati, 1942', *Royal Artillery Journal* 116 (September 1989), pp. 70–5.

Jeffrey, Keith. 'An English Barrack in the Oriental Seas? India in the Aftermath of the First World War', *Modern Asian Studies*, 5 (1981), 370–87.

———. 'The Eastern Arc of Empire: A Strategic View, 1850–1950', *Journal of Strategic Studies*, 5, 4 (1982), 531–45.

Keene, Donald 'The Barren Years: Japanese War Literature', *Monumenta Nipponica*, 33, 1 (Spring 1978), 67–112.

Kinvig, Clifford. 'General Percival and the Fall of Singapore', in Brian Farrell and Sandy Hunter (eds), *Sixty Years On: The Fall of Singapore Revisited* (Singapore: Eastern Universities Press, 2002), pp. 240–69.

Kent, D.A., '*The Anzac Book* and the Anzac Legend: C.E.W. Bean as Editor and Image-Maker', *Historical Studies* (*Australian Historical Studies*) 21, 84 (1985), 376–90.

Lau, Albert. 'The Colonial Office and the Emergence of the Malayan Union Policy, 1942–43', in R.B. Porter and A.J. Stockwell, *British Policy and the Transfer of Power in Asia*, pp. 95–125.

———. 'Malayan Union Citizenship: Constitutional Change and Controversy in Malaya, 1942–48', *JSEAS*, 20, 2 (September 1989), 216–43.

Lau, Albert and Yeo Kim Wah. 'From Colonialism to Independence', in Ernest Chew and Edwin Lee, *A History of Singapore*, pp. 119–21.

Lim Choo Hoon, 'The Battle of Pasir Panjang Revisited', *Pointer* 28, 1 (2002), http://www.mindef.gov.sg/safti/pointer/Vol28_1/1.htm.

McCarthy, John. 'Singapore and Australian Defence, 1921–1942', *Australian Outlook*, 25, 2 (August 1971), 165–80.

McCarthy, John. 'The "Great Betrayal" Reconsidered: An Australian Perspective', *Australian Journal of International Affairs* 48, 1 (May 1994), 53–60.

McCraig. Lieutenant-Colonel R. 'The Second World War The Far East: Part 2 The Gunners in Hong Kong, Singapore and Burma', *Royal Artillery Journal* 122 (Spring 1995), 11–18.

McCrane, James. 'The Influence of the Royal Engineers in Singapore', *The Veteran* 7 (August 2001), a publication of SAFRA (Singapore Armed Forces Association), 51–61.

Macleod-Carey, Lt-Colonel C.C. 'Singapore Guns', in *War Monthly* 1976, 35–9.

Malan, Colonel L. N. 'Singapore: The Founding of the New Defences', *Royal Engineers Journal* LII (June 1938), 213–35.

Murfett, Malcolm. 'Living in the Past: A Critical Re-examination of the Singapore Naval Strategy, 1918–1941', *War and Society*, 11, 1 (May 1993), 73–103.

Murphy, John. 'The New Official History', *Australian Historical Studies*, 26, 102 (1994), 119–24.

Norbury, Major H. 'An Exercise in Repository' *The Gunner* (November 1986), pp. 12–13. This deals with the recovery and moving of Singapore's coastal guns.

Ng Wei Kwang, Alec, and Toh Boon Ho, 'Yamashita and the Assault on Singapore: Was Yamashita's success a bluff that worked or the culmination of calculated risk-taking?', *The Veteran* 8 (August 2002), 86–94.

Ong, C.C. 'Major-General Dobbie and the Defence of Malaya, 1935–38', *JSEAS*, 5, 2 (1986), 282–306.

Parkinson, C. Northcote, 'The Pre–1942 Singapore Naval Base', *U.S. Naval Institute Proceedings*, 82, 9 (September 1956), 939–53.

Peden, G.C. 'A Matter of Timing: The Economic Background to British Foreign Policy, 1937–1939', *History* 69 (February 1984), 15–28.

Phan Ming Yen, 'The day Singaporeans called their Japanese occupiers fools', Life Section, *Straits Times* 12 Sept. 1995.

Positions east asia cultures critique 5, 1 (spring 1997). Special issue on 'The Comfort Women: Colonialism, War, and Sex'.

Porter, Catherine. 'Autopsies on the Southeast Asia Debacle: A Review Article', *Pacific Affairs* 16, 2 (June 1943), 206–15.

Pritchard, John. 'Winston Churchill, the Military, and Imperial Defence in East Asia', in, Saki Dockrill, (ed.), *From Pearl Harbor to Hiroshima*, pp. 26–44.

Ramli, Dol. 'History of the Malay Regiment', *JMBRAS*, 38, 1 (1965), 199–243.

Robbins, Cdr Charles B. 'Research Note: Spanish Heavy Coast Artillery in the Modern Era', *The Coast Defense Study Group Journal* 13, 2, pp. 92–7.

Saw Swee-Hock, 'Population Growth and Control', in Edwin Lee and Ernest Chew (eds), *A History of Singapore* (Singapore: Oxford University Press, 1991), pp. 219–41.

Sawyer, Lt-Colonel E. L. 'Prisoner of War in Changi', *Journal of the Royal Artillery* 124 (Spring 1997).

Simpson, Keith. 'Percival', in J. Keegan and W.P. Wilmott, *Churchill's Generals* (London, Weidenfeld and Nicholson, 1991), 256–76.

Sims, Philip. 'The Harbor Defenses of Singapore: Facing the Wrong Way?', *Coast Defense Journal* (Feb. 2001), 4–9.

Smith, R.B. 'Some Contrasts Between Burma and Malaya in British Policy in South-East Asia, 1942–1946', in R.B. Smith and A.J. Stockwell, (eds) *British Policy and the Transfer of Power in Asia: Documentary Perspectives* (London: SOAS, 1988).

Smith, Simon. 'Crimes and punishment: local responses to the trial of Japanese war criminals in Malaya and Singapore, 1946–48', *Southeast Asia Research* 5, 1 (March 1997), 41–56.

Stockwell, Anthony. 'British Imperial Strategy and Decolonization in South-East Asia, 1947–1957', in D. Basset and V. King, *Britain and South-East Asia* (Hull, Hull University Centre for South-East Asian Studies, Occasional Paper 13, 1986), pp. 79–90.

Tarling, Nicholas. 'Atonement Before Absolution: British Policy towards Thailand during World War Two', *Journal of Siam Studies*, 66, 1 (1978), 22–65.

Tawney, Lt-Colonel A. A. *The Gunner*, (February 1951).

Thio, Eunice. 'The Syonan Years, 1942–1945', in Ernest Chew and Edward Lee (eds), *A History of Singapore*, pp. 95–114.

Toh Boon Ho, book review of *Raising Churchill's Army: The British Army and the War Against Germany, 1919–1945* (Oxford: Oxford University Press, 2000), in *Pointer* 28, 2 (April-June 2002). *Pointer* is a journal of the Singapore Armed Forces, and can be found online at: http://www.mindef.gov.sg/safti/pointer/.

Turnbull, C.M. 'British Planning for Post-War Malaya', *JSEAS*, 5, 2 (1974), 239–54.

——. 'The Postwar Decade in Malaya', *JMBRAS*, 60, 1 (1987), 7–26.

Warren, Alan. 'The Indian Army and the Fall of Singapore', in Brian Farrell and Sandy Hunter (eds), *Sixty Years On: The Fall of Singapore Revisited* (Singapore: Eastern Universities Press, 2002), pp. 270–89.

Weinberg, Gerhard L. 'Some Thoughts on World War II', *The Journal of Military History* 56, 4 (October 1992), 659–68.

Wilberforce, Brigadier W.H.H., 'A Subaltern in pre-War Singapore'. *Royal Artillery* 122 (September 1995), 29–31.

Wilde, W.H., 'Mary Gilmore and 1942', *The Bulletin*, 22 July 1980, 77–81.

Wilkinson, Richard. 'Ashes to Ashes', *History Today* 52, 2 (February 2002), 36–42.

Wong Lim Ken. 'The Strategic Significance of Singapore in Modern History', in Ernest Chew and Edward Lee, *A History of Singapore*, pp. 17–35.

Yen Ching-hwang, 'The Overseas Chinese and the Second Sino-Japanese War, 1937–1945, *Journal of the South Seas Society* 52 (August 1998), 150–9.

Yeoh, P.K. 'Fortress Singapore', *Fort* 7 (1979), being the journal of the UK Fortress Study Group.

BIBLIOGRAPHY

Secondary sources theses, academic exercises and unpublished papers

Haron, Nadzon. 'The Malay Regiment, 1933–55: A Political and Social History' (Essex: PhD, 1988).

Kathiravelu, Singaram. 'Fortifications of Singapore, 1819–1942' (University of Malaya, Dept of History Academic Exercise, 1957).

Lim Wee Kiat, Edmund. 'Japanese War Memorials in Singapore: Commemoration or Tools of Propaganda? (National Institute of Education, Nanyang Technological University, Singapore: Academic Exercise, 1999).

Tan Sian Yeow, Terence. 'The War Crimes of the Japanese Officers involved in the *Sook Ching* Massacre' (Singapore: National Institute of Education, Nanyang Technological University, unpublished Academic Exercise, 2001).

Wai Koeng Kwok, 'Justice Done? Criminal and Moral Responsibility in the Chinese Massacres Trial, Singapore 1947', (Yale University: Genocide Studies Program Paper Paper No. 18, 2001).

Correspondence

Carmichael, Colonel Donald (RAOC). Correspondence with Commander C.B. Robbins, kindly supplied by the latter.

Gimblett, John. Including the kind provision of a copy of *The Changi Murals* (Singapore: Kok Wah Press, 1966?), sent with a guide to the Changi Murals for the Church of England in Singapore at Changi military base (1967 to 1970), 14 August 1999.

Lowe, James. Lumb Rossendale, England, 31 March 1998 (billeted at Changi 1948 to 1949).

Nixon, Roger. Research Assistant in London, especially for the Public Record Office, Kew Gardens, and Imperial War Museum.

Robbins, Commodore C.B. Information on coastal artillery including essential documents and correspondence.

Sissons, David, Australian and Japanese responses to the fall of Singapore.

Sundkuist, Dag. Information on various coastal guns.

Timbers, Major. Editor of *The Gunner*.

Yeo, Jimmy and Tresnawati, Fort Siloso, Sentosa Development Corporation, Singapore.

Video and film

Between Empires, VHS, (Singapore Broadcasting Corporation, 1992).
No Prisoners, (Australian Broadcasting Corporation, Four Corners series, 2002).

Websites

Coast Defense Study Group (United States of America): http://www.cdsg.org/
Fort MacArthur Museum site (Los Angeles, USA): http://www.ftmac.org/
Fort Siloso (Sentosa, Singapore): http://www.fort.com/
Fortress Study Group (United Kingdom): http://www.fortress-study-group.com/
Hong Kong Museum of Coastal Defence: http://www.lcsd.gov.hk/CE/Museum/Coastal/english/aboutus.html

INDEX

Pages with illustrations or maps appear in bold

15 inch guns *see also* Fortress Singapore 21, 33–4, **33–6**, 96, 97–8, 100–1, **107–10**, **116–18**, 129, 130–2, 199, 204–5
   anti-aircraft 127
   arc of fire 110–16, 121–2, 130, 204–206
   barrel life 205
   calculation of arc of fire 250n77
   construction 24–5, 33–4, 97
   destruction 25, 105, 162
   Dover guns 102
   gun manuals for arc of fire 204, 246n53, 250n77
   Japanese assessments 105–6
   myths 102–4
   plans for Blakang Mati battery 242n13
   railway 35–6
   Spain, Vickers-Armstrong 15 inch guns in 205, 270n3
   statistics 204–6
   war diaries 199
5th Column *see intelligence*

ABDA xxi, xxii, 79
Adnan Saidi, Lt 180–1, 252n96
Appeasement 2
Aircraft and Airpower *see also* Royal Air Force and Japanese airpower 5, 41, 44, 195–7
   aerodromes 39–40, 44, **45**, 72 (central Malaya)
   Bomber offensive in Europe 40, 49
   bombing 17, 66, 76
   Borneo, diversion of Japanese airpower to 77
   Buffalo versus *Zero* 197, 230n39–40
   estimates of Malayan requirements 40–1, 85
   Hurricane 5, 90, 190
   Japanese 8, 65
   Middle East 50–1, 66
   production 50
   Soviet Union 54, 90
   Thai airfields 42
aircraft carriers
   British 67–8, 232n50–1
   Japanese 31, 68, 87, 231n48–9, 232n50
airfields 44
   Central Malayan airfields impact on tactics 72
Air-raids 17, 19, 23
   Goh Sin Tub's poetry on raids 220n11
alcohol 56
Aldrich, Richard 8
Allen, Louis 7, 9
Amagi class battleships 31
Anglo-German Naval Agreement of 1935 31
Anglo-Japanese Alliance of 1902 30
anti-Japanese action 18
Atlantis 90
Australia
   commemoration *see* Commemoration
   class image *vis-à-vis* Britain 153, 262n71
   conservative coalition governments (interwar) 6
   Digger 7
   Empire Air Training Scheme and pilots 6, 50
   'Great Betrayal' by Britain 5
   Labor Party 6, 216n30

INDEX

Liberal Party 6, 216n30
nationalism 7
Singapore Naval Base 21-2
strategy 6-7
Australian Army (Australian Imperial Forces – AIF)
  Battalions
    2/4 Machine-Gun Battalion 190
    2/18th Battalion 263n76
    2/19th Battalion 157 footnote, 263n76
    2/20th Battalion 263n76
    2/29th Battalion 157 footnote
    2/30th Battalion (Gemencheh) 75
  Brigades
    22nd Brigade AIF 68, 74, 82
    27th Brigade AIF 68, 74, 76, 82
  casualties 159, 263n76
  Divisions
    7th Armoured Division 191
    8th Division 159, 161
  desertions *see also* troop performance 6, 86-7, 158-62, 264-5n83-7
  mateship *see* Commemoration, Australia
  numbers 188
  performance 6-7, 76-7, 85, 86-7, 123, 152-3, 158-62, 190, 260n70-1
Automedon, S. S. 90-91

Bakri 75
Balkans 51
Barbarossa *see also* Germany and Soviet Union 52, 54
Barber, Noel 8
Bataan 87, 140
batteries *see* Fortress Singapore
Batu Pahat 77
Bean, C. E. W 6, 215n28
Bennett, General Gordon 7, 9, 82, 154, 170 footnote, 183, 218n47
  biodata 74
  commemoration 263n72
  preface to Tsuji's book 9
Best, Anthony 8
bicycles 65, 78, 233n68, 234n88
Binyon, Laurence 142
Blakang Mati *now called* Sentosa, *see under* Fortress Singapore
Blitzkrieg
  German 50-1

Japanese *Kirimomi Sakusen* (driving charge) 68, 71
Bond, General Lionel 41, 257n152
Borneo 39-40, 77
Bose, Subhas Chandra 70
Braddon, Russell 50, 143, 156, 233n78, 257n1, 258n7
Brewster Buffalo 66, 197, 230n40
British Army
  Battalions
    2nd Argyll and Sutherland Highlanders 60, 77, 159
  Brigades
    53rd Brigade 76, 190
  Corps
    III Indian Corps 77
  Divisions
    9th Division 68, 74, 80
    11th Division 58, 65, 68, 70, 74 (placed in reserve), 80, 83
    18th Division 80, 83, 190, 191
British troops
  artillery 78, 84 (impact on Japanese), 188
  British forces in December 1941 188-90, 194
  equipment 79
  life in Singapore 27
  numbers in Malaya 190, 227-8n10,
  numbers for Singapore defence 234n97-8
  organisational chart 194
  performance 78-9, 153, 157
  tactics 60, 78-9
  training 64
Brooke-Popham, Air Chief Marshal Sir Robert 41-2, 52, 54-5, 139
  appointment as Commander-in-Chief Far East 41-2
  bluffing the Japanese 29
  fighting retreat to cover airfields 72
  Krohcol delay 69-70
  Matador delay 54-5, 57-8
  Order of the Day 8 December 1941 61-2
brothels *see* prostitution
Bukit Chandu 180-1
Bukit Timah Hill *see also* Singapore 20, 82, 83-4, 119, 122-3
  Geographical significance and name 20
Burma 87, 154
  and the reinforcement of Singapore 6, 190-1, 216n32
  road 19

291

INDEX

Burma-Siam 'death' railway 163, 165, 171 footnote, 265n95

Callahan, Raymond 2, 184
Campaign School 7
casualties 159, 171, 190, 193
   Australian 159, 263n76
   Japanese 193
Cenotaphs 119, 147, 150, 169–70
Ceylon 68, 80
Changi 13, 23–5, **166–7**
   abandoned February 1942 84
   airbase construction 25
   airport 25, 222n28
   beach before development 21
   chapel 163, **164**, 165–7, 177–8
   development 13–14, 24, 223n8
   Fire Command 97–8
   living conditions 105
   murals 163–5, 167, **169**, 177–8
   POW 163–8
   prison construction 25, 167
   Probert's *History of Changi* 25
Changi tree 167, 266n97
chiefs of staff
   appeasement 2
   estimates of Malayan requirements 40, 197
   Fortress 132–7
   lost Malayan plans 90
   Matador and Thai operations 42, 44
   Middle East 43–6
   reinforcements for Malaya 45–6, 48–9
China 18, 30
   Japanese relations with 30
   Impact of campaign on Japanese attitude to Singapore 93
   Importance in Japanese-American relations 53–4
Chinese
   in Singapore 12, 14
Churchill, Sir Winston 39–41, 44–53, 183–7
   Australia 6, 154, 225n30
   critics 3–5, 6, 46, 50, 143, 151, 152–3, 183–7
   Dardanelles failure, impact on Singapore 102, 226n48
   Fortress Singapore perceptions *see separate entry*
   heart attack 78
   House of Commons 46, 50, 88–9
   Malayan campaign tactics 77–8, 132–3
   Matador versus withdrawal 44–50, 77, 132, 138–40
   Middle East and Soviet preference for reinforcements 40–1, 44–6, 88–90
   Royal Navy primary in eastern defence, 1940 41
   'sinister twilight' 27
   surrender, aversion to 56–7, 80
   strategic gamble 4, 48–53, 226n46, 226n50
   United States in his calculations 48, 51–3, 54, 78
   writings 39, 110–11
civilian war memorial 174, 175, **176**, 179, 181
Coastal guns *see under* Fortress Singapore, batteries 21
Colonialism 7
comfort women *see* prostitution
Commemoration *see also* Changi 11, 142–82
   Australian 152–62
      Anzac myth 155, 158, 161, 186, 261n52, 262n71
      Australian War Memorial 162
      daffodils 155
      Gallipoli 153, 155, 186, 243n22, 261n52
      Great Betrayal 153–62
      Grim Glory 156
      HMAS *Australia* 154–5
      mateship 157, 215n28, 262–3n71, 262n71
      nationalism 152–3
      official history 157
      Parit Sulong 76–7, 157
      Pilgrimage to Singapore 158
      poetry 154, 261n56
      POWs 156, 258n7
      song (*Waltzing Matilda*) 157–8
      veterans 156–9, 183
   British 149–53
      15 February 150–1
      12 September 149–50
      11 November 150
   Changi chapels 163, **164**, 165–7, 177–8
   Changi murals 163–5, 167, **169**, 177–8
   Changi POW camp 163–8
      POW memorial under Japanese 147, 148
      veterans 152–3

INDEX

Cenotaphs 119, 147, 150, 169–70
  Japanese 143–8
    Ameratasu Omikami 144, 146
    Chidorigafuchi (Tomb of the Unknown Soldier) 259
    Jimmu 144
    Kigensetsu 83, 148
    schoolchildren 147
    Shinto 146, 259n16, 260n28
    Shrines and cenotaphs 119, 147, 260n28
    Syonan Chureito (*Light of the South Cenotaph*) 146–8, 165
    Syonan Jinja (*Light of the South Shrine*) 146–8
    Tenchôsetsu 148
    Yasukuni 146–7, 259n12–13
  Singaporean 171–82
    Battle of Bukit Timah 268n132
    Civilian War Memorial 174, **175**, 176, 179, 181
    Fort Siloso 176–7, 181, 269n143
    Kranji 170–1, 179
    national defence 178–81
    nationalism 176
    Overseas Chinese Volunteer Force 170
    poetry 142, 175
    schoolchildren 11, 147, 177–80, **181**, 219n53, 269n143
    Siglap **173**
    television 179–80, 266n106
    textbooks 268n128, 268n140
Commonwealth
  appeasement 2
communists *see* Malayan Communist Party
confidence *see* propaganda
Cornford, Roy 264n83
Corregidor 87, 105, 129, 130, 140
Crete 51
Curtin, John 6, 154

Dalforce *see* Overseas Chinese Volunteer Force
Dalley, Colonel 189
Dardanelles 102, 226n48
Darwin 87
Day, David 6, 215–16n30
Decolonisation
  Australia and the Fall of Singapore 7
desertion and stragglers
  Australian 6, 86–7, 158–62, 264–5n83–7, *passim*

British 85, 91–2
Dill, General Sir John 45–6, 48–9, 90
Dobbie, Major General William 39–40, 49, 140
Dollar arsenal *see* economics
Duff Cooper 85

economics
  conservative criticism of money squandered on social expenditure rather than defence 213n13
  constraints on British strategy 2–4, 15, 29, 88
  dollar-earnings 15, 27, 106
  Malayan 14–15
  Naval Base cost 22
  rubber 14
  Singapore 15, 17
  tin 14
Egypt 49, 51
El Alamein 51, 237n138
Elphick, Peter 7, 158, 160
Empire Air Training Scheme 6
Ethelred the Unready 5, 151
Ethnocentrism *see* Race
european 26–27
  civilians 26–7
  officials 26
  troops 26–7
Ex-Service Comrades Association 151

Far East Prisoners of War Association 153
Farrell, Brian 4, 6, 184, 265n87
Federated Malay States Volunteers 70
Ferris, 8, 217n37–8
finance *see* economics
Fire Commands *see under* Fortress Singapore
Fort Siloso Artillery Park (historical attraction) *see also* Fortress Singapore, batteries, Siloso 105, 176–7, 181, **182** (Siloso Live!), 203, 219n53, 241n12, 244n36, 269n143
Fortress Singapore *see also* 15-inch guns 9–10, 33–8, **34–7**, 48, 95–141, **108–10**, 185–7
  AMTB *see* close defence *below*
  anti-aircraft 127, 130
  arc of fire 110–15, **120**, 121, 123, 126, 127, 130–2, 133, 204–6

293

INDEX

ammunition 111–15, 119, 126–7, 131, 134, 136, 208
batteries (*for general information on battery organisation see* 209–10)
  Berlayer 103, 121, 127
  Buona Vista 101, 111–12, 121, **122**, 122–3, 124
  Connaught 38, 85, 94, 121, 124, **125**, 126, 128, 130, 132, 200
  Johore xiii-xiv (rediscovery), 33, 34, 98, 111–12, 113–14, 115 (origin of name), **116–18, 119, 120**, 180, **199**
  Labrador 121, 124, 126, 127, 129, 201–2
  Pasir Laba 123–4
  Pengerang 100
  Pulau Sjahat **101**
  Serapong 128
  Siloso **100**, 105, 121, 127, 128, 129, 176–7, 181, 182, 203, 219n53, 244n36
  Tekong 115, 128, 132, 134
Blakang Mati, Pulau (*island of, now Sentosa*) 85, 94 (*Sook Ching*), 97, 98, 100, 124, 126–8, 162–3, 182, 241n12
Changi Fire Command 36, 98–100, 115, 128, 210–11
Churchill's perceptions of 48, 79, 95–6, 102, 104, 110, 131–41
close or harbour defence system 98, 207–10
cost 96, 243n29
definition 34–7
development 33–4, 96–8, 223n8
Faber Fire Command 36, 98, 100, 121, 123, 126, 128, 209–10
Field fortifications 131–8
fire direction 98
guns of Singapore 1942 **99**
guns versus air debate 3, 33
history of coastal guns in Singapore 241n12
HMS *Singapore* concept 97–8, 205, 242n15
HMS *Terror* 207
Japanese assessments 105, 124–6
Japanese utilisation 121
Japanese landing craft, mistaken reports of destruction 129
MacCleod-Carey 126, 129

Matador, relationship to 114, 131–3
Mount Faber 84, 124, 127
myths 95, 102–14, 131–2
naval role 128–30
postwar fate, xiii-xiv, 162–3, 167, 176–7, 180, **182**
war diaries 114–31, 198–203
Four Corners (Australian Broadcasting Corporation current affairs programme) 160, 264n83, 265n87
France
  fall of 91
Frei, Henry 9, 219n49

Gemas 73–7, 78
  retreat to Gemas from Slim River 73
Gemencheh 75
Germany 31–2, 50–1, 88, 91
Gibraltar 95
Gillman Commission 24, 97, 178, 223n8, 240n7–9
Gilmore, Dame Mary 154, 216n56
Glossary 211
Glover, E. M. 19, 103
Goh Sin Tub 142,
  'Remember that December', on air-raids 220n11
  'Re-union with Jack' 142
Grand Strategy argument 2, 4
Greece 51
Gunboats 22, 77
  Dragonfly 77
  Scorpion 77
Guns versus air debate 3, 33, 96–7
Gurun 71, 132n62

Hainan 40
Heenan, Patrick 90, 237n140
Historiography 1–9, 184–5
Hitler 4
HMAS *Australia* 154–5
HMS *Ark Royal* 68
HMS *Barham* 98
HMS *Eagle* 23, 68
HMS *Hermes* 68
HMS *Indomitable* 67–8
HMS *Prince of Wales* 32, 67–8, 138
HMS *Queen Elizabeth* 98
HMS *Repulse* 32, 67–8, 138
HMS *Singapore* concept 97–8, 205, 242n15
HMS *Terror* 207

INDEX

Hong Kong
  ban on military development from 1920s 31
  coastal artillery 130
  contribution to naval base 21
  forces in 1941 2
Hong Kong and Singapore Royal Artillery 124, 126, 127
House of Commons 4, 46, 49–50, 143, 151
House of Lords 5, 151
housing
  Naval base 23–4
Hurricane fighter aircraft 5, 90

Images of Singapore 177
Imperialism *see* Colonialism and Decolonisation
Indian Army 60–1, 70–1, 127
  Battalions
    1st Hyderabads 61
    1/14th Punjab 70
    2/1st Gurkhas 70
  Brigades
    6th Brigade 71
    6/15th (amalgamated) Brigade 71, 82
    12th Brigade 73, 82
    15th Brigade 51, 77
    22nd Brigade 77
    28th Brigade 73
    44th Brigade 82, 123, 190
    45th Brigade 73, 76, 190, 233n78
  performance 85, 229n20, 233n78
  propaganda, effect of Japanese 60–1
  racial perceptions as gunners 252n99
Indian National Army 70
Indian civilians in Singapore 19
Indochina 39, 41, 48, 52
intelligence 7–8, 52, 217n37–8, 226n48
  Aircraft 79
  British intelligence on Japan 8
  Far East Combined Intelligence (Far Eastern intelligence) 8
  fifth column 72
  lost Malayan plans (*Automedon*) 90–91
  Japanese 7, 90
  spies 7, 90, 237n139
Ipoh 71
Italy 51

Japan
  advance across Asia towards Singapore 33, 39, 53–4
  artillery 80
  British estimates of capability and intentions 8, 30, 39–41, 49, 51–2, 90
  commemoration *see under* commemoration, Japan
  Japanese sources 8–9
  Kigensetsu 83
  landing in Malaya **58–9**
  'Official' histories 9
  planning 62–3
  propaganda 60–1, 259n16
  shrines 119, 259n16
  Singapore strategy 8
  Singapore surrender 86–8
  Sino-Japanese War 9, 30, 64
  Soviet Union in Japanese calculations 52
  spies, *see* intelligence
  Tenchōsetsu 148
Japanese airpower 66, 197, 230n1, 39–41
Japanese Army 192–3
  artillery 192
  bicycles 65, 78, 233n78, 234n88
  bridge repairs 65
  casualties 193
  divisions
    56th Division 58, 192
    5th Infantry Division 58, 64, 82, 192, 219n51, 260n26
    18th Infantry Division 58, 64, 82, 84, 126, 192
    Imperial Guards Division 58, 64, 82–3, 84, 192
  Frei, Henry on Japanese soldiers 9, 219n49
  numbers 58, 192–3, 227n8–10
  numbers for Singapore assault 234n97–8
  not using all forces available 87–8
  possibility of surrender to the British on 15 January 1, 86, 91–2
  quality 9, 219n49, 62–4
  reputation 56, 62–4
  strength in Malaya and Singapore 80, 228n10–11, 234n97–8
  tactics 62–3, 65 and 68 (*blitzkrieg* or *Kirimomi Sakusen* – driving charge), 70–1 (tanks) 74 (Slim River), 78
  tanks 192 *see also separate entry*

INDEX

training 238n149
theatre dominance 87–8, **89**, 236n130–1, 237n143
Japanese Navy
 aircraft carriers 31, 68, 87, 232n50
 strength 31, 68, 231n46, 231n48–9
 strength in relation to Fortress Singapore and coastal guns 33, 96
Japanese sources 9, 218n48
Jimmu Teneo 83
Jitra Position 69–71
Johore *see also* Gemas 73–7, **74**, 79
 Australians in 6, 68
 adviser 14
 battle for 73–7
 bombardment by coastal artillery 124, **125**, 130
 Causeway 14, 77–8, 79
 Churchill's preference for a retreat to 138–9
 Defence of 37
 fortifications 132
 geography 32
 role with Singapore as a last defensive zone 48
 Strait 20, 79–80, 98
 Sultan's palace 77, 80
Johore Battery *see* Fortress Singapore, batteries
Joint Planning Staff 183–5
jungle 78–9
Jutland 98

Kallang civil airport 24
Kampar 71–2, 157
Keating, Paul 5–7, 152–3, 159, 263n79
Kedah 69, 71
 need to screen by Matador 42–4
Kelantan 60
 airfields 44
Keppel Harbour 97, 100, 129
Ki-43 fighter 66, 230n40
Kigensetsu 83, 148
Kii class battleships 31
Kirby, S. Woodburn. 2, 59, 110, 190, biodata 213n12
Kirimomi Sakusen (blitzkrieg or driving charge) 68, 71
Kota Bharu 145
Kra *see* Songkhla
Kranji Memorial **160**, 168, 170–1, 179
Kroh 43

Krohcol 43–4, **43**, 54, **59**, 68–70
 cancellation on 8 December 65
Kuala Lumpur 64, 71–3
Kuantan 67
 fall of 74
Kuomintang 189
Kwa Chong Guan 178

Labour Governments 22, 32, 33, 97
Layton, Vice-Admiral Sir Geoffrey 61, 153
League of Nations 97
Leasor, James 8
Ledge, the 43–4
Lee Kuan Yew 176, 179

Macintyre 2
Malacca
 Straits Settlements, part of 14
Malay Regiment 80, 84–5, 126, 128, 180–1, 189
Malay States **13**
 British authority over 14
 contribution to naval base 21
Malay Sultans 14
Malaya
 east coast 14
 geography 37, 44
 Johore *see separate entry*
 population 15
 railway 14
 relationship to Singapore 13–14
 Residents 14
 Sultans 14
 territorial divisions **13**
 west coast 14
Malayan Communist Party 64–5, 151, 189, 230n31
Malayan People's Anti-Japanese Army 64–5, 150
Manchuria 97
Manila 87, 129, 140–1
Mant, Gilbert 156
Matador 5, 41–8, **43**, 54, 58–60, 68, 113, 131, 140, 185–6
 cancellation 57–60, 65, 228n13, 229n18
 chances of success 58–9, 70, 212n3, 228n12, 229n18
 Fortress Singapore, relationship to 114, 131–3
 geography 44

Japanese landings 59
  Plan Matador 43
  political aspects 54–5, 60
Mateship *see* Commemoration, Australia
Maxwell, Brigadier 82
Melbourne *Herald* 155–6
Menzies, Robert 48, 225n30
Mersing 77
Miao Xiu 172
Middle East 4–5, 39–42, 45–6, 49, 51
  Australian troops 6
  its effect on reinforcements for Malaya 4, 40, 44–6, 48–51, 66, 88–9
Midway, Battle of 68, 88
Monsoon 40, 44, 231n42
Morale 60–3, 65, 78–9, 105, 158–62, 262n71
Morrison, Ian 2, 80, 102, 113–14
Mountbatten, Admiral Lord Louis 149
Muar 76–7, 157, 190, 233n78, 257n1
Murdoch, Keith 155–6, 161
Murfett, Malcolm 6

Nagumo, Admiral 68
Nakajima Ki-43 fighter aircraft see Ki-43
Nagato 96
Naval Base 9–10, 20–1, 30–3, 80, 135
  building 31–2, 96
  completion 23, 32
  cost 22
  decision to build 31
  defence 21
  destruction 80
  docks 22–3
  floating dock 22
  location 20–1
  opening 23
  period before relief *see separate entry*
  size 23
Naval School or Singapore Strategy 2–3, 6, 30–3, 96, 102, 186, 242n15
New Zealand
  contribution to naval base 21
  pilots 50
  safety reliant on Royal Navy 48
Neidpath 2
Netherlands East Indies 66
Northern Africa *see* Middle East

oil 226n46
  significance for Singapore base 22
Onda, Shigetaka 9

Ong Chit Chung 5, 113, 178, 184
Operation *see separate entries*
Ovendale, Ritchie 2
Overseas Chinese Volunteer Force 64–5, 93, 170, 189–90

Page, Earle 5, 102, 269n1
Pan Shou 175
Parit Sulong 76–7, 157
Parkinson, C. N. 104
Parliamentary *see* House of Commons *and* House of Lords
Patani 43–4, 68–9, 70
Pearl Harbor 2, 48, 67, 77, 91
Penang
  evacuation 71
  Straits Settlements 14–15
Perak 71–3
Perak River 71
Percival, Colonel, later Lt-Gen 7, 39–40, 79–80, 83–4, 85, 136, 139, 235n115
  1937 appreciation on Japanese attack on Singapore 39, 42
  Krohcol delay 69–70
  Secret plans for a final perimeter defence in Singapore enacted prematurely 83
  surrender 57, 177
Period before Relief 32, 37, 96, 135
Philippines 2, 87
Poems *see also* songs
  Australian
    Dame Mary Gilmore's 'Singapore' (original title: 'General Bennett and his True Men') 154, 261n56
  British
    'Ode' from Laurence Binyon's 'The Fallen' 142, 143 *footnote a*
  Japanese
    'Corpses drifting swollen ' 62
    Haruo Sato's 'The Song of the Dawn of Asia' 144
    Tatsuji Miyoshi's 'The Fall of Singapore' 144
  Singaporean
    Goh Sin Tub's 'Remember that December', on air-raids 220n11
    Goh Sin Tub's 'Re-union with Jack' 142
    Pan Shou's unused epitaph to the Civilian War Memorial 175

Port Arthur 132, 136
POWs 92, 143, 147, 152–3, 156,
  Australian 262n71
Pownall, Lt-Gen. Sir Henry 79, xxi
Probert, H. A. 196, 215n24, 217n40
  History of Changi see also Changi
propaganda 29, 60–2
  Brooke-Popham's Order of the Day, 8
    December 1941 61
  Japan's *Read This Alone And the War
    Can be Won* 62–4
prostitution and forced sexual slavery
  brothels in prewar Singapore 17,
    222n39, 229n27
  'comfort' women 64, 229n28
Pulau Hantu 98
Pulau Ubin 80

Race 2, 7–8, 18–19, 61–5, 93, 216n34,
    221n16, 226n48
  Chinese 14
  European attitudes 27
  guns, gunners, and race 252n99
  Indians see separate entry
  Japanese attitudes towards 62–4, 70,
    93–4
  Malayan pattern 14
  Singapore 12
Raffles Hotel
  Ballroom wrecked 92
  dances 26–7
Raffles, Sir Stamford 15
Railway 14
Rape of Nanking 56, 64, 227n2
Reflections at Bukit Chandu *see* Bukit
    Chandu
reinforcements 190–1
riots 24
Roosevelt, F.D.R 53
Royal Air Force *see also* air-power 2, 33,
    42, 66, 195–7
  effect of having a RAF Commander-in-
    Chief 42
  guns versus air debate 33, 96–7
  performance 66, 197, 230n39, 39–41
  strength in Malaya 41, 49–50, 54, 65–6,
    85
  torpedo bombers 96
  view of 15 inch coastal artillery 33
Royal Navy 8, 30–33
  aircraft carriers 67–8, 232n50–1
  Far East Combined Bureau 8

Force Z 32, 67–8, 242n15
guns versus air debate 33
Italy 32
period before relief *see separate entry*
response to German naval power 30, 32
restrictions on building 30–1
rubber 14, 78
Russia *see* Soviet Union
Russo-Japanese War of 1904–5 30

Saito, Yoshiki 124
Sato, Haruo 144
Schoolchildren *see* Commemoration
Seabridge, G. W. 86
SEAC *see* Southeast Asia Command
Selerang Barracks 25
Seletar 24
Sembawang *see* Naval Base
Sentosa *see* Blakang Mati
Shanghai 97
Shimada, Major 78
Siam *see* Thailand
Siglap 'Valley of Death' 172, **173**, 174
Siloso *see* Fortress Singapore, batteries and
    Fort Siloso Artillery park
Simson, Ivan 136–8
Singapore *see also* Commemoration
    12–28
  Adam Road 84, 119
  Air-raids 17
  Alexandria Hospital 56–7, 85
  Alexandria Road 128
  battle for 79–86, **81**, 91–2
  Bukit Batok Park 148
  Bukit Panjang 83
  Bukit Timah, battle for 84
  Bukit Timah Hill 20, 82, 83–4, 119,
    122–3
  Bukit Timah Road 126, 130
  Bukom, Palau 128
  Causeway 14, 77–8, 79
  Changi *see separate entry*
  Chinatown 17
  Chinese High School 119
  city 12
  City Hall 149
  civilian labour 135, 137
  Cold Storage and food and drink 26
  defensive perimeter 91–2
  desertion and stragglers *see separate
    entry*
  geography 12–28, 134–5

INDEX

guns *see* Fortress Singapore
Jurong area 13
Jurong Line 82–3
Johore Strait 14, 20, 79–80, 98
Keppel Harbour 126, 129
Kranji River 82–83
Malayan links 13–14
Mount Faber *see under* Fortress Singapore
naval base *see separate entry*
Normanton 128
Pasir Panjang 83, 84, 119, 126
population 14–15
'race' and dialect groups 14, 18–19
Racecourse 126
Raffles College 84
Raffles Hotel *see separate entry*
railway 14
reservoirs 84
River 15–16
Robinsons 27
St Andrews Cathedral 92
Siglap 172, **173**, 174
Singapore City in 1941 **16**
Singapore Strategy 3–4, 6, 20–1
Sino-Japanese war, effect on Singapore 18, 56
social conditions 17, 26–7
stragglers 91
surrender 91–2 *see also under* Japanese, possibility of
Tengah Airfield 24, 113, 124, 130, 224n8
Thian Hock Keng temple 18
transport 14
water 85
Woodlands 13
Singapore Strategy *see* naval school
Singh, Captain Mohan 70
Singora *see* Songkhla *and* Matador
Sino-Japanese War 9, 17, 37, 189
Slim River 73–4, 78
Songkhla *see also* Matador 42–5, 57–60, 145
Songs
  Aikoku Koshin Kyoko (Look at the dawn over the eastern seas) 149
  Run Adolf Run 27
  Waltzing Matilda 157–8
Sook Ching 8, 93, 143, 150, 167, 171–4
  Palau Blakang Mati *now* Sentosa 94, 238–9n153
Southeast Asia Command 121, 149

Soviet Union 40, 46, 49–50, 52–3, 90, 226n50
  aircraft for and impact of these on Malaya 5, 49, 90, 215n24
  possibility of defeat by Germany 226n50
  widespread concern to put the Soviet Union first in 1941–2 50
spies *see* intelligence
Stewart, Lt-Col. Ian 60, 77–9
stragglers *see* desertion
Straits Settlement Colony 14–15
  contribution to naval base 21
Sultans 14
Sumatra 87, 236n131
Surrender 56–7
Syonan Chureito (Light of the South Cenotaph) 146–8, 165, 259n16
Syonan Jinja (Light of the South Shrine) 146–8, 259n16, 260n28
Syonan-to 57, 93–4, 257–8n3

Tan Cheng Lock 176
Tanks 49, 54, 58, 68, 70–1, 73, 192–3
  Gemas 75
  Slim River 78
Taoism 173–4
taxi-dancers 106
Tengah Airfield 24, 113, 124, 130, 224n8
Teo Chee Hean 179
Thailand
  defence of 5, 42
  Ledge, the 43–4
  police stop Krohcol 68–9
  possibility of invasion 44
The Gunner 104, 106, 128
Thomas, Sir Shenton 23
Thorne, Christopher 7
Tiger Beer 26
tin 14
Tojo, General Hideki 53
Total Defence 179
Trengganu 60
Trolak 73
Tsingtao 132
Tsuji, Col. Masanobu 8–9, 12, 58, 62–4, 71, 78, 83, 86, 93
  critique of his writing 256n148
  flight after the war 8
  on British tactic of fighting retreat 139
  on the Fortress and guns 102, 113, 139

on Singapore's importance 12
personality 9, 213n46–7
planning 62–3, 65, 78
withdrawal from planning staff over Kampar 71

United States of America 2, 44
A.B.C.1 'Hitler First' Plan 67
Anglo-American Alliance 78
attitude to Japanese advance towards Malaya 44, 51–4, 67
British expectations in response to Japanese action 48, 78

venereal disease 24, 63–4
Vlieland, C. A. 95
  Comparing Singapore to Isle of Wight 239n1

Waltzing Matilda 157–8
war crimes trials 172, 266n109, 239n153,
war diaries for coastal guns 198–203
Warren, Alan 7
Warren, Stanley 147, 165, 190
Washington Naval Limitation Treaty 30–1, 97, 154–5

Wavell, General Sir Archibald, Supreme Commander Allied Forces South West Pacific 56, 79, 131, 153, 158
Westforce 74
Wigmore, Lionel 6–7, 157, 215n28
  Australian moral ascendancy of the Japanese 262n70
Wildebeeste 66
women in Malaya 24, 27, 63, 64, 222n39, 229n27–8.

Yamashita, General Tomoyuki 9, 80, 86, 87, 91, 93, 147, 177
  trial and execution as a war criminal 266n109
Yamato 31
Yangtze 22
Yeo, George 179, 180–1, 268n137
  Bukit Chandu as Malay focus versus national memory
  memory of the war as a spur to nation-building 268n137
  heritage as a stir to patriotism 179
Yong Peng 76

Zero fighter aircraft 66, 197, 66, 230n40